Day by Day

THE NAMES OF GOD

Day by Day

THE NAMES OF GOD

Expositional Meditations

CHUCK GIANOTTI

EMMAUS
WORLDWIDE

Day by Day: The Names of God
Chuck Gianotti

email: crgianotti@gmail.com

Published by:
    Emmaus Worldwide
    PO Box 1028
    Dubuque, IA 52004-1028
    phone: (563) 585-2070
    email: info@emmausworldwide.org
    website: EmmausWorldwide.org

First Edition 2018
Reprinted 2021

ISBN 978-1-59387-293-9
eISBN 978-1-59387-465-0

Code: B-DBDNG

Copyright © 2018 Emmaus Worldwide

Other books by Chuck Gianotti:
    Biblical Foundations
    Cosmic Drama: Men, Women & the Church
    Day by Day: 1& 2 Corinthians
    Day by Day in Acts
    Day by Day in Galatians, Ephesians, Philippians & Colossians
    Day by Day in the Gospel of Matthew
    Day by Day: Growing in Faith (1&2 Thessalonians, 1&2 Timothy, Titus, Philemon)
    Day by Day in Hebrews
    Day by Day in Romans
    Day by Day in the Upper Room
    The Formation of the New Testament
    Leadership Qualities
    Leadership Principles
    Practical Ministry

All Scripture quotations, unless otherwise indicated, are taken from New American Standard Bible®, Copyright © 1960, 1962, 1963, 1968, 1971, 1972, 1973, 1975, 1977, 1995 by The Lockman Foundation. Used by permission.

All rights reserved. No part of this publication may be reproduced or transmitted in any manner, electronic or mechanical, including photocopy, recording, or any information storage and retrieval system including the Internet without written permission from the publisher. Permission is not needed for brief quotations embodied in critical articles and reviews.

Printed in the United States of America

To my parents, Jack and Margaret Gianotti, who exposed me to God and His Law through regular attendance at church and a strong moral upbringing. Because of this, I had no problem as a young adult with the concept of sin and my responsibility for it. That prepared me for exposure to the true gospel of grace, a different way to God than by religious works. I was a knowing sinner, unworthy of God, but in desperate need of forgiveness. My hope is that in the end they received the Savior as I did.

Acknowledgements

Writing a book is a team effort, and this book is no exception. Usually the only one identified is the author listed on the cover, but there are many hands involved that make a writing like this possible. Thanks to my editors, Ruth Rodger and Erica Fitzgerald, for rescuing my feeble attempts at writing and correcting my many errors. Their work is invaluable. Thank you to Jesse Fullan and the staff of Emmaus Worldwide for their work in pulling everything together into final form and publishing this book. My wife is my biggest encourager and supporter, reading every one of these meditations when they are in E-Med(itations) form, my daily blog where these writings originate—Mary, I can't thank you enough. You are God's primary helper in my life and ministry, and I highly esteem you as my life partner!

Most of all, ultimately, gratitude goes to the many-named and multi-faceted Creator God of the universe, Yahweh of Israel, the "I Am" of eternity. He is the grand subject of all Christian writings and especially this one that focuses on His extensive listing of names, epithets, and descriptions. Thank you, Lord; You are great!

Chuck Gianotti

Preface

These daily studies are generally divided into those occurrences found in the Old Testament and those found in the New Testament. Within that divide, related names are sometimes grouped together, and at other times the names are treated in alphabetical order. In a few instances, a single passage of Scripture may include multiple names, epithets and/or descriptions of God, and these are treated together in sequence. It would be impossible to be absolutely consistent apart from a pure alphabetical order or in order of first mention in the Bible, but those approaches seemed overly arbitrary.

Occasionally these meditations have drawn from outside sources. Where that happens, we have given appropriate citations. At times abbreviations helped us with space management. For example, TWOT stands for the "Theological Word Book of the Old Testament" by R.L. Harris, G. L. Archer Jr., B. K. Waltke (Eds), (Chicago: Moody Press). The usual abbreviations of English versions are used, for example, NASB (which is the default version used in these meditations), NIV, ESV, etc. Most readers should be familiar with these. Also, another convention adopted for the sake of space is referring to the Old Testament and the New Testament as "OT" and the "NT" respectively.

Notes for using this book

This Day by Day series fills a gap between the typical daily devotional readings (very brief) and in-depth commentaries (very long). It is designed to provide solid exposition in bite-sized portions for the busy Christian.

You will notice that these expositions correspond to a typical five-day work week. We suggest you conclude each reading with a few minutes in conversation with the Lord, using the prayer at the end of each day's meditation as a springboard for adding your own thoughts.

We have also included suggested readings for the weekends taken from the minor prophet books.

Table of Contents

The simplest way to study the names, epithets, and descriptions of God would be to take them in alphabetical order or in the order of first mentioned in the Bible. But grouping them linguistically or thematically, where possible, helps us see related meanings and nuances that might otherwise be missed. We have combined these approaches so that in addition to daily readings this book might also be used as a handy reference index.

To this end, we have divided our findings into Old Testament and New Testament occurrences. Within those two section, we bring together related names and name combinations. In a few instances, multiple descriptions are found in single passages, and therefore we treat these together. Finally we gather into simple alphabetic order the rest of the names, epithets, and descriptions of God that do not lend themselves easily to categorical classifications.

We trust the reader will appreciate the ordering of daily readings adopted here.

Introduction VII

Old Testament
    I Am/Yahweh 1
    Elohim Combinations 8
    Yahweh Combinations 25
    Adonai Combinations 45

    Alphabetical List 49
    Exodus 34:6-7 50
    "God of" Statements 65
    Psalm 18:2 106
    "My..." Statements 147

New Testament
    God (Theos) 182
    "I am..." Statements of Jesus 200
    Alphabetical List 214

Conclusion 311

Index 313

Introduction

The contemplation of God's names, epithets, and descriptions is one of the richest endeavors in biblical study. Many have taken up this challenge, and as a result there is no lack of books tackling this inexhaustible task—proof of the fascination this subject has engendered in God's people.

Mere humans have only a few names: our surnames, given names, middle names, nicknames, religiously given names, etc. Occasionally even an epithet can become the common way to refer to a person. But the list of "labels" assigned to God in Scripture is virtually unending, with every slight difference between one label and another sparking deep reflection on His character. That is why so many have undertaken the study—to gain and to share a deep appreciation of God as presented in Scripture.

So why another book on this subject? This one puts the study into the reading format characterized by the Day by Day series of expositional meditations. Therefore, it encourages daily meditation on the person and character of God as uniquely revealed in His names and epithets. Each page is dedicated to examining one of these "labels" set out for daily reading, five days a week, for one year – almost 260 in all. (A few names, like the primary one that God Himself gives, Yahweh, are afforded multiple pages, but each with a distinct perspective.)

This study has been more of a blessing to the present author than it could ever be to the readers. But nothing supersedes an author's thoughts and ideas better than those that arise in the reader's mind as a result. In that sense this book is a springboard, a catalyst of growth in your depth of knowing God and appreciating Him.

May you be blessed as you consider Him, for "Holy and awesome is His name" (Ps 111:9b).

WEEK 1, DAY 1

I Am • Yahweh

Then Moses said to God, "Behold, I am going to the sons of Israel, and I will say to them, 'The God of your fathers has sent me to you.' Now they may say to me, 'What is His name?' What shall I say to them?" God said to Moses, "I AM WHO I AM"; and He said, "Thus you shall say to the sons of Israel, 'I AM has sent me to you.' " God, furthermore, said to Moses, "Thus you shall say to the sons of Israel, 'The LORD, the God of your fathers, the God of Abraham, the God of Isaac, and the God of Jacob, has sent me to you.' This is My name forever, and this is My memorial-name to all generations." (Exodus 3:13-15)

Who is God? What is His name? In His own words, it is "I am" (vs. 14). But then He says in verse 15 that His name is "The LORD." So begins our study and meditation on knowing God through the study of His names. Clearly there is more to name that just knowing how to verbalize it and attach it to an individual. A name is a person's identity; it tells us about the person, who he or she is—especially in the ancient world, where a name often inherently described a person. Today we may give nicknames to people, like "Lefty" or "Happy," which tell us something of the person. Parents choose names for their children that embody their aspirations for their young one, choosing a name with a particular meaning or the name of an admired person.

God has chosen His own name, or rather, has given us His description embodied in the many names and epithets found in Scripture. The most important of them all is what we might call His personal name, the one that supersedes them all. Of course, the name of Jesus is the greatest name "under heaven that has been given among men by which we must be saved" (Acts 4:12), and it is the name before which every knee will someday bow and tongue confess (Phil 2:10-11). But the Scripture also says, "When all things are subjected to Him, then the Son Himself also will be subject to the One who subjected all things to Him, so that God may be all in all" (1 Cor 15:28). So even the name of Jesus will be subject to and superseded by "I am." In fact, Jesus even used the name "I am" of Himself, which infuriated the Jews of His day (Rom 8:28) because they took this for clear-cut blasphemy.

Jesus came to help us understand God. "No one has seen God at any time; the only begotten God who is in the bosom of the Father, [the Son] has explained Him" (John 1:18). "He is the radiance of His glory and the exact representation of His nature, and upholds all things by the word of His power" (Heb 1:3). "Before Abraham was, I am" (John 8:58). So we begin with the name of God, "I am."

My Lord and my God, help me be disciplined to continue this series of meditations to the end.

WEEK 1, DAY 2

I Am • Yahweh (cont.)

Then Moses said to God, "Behold, I am going to the sons of Israel, and I will say to them, 'The God of your fathers has sent me to you.' Now they may say to me, 'What is His name?' What shall I say to them?" God said to Moses, "I AM WHO I AM"; and He said, "Thus you shall say to the sons of Israel, 'I AM has sent me to you.' " God, furthermore, said to Moses, "Thus you shall say to the sons of Israel, 'The LORD, the God of your fathers, the God of Abraham, the God of Isaac, and the God of Jacob, has sent me to you.' This is My name forever, and this is My memorial-name to all generations." (Exodus 3:13-15)

A nation was being born; the usual protocol was for the people to choose a god. But breaking historical precedent, God, the Creator of the universe, was not chosen by the Jews. He chose them. While Abraham was the "father" of the Jewish people, Moses was the man under whom the Jewish people became a nation. It all began at the burning bush incident in the Sinai wilderness. Moses—who had fled Egypt toward the end of the 400 years of slavery of the descendants of Abraham, Isaac and Jacob—was tapped by God to lead them all out of Egypt and into the promised land of Canaan, from where Jacob and his 12 sons had earlier left during a famine.

After being in exile from Egypt and away from his Jewish kinsmen, Moses had one key question he anticipated they would ask (essentially): "What God told you to be our leader? What is his name?" It would take more than a mere man to lead them out of slavery in Egypt. Moses was convinced of the presence of deity, but how could he convince the Jews, who had not seen him for 40 years?

In accommodating Moses' concern, God graced him with the revelation that stands at the pinnacle of the uniqueness of Jewish monotheism. This God was different from all the other gods of the nations in the ancient world. As the story plays out, of course, it is revealed that this is the one and only true God: "Thus says the LORD, the King of Israel and his Redeemer, the LORD of hosts: 'I am the first and I am the last, and there is no God besides Me'" (Is 44:6). And this one true God became the absolute center of Jewish existence. The battle cry, or what Jews today call the Shema, was this: "Hear, O Israel! The LORD is our God, the LORD is one! You shall love the LORD your God with all your heart and with all your soul and with all your might" (Deut 6:4–5).

So what does His name, LORD, mean? What does God mean when He tells Moses, "'I AM WHO I AM'; and He said, 'Thus you shall say to the sons of Israel, I AM has sent me to you.' "?

Lord, help me discover more intimately who You are; so that I might love You with all my heart and with all my soul and and with all my might.

WEEK 1, DAY 3

The LORD Who Acts • Yahweh

God said to Moses, "I AM WHO I AM"; and He said, "Thus you shall say to the sons of Israel, 'I AM has sent me to you.'" ... 'The LORD ... has sent me to you.' This is My name forever, and this is My memorial-name to all generations." (Exodus 3:14)

"God" is not God's name. Neither is "Lord." His name is "The LORD." Notice the way that looks in print, in what we call small caps. That signals to English readers something is going on in the original language. This is because the Hebrew text in which the OT was written conveys an anomaly concerning this name. Some refer to it as "The Divine Name" or the Tetragrammaton (referring to the four consonantal letters making up the Hebrew name). It is variously translated as Yahweh or Jehovah, in attempt to reconstruct the sound of the name. What is going on here?

The original Hebrew was written with consonant letters only, with no vowels. It was meant to be read aloud, so the vocalization would be passed down audibly from generation to generation. However, when the Jews read the Scripture, they would not vocalize the name for God, where we see the English word LORD. Thus the vocalization of the word was not passed along. Whether this was due to reverence for the name of God or to superstition, the unfortunate event is that the sound, and therefore the vowels, have been lost to us.

After the time of Christ, Jews began to record the vocalization of the words of Scripture by adding what is called "vowel points," to preserve the vocalizations (and thus the vowels, which were inherently known through the oral readings). These points are small little marks (what the NT calls jots and tittles). However, since the Divine Name was never actually pronounced, the scribes borrowed the vowel points that naturally went with the Hebrew word for Adonai. The vocalization came to be rendered as Jehovah. But many scholars today, taking its association with the word "I am," use the vowels of that phrase to render the word sounding more like Yahweh (pronounced "yah-way").

Clearly to the Hebrew ear, God is using a play on words, associating Yahweh with "I am." He is Yahweh because He is "I am." This is the pattern often used with derivative names of God. For example, He provides, therefore, he is "Yahweh (Jehovah) Jireh," the God who provides. He is characterized by what He does. He does not just exist in and of Himself (though He does exist independently without any cause that brought Him into existence). His name means He is a living, acting presence in the universe, not a stagnant concept.

Lord, I am looking forward to knowing what You are like in action.

WEEK 1, DAY 4

The LORD Who Acts • Yahweh (cont.)

God spoke further to Moses and said to him, "I am the LORD; and I appeared to Abraham, Isaac, and Jacob, as God Almighty, but by My name, LORD, I did not make Myself known to them." (Exodus 6:2-3)

Hebrew language in the OT does not contain a word for the concept of self-existence, as many today like to think of "I am." That is more of a Greek philosophical concept. The Hebrew phrase means "to be actively present." An in-depth study of the Divine Name shows that it most likely means, "I am and will be present for you in what ever way you need Me to be." God acts on behalf of His creation and His people. He is an ever-present active and ultimate force in the universe. To put it in grammarian terms, He is the subject that needs no predicate. All things are qualified in some way, but God is ultimately without qualification. Theologians describe Him in terms of what He is not. For example, His power is without limit (or qualification). We attach qualifiers to relate this concept, such as "very powerful" or "more powerful than a hurricane." But these are wholly inadequate for giving God His just due. His power is so great that He created all things that are powerful, and so He is with out limit in His power.

The "I am" is the one "who gives life to the dead and calls into being that which does not exist" (Rom 4:17). "For in Him we live and move and exist…" (Acts 17:28). Job recognized that in His "hand is the life of every living thing" (Job 12:10). "He is before all things, and in Him all things hold together" (Col 1:17). These all coalesce into the meaning of the name Yahweh.

God said to Moses that He was now going to show Himself in the characterization of His name. He was going to show Himself to be Yahweh, the one who acts on their behalf. All the pagan gods did not act, for they were not real, but simply stone or wood statutes. God did not allow himself to be represented by any earthly images (see Exodus 20:4), because He is seen in what He does. And to Moses and the people of Israel, He was now going to deliver them from their Egyptian slavery.

While the name Yahweh does appear in Scripture before Moses' time (e.g. Genesis 2:4, 4:26), something new was going on. God was now making Himself known more fully than He did to Abraham, Isaac or Jacob. They knew Him primarily as "God Almighty," but their descendants would now begin to understand by His actions that He is "LORD" (Yahweh), the One who acts on their behalf to meet their needs. A new relationship was about to begin.

Lord, I am overwhelmed by the knowledge that You are the One who has committed to being there for me.

WEEK 1, DAY 5

LORD-Jesus Who Acts • Yahweh

Jesus said to them, "Truly, truly, I say to you, before Abraham was born, I am." Therefore they picked up stones to throw at Him, but Jesus hid Himself and went out of the temple. (John 8:58)

Was Jesus claiming to be God when He said, "Before Abraham was born, I am"? Literally, this should be rendered, "Before Abraham was (or came into being), I am." The connection to Exodus 3:14, "I am that I am," is often made, but the Jews of Jesus' day would have heard reflections of Isaiah 45:18 and 47:10, where the exact phrase is used in the same way. Through the whole section of Isaiah 40-49, the phrase "I am ..." is frequently used, as in "I am the LORD." Some scholars suggest that Isaiah was the reading in the synagogues during the Feast of Booths at that time (John 7:2, 37), so the connection would be unmistakable. The theme of Isaiah 40-49 asserts the absolute uniqueness of Yahweh. For example, "I am He. Before Me there was no God formed, and there will be none after Me. I, even I, am the LORD..." (Is 43:10–11, also Is 41:4; 44:6; 45:5-7, 18; 46:9; 47:10 and 48:12-13).

Jesus was therefore identifying Himself very much with Yahweh of Isaiah's writings in a way that made His listeners uncomfortable. Jesus had already said, a few verses earlier, "Unless you believe that I am He, you will die in your sins" (John 8:24). Although the English word "He" (italicized) shows in most translations, literally it reads, "Unless you believe that I am, you will die in your sins." And again, Jesus said, "When you lift up the Son of Man, then you will know that I am He ..." (John 8:28). Again, the "He" is not present in the original. Translators are attempting to fill in the sense of it, but we believe that the close proximity to John 8:58 requires us to note the formal absence of the predicate. We see "I am" (vs. 24), "I am" (vs. 28), and then finally "I am" (vs. 58). By this time, His listeners had had enough. Up until this point, there was sufficient ambiguity in the phrase, but when Jesus finally said, "Before Abraham was, I am," the full impact of what He was saying sunk in. They went to execute Him, clearly on the charge of blasphemy.

If Jesus had not intended His listeners to connect His use of "I am" with the "I am" of the OT (Yahweh), the strict monotheism of the Jewish faith would have required Him to clarify that point. But His lack of defending Himself speaks of His deity, as Yahweh of the OT. This is one of the most powerful testimonies of the deity of Jesus Christ. The Jews of His day understood this perfectly, and desired to kill him for it. Yet He is the God who will be there for His people, even for those who wanted to kill Him.

Lord, I thank You for seeking me even when I was rejecting You.

WEEKEND 1 READING
Hosea 1-2

PERSONAL REFLECTIONS

WEEK 2, DAY 1

Calling on the LORD • Yahweh

To Seth, to him also a son was born; and he called his name Enosh. Then men began to call upon the name of the LORD. (Genesis 4:26)

The first mention of the name of God, Yahweh, in Scripture is actually recorded in the second chapter of the Bible: "This is the account of the heavens and the earth when they were created, in the day that the LORD [Yahweh] God made earth and heaven" (Gen 2:4). So began Moses' second telling of the creation events. (While the original biblical languages did not use capitalization, we have adopted this tradition when referring to God.)

The first telling is the general layout of the six days of creation, whereas the second telling focuses on the details of the sixth day, in particular the creation of Adam and Eve and their assignment as God's representatives in the world. His work of creation in general was as Elohim, but when He began interacting with His image bearers, He acted not simply as Creator, but as Yahweh, the God who acts in a real way on their behalf.

The point is that God is personal, not just an abstract, omnipotent Creator who fashioned the world like a wind-up toy and threw it out to run on its own. He is the One who acts on behalf of His people. Notice the very personal description of God coming down to fellowship with Adam and Eve: "They heard the sound of the LORD [Yahweh] God walking in the garden in the cool of the day..." (Gen 3:8a). He gave them a garden, every tree to enjoy, with only one exception. He provided Adam with a partner that was perfect for him. He gave Adam the supreme privilege of naming the animals, and He gave the two complete security with no fear or shame.

They knew innately that God was personal and was actively involved in their lives. After their sin, they instinctively knew that He was not turning a blind eye to their disobedience: "... and the man and his wife hid themselves from the presence of the LORD [Yahweh] God among the trees of the garden" (Gen 3:8b). They now feared His involvement in their lives. They knew Him to be the God who acts on their behalf.

Only after the birth of Seth, their third son, did "men began to call upon the name of the LORD [YAHWEH]" (Gen 4:26). This came after Cain's murdering his brother Abel, and the listing of Cain's genealogy. The clear implication is that the descendants of Seth, and not those of Cain, desired a relationship with God. This reminds us of what Paul wrote: "Whoever will call on the name of the Lord will be saved" (Rom 10:13).

Lord, thank You for the privilege of calling on Your name, for You are the God who acts in my life on my behalf.

WEEK 2, DAY 2

God in the Beginning • Elohim

In the beginning God created the heavens and the earth. (Genesis 1:1)

The first reference to God in Scripture shows Him as an acting, creating God. (We will come back to the name Yahweh later in our readings.) The word "Elohim" in Genesis 1:1 is a fairly generic term for deity, used commonly in the ancient world of that which people conceive of as beyond the natural realm of the world, with super-human powers, that which controls the human and physical world. Often "elohim" was the tag used to imagine or believe there was some personal force behind the non-human controllable events of nature, such as weather. Every nation had its "elohim" (expressed of course in its own terminology). When wars were fought and won, the elohim of the victorious people was given the credit. The Hebrew word "elohim" was used for those so-called gods as well. For example, the second of the 10 commandments says, "I am the LORD your God ("Elohim") who brought you out of the land of Egypt, out of the house of slavery. You shall have no other gods ("elohim") before Me" (Ex 20:2-3).

But Elohim of Israel was not a limited territorial deity—He was Elohim over all creation. As John wrote in his gospel account, using the Greek equivalent, "… the Word was God [Theos]… All things came into being through Him and apart from Him nothing came into being that has come into being" (John 1:1, 3). The Elohim of Genesis 1:1 is not an abstract concept, like the Gnostics' concept of the Absolute One, too distant or too holy to actually create that which is material. Nor was He a deity subject to human foibles and capricious behaviors. Since Elohim created all things, there is nothing before Him or above Him. He answers to no one. While some may charge Him with capriciousness, lacking any accountability, He is in fact accountable, but only to Himself.

At this juncture, we only suggest that if there is any goodness (or sense of goodness) in the world, then He is the author of it, and therefore must be good. Thus, He cannot be capricious. God is the Creator of all beauty and all that is good. In its original state, at every turn, His creation was declared to be "good" (Gen 1:4, 10, 12, etc.). And after completing His creation, including humans, He declared, "It was very good."

Theologians point out that Elohim created "ex nihilo," out of nothing. There was no pre-existent material, and creation is not an extension of God Himself (pantheism). He spoke it into existence. If anything exists, then it exists because He thought of it and created it.

Lord, my Creator, though You created everything that exists, You thought of me and created me personally. I look forward to knowing You more.

WEEK 2, DAY 3

God in the Beginning • Elohim (cont.)

Then God said, "Let Us make man in Our image, according to Our likeness... The LORD God said, "Behold, the man has become like one of Us..." (Genesis 1:26, 3:22)

"Elohim" is a plural word, Hebrew scholars tell us. Some today are quick to think the roots of the Jewish faith give evidence of an original polytheism, a belief in many gods. Indeed, the accepted belief of the modern religious studies holds that polytheism has a longer history than monotheism, the belief in one God. Jewish monotheism, in this thinking came much later in history, largely due to the influence of Moses and his insistence on a staunchly held belief in one and only one deity. It is true that the Jews stood out among ancient religions in their tenacious monotheism. In fact, in Roman times, Jews and Christians were considered atheists, because they did not believe in the pantheon of Greek and Roman gods, and held only to their god (sic), Yahweh.

So does the use of the plural "Elohim" give evidence of an early polytheism that sort of slipped in to Genesis? Hardly so! The fact that the Jews were so ardently monotheistic would tell us that such an interpretation would be inconceivable. When Jesus took on the name "I Am" (John 8:58), the Jews were quick to pick up stones to kill Him for blasphemy. The death penalty for anyone who held to or worshipped any other gods was death (Deut 17:2-5). Every Jewish child knew the Shema by heart, the rallying cry of their unique monotheism, "Hear, O Israel! The LORD is our God, the LORD is one!" (Deut 6:4). Hardly could any Jewish writings therefore speak of God in polytheistic terms.

So what do we make of the plural term "Elohim," and the plural pronouns God uses of Himself? It may be helpful to know that since God's ways and thoughts are above ours, it makes sense that His self-references are above our usual ways of thinking. The concept of singularity and plurality simply cannot apply in the usual ways. In fact, the Scripture refers to God in the singular—"God created man in His own image..." (Gen 1:27)—and God Himself uses the singular pronouns, "Have you eaten from the tree of which I (singular) commanded you not to eat?" (Gen 3:11). God also uses the plural pronouns: "Let Us make man in Our image..." (Gen 1:26). In fact, "Elohim" is most of the time used as a singular term.

We take it, then, that "Elohim" as a plural word refers to the vast superiority of God, who cannot be described easily or in simple terms. As theologians say, it is the plural of majesty.

Elohim, show me all Your greatness and majesty that I might worship You more.

WEEK 2, DAY 4

LORD God • Yahweh Elohim

This is the account of the heavens and the earth when they were created, in the day that the LORD God made earth and heaven. (Genesis 2:4)

Two of the most significant terms for God, "Elohim" and the divine name, Yahweh, are found in precise combination "Yahweh Elohim" 37 times, plus a few instances where the terms are reversed. All the major English translations render this couplet as "the LORD God." Early in the biblical record, the two terms are associated to make sure it is understood that the Creator God of the universe is none other than Yahweh of Israel. Although Adam and Eve probably didn't know that terminology for God, since the formation of Israel was far distant in the future, Moses, who is the human author of Genesis, establishes the connection. So we might say the account of creation is the record of Israel's God moving in the beginning.

The Jews were unabashed in proclaiming that their God was the true God over all, not just a territorial deity. The message to the world was from the God over all creation, the true Deity who created the universe—that was whom the Jew worshipped. Modern scholars of comparative religion like to view the Jewish God Yahweh as one of many representations of deity in the ancient world. However, Yahweh was not a human creation devised by Jews coming out of Egyptian slavery to establish their own uniqueness as an emerging nation with their own unique god. When Moses met Him in the Sinai desert, it was "God ["Elohim" who] called to him from the midst of the bush" (Ex 3:4). The voice said, "I am the 'Elohim' of Abraham, the 'Elohim' of Isaac, and the 'Elohim' of Jacob" (Ex 3:6). And this "Elohim" identified Himself by name, Yahweh (Ex 3:14-15).

Conversely, it was Yahweh of Israel who created the heavens and the earth, as our verse for today indicates. He is the LORD God, that is, Yahweh Elohim. Twenty times we find this connection being made in Genesis 2-3 alone, irrevocably tying Yahweh to the creation account and the fall into sin of humans. The Creator God is not an impersonal deity detached from people, His image bearers. Rather it was "Yahweh Elohim" [who] "… formed man of the dust from the ground, and breathed into his nostrils the breath of life" (Gen 2:7). And it was "Yahweh Elohim" who confronted Adam and Eve when they sinned (Gen 3:8-9). Interestingly, Satan, as personified in the serpent only refers to God as "Elohim," exhibiting a distinct lack of relationship with Him. By extension, therefore, the God we worship as Christians is the Lord God, Yahweh Elohim over all the universe.

LORD God, I am overwhelmingly privileged that You reveal Yourself to me.

WEEK 2, DAY 5

God of Hosts • Elohim Sabaoth

"Therefore, I will make you go into exile beyond Damascus," says the LORD, whose name is the God of hosts. (Amos 5:27)

Amos was not a man of high religious standing. By his own writing, "I am not a prophet, nor am I the son of a prophet; for I am a herdsman and a grower of sycamore figs" (Am 7:14). He is not tied to any famous personage or else it would be stated. He forever stands as a testament of what God can do through an ordinary person who is willing to be used by Him.

He lived in a time of relative affluence well after the civil war and subsequent split in the nation of Israel during the time of Solomon's son, Rehoboam. The nation's wealth grew because of its location along the major trade route between Egypt and Syria. The moral climate, however, declined into selfish materialism where the rich oppressed the poor. Amos was commissioned to preach righteousness and warn of coming judgment by God, first against the northern kingdom (often called Ephraim, but sometimes called Israel) and also the southern kingdom of Judah, where the Davidic dynasty continued on.

The name Yahweh is mentioned 78 times in the book of Amos, and very pointedly: "The One who builds His upper chambers in the heavens and has founded His vaulted dome over the earth, He who calls for the waters of the sea and pours them out on the face of the earth, The LORD is His name" (Amos 9:6). Repeatedly, Amos appends to his proclamations, "Declares the LORD" or "Thus says the LORD" (Amos 5:3). Amos' God, Yahweh, is authoritative over all.

Yet despite their heritage of the Law, the David kingdom and the prophets before Amos, God's people continually strayed into idolatry. Amos rebuked them, "'Did you present Me with sacrifices and grain offerings in the wilderness for forty years, O house of Israel? You also carried along Sikkuth your king and Kiyyun, your images, the star of your gods which you made for yourselves'" (Amos 5:25–26). "'Therefore, I will make you go into exile beyond Damascus,' says the Lord, whose name is the God of hosts" (Amos 5:27).

Few commentators give much time to this name of God, "Elohim Sabaoth," which occurs only here in the Bible. Its significance is found, though, in the anticipation of God using the military of another nation to take Israel into captivity. (The term "hosts/sabaoth" is used mostly for military troops.) He is God of hosts (sometimes translated "God Almighty"), and He will use whatever means suitable for accomplishing His purposes, even punishing His people. Yes, sometimes God uses evil people and nations to accomplish His purposes.

Lord, God of hosts, I confess the idolatry in my life when I make other things more important to me than You.

WEEKEND 2 READING
Hosea 3-4

PERSONAL REFLECTIONS

WEEK 3, DAY 1

God Most High • El Elyon

And Melchizedek king of Salem brought out bread and wine; now he was a priest of God Most High. He blessed him and said, "Blessed be Abram of God Most High, Possessor of heaven and earth; And blessed be God Most High, Who has delivered your enemies into your hand." [Abram] gave him a tenth of all… Abram said to the king of Sodom, "I have sworn to the LORD God Most High, possessor of heaven and earth that I will not take a thread or a sandal thong or anything that is yours, for fear you would say, 'I have made Abram rich.'"(Genesis 14:18)

Enigmatic character that he is, Melchizedek reveals a portal to understanding God in a unique way. To be sure, the Book of Hebrews describes Melchizedek in a way that makes the comparison with Christ unmistakable. He was the "king of righteousness and … king of peace" (Heb 7:2). He had no parentage, is apparently eternal in nature, and was "like the Son of God" (Heb 7:3). Jesus' priesthood, which the writer of Hebrews makes clear was greater than the Levitical priesthood, was said to be "according to the order of Melchizedek" (Heb 6:20). We conclude that Abraham (i.e. Abram) had found himself in the presence of the pre-incarnate Christ.

Now Melchizedek-Christ was a priest of "God Most High," or in the original Hebrew, "El Elyon." The Hebrew term "El" is a shortened form of "Elohim," the generic reference to deity. By combining it with "Elyon," which means "most high," Melchizedek identifies with not just a localized tribal deity, but with the God who is Most High, the One of whom no one else can be said to be higher. In other words, Melchizedek is the mediator between the Creator God of the universe and humans.

Of course, Abraham did not fully recognize this, but in responding to the other king, the King of Sodom, he made an interesting expansion on Melchizedek's reference to God. He added the personal, divine name, Yahweh, and spoke of the LORD (Yahweh) God Most High. Abraham was tenacious to remove any hint of ambiguity; there is one and only one God to whom he gave allegiance, and that was Yahweh, for He is the Most High God over all. So Abraham made an oath to Yahweh that he would not be beholden to the king of Sodom. He took seriously the fact that God had sent him from his home country and led him to the land of Canaan, and would provide for him. As he became wealthy, it was not because of earthly financial support. In fact, Abraham gave 10 percent of his war spoils to Melchizedek. One wonders whether the contrast of the King of Salem (Melchizedek-prefigured Christ) is meant to prefigure Satan as the King of Sodom tempting us to be controlled by earthly wealth.

Lord, help me to remain loyal to You, for You supply all my needs.

WEEK 3, DAY 2

The Most High • Elyon

The oracle of him who hears the words of God, and knows the knowledge of the Most High, who sees the vision of the Almighty, falling down, yet having his eyes uncovered. (Numbers 24:16)

While the term "Elyon" is connected with "Elohim," the Creator God, as we saw previously, most of the time "Elyon" is used by itself as a descriptor of God. He is "The Most High," above all that is and will be. In the ancient world that meant He was greater than all other so-called gods.

In light of the biblical teaching that there is one and only one God, then what do we make of the Bible's frequent references to gods of other nations? The prophets of Scripture often resorted to polemics, an attack against the false beliefs of the pagan world around them. The pagans considered their gods (as depicted by their wooden, stone or metal idols) to be real and powerful. But, "Thus says the Lord … 'I am the first and I am the last, and there is no God besides Me'" (Is 44:6). The language of the prophets does speak of those other gods but in a pejorative way. Essentially they say, "Whatever you believe your gods to be, they are nothing compared to the Most High God whom we worship."

Indeed, Paul writes, "There is no such thing as an idol in the world, and that there is no God but one" (1 Cor 8:4b). That doesn't mean that worship of other gods is innocuous, for God considers it the height of evil. Indeed, the commands given to Moses begin with "I am the LORD your God … you shall have no other gods before Me." To put belief in other gods in the same category with belief in the Most High in any sense is to compete directly with God. In fact, it is Satanic. Paul writes, "The things which the Gentiles sacrifice, they sacrifice to demons and not to God; and I do not want you to become sharers in demons" (1 Cor 10:20). Satan himself, as personified in the king of Babylon in Isaiah's prophecy, had as his supreme goal to compete with God and to win out over Him: "I will ascend to heaven; I will raise my throne above the stars of God, and I will sit on the mount of assembly in the recesses of the north. I will ascend above the heights of the clouds; I will make myself like the Most High (Elyon)" (Is 14:13–14).

In the end, believers in the Most High have much to be encouraged by. In Daniel's end-time prophecy, he speaks four times of the "saints of the Highest One (Elyon)," believers who will be persecuted in a great tribulation but who will then reign in the everlasting kingdom over all the earth (Daniel 7).

Lord, when all is said and done, we will reign with You, our Most High One. There is no greater worship than to worship You.

WEEK 3, DAY 3

Mighty God of Israel • El Elohe Yisrael

Then he [Jacob] erected there an altar and called it El-Elohe-Israel. (Genesis 33:20)

Epithets about God are found in various combinations. While "Elohe-Israel" occurs 191 times in Scripture, we find it prefixed with "El" only here in Genesis 33:20. While the distinction may seem small, the event precipitating it is not. The Oxford English dictionary defines epithet as "an adjective or phrase expressing a quality or attribute regarded as characteristic of the person or thing." Something had happened to Jacob, the son of Isaac and grandson of Abraham, to cause him to build an altar and call it by this name.

The story began when Jacob had fled from his brother Esau, after conniving to steal the latter's birthright for the mere cost of some porridge. Jacob's sense of value clearly eclipsed Esau's, who when famished opted for some food at the expense of losing what was rightfully his as the firstborn. Jacob fled the land of Canaan, under advice from his father and mother, to find a wife among the distant relatives. Isaac blessed him, "May [God Almighty/El Shaddai] bless you and make you fruitful and multiply you, that you may become a company of peoples. May He also give you the blessing of Abraham, to you and to your descendants with you, that you may possess the land of your sojournings, which God gave to Abraham" (Gen 28:3-4).

As he left, Jacob saw in a dream a ladder with angels on it. Above the ladder was God saying, "I am the LORD, the God of your father Abraham and the God of Isaac; the land on which you lie, I will give it to you and to your descendants. At that time, Jacob wasn't even married, let alone a father. Your descendants will be like the dust of the earth ... Behold, I am with you and will keep you wherever you go, and will bring you back to this land; for I will not leave you until I have done what I have promised you" (Gen 28:12-15).

Jacob then made a vow: "If God will be with me ... and I return to my father's house in safety, then the LORD will be my God" (Gen 28:21). Well, he was gone 20 some years (Gen 31:41), and the first thing he had to do upon arrival was to face his brother, Esau. But not before wrestling with the angel of the LORD, an event that left him hobbling the rest of this life. After an unexpectedly pleasant reconciliation with his brother, Jacob "erected an altar and called it El-Elohe-Israel [or Yisrael]." He kept his vow because God had kept His promise to bring Jacob back safely. He was now ready to worship his father's God, but now El-Elohe-Israel was his God! The God we worship today is that same God of the patriarchs.

Lord, I too worship You as the Mighty God whom Jacob/Israel worshipped.

WEEK 3, DAY 4

Mighty One, God, the LORD • El Elohim Yahweh

"The Mighty One, God, the LORD, the Mighty One, God, the LORD! He knows, and may Israel itself know. If it was in rebellion, or if in an unfaithful act against the LORD do not save us this day!" (Joshua 22:22)

God is addressed in an expansive way; in the original Hebrew the phrase "El Elohim Yahweh" is repeated twice. We sit up and take notice at such an obvious reiteration as this, and sense intuitively the passion in this exhortation. But why the passion?

The back story is about Israel taking possession of the Promised Land and surrounding areas. Moses had passed from the scene, and now Joshua successfully led the charge, with the conclusion that:

"The LORD gave Israel all the land which He had sworn to give to their fathers, and they possessed it and lived in it. And the LORD gave them rest on every side, according to all that He had sworn to their fathers, and no one of all their enemies stood before them…" (Joshua 21:43–44)

Now some of the tribes that had previously asked for their portion—Reuben, Gad and the half-tribe of Manasseh—requested permission to return to their assigned land to begin living there. Joshua had reminded them of their commitment to the Law of Moses, blessed them and sent them on their way (Josh 22:5). But this precipitated a problem of geographical proximity.

These two and a half tribes built a large altar, and this upset the rest of Israel, for it looked like they were resorting to idol worship (Josh 22:10). As a prelude to war against them, Israel sent the high priest and ten tribal chiefs to rebuke them for rebelling against the LORD. They rehearsed God's judgment against Israel over their turn to idolatry at Peor in the wilderness wanderings (Num 25:1-9) and the sin of Achan (Josh 7:1-6), demonstrating that God will judge the nation for their collective sin, as well as the sin of one individual. So Israel as a whole rightly feared what God might do to them all, because of the sin of these two and a half tribes.

One can now understand the passion in the spokesmen for the two and a half tribes. They had not rebelled against El Elohim Yahweh. Absolutely not! If they had, then rightly they should be shown no mercy. Rather, their actions were to guard against the tribes west of the geological divide called the Jordan River, ostracizing them from the worship of Yahweh. So they built the altar as an enduring "witness between us that the LORD is God" (Josh 22:34).

Lord, I resolve to worship You and You alone, even when I am separated physically from other Christians.

WEEK 3, DAY 5

Mighty God • El Gibor

For a child will be born to us, a son will be given to us; And the government will rest on His shoulders; And His name will be called Wonderful Counselor, Mighty God, Eternal Father, Prince of Peace. (Isaiah 9:6)

A remnant will return, the remnant of Jacob, to the mighty God. (Isaiah 10:21)

Twice we find God referred to as "El Gibor," translated like other phrases as "Mighty God." Both times, Isaiah uses it to emphasize the military-like strength of God. With the Babylonians poised to war against Israel, Isaiah was God's point man for warning of judgment. The Lord was not at all averse to using natural calamities (plagues, pestilence, famine, etc.) or even other nations to execute His justice against Israel when they sinned. Isaiah warned them of the latter, namely the Babylonians.

To be defeated in war in the ancient world was horrifying. The victorious nation had complete control and often ultimate caprice in how they treated the vanquished nation. The Babylonians, as was not unusual, not only destroyed the city of Jerusalem and the LORD'S temple, but they enslaved the Jewish populous—indeed, the spoils of war included "free" laborers. It was the winners' right, because of their might. That was the internationally understood rule of the day. Who was going to disagree with the victors?

What would cause God to warn through Isaiah and eventually bring about such drastic measures as military defeat and captivity in His dealings with Israel?

"Alas, sinful nation, people weighed down with iniquity, offspring of evildoers, sons who act corruptly! They have abandoned the LORD, they have despised the Holy One of Israel, they have turned away from Him." (Is 1:4)

"What are your multiplied sacrifices to Me?" says the LORD ... "I take no pleasure in the blood of bulls, lambs or goats ... So when you spread out your hands in prayer, I will hide My eyes from you; yes, even though you multiply prayers, I will not listen. Your hands are covered with blood." (Is 1:11, 15)

In the face of all this, God offers hope. He is the Mighty God, El Gibor, who can militarily destroy the Babylonians as easily as He can use them to punish Israel. He can and will save the remnant of the faithful, through the coming Messiah, for He is the Mighty God, El Gibor!

Lord, I know You can bring external judgments into my life if You desire. I thank You for Your grace and mercy, which give me hope even when I sin.

WEEKEND 3 READING
Hosea 5-6

PERSONAL REFLECTIONS

WEEK 4, DAY 1

God Who Sees • El Roi

Then she called the name of the LORD who spoke to her, "You are a God who sees"; for she said, "Have I even remained alive here after seeing Him?" Therefore the well was called Beer-lahai-roi... (Genesis 16:13)

Elohim in its short form El combines with other terms to expand on the understanding of God. We have already seen that Elohim is Yahweh, the God who is active in the lives of people. Here we are presented with God as all-seeing. The story is familiar to us, but was a unique experience for Hagar, the outcast woman and one-time amour of the patriarch Abraham.

Hagar's story portrays a sad life that found hope in God. When Sarah, because of advancing age, lost hope of giving Abraham the child promised him by God, she devised a "next-best-plan" to give her servant-girl to Abraham to have sex with, in hopes of pregnancy through her. The resulting pregnancy only created resentment toward Sarah by Hagar, seemingly the natural outcome of human relationships and jealousy. So Sarah campaigns to have Hagar cast out.

Driven out on her own with her child, Ishmael, Hagar had no way to provide for her child, no protection from any unprincipled man who would come upon her. There were no women's shelters nor policing by a centralized government. It must have been a horrifying experience.

Your doctor calls and says, "Please come in to discuss the results of the MRI; it doesn't look good." Your employer calls you in with a glum look, pink slip in hand. Your spouse serves you with divorce papers. The police phone to tell you your son or daughter has been in an accident. Your long-kept secret sin is about to be exposed. The dream you have worked for all your life comes crashing down in complete and utter failure. If you have experienced any of the above you understand Hagar's experience. Horrifying. You wish you could become invisible and escape from everyone and everything. How can you ever go back to normal life again? But God intervened.

"The angel of the LORD found her by a spring of water in the wilderness..." The important thing to Hagar was not so much the promise of many descendants (Gen 16:10, which we note is a similar promise to Abraham about his other son, Isaac). Rather, what was most noteworthy was that this individual before her was no mere messenger of God. She had been in the very presence of El Roi, literally translated "the God who sees." And she lived to tell about it! That is a promise to us as well. When we feel left out, outcast, marginalized or otherwise completely unnoticed, God sees, and He still has a purpose for us in this world and promises for us that give us hope.

Lord, You are the One who sees and knows me, and You do not reject me.

WEEK 4, DAY 2

God Almighty • El Shaddai

When Abram was ninety-nine years old, the LORD appeared to Abram and said to him, "I am God Almighty; walk before Me, and be blameless." (Genesis 17:1)

One of the more well-known names for God, "El Shaddai," simply means God Almighty. This was the name by which Abraham came to know God. As mentioned before, the name "Yahweh" was known in Abraham's time, but God had not revealed the true nature or character of His name. It was later that God spoke to Moses, "I am the Lord; and I appeared to Abraham, Isaac, and Jacob, as God Almighty, but by My name, LORD, I did not make Myself known to them" (Ex 6:2–3). Abraham did not consciously know Him as the God who was committed to acting on his behalf but simply as a deity whose abilities were without limit.

If we take the genealogical accounts literally, Abraham was the 10th generation from Noah, and Noah's father was born before Adam (of the Garden of Eden fame) died. This infers that Noah was alive for the first 58-60 years of Abraham's life, and therefore Abraham would have learned about the flood from those who built the ark! And Noah was only one generation removed from direct contact with Adam. However, the family line strayed from the Creator God, Elohim, into idolatry (Josh 24:2), probably leaving Abraham with only a faint memory of the God of his ancestors.

Genesis 12:1 records that it was the LORD (Yahweh) who called him out of his paganism and gave him the pivot promises that would affect the entire human race (Gen 12:1-3). We must remember that Moses wrote this account, many years later, and Moses knew God as Yahweh, and thus used that name in recording the account. Abraham though did not know Him in the character of that name; nonetheless, God was indeed acting in the character of that name.

To Abraham (called here Abram), God revealed Himself by the name "God Almighty," El Shaddai. Melchizedek, the priest of God Most High, had already introduced God to him as "God Most High," El Elyon (Gen 14:18-19), But when he was 99 years old, God promised him a son by Sarah, his 90-year-old wife. Even in those days of longer life spans, they were long past childbearing age. But as Jeremiah wrote much later, "Behold, I am the LORD, the God of all flesh; is anything too difficult for Me?" (Jer 32:27). God showed Himself to be almighty in overriding the normal course of nature and caused Sarah to become pregnant! Impossible for them, but not for God Almighty.

Lord God Almighty, I do believe that nothing is impossible for You. I trust You in my present circumstance. I believe; help my unbelief!

WEEK 4, DAY 3

God • Elah

"Thus they answered us, saying, 'We are the servants of the God of heaven and earth and are rebuilding the temple that was built many years ago, which a great king of Israel built and finished.'" (Ezra 5:11)

The term "elah" is an Aramaic designation for God. While the major languages in which the Bible was originally penned were Hebrew (OT) and Greek (NT), a few short passages were actually written in Aramaic, a cognate language to Hebrew. "Elah" occurs only in those passages and seems to be equivalent to the Hebrew term "elohim." The prophet Jeremiah declared unequivocally in Hebrew, "The LORD is the true God [Elohim]; He is the living God [Elohim] and the everlasting King. At His wrath the earth quakes, and the nations cannot endure His indignation" (Jer 10:10). But then in the next breath, he switches to Aramaic so that pagans can read in their own language the indictment against the worship of any other gods: "Thus you shall say to them, 'The gods [elah] that did not make the heavens and the earth will perish from the earth and from under the heavens'" (Jer 10:11). Aramaic was the "lingua franca" of the day, the universally spoken language at that time, and so it would have been easy for Jeremiah to slip into that language for its emotional impact. In contrast to the Creator and living Yahweh Elohim of Israel who controls all, the elah of the pagans are nothing.

However, the term elah is used elsewhere of Yahweh Himself. The more frequent use of the term comes in the Aramaic sections of Daniel (chapters 2-7) and Ezra (4:8–6:18 and 7:12–26), who wrote during and at the end of the Babylonian-Medo-Persian captivity of Israel. Again, Aramaic was the common language at that time, and these two prophets chose to write much of their prophecies in that language.

The prophets had no problem adopting the terms for deity used by the surrounding culture. Some "purists" might argue against this, thinking it causes confusion. But the prophets made sure there was no ambiguity. In fact, Ezra uses the term LORD (Yahweh) 38 times and Daniel 29 times. They were saying in effect, yes, there is an Elah, and His name is Yahweh. Paul did something similar, as the book of Acts records: "Men of Athens, I observe that you are very religious in all respects ... For while I was passing through and examining the objects of your worship, I also found an altar with this inscription, 'TO AN UNKNOWN GOD.' Therefore what you worship in ignorance, this I proclaim to you" (Acts 17:22–23). A parallel today might be the use of "Allah" as a reference to God when witnessing to Muslims.

Lord, by any other name, You are still the LORD, Creator of everything.

WEEK 4, DAY 4

God Most High • Elah Illai

Then Nebuchadnezzar came near to the door of the furnace of blazing fire; he responded and said, "Shadrach, Meshach and Abednego, come out, you servants of the Most High God, and come here!" Then Shadrach, Meshach and Abednego came out of the midst of the fire. (Daniel 3:26)

The phrase "elah illai" is used in the mouth of Nebuchadnezzar (Dan 3:26). The issue giving rise to this description of God has to do with Nebuchadnezzar's exaltation of himself—he needed to learn that the God Daniel worshiped was supreme over all, including the king of Babylon.

Nebuchadnezzar was the most powerful man in the world at that time. Under his authority the Babylonian armies ransacked Jerusalem and took the Jews away captive (roughly B.C. 605). His policy was to resettle the defeated populaces into other conquered lands, making them easier to control by separating them from their ancestral lands and presumably from their geographically associated gods.

However, in taking the Jews captive the king found himself confronted with an "elah" (God) that was "illai" (Most High). As noted previously, this section of Scripture is written in Aramaic, and "elah" was a term of deity in use by the Babylonian culture. When Shadrach, Meshach and Abednego refused to worship the 90-foot-high golden image of Nebuchadnezzar, they were angrily thrown into an incinerator that was excessively stoked in keeping with his extreme anger. But when the king saw they were unhurt, he called out to them, "You servants of the Most High God." The most powerful man on earth came to recognize that the Jewish God was greater than all Babylonian gods. Yet the king did not humble himself to worship Elah Illai, God of the Jews.

But God was gracious to Nebuchadnezzar, by his own testimony. At the height of arrogance, he said, "Is this not Babylon the great, which I myself have built as a royal residence by the might of my power and for the glory of my majesty?" (Dan 4:30). As a direct result, God instantly struck him with insanity, causing him to act like an animal for seven years (Dan 4:33) until: "At the end of that period, I, Nebuchadnezzar, raised my eyes toward heaven and my reason returned to me, and I blessed the Most High and praised and honored Him who lives forever; for His dominion is an everlasting dominion, and His kingdom endures from generation to generation" (Dan 4:34). This is but a foretaste of what Paul wrote: "Every knee will bow…and tongue confess…that Jesus Christ is Lord, to the glory of God" (Phil 2:10-11).

Lord, I believe You humble those who exalt themselves, so therefore I confess my exaltation of myself. You are the Most High God, and I lift my eyes to You.

WEEK 4, DAY 5

God • Eloah

"Can mankind be just before God? Can a man be pure before his Maker?" (Job 4:17)

The term "eloah" seems to be a variation on the more common term, "elohim," and is universally translated generically as "God." What is particularly noteworthy is that of the 58 times it occurs in Scripture, 41 are in the book of Job. Scholars widely believe that Job lived before the time of Abraham, probably after the tower of Babel incident. He lived for well over 140 years (Job 42:16), a longevity that was on par with the time of the patriarchs. But there is no mention of the Mosaic Law or the Levitical priesthood. There is no clear mention in the book of his being a Jew. However, the writing of the book may have taken place much later, and on the question of authorship scholars disagree: some believe it was Job himself who penned it, while others think its poetic form points to Solomon. Its divine inspiration is verified by the apostle Paul, who quotes from it as Scripture in 1 Corinthians 3:19-20, where he puts it on the same level as the Book of Psalms, and James refers to Job as an historical character in James 5:11.

Job wrestled with Eloah, plumbing the depths of the Almighty about the meaning of life and its suffering. He did not see the events of his misery as the result of fate, but as the cause being Eloah, that is, the God of the universe. In his first mention of God by this term, we find Job cursing the day he was born:

Afterward Job opened his mouth and cursed the day of his birth. And Job said, "Let the day perish on which I was to be born, and the night which said, 'A boy is conceived.' "May that day be darkness; let not God [Eloah] above care for it, nor light shine on it."' (Job 3:1–4)

Though he cursed the day he was born, and though he was tempted by his wife to curse God (Job 2:9), Job refused to curse his Creator! Whatever we say about Job, he was a man of spiritual integrity and honesty (Job 1:1, 2:9). In the end, like a dog chasing a car doesn't know what to do when the cars stops, Job was completely dumbfounded when Eloah stopped and graced him with a response. With his proverbial tail between his legs, Job answered:

"Will the faultfinder contend with the Almighty? Let him who reproves God answer it." Then Job answered the LORD and said, "Behold, I am insignificant; what can I reply to You?" (Job 40:2-4).

Lord God Eloah, I submit my deepest anguish to You, in honesty and integrity.

WEEKEND 4 READING
Hosea 7

PERSONAL REFLECTIONS

WEEK 5, DAY 1

LORD God Most High • Yahweh El Elyon

Abram said to the king of Sodom, "I have sworn to the LORD God Most High, possessor of heaven and earth, that I will not take a thread or a sandal thong or anything that is yours, for fear you would say, 'I have made Abram rich.'" (Genesis 14:22–23)

Found only here in Scripture, this particular name of God shows Abraham's allegiance unambiguously. He and his men had fought against a consortium of kings who had captured another group of kings, which involved the rescue of Abraham's nephew Lot and his family. After Abraham's military intervention, two of the "rescued" kings came to meet him.

We have already seen in our discussion of the name "El Elyon" that the king of Salem, Melchizedek, worshiped God Most High (El Elyon) and recognized that Abraham was a believer in the same God Most High (Gen 14:18-20). The patriarch validated this connection by giving Melchizedek a tithe (10 percent) of the spoils of war from the recent military engagement.

But there was another king involved, the king of Sodom, to whom Abraham reacts much differently. Whereas King Melchizedek brought out food and drink for Abraham, the king of Sodom brought out demands to Abraham: "Give the people to me and take the goods for yourself" (Gen 14:21). By rights, according to the custom of the day, the victor or rescuer, being in the obviously stronger position, dictated the terms of agreement.

Abraham's response was crystal clear: he had an undying allegiance to the LORD God Most High, Yahweh El Elyon. He would not be beholden to an earthly king. The name of God he used was similar to the one used before, but now he felt it important to add "Yahweh," God's personal name. Abraham previously had no qualms about receiving some wealth from Pharaoh in Genesis 12, but that was under the ruse that Sarah, his wife, was his sister—a plot Abraham used to protect himself while he fled Canaan during a famine. He was still learning about God's faithfulness to His promise to make Abraham into a great nation. So now, when the king of Sodom offered to give Abraham all the spoils of war (except the defeated people), the patriarch adamantly refused. He would trust only in God for his blessings.

Abraham was growing in his faith, and the God he followed is not just a generic superpower or super authority, but He is Yahweh El Elyon. He is personal, and He has a name. Today, people easily sprinkle "god" in their conversations without knowing much about the true God. The true God is not just a nebulous, undefined deity-belief, but He is real, and He is person.

Lord, I want to help others know You, not just as "god" but as the true God of the universe. Help me be courageous to use Your name when witnessing.

WEEK 5, DAY 2

The LORD, Everlasting God • Yahweh El Olam

Abraham planted a tamarisk tree at Beersheba, and there he called on the name of the LORD, the Everlasting God. (Genesis 21:33)

For those raised in a "Christian" culture where the Judeo-Christian concept of God pervades our background, the default understanding is that He is everlasting. What's to study about that? But like many things in our background, such things can become caricatures of God at best or meaningless at worst, without some considered reflection.

In this Yahweh-El combination, the English translations are evenly split in rendering the term "olam" as either "everlasting" or "eternal." In English, the former has the sense of future time without end, whereas the latter includes time past, as in "eternity past and eternity future." The Hebrew term can be used in either way depending on the context. The psalmist puts it this way: "Blessed be the LORD God of Israel from everlasting ('olam'), and to everlasting ('olam')" (Ps 41:13). Clearly God is eternal in nature, having no beginning or end (see Heb 7:3 for a similar statement about Jesus Christ's eternality).

The context of our passage, Genesis 21:33, finds Abraham having a conflict with Abimelech, a king in Canaan. In those days, the land was composed of small kingdoms, which were essentially fiefdoms. Abraham had developed a relatively large and powerful entourage of family, servants and others who attached themselves to him. As is typical between rival powers, conflict arose—an issue concerning water rights, the ownership of a certain, strategic water source (Gen 21:25). In ancient times, water access was critical for the agrarian life and commerce.

Abimelech came to understand that indeed the well belonged to Abraham, and with Abraham's goodwill gift, they made a formal agreement and parted company. Abraham attached great significance to this event, as seen by his calling on the "name of the LORD, the Everlasting God." This area later became the city of Beersheba, situated on the southernmost boundary of the land.

Abraham had not yet established possession of the entire land promised by God, but he now had a toe-hold, having taken his place as a power to be reckoned with in the land. Permanence had to do with how long you could maintain military control over your land and property. Survival of the strongest was the rule of the day. Abraham, in a statement of faith, worshiped not just a regional god, like the Philistines around him. He believed that God was everlasting and was able to preserve him in the land.

Lord, trials and difficulties come and go. But You are an everlasting God, the same yesterday, today and forever. I trust in You as my eternal anchor.

WEEK 5, DAY 3

Lord God of Hosts • Yahweh Elohim Sabaoth

[Elijah] said, "I have been very zealous for the LORD, the God of hosts; for the sons of Israel have forsaken Your covenant, torn down Your altars and killed Your prophets with the sword. And I alone am left; and they seek my life, to take it away." (1 Kings 19:10)

"Be careful" is the phrase that comes to mind when reading passages like this one, where people proclaim their fidelity to God and at the same time complain about their situation to God. Clearly the Lord knows whether we are faithful or not. Job, in his wrestling with God, strenuously asserted what God already knew about him, that he was "blameless, upright, fearing God and turning away from evil" (Job 1:1). Habakkuk asserted his fidelity to the purity of God and even challenged God with it: "Your eyes are too pure to approve evil, and You cannot look on wickedness with favor. Why do You look with favor on those who deal treacherously? Why are You silent when the wicked swallow up those more righteous than they?" (Hab 1:13).

Elijah had the temerity to claim he was the only one of all Israel who had stayed true to God. God had called upon him to warn the people of Israel about His impending judgment if they didn't correct their ways. Instead, he lost his bearings by focusing on his own struggles. In his thinking, why wasn't God faithful to Israel? Why wasn't God turning people around? Despite Elijah's commissioning, he feared the worst: not only that Israel would be a lost cause, but that because of his ministry, he would die. He was without hope.

How ironic, then, that he should address God as Yahweh Elohim Sabaoth, the Lord God of Hosts (or Almighty)! In his own mouth was the answer to his hopelessness. The God who called him to service was THE God of Israel; Yahweh was His name. He has at His service the armies of heaven, and He can turn the armies of men to do His will. How can one be hopeless when one believes in a God like that, as Elijah confesses with his own mouth? He seemed to be appealing to God: "Do something, God! That's what You do, but that doesn't seem to be what You are doing now. And now I'm going to die as a result."

Today, we know God through "the Lord Jesus Christ, the Son of God," His full title, if you will. The words can form easily in our mouths, but do we really believe here and now, in this situation, that He is Lord? That He is the Christ, God's Messiah, to free us from all kinds of slavery? That He is God in the flesh, Jesus, the second person of the Trinity? If we do, there is hope!

Lord Jesus Christ, I believe in You, here and now. There is no power on earth that can circumvent Your plan. In You I place my hope.

WEEK 5, DAY 4

LORD Most High • Yahweh Elyon

I will give thanks to the LORD according to His righteousness and will sing praise to the name of the LORD Most High. (Psalm 7:17)

Names of God occur in various permutations—in our verse, Psalm 97:9, occurs God's formal, personal name "Yahweh" tagged with "Elyon," which translated means "the most high." Technically we could say the psalm writer is simply expressing his highest regard for God. However, theology is never forged in a bland, academic vacuum. There is context; there is a story behind his exclamation.

This poem by David was turned into a song for Israel's worship; it provides God's people a rehearsal of a godly man's response to the feeling of being harassed and fearful. As with many Christian hymns and songs, we repeat great truths frequently to remind ourselves how we too should act in similar circumstances. As the apostle Paul writes, "Let the word of Christ richly dwell within you, with all wisdom teaching and admonishing one another with psalms and hymns and spiritual songs, singing with thankfulness in your hearts to God" (Col 3:16). David teaches and admonishes us that we can take refuge in God because He is the LORD Most High.

Can we not all relate to his opening line? "O Lord my God, in You I have taken refuge" (Ps 7:1). One does not turn to God for refuge when one can defend oneself. And what better place can one turn for refuge than the Most High? While the real possibility of physical harm begets the desire for physical protection, our inner fears are too often what drive us. It's at that level David writes. If the physical harm resulted from God's justice for David's own evil behavior, then the consequences would be justified, and David would accept that (Ps 7:3-5). However, that is not the case, at least that David is aware of, so he calls upon the God in whom he has taken refuge.

What he calls for is vindication, as one who has lived a righteous life. "My shield is with God, who saved the upright in heart. God is a righteous judge, and a God who has indignation every day" (Ps 7:19-11). God will bring appropriate, or teleonic, justice to those who do evil: "He has dug a pit and hollowed it out, and has fallen into the hole which he made. His mischief will return upon his own head..." (Ps 7:15–16).

So David, and we along with him, can be thankful that the God we worship and follow is far above all unrighteousness. Everything will have its just consequences, and those consequences will be eternally appropriate.

Lord, I don't need to fear when I am being harassed, because I have taken refuge in Your righteousness. Therefore, I praise You as the LORD Most High.

WEEK 5, DAY 5

LORD of Hosts • Yahweh Sabaoth

Now this man [Elkanah] would go up from his city yearly to worship and to sacrifice to the LORD of hosts in Shiloh. And the two sons of Eli, Hophni and Phinehas, were priests to the LORD there. (1 Samuel 1:3)

The time of the judges was drawing to a close, with the last one, Samuel, occupying the swing position as the people of Israel moved into the time of the kings. The book of 1 Samuel records how this transition took place, the story beginning with a godly couple to whom Samuel was born.

Elkanah was an ardent worshiper of Yahweh Sabaoth, the LORD Almighty. Every year he would make pilgrimage to Shiloh, where the tabernacle and the Ark of the Covenant were kept. There he meticulously offered sacrifices to God. His wife Hannah was childless and was provoked bitterly by Elkanah's other wife (this was during a time when God overlooked having multiple wives). Elkanah tried to compensate Hannah by giving her a double portion of the sacrificial food. His response, we might think somewhat arrogantly today, was this: "Hannah, why do you weep and why do you not eat and why is your heart sad? Am I not better to you than ten sons?" (1 Sam 1:8). Giving him the best possible benefit of the doubt, though, what he seemed to be saying is, "You, Hannah, are my favorite wife, and have more of me than my other wife."

However, Hannah continued to be deeply distressed and wept bitterly. In praying to God, she addressed Him, "O LORD of Hosts [Almighty]." She bargained with God that if He gave her a son, she would dedicate that son to God as a Nazarite, one who would be dedicated to God entirely (1 Sam 1:11). She prayed so emotionally that the high priest, Eli, thought she was drunk. But eventually he began to understand and sent her away in peace.

We see similar name combinations elsewhere in Scripture: "Yahweh Elohim Sabaoth" and "Elohim Sabaoth." In one regard, they could be viewed simply as stylistic variety, and that may be so. But their particular use brings insight into the passages in which they occur. First, we see that Elkanah and Hannah are worshipers of Yahweh, the personal God of Israel, not a generic god like the pagans worship. Even in the spiritually dark time of the judges (see the Book of Judges) there were still those who worshiped Yahweh, carrying on faithfully in the worship patterns He had given to Moses. Second, Elkanah and Hannah knew Him as the God of Hosts (which can also be rendered "Almighty"). He has at His disposal all the angelic forces and every power on earth. Who better to pray to for a supernatural pregnancy than Yahweh Sabaoth?

Lord, in whatever circumstance I find myself, I have complete confidence that You lack no resource in meeting my need, because You are Yahweh Sabaoth.

WEEKEND 5 READING
Hosea 8

PERSONAL REFLECTIONS

WEEK 6, DAY 1

THE LORD Is There • Yahweh Samah

"The city shall be 18,000 cubits round about; and the name of the city from that day shall be, 'The LORD is there.' " (Ezekiel 48:35)

The book of Ezekiel is well known for its sci-fi-like visions of four-faced and four-winged angels, choreographed spinning wheels with rims populated of eyes (Ezekiel 1), and a clip of the noisy reconstruction of human bones (Ezekiel 37). Hollywood graphics hold nothing to this prophet. But the book has more depth than just entertainment for the fantasy seekers.

Ezekiel's ministry overlapped the fall of Jerusalem and early days of the Babylonian exile. God's people were under serious judgment for their continued disobedience and idolatry. One of the most tragic images in Scripture is that of the Spirit of God leaving the temple sanctuary. A little backstory: Moses had seen His glory on Mt. Sinai hundreds of years earlier, and after the people sinned he pleaded with the Lord, "If Your presence does not go with us, do not lead us up from here" (Ex 33:15). God's presence took up residence, as it were, among them as depicted by a cloud in the tabernacle (Exodus 40) and later in the temple (1 Kings 8). Now in Ezekiel's day, God's presence was leaving the temple because of their unrelenting sinfulness!

Ezekiel wrote, "The hand of the LORD God fell on me," and in a vision, he recognized that "the glory of the God of Israel was there" (Ezek 8:1-4). He saw that the elders of Israel were each secretly worshiping their idols, saying, "The LORD does not see us; the LORD has forsaken the land" (Ezek 8:12); and the priests had arrayed themselves "with their backs to the temple of the LORD and … were prostrating themselves eastward toward the sun (Ezek 8:16)!

Ezekiel saw in the vision, "Then the glory of the LORD [Yahweh] departed from the threshold of the temple … rose up from the earth … and stood still at the entrance of the east gate of the LORD'S house … The glory of the LORD went up from the midst of the city …" (Ezek 10:18-19, 11:23). On a personal level, this had been Kind David's greatest fear: "Do not cast me away from Your presence and do not take Your Holy Spirit from me" (Ps 51:11). And now, in Ezekiel's time, the LORD's presence was being taken away from Israel!

But there is coming a day when "the name of the city from that day shall be, 'The LORD is there.' " (Ezekiel 48:35). Until then, we have the presence of the glory of God in the person of Jesus: "And the Word became flesh, and dwelt among us, and we saw His glory, glory as of the only begotten from the Father, full of grace and truth" (John 1:14).

Lord Jesus, You are here, Immauel, God with us. Help me to see and sense and believe in Your very real presence with me, and with us as a church.

WEEK 6, DAY 2

THE LORD Our Provider • Yahweh Jireh

Abraham called the name of that place The LORD Will Provide, as it is said to this day, "In the mount of the LORD it will be provided." (Genesis 22:14)

Pivotal in biblical history is the event in our passage today, Abraham offering up Isaac, his promised son. Abraham had waited long for God's promise of descendants, but he believed.

> *The word of the LORD came to him, saying, "... one who will come forth from your own body, he shall be your heir ... Now look toward the heavens, and count the stars, if you are able to count them." And He said to him, "So shall your descendants be." Then he believed in the LORD; and He reckoned it to him as righteousness. (Gen 15:4–6)*

God reaffirmed the promise made long before, but now Abraham was pushing 80-90 years old and it had not happened yet, not even the first descendant! But against all human sensibilities, Abraham dared to believe with an audacious, unwavering faith. And, note it well, God "reckoned it to him as righteousness." Yes, this was absolutely pivotal, as our salvation today is rooted in this very event! Righteousness is not something earned or merited, but comes from the promises of God. We are blessed in salvation today through faith, just as Abraham was blessed through His faith in God's promises.

Fast forward, Isaac was born when Abraham was 100 years old (Genesis 21), becoming for us the supreme example of patience waiting for God's promises to be fulfilled! Continuing ahead, when Isaac became a boy old enough to carry wood, God commanded Abraham to sacrifice him as a burnt offering. Today, we recoil at such a command, but God who gives life and takes life (and does so every time someone dies) can command the taking of life. Lest we bog down, we must note the point of the story is that God was testing Abraham's faith. Would he choose familial feelings over faithful obedience?

Did Abraham know exactly what God was going to do when he told his unsuspecting son, "God will provide for Himself a lamb for the burnt offering, my son" (Gen 22:8)? The writer of Hebrews said, "He [Abraham] considered that God is able to raise people even from the dead, from which he also received him [Isaac] back as a type" (Heb 11:19). Just as Abraham lifted his knife to begin the sacrifice, the Angel of the LORD stopped him, and provided an animal for sacrifice instead. I am sure to his great relief and joy, Abraham assigned this epithet to that place of sacrifice: "The LORD Will Provide" (Yahweh Jireh).

> *Lord, I commit to obeying You in faith, no matter how difficult Your command, because I believe that You are Yahweh Jireh, the One who Provides!*

WEEK 6, DAY 3

The LORD Our Sanctifier • Yahweh Macaddeshkem

The LORD spoke to Moses, saying, "But as for you, speak to the sons of Israel, saying, 'You shall surely observe My sabbaths; for this is a sign between Me and you throughout your generations, that you may know that I am the LORD who sanctifies you.'" (Exodus 31:12–13).

Capstone of the Law was the sabbath law. What began with "I am the Lord your God…you shall have no other gods before Me" (Ex 20:2-3), climaxes with God's desire for the sanctity of His people. Immediately after giving this last commandment, God "gave Moses the two tablets of the testimony, tablets of stone, written by the finger of God" (Ex 20:18).

Keeping the seventh day of the week special was God's way of reminding them ("a sign") of their specialness in His eyes. In fact, His command to keep the sabbath day holy was His activity of sanctifying them. And when they kept this law, they were entering into that sanctification. There is always the human part that cooperates and comes alongside the divine part. As Paul says, "If we live by the Spirit, let us also keep in step with the Spirit" (Gal 5:25).

God was serious about this and imposed capital punishment for its violation: "Therefore you are to observe the sabbath, for it is holy to you. Everyone who profanes it shall surely be put to death; for whoever does any work on it, that person shall be cut off from among his people" (Ex 31:14). If someone did work on the sabbath, the Law said they should immediately die! Yet they were told to "celebrate the sabbath throughout their generations as a perpetual covenant" (Ex 31:16). It's hard for us today to fathom living under this kind of law.

So why don't we "celebrate" the sabbath today? Christians set aside Sundays for worship, ostensibly to commemorate Christ's resurrection on the first day of the week. Some have even applied the sabbath laws to preclude working on Sundays. But of poignant interest is the striking absence of support for the sabbath laws by our Lord Jesus Christ or His disciples, even while we see the other nine commandments affirmed throughout the New Testament.

What does this sabbath law in the OT tell us about God that is unchanging? He is still the God who sanctifies (Heb 2:11); He sets His people apart as special. It begs the question: what activities, behaviors and attitudes is He working in our lives that we need to keep in step with? If we do not cooperate with Him, we may not face physical death, but we will experience the death of our spiritual growth. He wants us sanctified; that is serious business!

Lord, You have commanded me, "Be holy, for I am holy." That is my desire and my hope; I want to keep in step with what You desire for my life.

WEEK 6, DAY 4

The LORD Our Banner • Yahweh Nissi

Moses built an altar and named it The LORD is My Banner; and he said, "The LORD has sworn; the LORD will have war against Amalek from generation to generation." (Exodus 17:15–16)

Banners in the ancient world showed prominently during war. They were the rallying symbol, the flag if you will. As long as the banner was up and moving forward the armies pressed on. When it fell, someone else would pick it up and carry it forward. The person carrying it, though obviously limited in his own personal engagement with the enemy, was performing a task much greater than himself. For if the banner fell and stayed down, that meant there was no one who believed in the effort enough to pick it up again; the will to fight was lost, every man fended for himself, and that was when the cause was lost. Some armies collected the banners of their defeated foes as prizes.

When Moses named an altar "The LORD is my Banner" he was acknowledging that Yahweh was the rallying flag. As surely as there is a God above and His name is Yahweh, there could be no defeat for Israel. The problem was that often Israel didn't really believe that. They wanted God as their banner only when a battle turned against them; then they cried out for His help. But they often strayed and worshipped other gods, like the golden calves of Egypt.

The back story to our passage today takes place during the exodus trek from Egypt to the promised land of Canaan. Moses' understudy, Joshua, was commanding the troops in a fight against their perennial enemies, the Amalekites (possibly descendants of Esau, brother of Jacob, as seen in Genesis 36:12). Moses stationed himself on a hilltop in sight of the troops, holding his hands up. When Moses' hands were up, the battle went in Israel's favor. When down, the Amalekites prevailed. Moses was a kind of banner, a rallying symbol. We are not told whether the troops would occasionally look over their shoulder to see if Moses' hands were up, or whether God responded to Moses' hand position.

What we do know is that after Israel won the battle, Moses put it all together clearly. He himself was not the banner, "The LORD is my Banner." And as the leader of Israel, this meant the LORD was Israel's banner. Today, our banner is the Lord Jesus Christ. When Jesus lifted the bread and cup and said, "Do this in remembrance of Me," He presented Himself as our banner, our rallying point, with the Lord's Supper being our symbol by which we remember Him. We do well to follow the early church, of whom it is written, "They were continually devoting themselves ...to the breaking of bread" (Acts 20:42).

Lord, when I am feeling defeated, I have only to set my mind on You, my banner.

WEEK 6, DAY 5

The LORD is My Shepherd • Yahweh Ra'ah

The LORD is my shepherd, I shall not want. (Psalm 23:1)

One of the most beloved portions of all Scripture, Psalm 23 has brought comfort to millions through the years, especially at times of loss and grief. As A.F. Kirkpatrick says in his commentary, The Book of Psalms, "Each sheep can claim the care which is promised to the whole flock." The benefits from these promises come from knowing Yahweh Ra'ah, "The LORD is my Shepherd." Nowhere do we see the meaning of His name Yahweh more poignantly expressed in such personal terms. Now we know Him through Jesus, who appropriated this title: "I am the Good Shepherd" (John 10:11).

In this psalm we see the benefits of knowing Yahweh Ra'ah:

- Contentment – "I shall not want" even in the midst of many needs.
- Relief – "He makes me lie down in green pastures" even when life seems hard and barren.
- Peace – "He leads me beside quiet waters" when life is in turmoil.
- Revival – "He restores my soul" when I struggle spiritually (Ps 19:7).
- Guidance in right living – "He guides me in the paths of righteousness" when the way forward seems convoluted.
- His purpose in our lives – "For His name's sake" not mine.
- Confidence to replace fear – "Even though I walk through the valley of the shadow of death, I fear no evil" when things threaten me.
- His protective presence – "You are with me," assuring me when I feel vulnerable.
- His concern for my well-being – "Your rod and Your staff, they comfort me" when I feel unloved or uncared for.
- His enjoyment of me – "You prepare a table before me in the presence of my enemies" when I feel marginalized.
- His fellowship – "You have anointed my head with oil" when I feel unacceptable (Ps 133).
- His blessing – "My cup overflows" even in the midst of earthly deprivation.
- Hope for this life – "Surely goodness and lovingkindness will follow me all the days of my life" when the outlook seems grim.
- An assured eternity – "And I will dwell in the house of the LORD forever." Amen!

Lord, You are my Shepherd. Thank You for Your real presence in my life.

WEEKEND 6 READING
Hosea 9

PERSONAL REFLECTIONS

WEEK 7, DAY 1

The LORD Is Our Healer • Yahweh Rapha

And [Moses] said, "If you will give earnest heed to the voice of the LORD your God, and do what is right in His sight, and give ear to His commandments, and keep all His statutes, I will put none of the diseases on you which I have put on the Egyptians; for I, the LORD, am your healer [Rapha]." (Exodus 15:26)

Oh that we believers in Christ would be preserved from ever getting sick. The reality is that we live in a fallen world (see Rom 8:22) that will be renewed only at the coming of "a new heaven and a new earth" (Rev 21:1). So what do we make of our passage in Exodus 15:26? Can we believers today claim healing whenever we want it? Many today would say yes, and use verses like Isaiah 53:5 as support: "And by His scourging we are healed." Indeed, Jesus Himself said that His followers would do greater works than He did (John 14:12). And Peter's quote from Joel in his Pentecost sermon gives evidence of the miraculous effects of following Christ (Acts 2:17).

Oh that the miracle purveyors were right about their interpretation of these things! Hospitals would be much emptier with Christians cured of illness. We would never have cancer, diabetes, permanent injuries, congenital deformities or other debilitating maladies. Following that reasoning, we would never die, for we Christians would be freed from the ultimate disease, namely death and its sting (1 Cor 15:55-56). But in the end, something gets all of us! Even many so-called "faith-healers" wear glasses and suffer from the common cold.

So what then does it mean that the LORD is our Healer? In context, Moses declared this specifically for the Jewish people during the Exodus period of Israel. They were on their way to the promised land that would be everything Egypt was not. Etched permanently in the collective memory of the Jews were the ten plagues that had devastated the Egyptians leading up to the Exodus. The promised land of Canaan would be a land flowing with "milk and honey." Yes, God promised they would experience the ultimate earthly environment, maybe even similar to the Garden of Eden. But His healing would require their hearing and obedience. Complete obedience. Of course, obedience was in short supply, and the Jewish people fell far short, so they lost their reward of God's healing.

God's character as Yahweh Rapha, however, still stands. For example, in context, He had just healed the bitter water at Marah to provide for their thirst (Ex 15:21-25), despite their complaining. God can and at times does heal all our diseases (Ps 103:3), but never because we deserve it. He heals because of His grace and mercy. And He has healed us of the greatest disease of all: Sin.

LORD Rapha, I thank You eternally for healing me from the spiritual-life-killing disease of sin, through Your forgiveness and the new life You give.

WEEK 7, DAY 2

The LORD of Hosts • Yahweh Sabbaoth

In the year of King Uzziah's death I saw the Lord sitting on a throne, lofty and exalted, with the train of His robe filling the temple. Seraphim stood above Him, each having six wings: with two he covered his face, and with two he covered his feet, and with two he flew. And one called out to another and said, "Holy, Holy, Holy, is the LORD of hosts [Sabbaoth], the whole earth is full of His glory." (Isaiah 6:1–3)

Uzziah had not learned that the God of Israel, Yahweh, was holy, and that He was the one who sets the terms for approaching Him. Uzziah was king of Judah during the split-kingdom era. Though he was a descendant of the "God's-heart" King David, he became arrogant and presumed upon God's holiness. He had earthly power and now he wanted spiritual power too, so he attempted to do what God had authorized only the priests to do: enter the temple to burn incense. Who on earth could oppose this king, who commanded the hosts (armies) of Israel?

But Uzziah's presumptuous actions transgressed an authority far greater than his own. (2 Chron 26:16-23). When he raged against the priests for resisting his self-acclaimed prerogative, God plagued him with the dreaded leprosy, and he was saddled with the social stigma until his death. Despite his arrogance and earthly power, his memorial was simply, "He is a leper," and he lived out his days in isolation (2 Chron 26:21-23).

Notice that our passage begins, "In the year of King Uzziah's death" (Isaiah 6:1). The unholy Uzziah died, and the vision of a thrice-holy Yahweh of Hosts is revealed. He who was a leper versus He who is absolutely holy; he who was untouchable because of his contagion of sin versus He who is unapproachable because of His perfection. An earthly king in command of Judah's armies versus the LORD of celestial armies, Yahweh of Hosts. He who would presume to take over the temple versus He who dwelt in the temple. He who was rebuffed by the priestly attendants versus He who was worshipped and adored by the angelic attendants. What a contrast, indeed.

The LORD Sabbaoth is "lofty and exalted" sitting on a throne, His authority unmitigated and unchallenged. "The train of His robe [filled] the temple"—no unholy feet could possibly stand in His presence, for that would be holy ground. Godly men, unlike Uzziah, shrink back from presuming upon God's holiness. Moses, when confronted with God in the burning bush, was told, "Do not come near here; remove your sandals from your feet, for the place on which you are standing is holy ground" (Ex 3:5).

Lord, You are holy; I often live an unholy life. How can I ever approach You?

WEEK 7, DAY 3

The LORD of Hosts (cont.) • Yahweh Sabbaoth

And the foundations of the thresholds trembled at the voice of him who called out, while the temple was filling with smoke. Then I said, "Woe is me, for I am ruined! Because I am a man of unclean lips, And I live among a people of unclean lips; For my eyes have seen the King, the LORD of hosts [Sabbaoth]." Then one of the seraphim flew to me with a burning coal in his hand, which he had taken from the altar with tongs. He touched my mouth with it and said, "Behold, this has touched your lips; and your iniquity is taken away and your sin is forgiven." (Isaiah 6:4–7)

Inanimate objects in the Lord's presence "trembled" when He spoke. Unlike Uzziah's false confidence, maybe even swagger, the "thresholds" (also translated "doorposts" or "door sockets" as in the NIV) move at the Lord's voice. The sound and light show exceeded anything modern computer animation could ever attempt. One of the most revered men in biblical history began to quiver with the awful response, "Woe is me, for I am ruined." The Hebrew word has a sense of causing to cease to exist. Isaiah felt himself disintegrating.

The absolute discord was immediately and intuitively obvious. Isaiah's reaction was not a logical deduction, nor was it simply a moral conclusion he came to after some time of reflection. It was more like two magnets that repel each other. Imagine the repelling force between the two beings so great that the force itself destroys the lesser magnet. This was Isaiah's reality when he said, "I am ruined." Holiness and sinfulness simply cannot abide peacefully together. That which is unholy will be destroyed by the holiness of God.

Nothing shows the sinfulness of a human being more than exposure to God's holiness, and Isaiah felt this deeply. This notion is not subject to the mental cud-chewing of philosophers or ivory-tower theologians. It will be the horror of those who are lost in their sin when they stand before God, as described by the apostle John: "Then I saw a great white throne and Him who sat upon it, from whose presence earth and heaven fled away … and I saw the dead, the great and the small, standing before the throne …" (Rev 20:11-12).

Better to come before the throne of Yahweh Sabbaoth, the LORD of Hosts, now—willingly—rather than wait for the final judgment. The only way to do that is God's way. God provided for Isaiah. His problem was "unclean lips," for which the angel touched his lips with a burning, hot coal, picturing that his sins were forgiven. Today, we can come before our holy God's throne because God sent His Son to be our burnt offering, that is, to take away our sin.

LORD Sabbaoth, You are so absolutely holy, and You have prepared me to come into Your presence by taking my sins away. What more could I ask?

WEEK 7, DAY 4

The LORD Our Peace • Yahweh Shalom

When Gideon saw that he was the angel of the LORD, he said, "Alas, O Lord GOD! For now I have seen the angel of the LORD face to face." The LORD said to him, "Peace to you, do not fear; you shall not die." Then Gideon built an altar there to the LORD and named it The LORD is Peace. (Judges 6:22–24)

Gideon, the fifth of 15 judges of ancient Israel, which included such luminaries as Samson and the prophet Samuel, followed the lone woman judge. While the vast majority of leaders recorded in Scripture were men, God at times raised up women. In Deborah's time, the men of Israel were weak-kneed and would not even go to battle unless she was with them (presumably not because of any physical or military prowess on her part). So after her death, Gideon's military strategies and exploits made him stand out for extended treatment by the writer of the Book of Judges.

Against the backdrop of the Midianites' assaults on Israel, God sent "The angel of the LORD [Yawheh]" to a humble farmer named Gideon to lead His people to victory over the enemy. The evidence shows that this was no ordinary angel but a pre-incarnate appearance of Christ. First, the way this phrase "angel of the LORD" is used in Scripture (see Gen 16:7-11; 22:11-15, etc.) points toward God Himself. For instance, to Moses the angel of the LORD appeared in a burning bush, but the voice was identified as that of God Himself (Ex 3:2-3, 6). Second, the angel of the Lord is treated with greater deference in Scripture than common angels. And finally, there is no mention of the angel of the Lord after the incarnation of Jesus Christ.

In response to the Lord's commissioning him, Gideon was overwhelmed and greatly feared for his life (possibly due to fear of dying in battle, but more surely due to being in the Lord's presence, similar to Isaiah's fear in Isaiah 6:5). "Alas, Lord GOD! For now I have seen the angel of the Lord face to face" (Judges 6:22). The Lord responded, "Peace to you, do not fear; you shall not die." What comforting thoughts for the fearful farmer.

At this, Gideon built an altar, a common memory device in OT Israel, and called it "Yahweh Shalom" or "The LORD is Peace." By inferential application we too can say the LORD is our Peace. This reminds us of our Lord in the upper room the night before He died: "These things I have spoken to you, so that in Me you may have peace. In the world you have tribulation, but take courage; I have overcome the world" (John 16:33).

Lord, help me to see the peace You bring to my life, despite anxious fears that can so easily consume me.

WEEK 7, DAY 5

The LORD Who Is Present • Yahweh Shammah

"The city shall be 18,000 cubits round about; and the name of the city from that day shall be, 'The LORD is there [Shammah].' " (Ezekiel 48:35)

In this last verse in the book of Ezekiel, his vision injects hope into the people of Israel, now in Babylonian exile. The nation had been ransacked, Jerusalem destroyed, and its people taken into captivity, echoing their slavery in Egypt many centuries earlier. The book was written to the captives, clearly denouncing the practices that had led to the destruction of Jerusalem—primarily their unfaithfulness to Yahweh and their turning to pagan gods. Yet the book is all about the Lord's faithfulness to Israel. From His Glory departing the temple and the holy city of Jerusalem (Ezekiel 11:23) to His Glory returning to dwell in a new temple (Ezekiel 43:2-5; 44:4) in the millennial kingdom, Yahweh will never completely or permanently abandon His people.

In the final vision of the book (Ezekiel 40-48), God reveals a picture of the land of Israel when the people would be restored to it. About the inner sanctuary of the temple we read, "Son of man, this is the place ... where I will dwell among the sons of Israel forever" (Ezek 43:7). In our verse today, Jerusalem is characterized by the name given it: Yahweh will be present there.

We take this vision to portray the millennial kingdom of Israel, God Himself being permanently present in the earthly Jerusalem. Some refer to the reign of King David as the godliest era in Israel's history, and others refer to Solomon's reign as the "golden age" of Israel. However, the coming millennial era will be the ultimate kingdom of God on this present earth and will extend 1,000 years (Revelation 20:7), with the Lord's glory present in Jerusalem in a very real way. This era will conclude with a final eschatological battle when the devil and his demonic armies will be finally and forever defeated (Rev 20:7-10). The "Great White Throne" judgment (Rev 20:11) will bring to a close the time of this present earth's history. God then will make a new heaven and a new earth (Rev 21:1). A new Jerusalem will come down from heaven with this description: "I saw no temple in it, for the Lord God the Almighty and the Lamb are its temple" (Rev 21:22). The Lord will be there, forever and forever. That is what Ezekiel's prophecy conveys to us. That is the hope of Israel

Today, we have the Lord's presence with us continually. He came as Immanuel (literally, "God with us"). He promised, "I will never desert you, nor will I ever forsake you" (Heb 13:5) and assures His followers, "I am with you always, even to the end of the age" (Matt 28:20). Nothing can ever separate us from the love of God (Romans 8:38-39).

Lord, when I feel alone and abandoned, I know You are always present with me.

WEEKEND 7 READING
Hosea 10

PERSONAL REFLECTIONS

WEEK 8, DAY 1

The LORD Our Righteousness • Yahweh Tsidkenu

"Behold, the days are coming," declares the LORD, "When I will raise up for David a righteous Branch; and He will reign as king and act wisely and do justice and righteousness in the land. In His days Judah will be saved, and Israel will dwell securely; and this is His name by which He will be called, 'The LORD [Yahweh] our righteousness [tsidkenu].'" (Jeremiah 23:5–6)

Hope of the future had kept God's people from complete collapse into despondency. The ray of light at the end of the proverbial tunnel, the sliver of hope to which one holds, the strong cord on which one desperately hangs? No! Rather, an anchor, a solid reference point as history careens along in this fallen world. From the seed promise in Eden (Gen 3:15) until the coming of the Messiah and His promised return, God has left His golden trail of hope.

During Israel's darkest times, the downline of King David's dynasty had turned away from God with exacting punishments. King Jehoiakim (also called Coniah or Jeconiah) was the 20th generational king in the line of David, and under his watch Israel surrendered to Babylon, the treasures of the temple were removed, and the people taken into captivity. His punishment was that none of his physical descendants would ever carry on the throne of David (Jer 22:28-30, 36:30). The promise to David seems to have come to an end: "He [Jehoiakim king of Judah] shall have no one to sit on the throne of David …" (Jer 36:30).

But God's promise to David was binding: "Your house and your kingdom shall endure before Me forever; your throne shall be established forever" (2 Sam 7:16). How could this be, if it came to an end with Jehoiakim, the kingly line? What about Jesus being a descendant of David and therefore King of Israel? While the details exceed the scope of this essay, the resolution is found in the two genealogies of Jesus. The blood line, His physical lineage, came through Mary, whose line traced back through King David's son, Nathan (Luke 34:31). But Jesus' kingly line was traced back to Jehoiakim (Matt 1:11, there called Jeconiah) through His adoption by Joseph, Mary's husband. David's promise was fulfilled then despite the curse on Jehoiakim, which endured.

The point in Jeremiah, though, is that despite the curse discontinuing the Davidic line through unrighteous Jehoiakim, the promise to David still goes on. What a grand hope this was in the darkest time of Israel. God will revive the great promise that a descendant of David would reign with wisdom, justice and righteousness. His name will be "The LORD our righteousness."

Lord, when the world judges Christians as immoral hypocrites, I take refuge in You, my Righteousness.

WEEK 8, DAY 2

LORD • Yah

"Behold, God [El] is my salvation, I will trust and not be afraid; for the LORD [YAHWEH] GOD [YAH] is my strength and song, and He has become my salvation." (Isaiah 12:2)

This one verse contains three names of God, with "Yah" representing a shortened form of "Yahweh." The NIV translates the verse, "... for the LORD, the LORD Himself, is my strength ..." seeing both terms as referring to the divine name Yahweh. Shortening the name—and using it alongside the longer form—fits the poetic structure of the passage in which our verse is found. We are reminded of Moses' song: "The Lord is my strength and song, and He has become my salvation; this is my God, and I will praise Him; my father's God, and I will extol Him" (Ex 15:2, see also Ps 118:14). Yah is to be praised precisely because it is in His nature to give salvation and strength to those who trust in Him. Hardly can this be uttered without singing its truth.

The meaning of the word "Yah" basically draws from the term "Yahweh." However, our interest is found more in the term's later use in a more recognizable form, the Hebrew word combination "hallel-u-jah." In most English translations this is rendered, "Praise the LORD." The first part of the word, "hallel," means "praise." The "u" indicates a grammatical imperative or command, and "jah" renders the Hebrew "Yah." So when the world exclaims "Hallelujah," from the lips of the unsaved comes praise for Yahweh!

The LORD is worthy to be praised, as seen in Psalms (for example, 104:35; 105:45; 106:1, 48; 111:1; 112:1; 113:1, 9; 115:18; 116:19; 117:2; 135:1, 3, 21; 146:1, 10; 147:1, 20; 148:1, 14; 149:1, 9; 150:1, 6). Sometimes the psalmist calls others to praise, while at times he challenges himself to praise the LORD.

Who can think of this word without the background echo in our minds of Handel's famous oratorio, The Messiah, in particular the grand finale?

Hallelujah: for the Lord God Omnipotent reigneth
The kingdom of this word is become the kingdom of our Lord, and of His Christ; and He shall reign for ever and ever.
King of Kings, and Lord of Lords.

Theology is the study of God; doxology is the praise of God. The study of God has no valid purpose unless it leads to praising Him. If it doesn't, then we don't understand Him. Yah is to be praised because He is the One who gives us salvation and strength. To do anything else is to miss the point of theology.

Hallelujah! You, my God, shall reign for ever and ever!

WEEK 8, DAY 3

Lord • Adonai

He [Moses] said, "If now I have found favor in Your sight, O Lord [Adonai], I pray, let the Lord [Adonai] go along in our midst, even though the people are so obstinate, and pardon our iniquity and our sin, and take us as Your own possession." (Exodus 34:9)

While Moses was receiving the Law from God on Mt. Sinai over the course of 40 days (Ex 24:18), the people turned away from God to idolatry (Ex 32:1-6), breaking the first of the commandments Moses was receiving: "I am the Lord your God ... You shall have no other gods before Me. You shall not make for yourself an idol ... you shall not worship them or serve them ..." (Ex 20:2-5). How quickly do people abandon God, whom they cannot see, for man-made images they can see and touch!

The Lord had pre-warned Moses of this betrayal of loyalty and sent Moses down "at once" (Ex 32:7) to convey His message: "Let Me alone, that My anger may burn against them and that I may destroy them; and I will make of you [Moses] a great nation" (Ex 32:10). Moses, in his absolute loyalty and devotion to God, intercedes—not on behalf of the people, but on behalf of God! If God were to destroy the Jews, Moses pleaded, the Egyptians would think Him to be an evil god who simply devised the exodus from Egypt as a means of killing them. As a result, "The LORD changed His mind." But Moses was mad at the people, throwing down the newly minted tablets of the Law, shattering them to shards (Ex 32:14).

A short time later, we find Moses again pleading with God to forgive the people or to take his life instead. In the end, God did destroy some of the people, the ones who actively engaged in the idol worship, but spared the innocent ones. God then said He would send an angel before them into the Promised Land, implying that He Himself would not go with them. Moses responded, "If now I have found favor in Your sight, O Lord, I pray, let the Lord go along in our midst, even though the people are so obstinate, and pardon our iniquity and our sin, and take us as Your own possession" (Ex 34:9, see also Ex 33:12-18).

After Moses replaced the tablets on Mt. Sinai, he saw the Lord as being "compassionate and gracious, slow to anger, and abounding in lovingkindness and truth..." (Ex 34:6). He therefore appealed again to the Lord, as Adonai (which carries the sense of a master with authority), to go with Israel despite their being obstinate.

Lord Adonai, You have the power and strength to lead me, despite the weakness of my loyalty and resolve in following You.

WEEK 8, DAY 4

Lord GOD • Adonai Yahweh

Joshua said, "Alas, O Lord GOD [Adonai Yahweh], why did You ever bring this people over the Jordan, only to deliver us into the hand of the Amorites, to destroy us? If only we had been willing to dwell beyond the Jordan!" (Joshua 7:7)

Even great leaders sometimes question God when suffering defeat. Under Joshua's leadership, Israel's first military foray into the Promised Land went down as a wild success, totally obliterating Jericho. They had seen God divide the Jordan River for their miraculous crossing, and then witnessed the great walls of the fortified city miraculously fall. God's promise held true:

"No man will be able to stand before you all the days of your life … I will be with you; I will not fail you or forsake you … you shall give this people … the land which I swore to their fathers to give them" (Josh 1:5–6).

Confidence ran high. Word on the street, as Rahab the woman of Jericho earlier put it, was this: "The terror of [Israel] has fallen on us … all the inhabitants of the land have melted away before you" (Josh 2:9). They must have thought, "If God be for us, who can stand against us?" as the apostle Paul would later write (Rom 8:31). Indeed, "The LORD was with Joshua, and his fame was in all the land" (Josh 6:27).

But—and this is the pivotal word, "but," in the very next verse—after proclaiming God's faithfulness to Joshua, our text tersely points out: "But the sons of Israel acted unfaithfully…" (Josh 7:1a). This is the eternal exception, the fulcrum of God's relationship with His image bearers: He is gracious, working on our behalf, and we are to be faithful to Him, trusting His word. God brought defeat where He had promised victory. "Therefore the anger of the LORD burned against the sons of Israel" (Josh 7:1b), resulting in complete disaster in their second military offensive, at the hands of the army of Ai.

Joshua was devastated and began to question God. Notice, he went directly to the ultimate source that had animated him from the beginning, the Lord GOD, Adonai Yahweh, as we read in Joshua 7:7. He did not blame a faulty battle plan, nor regress into self-doubt. He understood the divine dimension in the event, and it didn't make any sense at all. Why would the Lord GOD bring defeat when He had promised victory? He soon discovered there was sin in the camp and that one person's sin affected the whole nation (Josh 7:20-26). Though we may use our human reasoning to understand failure, we must look to the Lord GOD, Yahweh Adonai. He ultimately controls the destinies of all men, both great and small.

Lord, in life's confusing defeats, help me understand Your guiding hand.

WEEK 8, DAY 5

Adonai Yahweh Sabbaoth

"What do you mean by crushing My people and grinding the face of the poor?" declares the Lord GOD of hosts [sabbaoth]. (Isaiah 3:15)

Used primarily around the Babylonian exile, this extended fusion of divine names was reserved by the prophets Isaiah and Jeremiah for terse charges against Israel. God's decadent and faithless people were accountable to the covenant-keeping Master of the universe, who always acts on behalf of His people, who has at His disposal all the angelic forces, and who can marshal any army on earth for His purposes. The LORD God of Hosts is not to be taken lightly when He speaks: Adonai Yahweh Sabbaoth!

Who was God speaking to in Isaiah 3:15? None other than "the elders and princes of His people" (Is 3:13). What was their offense? Unfaithfulness to God, which led to the oppression of others and obsession with self.

God described the actions of Israel's leaders and prominent men as "crushing My people and grinding the face of the poor." Meanwhile, the women were caught up in their sexual allurement: "The daughters of Zion are proud and walk with heads held high and seductive eyes, and go along with mincing steps and tinkle the bangles on their feet … the LORD will take away the beauty of their anklets, headbands, crescent ornaments, dangling earrings, bracelets …" (Is 3:16, 18-26). God's people had become self-obsessed and with little care for anyone else, especially society's most vulnerable. God repeatedly portrayed their idolatry using the metaphor of divorce. Their unfaithfulness to Him showed in their callousness toward others, excessive narcissism and extreme self-interest.

The Christian movement in recent history has struggled with the role of social involvement, despite such a clear window into God's heart in passages like Isaiah 3:15. Early 20th century saw a move toward more social engagement, but was accompanied unfortunately with an abandonment of the Gospel of Jesus Christ. In response, conservative evangelicals attempted to counter the liberal movement away from the purity of the Gospel. "Social gospel" became a derisive term, and efforts to relieve earthly human suffering were replaced by an exclusive focus on the eternal suffering of hell, the spiritual need for salvation from God's anger, and entrance into His eternal rest.

Yahweh Adonai Sabbaoth cares for the poor and disadvantaged, and we should not take that lightly. Did not Jesus teach, "… inasmuch as you did it to one of the least of these My brethren, you did it to Me" (Matt 25:40 NKJV)?

Lord, I confess my inordinate attention to myself at the expense of those around me who are disadvantaged.

WEEKEND 8 READING
Hosea 11

PERSONAL REFLECTIONS

WEEK 9, DAY 1

Ancient of Days

"I kept looking until thrones were set up, and the Ancient of Days took His seat; His vesture was like white snow and the hair of His head like pure wool. His throne was ablaze with flames, its wheels were a burning fire. A river of fire was flowing and coming out from before Him; thousands upon thousands were attending Him, and myriads upon myriads were standing before Him; the court sat, and the books were opened." (Daniel 7:9–10)

A vision of four beasts begins a series of revelations given to the prophet Daniel. Startled, Daniel describes the images as "dreadful and terrifying" (Dan 7:7). He writes, "My spirit was distressed within me, and the visions in my mind kept alarming me" (Dan 7:15). Future history was unfolding before his eyes, a succession of four empires, which prophetic scholars have identified as the Babylonian, Persian, Greek and Roman empires (the last of which will be revived at some future time).

Not only did Daniel live through the instability of successive kingships during his own life in exile from the land of Israel, but the future the world was in for continual disruption through international conflict and domination. The march of humanity does not bode well for ever arriving at "peace." That is an extremely disconcerting thought, especially for the people of Israel, who had been promised world prominence and blessing through their ancestor Abraham (Gen 12:1-3). What little memory of that vow, that pledge God had made so long ago to the patriarch and his descendants was surely faded in their present experience of successive oppressions of foreign control.

In the midst of what might have seemed like depressing prospects of continued domination by powerful empires, we find enthroned over that future history the enigmatic "Ancient of Days," who has been enthroned since ancient times. In the ancient world where age was respected for its accumulated wisdom and stature, this One that Daniel saw eclipses all wisdom and stature. Notice how He is described: clothes of pure white, indicating absolute purity; His throne engulfed in flames, a sign of fierce judgment. The record books were opened, for He is the one who "came and judgment was passed in favor of the saints of the Highest One, and the time arrived when the saints took possession of the kingdom" (Daniel 7:22). There is hope, because God will come and His people will reign with Him over all. The Ancient of Days is not limited by the sequential flow of time and history or the machinations of human hearts. We today also have the One who is the first and the last, the Alpha and Omega (Rev 1:8). History is controlled by Him whose name is "the Ancient of Days."

Lord, I have no fear of the future in You, because You are the Ancient of Days.

WEEK 9, DAY 2

Compassionate and Gracious God

Then the LORD passed by in front of [Moses] and proclaimed, "The LORD, the LORD God, compassionate and gracious, slow to anger, and abounding in lovingkindness and truth; who keeps lovingkindness for thousands, who forgives iniquity, transgression and sin; yet He will by no means leave the guilty unpunished, visiting the iniquity of fathers on the children and on the grandchildren to the third and fourth generations." (Exodus 34:6–7)

Expansive descriptions of God's character are not more succinct anywhere in Scripture as in our verse today. The Lord opened Himself to Moses for an intimate insight into what He is really like, and in the recording of that revelation in Scripture we are privileged to listen in over Moses' shoulder. This was not a theology lesson to be memorized for future examination. Rather, "the LORD used to speak to Moses face to face, just as a man speaks to his friend" (Ex 33:11). I believe this is the kind of communication God intended in the Garden of Eden, when He came down to walk "in the garden in the cool of the day" to spend time with Adam and Eve. He always wants to reveal Himself to His image bearers but will only do so when we are in right relationship with Him. Moses had that with God, an open-faced, transparent friendship, as God called it.

Everything Moses learned about God was true of Him back in the Garden but was obscured by sin. God's compassion and grace are seen in His provision of a future seed that would crush Satan—though Adam and Eve heard of this in cryptic form (Gen 3:14-15). They were driven from the Garden, a gracious move of God to keep them from eating of the tree of life and living forever in a fallen state (Gen 3:22-23).

The backstory to Moses' receiving this revelation of God's character was the formation of the second set of the tablets of the Law. Moses had shattered the first set, made by God (Ex 24:12, 32:16), upon seeing the licentious idolatry the people of Israel had come to engage in while he was on Mt. Sinai receiving the Law (Ex 32:19). Moses returned to God and pleaded on behalf of the people for forgiveness. But if God would not forgive, Moses offered to be blotted out of "Your book which You have written" (Ex 32:32). In other words, Moses would not go further in following God if the people were wiped out by God's anger. Furthermore, Moses would not continue on without God's presence (Gen 33:15). He would rather die instead. Having demonstrated that Moses had a heart like God's, the LORD said, "You have found favor in My sight and I have known you by name" (Ex 33:17).

Lord, help me love Your people and not reject them because of their sin.

WEEK 9, DAY 3

Compassionate and Gracious God (cont.)

Then the LORD passed by in front of [Moses] and proclaimed, "The LORD, the LORD God, compassionate and gracious, slow to anger, and abounding in lovingkindness and truth; who keeps lovingkindness for thousands, who forgives iniquity, transgression and sin; yet He will by no means leave the guilty unpunished, visiting the iniquity of fathers on the children and on the grandchildren to the third and fourth generations." (Exodus 34:6–7)

A personal relationship was developing, upon which Moses hazards a request: "I pray You, show me Your glory!" To this request, God responded, "I Myself will make all My goodness pass before you, and will proclaim the name of the LORD before you; and I will be gracious to whom I will be gracious, and will show compassion on whom I will show compassion" (Ex 33:19). So much "theology" is wrapped up in this statement, but we focus on His compassion and grace.

So God set Moses in "the cleft of the rock" and allowed him to see God's back but not His face (Ex 33:22-23). Our visual limitation in picturing this should not spoil the point: God was going to show Himself to Moses in a moderated but unprecedented way—a full and complete vision of God no mere human could handle (Ex 33:20).

So Moses was instructed to create a new set of tablets; he ascended Mt. Sinai again and "called upon the name of the LORD" (Ex 34:1, 5). What God had previewed for him now took place: "The LORD passed by in front of Him and proclaimed, 'The LORD, the LORD God, compassionate and gracious.'" Keep in mind, at this point God had not yet exacted punishment on those who engaged in idolatry among the people of Israel. The reality of His promise to Moses of going with them into the Promised Land had not yet materialized. But at this juncture, God took Moses into His confidence to reveal what kind of God He is. To present-day ears, this may seem academic, but Moses' quest in life was to continually discover the answer to the question he had asked God at the burning bush: "They may say to me, 'What is His name?' What shall I say to them?" (Ex 3:13). The thrust of the question was this: "What kind of name or character is this God you want us to follow, Moses?" Very possibly the question Moses imagined of the others was in reality his question: What kind of God are you?

Like Moses, the believer's life today is a journey of discovering what kind of God is the one he serves. Paul phrased it "that I may know Him" (Phil 3:10). Peter wrote, "…grow in the grace and knowledge of our Lord and Savior Jesus Christ" (2 Peter 3:18). He is a compassionate and gracious God.

Lord, I want to know You, Your compassion and Your grace.

WEEK 9, DAY 4

Slow to Anger

Then the LORD passed by in front of [Moses] and proclaimed, "The LORD, the LORD God, compassionate and gracious, slow to anger, and abounding in lovingkindness and truth; who keeps lovingkindness for thousands, who forgives iniquity, transgression and sin; yet He will by no means leave the guilty unpunished, visiting the iniquity of fathers on the children and on the grandchildren to the third and fourth generations." (Exodus 34:6–7)

A bad rap is what nominal Christians and non-Christians alike place on the God of the Old Testament. It usually sounds something like this: The OT God is angry, vicious and capricious, but God in the NT is kind, loving and gentle—a turn-the-other-cheek sort of God. Hardly could this be further from the truth.

To be sure, the God of both Testaments is one and the same God, and His character does not change between the two. Indeed, NT passages like Matthew 25:41, Luke 12:48, Hebrews 10:27 and 12:29, 2 Peter 3:7, and the prophecies of Revelation all show God's character in depictions of His burning anger. However, the God of the Bible is not a deity who flies off the handle at the least provocation or on a whim. He is "slow to anger," as our passage above points out. This is God's own assessment.

Remember, God had told the first humans that in the day they ate from the forbidden tree, they would die. However, when that fateful time came, He did not snuff out their lives, but delayed the punishment. He was gracious in not allowing them to eat of the tree of life, so that they would not live forever in a fallen, rebellious state. All along, God showed Himself to be slow to anger. The interaction with Moses following the people's turn to idolatry is a case in point. While God was in fact angry with them for their bold-faced rejection of Him and their turning to other so-called gods, He could have snapped His finger or merely spoken them into oblivion. But instead, He engaged Moses in conversation to contextualize His character. He is "compassionate and gracious, slow to anger."

Throughout Israel's history of rebellion—lip service to Yahweh and continuous forays into idolatry, not to mention their treatment of the poor and disadvantaged—God kept stalling to give them time to repent. From the time of David through the 20 kings of Judah, only a few (three) were godly kings, yet it wasn't until the last one that God finally sent them into exile. Yes, God is slow to anger, slow to act on His anger. I am so glad—otherwise you and I would be long gone to judgment.

Lord, help me never to take Your slowness to anger for granted. For You are quite capable of terrifying wrath, but have graciously held it back from me.

WEEK 9, DAY 5

Abounding in Lovingkindness and Truth

Then the LORD passed by in front of [Moses] and proclaimed, "The LORD, the LORD God, compassionate and gracious, slow to anger, and abounding in lovingkindness and truth; who keeps lovingkindness for thousands, who forgives iniquity, transgression and sin; yet He will by no means leave the guilty unpunished, visiting the iniquity of fathers on the children and on the grandchildren to the third and fourth generations." (Exodus 34:6–7)

Lovingkindness carries great significance. Some have suggested it is the OT equivalent of the NT word "agape." But this comes short. The Hebrew term is "hesed," and along with "truth" is translated variously as lovingkindness and truth (NAS), love and faithfulness (NIV), steadfast love and faithfulness (ESV), loyal love and faithfulness (NET), unfailing love and faithfulness (NLT) or goodness and truth (NKJV).

The sense of the word combination lends itself to that affection and action of God toward those with whom He has entered into a covenant. In that sense, the emphasis is on His faithful loyalty. The first time the word occurs in Scripture, we find it in the mouth of Abraham's servant, when he was looking for a wife for Isaac: "O Lord, the God of my master Abraham, please grant me success today, and show lovingkindness [hesed] to my master Abraham" (Gen 24:12). The servant was recalling in his request to God to act toward Abraham with love because of the promise God had made to the patriarch of a line of blessing through Isaac. If the blessing through Abraham's seed was to continue on, then his only legitimate son must have children, and therefore would need a wife. So the use of "hesed" was significant; God's love toward Abraham was based on His covenant with the patriarch.

The Lord "extended [hesed]" to Joseph (Gen 39:21), for the divine plan to preserve the descendants of Abraham was to raise up Jacob's second-youngest son to rescue the whole family from famine and death; thus the promise to Abraham would continue on to fulfillment.

Yet it may be that God's love is rooted in His character and that His covenant relationship with people is an expression of His "hesed." Because He loves, He uses a covenant to formalize the commitment. We see through the OT God showing Himself as One who loves and is loyal to those He loves and will steadfastly keep His commitment to them, as expressed in the covenants.

Our belief in a God of "hesed" strengthens us to resist the normal human responses to suffering of bitterness, complaint, anger. His goodness (to use the NKJV translation) anchors in eternity. For NT Christians, that love finds its expression in God's ultimate act of love, the death of Jesus Christ for us.

Lord, no matter how difficult my life, Your "hesed" is working for my good.

WEEKEND 9 READING
Hosea 12-13

PERSONAL REFLECTIONS

WEEK 10, DAY 1

The Forgiving God

Then the LORD passed by in front of [Moses] and proclaimed, "The LORD, the LORD God, compassionate and gracious, slow to anger, and abounding in lovingkindness and truth; who keeps lovingkindness for thousands, who forgives iniquity, transgression and sin; yet He will by no means leave the guilty unpunished, visiting the iniquity of fathers on the children and on the grandchildren to the third and fourth generations." (Exodus 34:6–7)

Standing "in the cleft of the rock," covered over with God's hand, only seeing God's back (Ex 33:22-23), Moses receives this monumental and comprehensive revelation of the LORD'S character. Lest anyone think God in the OT is unforgiving, we can see by God's own self-description, He "forgives iniquity, transgression and sin." He leaves nothing beyond His reach.

God's compassion, grace and lovingkindness are not theoretical, but outcome-focused. They lead to forgiveness. That God abounds in truth means His forgiveness is not naïve, but well informed of the magnitude of our offense against Him. Forgiveness, if it means anything, tells us that we are in dire need of God dealing with our affront to Him. We know we have sinned against Him; He knows we have sinned against Him. His forgiveness is not superficial like the way we humans brush off our sins against each other. When someone asks forgiveness (rare as that may be), we tend to respond, "Don't worry, I haven't thought at all about it," as though we are above being offended or don't want to sound judgmental in acknowledging offense.

With God our sin is an offense—He is offended. That is not a weakness in Him. That is the truth, and God is truth. Our sin goes deep: "The heart is more deceitful than all else and is desperately sick; who can understand it?" (Jer 17:9). That sets the tone for understanding the depth of His forgiveness. We have no fear that He may say "No big deal" yet continue to hold it against us (like we humans do with our superficial forgiveness). We are reminded of what the psalmist wrote: "As far as the east is from the west, so far has He removed our transgressions from us" (Ps 103:12).

What has He forgiven us for? 1) Iniquity – we have bent, twisted and distorted our relationship to God; 2) Transgression – we have violated His commands for us, and therefore have breached our relationship with Him; 3) Sin – we have missed the mark and come short of the way God wants us to live. For all of this, He forgives, because it is in His nature to forgive. And since we are His image bearers, we too should, by nature, forgive others for their offenses against us.

Lord, help me forgive others for their sins against me, as You have forgiven me.

WEEK 10, DAY 2

The God Who Punishes the Wicked

Then the LORD passed by in front of [Moses] and proclaimed, "The LORD, the LORD God, compassionate and gracious, slow to anger, and abounding in lovingkindness and truth; who keeps lovingkindness for thousands, who forgives iniquity, transgression and sin; yet He will by no means leave the guilty unpunished, visiting the iniquity of fathers on the children and on the grandchildren to the third and fourth generations." (Exodus 34:6–7)

God's forgiveness does not mean He is a pushover! Jonathan Edwards captured this truth in his famous sermon, "Sinners in the Hands of an Angry God." His imagery of hell was typical of the Great Awakening in the 1700s in colonial New England and, to some critics today, represented the horrific scare tactics of the Puritan mindset. One cannot help make the connection with such Medieval writings as Dante's "Inferno," with its fanciful, detailed pictures of purgatory, hell and eternal suffering. Many relegate such things to be artifacts of past ignorance of the uninformed, or manipulative tools in the hands of a power-hungry institutionalized church to control the masses.

While we may acknowledge excesses and abuses from the past, we must resist the urge to swing the pendulum to the other extreme, which negates God's seriousness about sin and toward sinners. He holds His image bearers accountable for sin. In today's passage, this comprehensive self-description presents clearly and unequivocally, "The LORD ... will by no means leave the guilty unpunished" (emphasis added). There are enormous consequences to sin.

In context our passage speaks of God's temporal punishment, namely that our sin has generational consequences. Our behavior affects our children and grandchildren—those who come after us. While thinking Christians debate issues of fairness and contrasting passages (see Deut 24:16, 2 Kings 14:6, 2 Chron 25:4, John 9:3), the fact of the matter is God's compassion, grace and lovingkindness do not negate His willingness to punish. Even Jesus spoke of eternal consequences in hell and frequently used imagery of fiery punishment.

What then determines whether God forgives or punishes? That is left for other Scriptures to delineate. God is satisfied in His revelation to Moses to simply outline His character. He is all those things rolled into one, as it were, with no inherent contradiction or tension. Moses, upon understanding this, "made haste to bow low toward the earth and worship" (Ex 34:5). In our growing understanding, we want to study, ask hard questions and wrestle with what we find out about God. But above all, our search should lead to humble worship!

Lord, I bow before You and worship You as my Lord and my sovereign God!

WEEK 10, DAY 3

The Cornerstone

The stone which the builders rejected has become the chief corner stone. (Psalm 118:22)

Construction term that it is, the "cornerstone" metaphor is used in all three synoptic gospels (Matthew, Mark and Luke), by Peter in his second great Jerusalem sermon (Acts 4:11) and years later in his first letter (1 Peter 2:7), and also by Paul (Eph 2:20). God is always building, and He begins with Christ, the chief cornerstone. And that is where the world begins to deconstruct God's work.

The "cornerstone" in the ancient world has been described by interpreters variously as 1) the foundation stone, the first laid stone that sets the orientation of the entire building, 2) the keystone at the top of the arch, without which the arch would fall, and 3) the crowning capstone, like the pinnacle of a pyramid or the top of a corner. The qualifier "chief" tells us that it is the most important stone in a wall. One pictures a stone mason building a wall, sorting through the stones to arrange them into a perfect wall. At every juncture he rejects the one perfect stone as unsuitable. Think of the horror when the building collapses due to the builder's irrational rejection of the best stone for the task.

That this verse (Psalm 118:22) is used by the NT writers to depict the rejection of Christ by the Jewish people is clear. What is ironic is that the origin of this metaphor is found in a psalm of thanksgiving. As we read through Psalm 118, it begins with a general expression of gratitude to the LORD [Yahweh] for His lovingkindness ("hesed"). Then the psalm writer gives the specifics for which he is thankful: "From my distress I called upon the LORD; the LORD answered me and set me in a large place. The LORD is for me; I will not fear; what can man do to me?" (Ps 118:5-6). He goes on to express his confidence in the LORD in the face of his enemies (Ps 118:10-13) and exclaims, "The LORD is my strength and song, and He has become my salvation" (Ps 118:14). Then he prays, "Open to me the gates of righteousness; I shall enter through them … This is the gate of the LORD; the righteous will enter through it" (Ps 118:19-20).

Then abruptly comes verse 22 and the rejected cornerstone. But the tone is one of jubilation. The focus is not on the rejection of the stone, but on the fact that what was rejected has been made the chief stone of all. God, to the complete contrast of human expectation, chooses to glorify Himself in the things humans reject. Does this not picture the return of Christ, the Lamb who was slain, the stone that was rejected, in the last day coming in glory?

Lord, though the world rejects You, I accept You. You are my Cornerstone!

WEEK 10, DAY 4

The Cornerstone (cont.)

The stone which the builders rejected Has become the chief corner stone. (Psalm 118:22)

One would naturally think that if the story were invented by human creativity, the rejected stone would roll back over the building and the builder and destroy them all. That would be the natural storyline, one of rightful vengeance and justice. That is what makes this description of God so amazing. No attempts at eliminating God from the story (or the building in the metaphor)—or even recasting the plot line, as many today try to do with their various religions, sects or deviant theologies—none of these changes God's plan or His character. Reject Him all you like, distort His picture with idols or skewed theologies, reduce Him through human philosophies and academic elitism or religious ritualism and legalism—but God remains God. He, and He alone, defines and describes for us who He is.

Rejection comes in many forms. The apostle John in the prologue to his gospels put it this way: "He came to His own, and those who were His own did not receive Him" (John 1:11). Upon Jesus' so-called "triumphal entry" into Jerusalem the week before He died, the crowds lined the street as He rode on a donkey. Psalm 118 was very much on their minds, but not the part about the rejected cornerstone. Rather, they called out essentially a quotation from later in Psalm 118.

Psalms 113-118 form what is called the Hallel psalms, or Songs of Praise, which were traditionally sung at the three great festivals of Israel, including the Passover. According to Jewish historians, the last of these, Psalm 118, was intended to be sung as Jewish pilgrims ascended to the temple. In this context one can imagine the irony soon to be upon them of the "stone which the builders rejected" (Ps 118:22). In the mouths of those laying palm branches before the Lord, we hear Psalm 118:25-26 echoed: "Hosanna to the Son of David; Blessed is He who comes in the name of the Lord; Hosanna in the highest!" (Matt 21:9). "Hosanna" is a rough Greek transliteration of the Hebrew, "O Lord, do save ..." (Psalm 118:25). This cry for help morphed over time into a word of praise to God, as the crowds then used it. "Blessed is He who comes in the name of the Lord" (Matt 21:9b) is a direct quote from Psalm 118:26.

> *The very One whom they praised became the One whom they rejected. The Chief Cornerstone. "Now to you who believe, this stone is precious. But to those who do not believe ... 'A stone that causes people to stumble and a rock that makes them fall.'" (1 Peter 2:7-8).*

Lord, You are my precious Cornerstone. I stand firm, for I am aligned with You.

WEEK 10, DAY 5

The Defense of My Life

The LORD is my light and my salvation; whom shall I fear? The LORD is the defense of my life; whom shall I dread? (Psalm 27:1)

The Book of Psalms has provided comfort and encouragement to many believers through the centuries. In discouragements, sufferings, fears and anxieties we can turn to what can be called "God's handbook for godly emotions." The psalmist pens our feelings for us; we see that the cry of our heart to God does not betray a spiritual inferiority or lack, but expresses our faith along with our honesty to God, who does listen and care for us.

David, the human author of our passage for today, begins with an assertion of faith. Why would he do this? He will get to his lament for help soon enough, but he begins from a position of faith. In particular, a faith in the kind of God he needs for his particular need. He speaks in general terms about evildoers and enemies that "encamp against me" (Ps 27:3). He asks that he might "dwell in the house of the LORD all the days of my life." Such a request would not even enter his mind if there wasn't some trace of doubt. Thus, he affirms faith most likely for his own self-encouragement, to trust in the "defense of my life."

He writes to an unseen audience, for us who read the psalm. But surely he writes rhetorically to himself, similar to other psalms, like Psalm 42:5 where he intones, "Why are you in despair, O my soul? ... Hope in God, for I shall again praise Him for the help of His presence." So here, we might sense David saying to himself, "Trust in the Lord, O my soul, for He is the defense of my life. You have nothing to dread."

To dwell in the house of the Lord (see Ps 23:6) does not point to the physical temple, which was not built until David's son's reign. Rather, David seeks to enjoy the very presence of the Lord, to transcend his earthly circumstances, to not be knocked off his real and ultimate goal. He wanted to understand properly and respond to appropriately the ugly things of life by seeing them through the lens of God's beauty. He writes in order "to behold the beauty of the LORD" (vs. 4). He did not want to live in fear, but wanted his "head ... lifted up above my enemies" (Ps 27:6)

Our defense against earthly difficulties is to not always be rescued from those situations, but rescued within those difficulties. A defense is only needed when an enemy is present. Peter did not pray that the storm would be removed, but that he could walk on water and be with Jesus in the storm. No matter our circumstances, suffering, discouragement, fear or anxiety, the LORD is our defense, and He will lift up our heads to see the beauty of the LORD.

Lord, my one desire is to see my difficult circumstance through Your beauty.

WEEKEND 10 READING
Hosea 14

PERSONAL REFLECTIONS

Everlasting God, LORD, Creator • Elohim Olam Yahweh Bara

Do you not know? Have you not heard? The Everlasting God, the LORD, the Creator of the ends of the earth does not become weary or tired. His understanding is inscrutable. (Isaiah 40:28)

Comprehensive in scope, this description or name combination of God stands in stark contrast to all the false gods Israel had run after in their idolatrous fall away from the LORD. Isaiah 40 begins the grand polemic against the notion of other gods that extends through chapter 48. Throughout this section, God declares through Isaiah His absolute uniqueness and greatness:

"I, the LORD, am the first, and with the last. I am He." (Is 41:4)

"I am He. Before Me there was no God formed, and there will be none after Me. I, even I, am the LORD, and there is no savior besides Me." (Is 43:10–11)

"Thus says the LORD, the King of Israel and his Redeemer, the LORD of hosts: I am the first and I am the last, and there is no God besides Me." (Is 44:6)

"I am the LORD, and there is no other; besides Me there is no God ... there is no one besides Me. I am the LORD, and there is no other ... I am the LORD who does all these." (Is 45:5–7)

"I am the LORD, and there is none else." (Is 45:18)

"For I am God, and there is no other." (Is 45:22)

"I am God, and there is no other; I am God, and there is no one like Me." (Is 46:9)

"I am, and there is no one besides Me." (Is 47:10)

"I am He, I am the first, I am also the last. Surely My hand founded the earth, and My right hand spread out the heavens." (Is 48:12–13)

He is the absolute God, the Creator of the universe, all that exists. There is nothing greater than He. Through faith in this One, we can run the race of life with endurance in this fallen and tempting world. "Those who wait for the LORD will gain new strength; they will mount up with wings like eagles, they will run and not get tired, they will walk and not become weary" (Is 40:30–31).

Lord, by faith I believe and trust in You, the absolute Creator of everything.

WEEK 11, DAY 2

God, the Faithful God • Elohim El Han-Emen

"Know therefore that the LORD your God, He is God [Elohim], the faithful [Han-Emen] God [El], who keeps His covenant and His lovingkindness to a thousandth generation with those who love Him and keep His commandments; but repays those who hate Him to their faces, to destroy them; He will not delay with him who hates Him, He will repay him to his face." (Deuteronomy 7:9–10)

Emphasis here falls on His faithfulness. The Hebrew word "emen" will be recognized in its derivative rendered in the NT as "amen," which Jesus used frequently. According to the Theological Wordbook of the Old Testament, "The meaning of the root is the idea of certainty. And this is borne out by the NT definition of faith found in Heb 11:1."

If there is one thing that can be counted on in this world, it is that God is faithful. What He says is certain. When He makes a covenant, we can count on God to be faithful to fulfill the covenant. When He says He will keep His lovingkindness "to a thousandth generation," He means it and it will happen. This is bedrock to the dispensational eschatological belief that God still has a plan for Israel that will be fulfilled at some future time. How do we know this? Because God made a covenant with Abraham and to His descendants, and with David, for a land and the reign of a king in David's place.

God promises to reward those who "love Him and keep His commandments" and to destroy those who "hate Him." The popular saying goes like this: "There are only two things in life that are certain: death and taxes." But that is wrong; even more than death and taxes, God's Word is certain.

The word "emen" describes God in two other places as well. "The Rock! His work is perfect, for all His ways are just; a God of faithfulness and without injustice, righteous and upright is He" (Deut 32:4). His work and ways, righteousness and uprightness are assured and fixed. They can be no other way, for God does not change (Ps 55:19).

"Ephraim surrounds Me with lies and the house of Israel with deceit; Judah is also unruly against God, even against the Holy One who is faithful" (Hosea 11:12). God's holiness is certain, non-ambiguous. To every description of God, we can say, "Amen and amen." For every word spoken by Jesus, we could rejoin, as He often did, "Truly, truly" (which is how some English translations render, "amen, amen." When our hearts begin to doubt because of the words of others, let the words of Scripture ring deeply in us: "Their unbelief will not nullify the faithfulness of God ... Rather, let God be found true, though every man be found a liar..." (Rom 3:3–4).

Faithful Lord, I trust in Your Word, which is true and never changing.

WEEK 11, DAY 3

The Fear of Isaac • Pahad Yishaq

"If the God of my father, the God of Abraham, and the fear [pahad] of Isaac, had not been for me, surely now you would have sent me away empty-handed. God has seen my affliction and the toil of my hands, so He rendered judgment last night." (Genesis 31:42)

"[Laban said] The God of Abraham and the God of Nahor, the God of their father, judge between us." So Jacob swore by the fear of his father Isaac. (Genesis 31:53)

Found only in these two verses in Scripture, we discover an interesting description of God. The backstory has it that Jacob fled his fraternal twin brother Esau in fear and landed in his uncle Laban's sphere of influence. After spending 20 years in servitude to Laban and acquiring his two daughters as his wives, and after God blessed his animal husbandry efforts, Jacob prospered to the point where he was no longer indebted to his uncle.

Just before Jacob returned to the land of his father Isaac and grandfather Abraham to face his estranged brother Esau, we come across the final conversation between him and Laban. Jacob refers to the "God of my father, the God of Abraham, and the fear of Isaac." This seems an odd thing to say, because Jacob's father was, in fact, Isaac. Jacob may have had reason to fear his father, for 20 years earlier he deceived Isaac into giving him the coveted birthright and blessing that was rightfully Esau's. However, the construction of the sentence leads us to see that Jacob was possibly referring to God as "The Fear of Isaac."

We can see this in Genesis 31:53, where "Jacob swore by the fear of his father Isaac." The contrast is unmistakable: Laban appealed to pagan gods. To be sure, Laban referenced the God of Abraham, but he also referenced the gods (plural) of Nahor (Abraham's brother, also Laban's grandfather), and the gods (plural) of their father (Terah)! While the OT routinely refers to the true God with "elohim" used as a plural of majesty, never is "elohim" used in that sense with pagan gods. This is further supported by Jacob's contrasting response in swearing "by the fear of his father Isaac" (using a singular construct).

Jacob clearly came to know the true God as the "Fear of Isaac." He is the one to be respected and feared above and apart from any other gods (or concepts of the divine). Jacob was committed to standing or falling on His belief in and submission to Him. The Law of Moses later encapsulated this succinctly: "Now, Israel, what does the LORD your God require from you, but to fear the LORD your God, to walk in all His ways and love Him, and to serve the LORD your God with all your heart and with all your soul ..." (Deut 10:12).

Lord, I commit to live in submission to You, for You are "The fear of Isaac."

WEEK 11, DAY 4

The Forgiving God • Eloah Selihah

"They refused to listen, and did not remember Your wondrous deeds which You had performed among them; so they became stubborn and appointed a leader to return to their slavery in Egypt. But You are a God of forgiveness, gracious and compassionate, slow to anger and abounding in lovingkindness; and You did not forsake them." (Nehemiah 9:17)

"Forgiveness" as a rending of the Hebrew word "selihah" is only used in Scripture of God's activity, never of a human activity toward another human. There are words that apply to human forgiveness, but not this one. This is the sole prerogative of the Creator God of the universe (see also Psalm 130:4, Daniel 9:9). The word means "an act in which a mistake or offense is no longer considered or held against another." The God of the Old Testament, as Nehemiah lays out for us, is described in similar terms as the God of the New Testament—and of course that would be true, for they are one and the same. Dismissing the OT God as a product of medieval scare-mongering has no place in responsible biblical study.

He is not only forgiving, but is also "gracious and compassionate, slow to anger and abounding in lovingkindness." We have seen these descriptions elsewhere (see Ex 34:7) in slightly different form. We focus here on His character of forgiveness, in part because that is a cornerstone to our evangelical beliefs. At the core, we are sinners separated from God, and what we need most is His forgiveness. David captures this most eloquently when he writes:

Wash me thoroughly from my iniquity and cleanse me from my sin. For I know my transgressions, and my sin is ever before me. Against You, You only, I have sinned and done what is evil in Your sight ... (Ps 51:2–4)

It is in God's very nature to forgive. That was so in the Garden when Adam and Eve questioned His goodness and chose to obey the lie of Satan that they would become like God by eating the forbidden fruit. As God drove them out of the Garden, He did not abandon His character as a forgiving God, but rather preserved the opportunity for His image bearers to fully embrace their need of forgiveness. In fact, the entire Scriptures lead us to see God in His essential character as a forgiving God. The history of Israel is all about experiencing God's forgiveness. The Law of Moses was based on God providing a method through the sacrifices to bring about His forgiveness, or at the least His temporary stay on judgment, until the perfect sacrifice would come, the Lamb of God. Through Christ we see that character in all its glory.

Lord, thank You for Your immeasurable and infinite forgiveness!

WEEK 11, DAY 5

The God of the Patriarchs

He said also, "I am the God of your father, the God of Abraham, the God of Isaac, and the God of Jacob." Then Moses hid his face, for he was afraid to look at God." (Exodus 3:6)

Thirteen times in the Bible, both Old Testament and new, this phrase occurs, with slight variations: "The God of Abraham, Isaac and Jacob." Moses received the first mention in the wilderness during the burning bush incident. Chronologically, we must remember, this came after 400 years of silence from God, a particularly dark period in the history of God's people.

God had spoken to Abraham, the revered ancestor of the Jewish people, giving him a promise in three parts. He would give Abraham and his descendants their own land (what is called "the Promised Land"), they would increase to become a great nation, and God would bless the entire world through them (Gen 12:1-3). In time, Abraham had a son Isaac, and then Isaac had a son Jacob (who was later renamed by God as Israel). Jacob in turn had 12 sons, whose descendants are aligned into the 12 tribes or family clans of Israel.

These sons along with Jacob relocated to Egypt during a time of great famine, where they ended up remaining for 400 years. During that time, there was no communication from God until the time leading up to the Exodus (the great movement of the descendants of Jacob out of Egypt to the Promised Land) under Moses' leadership. This is, in summary form, the genesis of the Jewish people—they are all descendants of Abraham, Isaac and Jacob (who are called "the patriarchs"). While individual Jews identified with one of the 12 tribes from which they were descended, all were linked to Abraham, Isaac and Jacob.

Continuity with God's dealings with the great Jewish patriarchs was therefore paramount for Moses' commissioning to lead God's people out of Egyptian slavery and to begin forming the nation of Israel. This was not to be a new religion, with new gods. Theirs would be the same God as that of Abraham, Isaac and Jacob. Four hundred years did not change God, for the history of humanity is not about people evolving in their construct of deity. But unfolding of history is really about the God of the universe invading our fallen, dark world to reveal Himself and His requirements for His creation, His image bearers. We don't define Him; He reveals Himself. And today, He continues to reveal Himself, the same One who revealed Himself to Abraham, Isaac and Jacob. We worship the same God they worshipped.

*Lord, You are the God of Abraham, Isaac and Jacob—and
I worship You as the same One they worshipped.*

WEEKEND 11 READING
Joel 1

PERSONAL REFLECTIONS

WEEK 12, DAY 1

The God of Abraham • Elohim Abraham

He said also, "I am the God of your father, the God of Abraham, the God of Isaac, and the God of Jacob." Then Moses hid his face, for he was afraid to look at God." (Exodus 3:6)

It all began with Abraham—the continuity of faith that extends to our present day. Our faith is one and the same with his. When Moses was commissioned at the burning bush to lead God's people out of Egypt after 400 years of silence from God, he wasn't called to begin a new religion. His role, though, was different from Abraham's. While God called Moses to communicate the Law to Israel in its nation-formative years, Abraham is rightly called the father of faith. God made this absolutely clear to Moses.

Abraham is the first of the big names of faith in biblical history that also include Moses and King David. The list begins with Abraham and leads to the greatest, of course: the Lord Jesus Christ, who was God in the flesh.

When Abraham first appears in the Scripture, 11 chapters of the Bible had already happened, including the history of creation and the fall, the Tower of Babel, the flood and Noah. However, God's program of faith began with Abraham, first introduced at the end of the genealogy of Noah's son Shem (Gen 11:26).

God's three-fold promise to Abraham of a land, seed (descendants) and blessing form the foundation of everything else God does in biblical history. Israel still has a future in the physical land of promise. Abraham's descendants, the Jews, are still a large, recognizable people group. Through his descendants came the "seed," Jesus Christ, who is the blessing for all the world. Paul in his grand polemic writes to the Galatians:

Abraham believed God, and it was reckoned to him as righteousness. Therefore, be sure that it is those who are of faith who are sons of Abraham, (Gal 3:6–7)

Christ redeemed us from the curse of the Law, having become a curse for us—for it is written, "CURSED IS EVERYONE WHO HANGS ON A TREE"— in order that in Christ Jesus the blessing of Abraham might come to the Gentiles, so that we would receive the promise of the Spirit through faith. (Gal 3:13–14)

Today, we believers in Christ worship the God of Abraham. The God who justified Abraham through faith is the same God who justifies us through faith.

Lord, though time and culture have changed, You remain the same today as in Abraham's day. Time has not changed You or the role of faith in coming to You.

WEEK 12, DAY 2

The God of Isaac • Elohim Yishaq

He said also, "I am the God of your father, the God of Abraham, the God of Isaac, and the God of Jacob." Then Moses hid his face, for he was afraid to look at God." (Exodus 3:6)

Abraham had many sons by at least three different women: Ishmael by the servant girl Hagar, Isaac by Sarah, his wife, and six sons by Keturah, his second wife (Genesis 25:1-2). Little is known about Ishmael, though he did go on to have a large family and many descendants. We hear less of the other six sons. But it was the God of Isaac that Moses was to follow, not the God of Ishmael or of the other half-brothers. Clearly, the Lord was etching out a line of orthodoxy. Isaac was the favored son and treated as the firstborn (Genesis 25:5-6), for he was the child of promise, and God's plan for His people was for those whose descent came from Abraham through Isaac:

"Sojourn in this land and I will be with you and bless you, for to you and to your descendants I will give all these lands, and I will establish the oath which I swore to your father Abraham. I will multiply your descendants as the stars of heaven, and will give your descendants all these lands; and by your descendants all the nations of the earth shall be blessed; because Abraham obeyed Me and kept My charge, My commandments, My statutes and My laws." (Gen 26:3–5)

Yet despite the same promise from God and despite his own father's actions of doubt in God's protection, Isaac fell to the same temptation. He, too, doubted God's protection, passing off his wife as a sister to safeguard himself from being killed by the jealous men where he lived. Yet God was faithful to His promise:

Now Isaac sowed in that land and reaped in the same year a hundred-fold. And the LORD blessed him, and the man became rich, and continued to grow richer until he became very wealthy... (Gen 26:12–13)

Later, when Isaac was fearful again, God reassured him:

"I am the God of your father Abraham; do not fear, for I am with you. I will bless you, and multiply your descendants, for the sake of My servant Abraham." (Gen 26:24)

With the God of Abraham and the God of Isaac, we have no need to fear anything. For He is our God as well.

Lord, thank You for the security I have in You. I have no need to doubt or fear.

WEEK 12, DAY 3

The God of Jacob • Elohim Yaaqob

He said also, "I am the God of your father, the God of Abraham, the God of Isaac, and the God of Jacob." Then Moses hid his face, for he was afraid to look at God." (Exodus 3:6)

God revealed Himself in the line of orthodoxy first to Abraham, then to Isaac, and third to Jacob. This threefold declaration riveted Moses in front of the burning bush. The awesome God he must have heard about—the faint memory of the revered ancestors, the ancient patriarchs of his people—was revealing Himself to this man who had fled out of fear, having been rejected by the Egyptians and his own people. For 40 years Moses lived a quiet life in the wilderness tending sheep, getting married and having children. His identification with the descendants of Jacob must have become a distant memory.

If you recall the story of the last part of Genesis, Jacob, the son of Isaac, who was the son of Abraham, had 12 sons. Due to famine, they ended up in Egypt—a common theme among the patriarchs, who in doubt of God's protection fled from the land promised to them by God, to greener pastures, so to speak. In Jacob's case, his stay lasted longer than the famine—in fact, his descendants settled there for about 400 years! Their life became one of servitude, supplying the Egyptian overlords with construction materials for their great nation-building projects. Without their realizing, God was nation-building His own people, creating a foundational experience that would shape the rest of biblical history: the captivity by Egypt and deliverance from it (namely, the Exodus) was an object lesson of redemption from captivity by the world.

So after 400 years, when God commissioned Moses to lead His people out of Egypt back to the Promised Land, Moses must have known and understood the continuity with God's work in Abraham, Isaac and Jacob. This was not a new religion conjured up in the creative mind of Moses. There was absolutely no disconnect with God's work as expressed in the promise to Abraham, Isaac and Jacob.

Faith in God did not come easy for Jacob. As he fled Canaan out of fear of his brother, God spoke to him in a dream at Bethel:

> *"I am the LORD, the God of your father Abraham and the God of Isaac; the land on which you lie, I will give it to you and to your descendants. Your descendants will also be like the dust of the earth ... in your descendants shall all the families of the earth be blessed." (Gen 28:13–15)*

Lord, the God of Abraham, Isaac and Jacob, thank You for blessing me with salvation because of the promise You gave to the patriarchs.

WEEK 12, DAY 4

The God of Jacob (cont.) • Elohim Yaaqob

He said also, "I am the God of your father, the God of Abraham, the God of Isaac, and the God of Jacob." Then Moses hid his face, for he was afraid to look at God." (Exodus 3:6)

Jacob's faith in God did not come automatically; it was not inherited. In him we discover that every generation must believe in God for themselves. A godly heritage does not guarantee a godly life. In running for his life, Jacob took matters into his own hands to protect himself, rather than trust God. Of course, his life was built on greed and deception, as seen in his duping his brother Esau out of the inheritance. The irony was that God had pre-determined Jacob to be the child of promise (Genesis 25:23, Malachi 1:2-3, Romans 9:10-13). Sin does not lead to trusting God. So Jacob fled for his life in fear of Esau's revenge.

After God reiterated the Abrahamic promise to Jacob, the fleeing young man made a vow:

"If God will be with me and will keep me on this journey that I take, and will give me food to eat and garments to wear, and I return to my father's house in safety, then the LORD will be my God." (Gen 28:20–21)

During his time away, he came under the influence of "foreign gods" (Gen 35:4). But upon returning to the land of Canaan some 20 years later, he rid his household of all foreign idols and acknowledged God:

So Jacob said to his household and to all who were with him, "Put away the foreign gods which are among you, and purify yourselves and change your garments; and let us arise and go up to Bethel, and I will make an altar there to God, who answered me in the day of my distress and has been with me wherever I have gone." (Gen 35:2–3)

Then God appeared again to him and again rehearsed His promise made earlier:

"Your name is Jacob; you shall no longer be called Jacob, but Israel shall be your name ... I am God Almighty [El Shaddai]... a nation and a company of nations shall come from you, and kings shall come forth from you. The land which I gave to Abraham and Isaac, I will give it to you, and I will give the land to your descendants after you." (Gen 35:10–12)

Now as Moses was about to lead God's people back to the Promised Land, he was reminded that the God of Jacob keeps His promises.

Lord, thank You for Your promise never to leave me or forsake me (Heb 13:5).

WEEK 12, DAY 5

The God of Nahor? • Elohim Nahor

"The God of Abraham and the God of Nahor, the God of their father, judge between us." So Jacob swore by the fear of his father Isaac. (Genesis 31:53)

We include this description as a contrast. Jacob specifically does not swear by either the God of Abraham or the God of Nahor! While the same generic term for deity, "elohim," is used in both cases, it is highly questionable that Nahor's god was the same as Abraham's God. This is an important distinction in view of the monotheism of the Abrahamic faith being established. There has always and only been one true God; Jacob was challenged to take an oath to an ambiguous "god." He refuses.

Abraham and Nahor were brothers, whose ancestral line can be traced from Adam and Eve through Noah and his son Shem (there are a total of 10 generations between Noah and Abraham). Some time after the Noahic flood, God scattered the human race at the Tower of Babel through the confusion of languages; it is not hard to imagine the divergent imaginations of deity that would ensue, and the evolution of humanity away from God to idols.

God called Abraham out of the city of Ur (near the Tigris and Euphrates Rivers at the Persian Gulf in present-day Iraq). We learn later from Joshua: "Thus says the LORD, the God of Israel, 'From ancient times your fathers lived beyond the River, namely, Terah, the father of Abraham and the father of Nahor, and they served other gods'" (Josh 24:2).

So Abraham's background and upbringing was among idol worshippers, and by implication or association, he, too, probably had been an idol worshipper. But God revealed Himself to Abraham while still in Ur with the result that the man who would become the patriarch of future Israel stepped out in faith and headed for the land promised to him: "By faith Abraham, when he was called, obeyed by going out to a place which he was to receive for an inheritance; and he went out, not knowing where he was going" (Heb 11:8). We have no record of Nahor believing in the God Abraham had come to obey. In fact, Nahor was left behind in Haran, the temporary stopping place, when God fleshed out the three-fold promise to Abraham (Gen 12:1-4) and renewed the command to continue on.

Back to our passage for today, lest there be any confusion that they worshipped the same god, or two different gods on an equal plane, Jacob made clear to Laban that his theology rested with allegiance to the God of his father Isaac, which was, in fact, the God of Abraham. His God was not just Abraham's God (ambiguous as that may have been to Laban), but the God of Isaac.

Lord, help me know You and defend against false misrepresentations of You.

WEEKEND 12 READING
Joel 2

PERSONAL REFLECTIONS

WEEK 13, DAY 1

The LORD, the God of Heaven

The LORD, the God of heaven, who took me from my father's house and from the land of my birth, and who spoke to me and who swore to me, saying, 'To your descendants I will give this land,' He will send His angel before you, and you will take a wife for my son from there. (Genesis 24:7)

The ancient world considered heaven to be the abode of deity, a spiritual realm beyond the physical world. The phrase "the God of heaven" uses the generic term for deity, "elohim," and seems to be a reference to the supreme deity over all of heaven. Abraham distinguishes that deity by attaching the name "LORD" ("Yahweh Elohim Samayim").

This description or name of God seems to be used mostly in Scripture when involving those outside of the Abrahamic faith. Abraham referred to God in this way when directing his servant to find a wife for Isaac from among Abraham's relatives (Gen 24:2-4). Abraham's relatives would have been familiar with the general phrase "God of heaven," though there is no evidence they had abandoned paganism as Abraham had done. Thus he added the specificity ("Yahweh") to the generality.

Daniel, early in the Babylonian exile, addressed King Nebuchadnezzar, "You, O king, are the king of kings, to whom the God of heaven has given the kingdom..." (Dan 2:37). In using the generic "God of heaven," he was using common language the king would understand. Interestingly, the name LORD ("Yahweh") is not used in the book of Daniel until after chapter 8. When referencing the revelation of "the word of the LORD to Jeremiah..." (Dan 9:2), the book pivots toward end-time prophecies, with a clear emphasis to the Jews.

In 2 Chronicles 36:23, the Persian king Cyrus referenced God in this way ("the LORD, the God of heaven") when, after the Jews had been 70 years in Babylonian exile, he proclaimed that God had "appointed me to build Him a house in Jerusalem, which is in Judah." Ezra at the end of the exile quotes this proclamation as he writes about the beginning of the restoration of the Jews to the Promised Land from where they had been exiled (Ezra 1:2-3).

What do we make of all this? God reveals Himself in generic terms to all people. Indeed, scholars tell us every culture on the planet has a sense of deity. We need not be afraid to use generic language to convey basic ideas about God, but we should always tie those concepts back to the more specific knowledge we have of God. For Christians today, that would mean connecting God with Jesus Christ, who is the "exact representation of His nature" (Heb 1:3).

Lord Jesus, I want to make Your name and character known in my witness so that people can understand who God really is.

WEEK 13, DAY 2

The Lord, the God of All Flesh

"Behold, I am the LORD, the God of all flesh; is anything too difficult for Me?" (Jeremiah 32:27)

Scripture adorns the name of God, Yahweh, with various modifiers. These in no way reduce God, as though He needed modification. Rather, like a rainbow, the literary modifications used around His name help us focus on various aspects of His glory. The name "Yahweh" stands alone, for it encompasses God entirely. To be sure, no single literary term can capture God's glory entirely. We remember that when Moses saw the "backside" of God, what Moses saw was described in terms of God's character: "compassionate and gracious, slow to anger, and abounding in lovingkindness and truth ..." (Ex 34:6). There was no video camera to record the visual phenomenon. What he "saw" was a sort of prism-expanded perspective of God, like light being separated out into the colors of the rainbow. No wonder Ezekiel describes the Lord's glory…

> *"As the appearance of the rainbow in the clouds on a rainy day, so was the appearance of the surrounding radiance. Such was the appearance of the likeness of the glory of the LORD." (Ezekiel 1:28)*

In our passage today, we see the hue of God's sovereign power. The description "the God of all flesh" doesn't by itself denote a dynamite kind of power, but Jeremiah had just previously written, "Ah, Lord GOD [Adonai Yahweh]! Behold, You have made the heavens and the earth by Your great power and by Your outstretched arm! Nothing is too difficult for You…" (Jer 32:17). In that power, God was going to raise up Nebuchadnezzar and the Babylonians to defeat Israel and take them away into captivity. After years and years of idolatry and wicked behavior, God was finally going to make good on His promise of punishment. In the midst of that inevitability, God commands Jeremiah to buy some property in Judah! That might seem like buying a piece of the deck on the Titanic, except that God was planning to return the Jews to their land after the defeat and exile. In buying a piece of land, Jeremiah would be trusting in God, who had the power and ability to fulfill His promise to return them to their home after their punishment.

God poses a question intended to point out the ridiculousness of doubting Him: "Is anything too difficult for the God of all humanity?" Of course not! How could you even consider that? What a great promise is that!

> *Lord, I have nothing to fear because You are the God of all flesh, and nothing is impossible for You. I believe that.*

WEEK 13, DAY 3

The God of Bethel

"I am the God of Bethel, where you anointed a pillar, where you made a vow to Me; now arise, leave this land, and return to the land of your birth." (Genesis 31:13)

Far away from the land of his father, Isaac, and his grandfather, Abraham, Jacob found himself working for his uncle Laban (brother to his mother Rebekah) for 20 years and acquiring two wives, two mistresses (his wives' servant girls), 11 sons and one daughter. From our perspective today, this proved to be a classic dysfunctional family, with its intrigues, jealousy, fears, insecurities, and sibling rivalries at all levels. Yet in the midst of all this, God inserted Himself. Lest we become too bogged down in a debate on how a holy and righteous God could use such a messed up family like this, we might better muse on the question of what kind of people God routinely used.

Consider the apostles, a rag-tag collection of men, some uneducated, some fiery-tempered (James and John, the "sons of thunder" in Mark 3:17), impetuous (Peter), doubtful (Thomas), disloyal (Judas), etc. Think of Matthew, an extortionist tax collector or Paul, who by his own admission was "the chief of all sinners" (1 Tim 1:15). Why would God choose to use them? Consider even further why He chose to reveal Himself to you! As I write these words, the greatest question I ponder is, why did He choose to reveal Himself to me? How can we ever get over this wonderful, gracious, merciful movement of God toward any of us?

He chose to reveal Himself to lying, conniving Jacob—that is what God in His sovereignty did after Jacob lived for 20 years outside of the land of promise. Jacob had changed, though, and he acknowledged that "the God of my father has been with me…God did not allow [Laban] to hurt me" (Gen 31:5, 7). Then God spoke to Jacob in a dream, and Jacob was ready to listen. In identifying Himself as the God of Bethel, He reminded him of the vow made years earlier at Bethel as he fled the land of his fathers: "If God will be with me and keep me on this journey that I take … and I return to my father's house in safety, then the LORD will be my God" (Gen 28:20-21). God was now calling in that vow!

Jacob had already received the blessing from his father, Isaac: "May [God Almighty-El Shaddai] give you the blessing of Abraham, to you and to your descendants with you, that you may possess the land of your sojournings, which God gave to Abraham" (Gen 28:4). This was the expression of his father's faith; Jacob had to come to faith in and relationship to God for himself.

Lord, speak to me that my faith may come from my own encounter with You.

WEEK 13, DAY 4

The Voice of the LORD, the God of Glory

The voice of the LORD is upon the waters; the God of glory thunders, the LORD is over many waters. (Psalm 29:3)

Picture the psalmist David sitting on the side of a mountain in northern Israel watching a storm blow in off the Mediterranean Sea, across Lebanon, destroying the well-known "cedars of Lebanon" (Ps 29:5), over Mount Hermon (also called Serion), with lightning and mountain-shattering thunder. Animals are frightened into premature labor, and the trees left standing have had the bark ripped off (Ps 29:9). One terrific hurricane-level storm engulfs the land.

This "natural" phenomenon reminds David of the LORD, and he invites his readers to join him in worship:

"Ascribe to the LORD glory and strength. Ascribe to the LORD the glory due to His name; worship the LORD in holy array." (Ps 29:1-2)

When he hears the thunder, he thinks:

The voice of the LORD is upon the waters; the God of glory thunders, the LORD is over many waters. The voice of the LORD is powerful, the voice of the LORD is majestic. (Ps 29:3-4)

Truly, David's heart is so attuned to God that he sees with the perspective of the angels in Isaiah's lofty vision of God's throne room: "Holy, Holy, Holy, is the LORD of hosts, the whole earth is full of His glory" (Is 6:3). Everything, including a storm, shows forth the "God of Glory."

Rather than being overtaken with fear of this fierce natural occurrence or taken in by the demonstration of nature's power, David views the thunder and lightning as showing the Lord as "powerful" and "majestic" (Ps 29:4). It shows God's glory.

No, weather conditions are not a matter of natural occurrences, but are orchestrated by God, the Maker of all things, for "[t]he LORD sat as King at the flood; yes, the LORD sits as King forever" (Ps 29:10). Even more so, when we see such fierce things like thunder and lightning, we are reminded that "[t]he LORD will give strength to His people; the LORD will bless His people with peace" (Ps 29:11).

In the ancient world, when the nearby nations and the remnant of pagan worshipers still lingered in the land and worshiped local "gods" of nature, David worshiped the "God of Glory," who is Yahweh the LORD.

Lord, I will never fear "natural" catastrophes but see Your glory in them.

The God of Gods and Lord of Lords

"For the LORD your God is the God of gods and the Lord of lords, the great, the mighty, and the awesome God who does not show partiality nor take a bribe." (Deuteronomy 10:17)

Polytheism is the generic belief in many gods. Some religions have innumerable gods, like Hinduism. Abrahamic religions (Judaism, Christianity and Islam) are monotheistic, believing in one God. Islam accuses Christianity of worshiping three Gods, whom we call the Trinity. However, Christianity is rooted securely in OT monotheism. Nothing could be more fundamental than this: "Hear, O Israel! The LORD is our God, the LORD is one!" (Deut 6:4). The doctrine of the Trinity is properly stated: there is one God who exists in three persons; there are not three Gods. There is no logical contradiction in that statement, although the doctrine of the Trinity—like the doctrine of the incarnation, the notion of God becoming human, a part of His own creation—confounds human understanding. The Trinity is incomprehensible but not illogical: the Bible teaches that Jesus is God and the Holy Spirit is God, and along with the Father, the three are equally one God.

Now, the God of Israel (Yahweh) is the "God of gods and the Lord of lords." He is not just one of many, or a local god in the manner of the pagan religions of the day. Whatever the belief system, the God of the Bible is superior to all other divine or secular authorities. As Moses was reiterating the Law ("Deuteronomy" means "second Law" or the second reading of the Law) toward the end of the Exodus wanderings, just before the people would enter the Promised Land filled with pagans who worshiped many different so-called gods, he reminded them of the supremacy of Yahweh.

Yahweh is mighty and awesome. He is completely impartial and cannot be manipulated with bribes or anything else—in other words, He is completely just. He is not influenced by the self-effort of merit-based religious systems.

The pagans would perform all kinds of elaborate rituals to try to influence the gods of the weather and gods of the harvest. They would even sacrifice their children to their gods (Deut 12:31)! While we may not go to such extremes today, people still tend to see religion as a way to manipulate God, to coerce Him to do their bidding. But He is the God of gods and the Lord of lords, who does not, like pagan deities, stoop to our measly attempts to control Him.

He is Lord; we are not. And there is no other God. We had best simply align ourselves with Him, rather than He with us.

Lord, I submit to Your Lordship, for You are mighty and awesome.

WEEKEND 13 READING
Joel 3

PERSONAL REFLECTIONS

WEEK 14, DAY 1

The God of Israel • El Yisrael

O God, You are awesome from Your sanctuary. The God of Israel Himself gives strength and power to the people. Blessed be God! (Psalm 68:35)

Of course, He is the God of Israel; nothing could be more clear in the Old Testament. But we often overlook the obvious and miss its import. As David wrote this psalm he was concerned about God's "enemies" (Ps 68:1), the disadvantaged people in Israel, the armies who fled before Israel, and various deliverances. Interspersed, he wrote of God's worthiness to be praised, of God's protection and deliverance of His people. He spoke of Sinai: "The Lord is among them as at Sinai, in holiness. You have ascended on high, You have led captive Your captives; You have received gifts among men, even among the rebellious also, that the LORD God may dwell there" (Ps 68:17-18). The apostle Paul quoted this verse in Ephesians 4:8, speaking of God equipping the church with key spiritual gifts. And David invited all to "Sing to God, O kingdoms of the earth, Sing praises to the Lord, Selah" (Ps 68:32).

So what's the big deal about David's God being the God of Israel? Some in today's multi-religious culture would say David was limited to his provincial deity and was claiming in an uneducated or uninformed way, "Our God is better than your god. Did he not know that everyone has a right to worship their deity, and that all roads lead to the same god?" Or as one person put it, everyone may drink from a different well, but we are all drinking water.

On the contrary, David asserted that there is only one God, and He is the God of Israel. In other words, the Jew had it right! As Christians, we are not to simply take our seat among the pantheon of religious beliefs. We are not all on different roads leading to the same place. We worship the true God of Israel, who has now revealed Himself in the person of Jesus Christ. This is not a generic god toward whom all are ultimately working. He is the very specific God, who has revealed Himself to us. True, He is the God of all human beings, but as Judaism was the first to clearly present, belief in the God of Israel excludes all other religious belief systems.

A big discussion today surrounds whether Christians and Muslims worship the same God, only differently. But the One we Christians worship (who is the true God) is the God of Israel, who revealed Himself in Jesus Christ. Muslims do not worship this God. The consequences are significant: "There is salvation in no one else; for there is no other name under heaven that has been given among men by which we must be saved" (Acts 4:12).

God of Israel, I worship You and You alone, through Jesus Christ Your Son, for You alone give me strength and power as I face life situations.

WEEK 14, DAY 2

The LORD, God of Justice • Yahweh Elohim Mispat

Therefore the LORD longs to be gracious to you, and therefore He waits on high to have compassion on you. For the LORD is a God of justice; how blessed are all those who long for Him. (Isaiah 30:18)

Harkening back to Exodus 34:6-7 where God showed Moses His glory in the cleft of the rock, we again see Yahweh revealing Himself to be gracious, compassionate and righteous. In fact, He is "The LORD, God of justice." This is great news for all of humanity. For some, the greatness of this is good news, in that He will vindicate the innocent; but to others the greatness of this is bad news, for He will punish the guilty.

As for Israel, whom the Lord addresses through Isaiah here, there is coming a time when God will hear their cry over being oppressed, destitute and famished. The land once destroyed would again become plentiful and well-watered (important for an agrarian society). They will recognize that these things are not provided by the provincial gods they were continually tempted to worship, but come from the hand of Yahweh, God of justice (Isaiah 30:19-26).

But for the guilty, the prophet writes:

Behold, the name of the LORD comes from a remote place; burning is His anger and dense is His smoke; His lips are filled with indignation and His tongue is like a consuming fire; His breath is like an overflowing torrent, which reaches to the neck, to shake the nations back and forth in a sieve, and to put in the jaws of the peoples the bridle which leads to ruin. (Is 30:27–28)

"Justice" is a major theme of the book of Isaiah: the word itself occurs 26 times, and "righteousness" comes in 68 times in our English Bible (NASB). God is concerned about injustice by other nations against Israel, but also injustices within Israel. Early in the book, he wrote of Jerusalem, "How the faithful city has become a harlot, she who was full of justice! Righteousness once lodged in her, but now murderers" (Is 1:21). For, "He looked for justice, but behold, bloodshed; for righteousness, but behold, a cry of distress" (Is 5:7).

Yes, He is Yahweh, God of justice, and He requires us to be just in our dealings with others also. The prophet Micah intones this as well:

He has told you, O man, what is good; and what does the Lord require of you but to do justice, to love kindness, and to walk humbly with your God? (Micah 6:8)

Lord, since justice is so important to You, help me to mirror that characteristic toward others.

WEEK 14, DAY 3

The LORD, Rock of Israel • Yahweh Sur Yisrael

You will have songs as in the night when you keep the festival, and gladness of heart as when one marches to the sound of the flute, to go to the mountain of the LORD, to the Rock of Israel. And the LORD will cause His voice of authority to be heard, and the descending of His arm to be seen in fierce anger, and in the flame of a consuming fire in cloudburst, downpour and hailstones. (Isaiah 30:29–30)

The wind blows either with us or against us. When we ride a bike into the wind, we say the wind is against us. When we ride a bike in the other direction, we say the wind is with us. There is a big difference—not in the wind, but in the direction we are pedaling. The same is true of God; He does not change: "For I, the LORD, do not change ..." (Mal 3:6, see also James 1:17). The book of Isaiah contains two major themes: one of warning and judgment, and the other of promise of rescue and peace. In our passage we have both, and the way in which we experience God depends on how we respond to Him.

Some, like those in Israel who repent and turn to Him, will experience the peacefulness and joy of singing in the night, not guilt or the fear of punishment. There will be an inner "gladness" or joy when thinking of approaching God. In the words of the writer to the Hebrews, we respond positively to the invitation: "Therefore let us draw near with confidence to the throne of grace, so that we may receive mercy and find grace to help in time of need" (Heb 4:16). God's presence is a good thing, and we look forward to it.

Yet the presence of the same God can strike fear in the unrepentant sinner. Not because God has changed. A brick wall provides protection and security while creating an impenetrable barrier that would hurt us if we try to run up against it. Those Jews in Isaiah's time who continued to resist God's sovereign rule in their lives were beating their heads against an immovable, divine obstacle—and His name is "the LORD, the Rock of Israel."

The description of God when we resist Him is formidable: He is the "voice of authority," and He will be heard. You can count on that! "His arm" will express His anger. One can imagine the sword-wielding, muscular arm of a warrior descending on his foes. Such is God's judgment on those who do not humble themselves before Him. His anger is most aptly described in weather terminology, like a hail storm with lightning and thunder—the kind that would shake a man to his core.

We choose how we will experience the Rock—either with joy when we humbly repent, or with fear when we stubbornly resist.

Lord, I come humbly before You, submissive to Your rule in my life—and I joyfully enter with confidence into Your presence, for You are my Rock.

WEEK 14, DAY 4

The God of My Life • El Hayyay

The LORD will command His lovingkindness in the daytime; and His song will be with me in the night, a prayer to the God of my life. (Psalm 42:8)

A yearning for God, this psalm expresses the heart of many Christians for a deeper relaionship with God. It begins:

As the deer pants for the water brooks, so my soul pants for You, O God. My soul thirsts for God, for the living God; when shall I come and appear before God? (Ps 42:1–2)

The refrain echoes three times in Psalm 42 and 43 (considered "twin songs"):

Why are you in despair, O my soul? And why have you become disturbed within me? Hope in God, for I shall again praise Him for the help of His presence. (Ps 42:5, 11; 43:5)

The anguish of distance saturates virtually every verse: "my soul pants" (vs.1), "my soul thirsts" (vs. 2), "my tears" (vs. 3), "pour out my soul" (vs. 4), "despair" (vs. 5 & 6), "deep calls to deep" (vs.7), "mourning" (vs. 9), "shattering of my bones" (vs. 10), "despair" (vs. 11). Yet there is faith and hope intermingled. Truly this is the honest wrestling of a soul with itself, as the psalmist speaks faith into his own discouraged soul.

This song is attributed to a group of Levites called "the sons of Korah." This prescript before verse 1 is found in all of the ancient Old Testament manuscripts, so we take it to be divinely inspired. The "sons of Korah" are descendants of the Levite Korah, who rose against Moses and Aaron in the wilderness wanderings years earlier (Num 16:11-3). Because of Korah's insurrection,14,700 people died of the plague (Num 16:49), and God destroyed Korah and 250 others with an ancient version of a sinkhole (Num 26:9-11). But Korah's sons were spared—and now we see this psalm attached to his descendants. Does this not remarkably speak life-giving grace, that the descendants of someone like Korah would be used by God?

In an 11-verse song where God is referred to 13 times, the psalmist specifically calls out to "the God of my life." When depression sets in, and emotional concerns overwhelm your world, life seems more like a living death. The godly person combats depression with a prayer of hope in the God who is life itself. We are reminded of the Lord's disciples who, even though they did not have everything figured out, said to Him, "Lord, to whom shall we go? You have the words of eternal life" (John 6:68).

Lord, I look to You, the God of my life, for where else shall I turn? You are Life!

WEEK 14, DAY 5

God of the Hebrews • Elohim Ibbriyyim

"They will pay heed to what you say; and you with the elders of Israel will come to the king of Egypt and you will say to him, 'The LORD, the God of the Hebrews, has met with us. So now, please, let us go a three days' journey into the wilderness, that we may sacrifice to the LORD our God.'" (Exodus 3:18)

The Old Testament is filled with polemics. In contrast to an apologetic (a defense of one's faith), a polemic takes the offensive and goes up against other faith systems. Our present-day Western culture considers that all religions are equally valid, following the assertion that religion itself is a construct of human need and imagination. Further, the supposedly enlightened view is that all religious roads lead to heaven, in the way that all wells, though different in size and depth, are designed with the same thing in mind, namely, to provide water. Our culture views religion as man's effort to frame the unknown in a way that meets human emotional and physical needs.

However, God as recorded in the Bible doesn't sit back and wait for attacks on His existence or on the Jewish approach to knowing God. Rather He defines Himself and makes Himself known to humans. He does not leave it up to theologians or philosophers to create an image of Him according to their own earth-bound, limited, egotistical thinking. The 10 commandments of Exodus 20 begin with, "I am the LORD your God … You shall have no other gods before Me. You shall not make for yourself an idol, or any likeness of what is in heaven above …" (Ex 20:2-4). That includes any images of God, physical or imagined.

After the descendants of Abraham had spent 400 years in Egypt amidst rampant idolatry—the religion of their task masters—the LORD, the God of the Hebrews, intervened. He was not a creation of Moses' desert-baked imagination. He revealed Himself in a burning bush, and with instructions to lead the Jews away from their idol-worshiping masters, wanted everyone to know who He was. He is "the LORD," that is, Yahweh. And He is the Hebrew God. Not just any god—not just one on a level with other gods, maybe stronger—but Yahweh Elohim. Enough is enough; He was now going to intervene, and there would be no doubt about who He is.

Today, we Christians believe in the Yahweh, God of the Hebrews, as the one true God, who revealed Himself in our Lord Jesus Christ.

Lord, help me have the courage to make You known in this pagan culture in which I live. Reveal Yourself in me and through me so that others would see Christ because of me.

WEEKEND 14 READING
Amos 1

PERSONAL REFLECTIONS

WEEK 15, DAY 1

God of the Spirits of All Flesh

But they fell on their faces and said, "O God, God of the spirits of all flesh, when one man sins, will You be angry with the entire congregation?" (Numbers 16:22)

"May the LORD, the God of the spirits of all flesh, appoint a man over the congregation …" (Numbers 27:16)

Two significant events for the people of Israel require an address to God unique in Scripture, "God of the spirits of all flesh." We have seen in Jeremiah 32:27 the description, "I am the LORD, the God of all flesh; is anything too difficult for Me?" The totality and comprehensiveness of God's provenance is the focus. No human anywhere lives independently of God's sovereign rule. He is the Master of everything because He is the originator of everything: "All things came into being through Him, and apart from Him nothing came into being that has come into being" (John 1:3, see also 1 Cor 8:6, Col 1:16, Heb 1:2).

In the first event, Korah and 250 other Levites attempted a coup against Moses and Aaron, presumptuously charging them with arrogance and self-aggrandizing, ineffective leadership (Num 16:1-3). The insurrectionist seemed to sway the entire congregation of Israel against them, to the point where God was ready to destroy them all. Despite his own anger with them, Moses humbly pleaded with God to forgive the people's naivety in blindly following Korah and his company, and to deal only with the instigators of the mutiny. Rightfully, Moses recognizes he is appealing to the God who is over all flesh (a figure of speech referring to humanity, and in this case the whole congregation). God has the prerogative to do as He likes, and so Moses and Aaron fall prostrate.

Some have concluded from Moses' example that effective prayer turns the hand of God, but the text does not imply that. God acted in two steps. First God told Moses and Aaron to separate themselves from the congregation (Numbers 16:21), then through Moses he commanded the congregation to separate themselves from Korah and his fellow-mutineers (Numbers 6:24). Everyone individually had to decide whom he would follow—Korah and company or Moses and Aaron. Certainly the fear of the God of the spirits of all flesh became their reality (Number 16:35)!

The second time Moses addressed "the God of the spirits of all flesh" was at the end of his life, when he asked God to appoint a successor to him. This points to the need for divine appointment by the God who was sovereign over people who struggled with their own earthliness and fallen spirits.

Lord, You are the God of all flesh even when I fall to temptations of the flesh.

WEEK 15, DAY 2

God of Their Fathers

Then David said to all the assembly, "Now bless the LORD your God." And all the assembly blessed the LORD, the God of their fathers, and bowed low and did homage to the LORD and to the king." (1 Chronicles 29:20)

Connectedness. Spiritual heritage. Tradition. David instilled in God's people, the nation of Israel, a deep sense of continuity with the faith of "their fathers." That phrase refers to Abraham, Isaac and Jacob, the lineage which all Jews trace as theirs. David's God was not a new invention, nor an evolution or refinement of a humanistic construct of deity, as some academics and "experts" in the history or sociology of religion would have us to believe. His faith, like Judeo-Christian theism today, was based on the belief in one and only one God, rooted in the earliest revelation of Yahweh God to the man Abraham. Monotheism, the belief in one God, is in fact ancient.

Under David's leadership, God's promises to bless Abraham—particularly by possession of a promised land—had finally come to fruition. David essentially handed to his son, Solomon, a nation completely at peace in the Promised Land; the promise of complete possession was fulfilled. Solomon, after being installed as king, acknowledged, "[T]he LORD my God has given me rest on every side; there is neither adversary nor misfortune" (1 Kings 5:4). And David challenged the people to continue on the foundation, namely, to "bless the LORD your God," showing their allegiance to the God of their fathers.

Why is this point important for David to make? Or for us today, for that matter? Human nature, fallen since the Garden of Eden, drifts from God. The sinister nature of our darkened souls, against all logic and reason, looks for something new to capture our imaginations, emotions and energies. David understood that security and peace can easily ebb away. Prosperity and faith don't often mix well. Israel's history bears this out.

Solomon began his reign well but showed signs of spiritual slippage early on by marrying foreign women and eventually falling headlong into their idolatry-laden influence, embracing idols—despite all of God's abundant blessings. He lost his mooring, if not in the intellectual belief in the God of Abraham, Isaac and Jacob, then in his moral disobedience to God's law. Solomon wrote many of the biblical psalms and proverbs, and also the books of Ecclesiastes (the vanity of life under the sun) and the Song of Solomon (extolling love). But he ceased blessing the God of His fathers. The faith and humility he exhibited early in his life came to have little bearing in the outworking of his life, as he chased after new gods.

Lord, help me to grow in faith, the same faith as Abraham, Isaac and Jacob.

WEEK 15, DAY 3

God of Your Father

"Thus you shall say to Joseph, 'Please forgive, I beg you, the transgression of your brothers and their sin, for they did you wrong.'" And now, please forgive the transgression of the servants of the God of your father." And Joseph wept when they spoke to him. (Genesis 50:17)

On many levels this passage is startlingly pathetic. Joseph's brothers' character had not changed, and their attempts to deal with their insecurity were dysfunctional and misguided. Years earlier, they had sold Joseph into Egyptian slavery. They had been jealous over their father Jacob's favoritism for their kid brother and had perceived Joseph as pompous when he told them of a dream about his eventual prominence in the family. In time, a famine struck, and the brothers sought relief in the abundant Egyptian grain store. Unbeknownst to them, Joseph had risen from slavery to political power, becoming the second most powerful man in Egypt. In time, he graciously revealed himself to the brothers, and they, along with their father Jacob and families, moved to Egypt, where Joseph made sure they were well taken care of.

In time, Jacob died. He was the patriarch of the family—in the minds of the 10 brothers, the glue that held them all together. They feared that with father now dead, brother Joseph, with whom they had earlier dealt treacherously, might take revenge on them. Little did they know Joseph's heart and character! They plotted to give a message to Joseph, ostensibly from father, with a request to forgive the brothers. There is no evidence in the text that the message originated with Jacob, yet it was the best plan the brothers had to allay their personal fears. Their fear was understandable, but not because of any indication from Joseph that they should fear him. On the contrary, the fear arose from within themselves, which becomes clear as we examine this passage more deeply.

Notice the brothers could not bring themselves to ask for forgiveness themselves. What is essentially important here, and what I believe made Joseph weep, was this: they identified the God of Jacob ("God of your father") with Joseph, but not themselves! Had they known God like Jacob and Joseph did, they would have understood forgiveness and compassion. Jacob's life had been filled with deceit. But God's restoration and blessing, and finally the reconnection with Joseph, speak of a God whose blessings far outweigh any merit (or demerit) of ours. God continually raised up Joseph after deep-pit experiences, showing that He rescues those who are faithful to Him. If the God of Jacob and Joseph were their God, then they would have understood this and not feared.

Lord, because I have been forgiven, I have no fear—Your love eclipsed it.

WEEK 15, DAY 4

The LORD, God of Your Father David

"Go and say to Hezekiah, 'Thus says the LORD, the God of your father David, "I have heard your prayer, I have seen your tears; behold, I will add fifteen years to your life."'" (Isaiah 38:5)

Spiritual continuity continued throughout Israel's history. The religion of Israel did not evolve; God was and is the same as He was for Abraham, Isaac and Jacob; He was the same God for Moses and for David. Nothing revealed to any of the prophets or writers of Scripture differed from what had been made known before, though God progressively revealed more and more of Himself and His ways, adding to but never taking away. In fact, we say Judaism and Christianity are "revealed" religions, based not on human effort to discover God, but on God's initiative to reveal Himself to mankind.

Twelve hundred years after God called out Abraham, and about 300 years after David was anointed king over Israel, Hezekiah, the 14th king in the Davidic dynasty, "became mortally ill" and prayed for healing (Isaiah 38:1-3). Just previously, God had given a word through Isaiah at a time of threat against Jerusalem, "I will defend this city to save it for My own sake and for My servant David's sake" (Is 37:35). God's faithfulness was to David, and all the kings that followed him were referred to as reigning in the "house of David" (Is 7:13) and sitting "on the throne of David and over his kingdom" (Is 9:7). So when Isaiah came to Hezekiah with a message of healing, the message came from "the LORD, the God of your father David." He was one of the few "good" kings of Israel who "did what was good, right and true before the LORD his God" (2 Chron 31:20).

What is an illness to the God who had revealed Himself to the great king David before him? This was Yahweh, whose glory was more fully revealed when Moses was protected in the cleft of the rock when calling upon the name of the LORD (Exodus 34:5-6). It was this God, the true God revealed to the godly men who preceded Hezekiah, who healed him. The God of eternity injects Himself at various junctures in history. Life and events change, but He does not. And we today believe in and worship the same God as Hezekiah, David, Moses and Abraham. He continues to reveal Himself to us today. While the details and extent of His self-revelation may differ, the same One reaches into our lives as He reached into Hezekiah's. Like pinpoints of glory shining through the backdrop of history, God continues to speak to us today.

Lord, I desire to rise above history and connect to You, the God of Abraham, Moses, David and Hezekiah. You never change; You always remain the same, yesterday, today and forever (Heb 13:8).

WEEK 15, DAY 5

The LORD God, My God

Then David said to his son Solomon, "Be strong and courageous, and act; do not fear nor be dismayed, for the LORD God, my God, is with you. He will not fail you nor forsake you until all the work for the service of the house of the LORD is finished." (1 Chronicles 28:20)

The greatest thing a parent can do for his or her children is to pass on to them the historical faith they have in the true and eternal God. David set the example when he commissioned Solomon to succeed him as king of Israel. He challenged his son to "be strong and courageous." That was Solomon's responsibility. God's promise was explained this way: He would be "with you" and "not fail you nor forsake you." Does this not remind us of God's promise to Moses at his burning bush commissioning to lead God's people out of Egyptian slavery? "Certainly I will be with you…" (Ex 3:12). God likewise commissioned Joshua to take up after Moses: "Just as I have been with Moses, I will be with you; I will not fail you or forsake you" (Jos 1:5). Is this not a universal promise of commissioning by God? Think of Jesus who, when giving His disciples the "Great Commission," concluded with this: "Lo, I am with you always, even to the end of the age" (Matt 28:18-20).

The lesson we learn is that we can do nothing without the very real presence of the Lord; we need His commissioning, His authority for every act of service for Him. So we must always seek His leading and guidance.

There is also a lesson for parents here. A popular statement on parenting thought by some to be wise and astute says, "I will let my children decide for themselves and not influence them toward any particular religion or belief in a deity." If religion were just another of the social sciences, there would be no reason to pre-condition children in one way or another about belief in a deity. However, if in fact God truly exists and has revealed Himself in the Bible and through the history of Abraham, Moses, David, Jesus and the apostles, then it is paramount that we instill in our children the same historic belief we have come to realize in our own lives. If we believe in the truth, why should we allow them to wallow in agnosticism or even atheism, to wander along aimlessly influenced by anti-God rhetoric that passes as educated awareness? Indeed, someone will influence their beliefs; best it would be parents who have the knowledge of the true God of the universe. As David charged his son Solomon to live before the LORD his God, so we should charge our children to not only believe in God, but to live all out for Him.

Lord, You have given me a responsibility to teach my children about You. Help me teach them well, and help me teach them truth.

WEEKEND 15 READING
Amos 2

PERSONAL REFLECTIONS

WEEK 16, DAY 1

God of Truth

"Because he who is blessed in the earth will be blessed by the God of truth; and he who swears in the earth will swear by the God of truth..." (Isaiah 65:16a)

In our multi-faith, pluralistic world, the notion of absolute truth has suffered among the elites as an antiquated, uninformed perspective on life. With the making of many books there is no end (Eccl 12:12): with ideas and philosophies proliferating through internet blogs and news outlets of every conceivable stripe, everyone has a say. Social media, while giving a voice to every person who thinks he has something significant to say, seems to have taken on a personality of its own, like a mastermind manipulating and feeding the masses. What goes "viral" reflects the collective shouting down of that which is not popular or not trending, while promoting that which is threatening and non-threatening alike.

But in the storm-tossed sea of competing ideas, where is an anchor to keep a person from being swallowed up like sinking flotsam? Any mooring you choose will be buffeted by some faceless voice—nothing is sacrosanct anymore. So where does one turn, to stop the drunken swirl of worldly intoxication of untruth and the resulting animal-like retreat into one's own individual enclave, one's own personal "truth" mixed with self-gratification? After all, doesn't the philosophy of today have self as its ultimate goal? Everyone must define truth for himself, or so we are told.

The prophet Isaiah lived in a similar time, where people jettisoned God's truth for their own, albeit cloaked in religious activities. They had become:

"[a] people who continually provoke Me to My face, offering sacrifices in gardens and burning incense on bricks; who sit among graves and spend the night in secret places; who eat swine's flesh, and the broth of unclean meat is in their pots. Who say, 'Keep to yourself, do not come near me, for I am holier than you!' These are smoke in My nostrils, a fire that burns all the day." (Isaiah 65:3–5)

Who is to say what they were doing was wrong? The God of truth says so, that's who—He designed truth, He created it. He is truth. He is the anchor of reality for those who live by His Word. How blessed are those who separate from the popular thinking of the crowd. To "swear by" is to act upon the real existence of God. In Scripture, an oath is worded this way: "As the Lord lives I will do ..." When all is said and done, eternity will settle the record (Isaiah 65:17), because we believe there is an anchor of truth. That anchor is God.

Lord, You are my truth anchor in the fluid world of human philosophies.

WEEK 16, DAY 2

God Who Avenges

O LORD, God of vengeance, God of vengeance, shine forth! (Psalm 94:1)

Vengeance is not one of the softer descriptions of God, to be sure. To many, it smacks of medieval caricatures and oppressive, controlling religious institutions or fiery Bible-thumpers on the saw-dust trails. So what do we make of this verse in the inspired Word of God?

Some might offer that Psalm 94 is written from a human perspective, reflecting the anguished but misguided cry of an otherwise pious soul. Yet Psalm 22 rings out with a similar, but more familiar cry of anguish, "My God, my God, why have You forsaken me?" Can we not hear these words echo on the anguished lips of our Savior on the cross (Matt 27:46, Mark 15:34)? The book of Psalms is filled with similar prayers—one can hardly write them all off as being sub-spiritual. Nor can we appeal to the lack of authorial identity for this psalm, for we do not cast aspersions on the book of Hebrews for that reason.

In reality, it is good that God is vengeful. In order to see this, we need to simply read the rest of the psalm and open our eyes to the reality of our fallen world and the evil all around. We read of the proud, the wicked, those who speak arrogantly, those who vaunt themselves, those who crush the people of God, slay widows and immigrants and murder orphans. The psalm writer notes those who blatantly question God's ability to see and know everything. Do we really want a God who will not take revenge on these kinds of people? Certainly God is love, but some would have us believe that God is "only" love. He, however, is not one dimensional, and is not to be defined by a superficial concept of love that renders him a pushover, lacking strength or resolve to bring righteous judgment. He is the defender of the poor and the downtrodden, of the widow and the orphan, the oppressed and the neglected. How dare anyone abuse or take advantage of them with impunity, and get away with it "scot-free"? Do we want a God who turns a blind or callous eye to the injustices in the world?

The word vengeance in this context means "the act of harming someone in return for an injury or offense." God is holy and just. We humans are not. Our vengeance is subjectively tainted, while His vengeance is perfect and flows naturally from is His perfect holiness and righteousness. Thus, the Lord says, "Vengeance is Mine" (Deut 32:35, 41). Praise God that He will deal with unrighteousness and injustice and unholiness—definitively and decisively. That is our great hope—that in the end, what is right prevails, because He is a God of vengeance.

Lord, I so look forward to You righting all the wrongs, and setting straight the record of Your righteousness and holiness.

WEEK 16, DAY 3

God's Son

"I will surely tell of the decree of the LORD: He said to Me, 'You are My Son, today I have begotten You.'" (Psalm 2:7)

Do homage to the Son, that He not become angry, and you perish in the way, for His wrath may soon be kindled. How blessed are all who take refuge in Him! (Psalm 2:12)

To Christian ears, these verses out of our Old Testament (which Jews also hold to be the Word of God) bring to mind the Trinity, or at least the second person, the Son of God. Certainly, the New Testament quotes Psalm 2:7 at least four times, applying it to Jesus Christ. Some English versions (NASB, ESV, NKJV) capitalize "Son," while others do not (NIV, NLT); but since the original Hebrew in which this was written did not use capitals, such renderings are the translators' theological interpolations. What would these verses mean to the Jewish ear, in the Old Testament context?

The Jewish king is in view here, using an ancient Near East idiom of adoption language. The king was viewed as being adopted by God. We see this in the God's message to David about his son Solomon:

"I [God] will be a father to him and he will be a son to Me; when he commits iniquity, I will correct him with the rod of men and the strokes of the sons of men, but My lovingkindness shall not depart from him..." (2 Sam 7:14–15)

This makes perfectly good sense in the context of Psalm 2. Verse 7 then would refer to the coronation of the king. Verse 12 indicates that other nations must decide whether to honor ("do homage") the Jewish king or not, whether to join ranks with and come under the protection of Israel or suffer the animosity of the people of Yahweh. This fits well with the promise to Abraham, "I will bless those who bless you, and the one who curses you I will curse. And in you all the families of the earth will be blessed" (Gen 12:3).

The NT applies verse 7 Messianically, that is, to the ultimate Davidic King, the Lord Jesus Christ. This was made clear at Jesus' baptism when God's voice was heard: "This is My beloved Son" (Matt 3:16). The apostle Paul, from the get-go, applied Psalm 2:7 to Jesus' resurrection and proclaimed that His sonship was the fulfillment of "the promise made to the fathers" (Acts 13:30-33). The writer to the Hebrews uses Psalm 2:7 to proclaim the supremacy of Jesus over the angels and the Jewish priesthood (Heb 1:5, 5:5). Truly, the whole world hangs in the balance—depending on how they respond to the Son.

Lord Jesus, You are the Son-King who is coming to reign. Even so, reign now!

WEEK 16, DAY 4

Gracious and Compassionate God

"They refused to listen, and did not remember Your wondrous deeds which You had performed among them; so they became stubborn and appointed a leader to return to their slavery in Egypt. But You are a God of forgiveness, gracious and compassionate, slow to anger and abounding in lovingkindness; and You did not forsake them." (Nehemiah 9:17)

"Nevertheless, in Your great compassion You did not make an end of them or forsake them, for You are a gracious and compassionate God." (Nehemiah 9:31)

Not an uncommon epithet of God, this description evokes Exodus 34:6-7, where God reveals the back side of His glory to Moses in the cleft of the rock. That was just after Moses had led the people out of captivity to relocate in the Promised Land. Now in Nehemiah's time, just after returning to the land from their Babylonian-Assyrian captivity, the people acknowledged (in the Levites' words) that their God was gracious and compassionate. He never changes, even when disciplining His people for their wayward ways.

The Levites led the way in repentance with fasting, in sackcloth and with dirt upon them; they confessed their sins; they returned to reading the book of the Law of Yahweh; and they worshipped Yahweh (Neh 9:1-4). Then the Levites summarized biblical history, beginning with creation (vss. 5-6), the call of Abram who was renamed Abraham and God's promise to him (vss. 7-8), the Egyptian captivity (vs. 9), the Exodus (vss. 10-12), the giving of the Law to Moses (vss. 13-14), provisions of manna and water in the wilderness wanderings (vs. 15), and the people's rebellion against God (vss. 16-17a). But—and this is a great insight into their own history—in the midst of their rebellion, God was gracious and compassionate (vs. 17b). The history of God's dealing with His people, according to this account, amounted to this: God never left them, even when they blatantly engaged in idol worship!

Eventually, God did bring them into the Promised Land of Canaan (albeit 40 years later) and fulfilled His promises to Abraham of a huge descendancy living in the land (Neh 9:23-25). Yet, once settled in the land and enjoying the promises, they again strayed from God. Despite the Lord's many gracious and compassionate warnings of judgment, they continued in their sin, until He sent them into captivity again (Babylonian-Assyrian). Now, having returned to the land, the Levites reminded them they are there because God has always been and continues to be gracious and compassionate.

Lord, at times You chastise us for our sin, yet You are the God of the eons who works everything to our good, because You are gracious and compassionate.

WEEK 16, DAY 5

Gracious, Righteous and Compassionate God

Gracious is the LORD, and righteous; yes, our God is compassionate. (Psalm 116:5)

Our quest to know God returns to common themes, combined in various ways. In this single verse we have three adjectives (gracious, righteous, compassionate) and two nouns (LORD "Yahweh" and God "Elohim"). Here we see that the knowledge of God carries the psalmist along in his individual thanksgiving prayer. And what a prayer this is, for it provides for us poetic words that express the innermost struggle and relief of godly hearts.

Typical of many thanksgiving psalms, this one begins with an introduction (Psalm 116:1-12), followed by a problem (Psalm 116:3-4), then recognition and praise of His character as it relates to the writer's deliverance from his problem (Psalm 116:5-11), and finally, renewed commitment to God.

We know nothing of the particular problem the writer faced, except that it was death-threatening and caused great fear and distress (vs. 3, 7-8). What we do know is that he extolled God, rather than wallowing in the experience or in a pity party. Adversity became an opportunity for seeing God in greater glory. His response naturally followed, as he recognized the Lord's sovereign hand in it all. The cry for help was simply but earnestly put: "Then I called upon the name of the LORD: 'O LORD, I beseech You, save my life!'" (Ps 116:4).

He could do this because he knew the Lord, that He is gracious, righteous and compassionate. God may be known intellectually, but He is really known intimately through His actions, for His name Yahweh means He is a very real presence in our time of need. And the psalmist, in classical "self-talk," counsels his soul, "Return to your rest, O my soul, for the LORD has dealt bountifully with you" (Ps 116:7). All is well because the Yahweh is here. There is no need for worry or anxiety or fear. The psalmist provides an example of choosing to believe the divine perspective rather than the human perspective (vs. 10-11).

The thought of it all produces in the psalmist an overwhelming desire to renew his commitment to praise and worship God. "What shall I render to the LORD for all His benefits toward me? I shall lift up the cup of salvation and call upon the name of the LORD" (Ps 116:13-14). We, too, when tempted toward fear and anxiety, must instruct our souls by rehearsing God's character, challenging ourselves to believe in Him and not our human understanding, to dare to believe He is gracious, righteous and compassionate. So we call on the name of the Yahweh; we celebrate His "cup of salvation" and live out our redeemed lives, day by day.

Lord Yahweh, I choose to live the redeemed life and call on You every day.

WEEKEND 16 READING
Amos 3-4

PERSONAL REFLECTIONS

WEEK 17, DAY 1

God of Gods, Lord of Lords

"For the LORD your God is the God of gods and the Lord of lords, the great, the mighty, and the awesome God who does not show partiality nor take a bribe. (Deuteronomy 10:17)

Many Scripture passages drip with descriptions of God, and this is a key one. A rich tapestry, a colorful kaleidoscope, a rainbow of hues—this adds to a wonderful 360-degree picture of God. I resist calling Him "our God," for that implies there are others. But in contrast to other gods, who are merely imagined in people's minds, our God is the one and only true God. He is not what modern skeptics like to say He is—a fantasy of our imagination, designed in our unevolved minds to meet our emotional needs. Rather, He is there, as Dr. Francis Schaefer used to say. He is just as real, even more real, than you or I. All other imaginations of gods exist only in the minds of those who deny the true God.

In Egypt, the descendants of Abraham, Isaac and Jacob multiplied over 400 years, but they were surrounded by the paganism of Egypt. So when Moses led them in the Exodus, they became reacquainted with the God of their forefathers, through the giving of the Law at Sinai. And now, in the book of Deuteronomy, Moses is giving them a second telling of the Law; this is after 40 years of wandering in the Sinai desert, and just before entering into the Promised Land. When he addresses the people about God, Moses calls Him "your God," in contrast to the so-called gods worshipped by the Egyptians and the pagan inhabitants of the Promised Land they are about to enter.

Their God as Jews is also our God as Christians. He is Yahweh ("the LORD"), unique by His name and its meaning—He is the deity who is actively present, not just a religious construct. He is the "God of gods," par excellence. The 11th century theologian Anselm, in a carefully worded statement regarding "proof of God's existence," described God this way: He is "the Being than which none greater can be conceived" (the so-called "ontological" argument). If one could imagine something greater than God, then we would have to reframe our understanding of God to include that "thing" as well. He is without any further qualification or limit. Or to put it in Moses' terminology, He is "the God of gods." He is greater than all human imaginations of deity.

As God of gods, it follows that He also is Lord of lords. His authority supersedes all other authorities. This is the God the people of Israel were to follow and obey. He is the God we Christians follow and obey. And this goes against our humanistic grain of self-exaltation.

O God of gods and Lord of lords, I acknowledge You as my supreme allegiance.

WEEK 17, DAY 2

Great, Mighty and Awesome God

"For the LORD your God is the God of gods and the Lord of lords, the great, the mighty, and the awesome God who does not show partiality nor take a bribe." (Deuteronomy 10:17)

Yahweh God is not simply a remote, impersonal, austere deity that watches over the unseen affairs of the world. He is actively engaged in sensible ways—and by "sensible" we mean ways we can sense, either externally in the world around us or internally within ourselves. In other words, He is truly involved in our lives in ways that can be known. This does not negate faith, which is "the conviction of things not seen" (Heb 11:1b). Rather through faith, we bring the unseen, that which is hoped for, into our real experience. So we can say, "I know God. I really do."

Moses' description of God conveys this notion in everyday terms. The Hebrew word for "great" ("gadol") is a term used for physical growth of people and other living things (TWOT). In 1 Sam 26:24 the term is used "to set a high value on one's life." God is of highest value in terms of personal worth. We value humans differently depending on our relationships—for example, I mourn more deeply over a loved one who dies than over a stranger on the other side of the world whom I have never met. It may pain the idealistic humanist to acknowledge this, but we are selective in the value we place on others. But God is to be valued above all else. To value Him is to see Him as the greatest thing in our lives, that which completely consumes our allegiance.

He is also mighty (Heb: "gabar"), according to our verse today. It means one who is strong, and the word is "commonly associated with warfare and has to do with the strength and vitality of the successful warrior" (TWOT). As Israel was about to enter the Promised Land, there would be wars as they drove out the evil pagan nations. Because Yahweh is mighty, then His followers can also be mighty. David, later in biblical history, had his "mighty men" (2 Sam 23:8), but he also knew that greater yet, he had a mighty God: "Who is the King of glory? The LORD strong and mighty, the LORD mighty in battle" (Ps 24:8).

Moses also describes Yahweh as awesome (Heb: "yareh"). While God is certainly awesome in the popular present-day sense of being wonderfully amazing, the word used here actually contains a more arresting notion. It would be more akin to the phrase "shock and awe." The Hebrew concept involves fear and terror. God's might is "awe-inspiring," and if He is on our side, then our enemies (whether human or demonic) should rightly tremble. Our God is a great, mighty and awesome God! We believe that. I believe that!

Lord, I have nothing to fear because You are my hero and defender.

WEEK 17, DAY 3

Great God and King

For the LORD is a great God and a great King above all gods ... (Psalm 95:3)

Descriptions of God are well worth repeating, for how can one exhaust the greatness of God? The psalm writer was overcome with joy as he contemplated the LORD he worships. He begins his ode:

O come, let us sing for joy to the LORD, let us shout joyfully to the rock of our salvation. Let us come before His presence with thanksgiving, let us shout joyfully to Him with psalms. (Ps 95:1–2)

Four invitations invite the soul to delight in the "rock of our salvation." Have you ever noticed how the writers of Scripture just can't get over their appreciation for their salvation? The song never gets stale, the story never drones old—how God saved me. We are constantly reminded how wonderful it is that God, in His grace and mercy, reached into this lost world of sinners and redeemed us. When the world turned dark and oppressive in the Garden of Eden, God provided a suitable covering and prevented mankind from eating of the tree of life while in a fallen state. What a blessing that was, for it preserved the opportunity for restoration by not sealing man's fate eternally. God provided—and still provides—the opportunity for a rescue from fallenness.

When we fully consider the state of our condemnation, how can we be anything but continually thankful in God's presence? We are reminded of how unworthy we are. Modern psychologists may tell us such feelings of unworthiness are fostered by a repressive, puritanical society—but what is society but made up of human beings all of whom are fallen. Yes, we are indeed unworthy, and not because of false feelings of inferiority. We are infinitely inferior to a perfect and holy God. Religion may build on that to coerce and manipulate, but our God invites us into His presence. The remedy for our unworthiness is not to cast blame on other people or even on God. The remedy, rather, is to "... draw near with confidence to the throne of grace, so that we may receive mercy and find grace to help in time of need" (Heb 4:16).

There is no greater joy than that found in His presence, for His grace is greater than all our sin (Rom 5:20). Is He not great?! No wonder the psalmist continues: "Come, let us worship and bow down, let us kneel before the LORD our Maker. For He is our God, and we are the people of His pasture and the sheep of His hand..." (Ps 95:6–7). When we are captured by these thoughts, we join with the writer in proclaiming, "He is indeed a great God and King."

Lord, I do come into Your presence right now with thanksgiving and worship. You are the great and exalted God and King, the rock of my salvation.

WEEK 17, DAY 4

Rock of Our Salvation

O come, let us sing for joy to the LORD, let us shout joyfully to the rock of our salvation. Let us come before His presence with thanksgiving, let us shout joyfully to Him with psalms. (Psalm 95:1–2)

Rocks are sturdy, solid. Houses built on solid rock stand up much better than houses built on sand or even clay. Anchoring a guy line into a rock holds much better than tying it to a stick or a branch. Anchors keep boats from drifting away. Anchors are used to fasten objects to walls. To anchor something means to fix it so that it is immovable.

Thinking of God as our rock comes easily. He is our reference point for all of life and thinking. He is the absolute truth that the unbelieving world denies exists. And rightly so, for if one believes in the non-existence of God, then one must therefore believe in the non-existence of truth. I use the phrase "belief in the non-existence" advisedly, for indeed atheism is a belief system, make no mistake about it. What one chooses to believe becomes his anchor point for everything else in life.

As believers in Yahweh, our worldview begins with God. "In the beginning God …"—so begins our Scriptures (Gen 1:1). His existence is assumed, and from that everything else flows. John states it this way: "In the beginning was the Word and the Word was with God, and the Word was God" (John 1:1). This is the bedrock truth.

For Christians, this rock-solidness extends to our salvation. He is the Rock of our Salvation. If our house is built on this rock, then it will be immovable, unshakeable, and unassailable. While we recognize that Psalm 95 is Jewish Scripture, we are heirs of these truths along with them. Salvation for the Jews is ultimately rooted in God, and not in the shifting sands of their good works. Indeed, the Law of Moses provided a way of dealing with the inevitability of sin. The Day of Atonement, in particular—the catch-all, so-to-speak—was given as an annual reminder of sinfulness and the remedy that is found only in God through a sacrifice. In the NT, we discover that the sacrifice God accepts for complete forgiveness and thus salvation is found in Jesus Christ, who did not "… need daily, like those high priests, to offer up sacrifices, first for His own sins and then for the sins of the people, because this He did once for all when He offered up Himself" (Heb 7:26–27).

This salvation in Christ's completed and perfect sacrifice is our security and can never be taken away from us. We are assured forever; we are saved always; we are forgiven eternally. Because He is our Rock.

Lord, thank You for mty security, Your salvation. I shall never be moved.

WEEK 17, DAY 5

The LORD, Holy God

[God] struck down some of the men of Beth-shemesh because they had looked into the ark of the LORD ... The men of Beth-shemesh said, "Who is able to stand before the LORD, this holy God? And to whom shall He go up from us?" (1 Samuel 6:19-20)

"Holy," the word, clocks in as the quickest adjective that comes to mind when talking about religious things. It spills out easily in phrases like, "The church is a holy place." I remember from my childhood, renaissance art picturing "holy" people with halos above their heads, or "holy" objects as glowing, as if somehow imbued with a spiritual energy. Like many spiritual terms, the word shows up in common vernacular expressions of exclamation, like "holy cow."

The word itself "connotes the state of that which belongs to the sphere of the sacred" (TWOT). Something is holy if it is designed for use in relation to God. The word was not uncommon in ancient languages and dialects, and in some cases it was even used in reference to temple prostitution. Thus, the word is not specific to Judeo-Christian religion and does not necessarily carry a moral connotation, though it certainly may be used that way when rightly understood.

Our passage today contains an excellent example of a holy object, the Ark of the Covenant (not to be confused with Noah's ark of hugely different size). During the Exodus period, this elaborate box occupied the central position in the Most Holy place of the Tabernacle. Ornate, golden artistry covered it, capped with a covering called the "Mercy Seat," which was bookended by two gilded angel figures. The Ark represented the place of the Lord's presence, and to this place the high priest came yearly to make atonement. The Ark epitomized holiness, for it was set apart for use in worship of God (see 1 Kings 8:4).

The Ark was made from earthly materials. Its holiness did not constitute any change in the material properties of its makeup. What made it holy was that God had pronounced to the Jews that it had a singular, special purpose. The Philistines had stolen the ark in a previous battle but were now returning it to the Jews. When the men of Beth-shemesh, who should have known better (Num 4:15), audaciously opened the ark, God took their lives. In fact, that judgment extended to 50,000-plus people. This was indeed a holy object, and the Jews were to treat it the way God commanded. This was because the LORD God of the Jews, Yahweh, is holy. We dare not treat Him as common or use His name simply as an exclamation. The name "Yahweh" or "Jesus Christ" must never fall from a Christian's lips as an idle exclamation.

Lord Jesus, You are holy. I confess that too often I have taken You for granted, rather than treating You as more precious than gold or silver.

WEEKEND 17 READING
Amos 5

PERSONAL REFLECTIONS

WEEK 18, DAY 1

Holy One of Israel

I will also praise You with a harp, even Your truth, O my God; to You I will sing praises with the lyre, O Holy One of Israel. (Ps 71:22).

As common as the word "holy" is in Scripture, and as frequently objects associated with Israel's worship are called holy, in what sense can we use the same word of the most high God? To describe Him with similar words as earthly objects seems to diminish God. Is God holy just like the Ark of the Covenant is holy? That would be like saying the shadow of a beautiful building is as beautiful as the building itself.

When we use a word to describe God we mean to say, at the least, that God is better in the realm of that attribute. So God is holy like the Ark is holy, but "more" holy. But isn't God more than just "more holy"? He is absolute holiness. He defines holiness, epitomizes it, originates it, generates it and imparts it. He cannot be made unholy. His holiness is not just "better" or "more." It is a difference on the order of essence. Michelangelo, for example, was a Renaissance artist and his works are Renaissance art. The painter and his art of the same "genre," that is, are described as Renaissance. But the two are completely different in "kind." The artist is of a different essential nature than his art work, and this difference is of immense magnitude.

God, then, is holy of a different kind or magnitude. The holiness of things is a derivative of His holiness. He is completely separate from all things and stands unique. If "holy" is a word that "connotes the state of that which belongs to the sphere of the sacred" (Theological Wordbook of the Old Testament), God by definition is holy. He completely belongs to the sphere of the sacred because He IS the sacred. Nothing is sacred or holy apart from Him. Before anything else existed, there was God (Gen 1:1, John 1:1).

The psalmist extols God for His holiness. He writes from the vantage of old age (Ps 71:9) but has learned to continually call on the Lord for help in troubling times. The longer we live, the more we are immersed in this fallen world. Temptations to abandon faith in God—to stop trusting God, who doesn't always seem to answer our prayers or rescue us from difficulties—never stop piling on. Some things just seem to go on and on. The refrain of the world is, "God has forsaken him, pursue and seize him, for there is no one to deliver" (Ps 71:11). That is the world's wisdom, and it is easy to believe. But our God is holy; He is different from the world. Our hope is in Him. So in faith, we join the psalm writer's chorus and say ...

I will also praise You with a harp, even Your truth, O my God; to You I will sing praises with the lyre, O Holy One of Israel.

WEEK 18, DAY 2

God's Holy One

For You will not abandon my soul to Sheol; nor will You allow Your Holy One to undergo decay. (Psalm 16:10)

Psalm 16 has brought spiritual comfort to many believers through the years. It is a message of faith, an expression of trust, for all who struggle in our fallen world. Notice some of the more memorable sections:

"Preserve me, O God, for I take refuge in You." (vs. 1)

"You are my Lord; I have no good besides You." (vs. 2)

"As for the saints who are in the earth, they are the majestic ones in whom is all my delight." (vs. 3)

"The LORD is the portion of my inheritance and my cup." (vs. 5)

"The lines have fallen to me in pleasant places; indeed, my heritage is beautiful to me." (vs. 6)

"I have set the LORD continually before; because He is at my right hand, I will not be shaken." (vs. 8)

But what do we make of verse 10? In Peter's great Pentecost sermon, he lifts this verse out of its context and applies it to the resurrection of Jesus Christ (Acts 2:27). So does the apostle Paul on his first missionary tour, where he preached in the synagogue at Pisidian Antioch (Acts 13:35). There he made the distinction that this applies to our Lord's resurrection.

Yet, the verse does situate itself in the very personal psalm of David's own experience. In its original context, David's body did experience decay. In fact, Paul made the very point that "David ... was laid among his fathers and underwent decay; but He whom God raised did not undergo decay" (Acts 13:36). So how could David have included Psalm 16:10?

Clearly, David would not refer to himself definitively as "Your Holy One." He probably knew he was speaking prophetically that he would ultimately be raised from the dead, because there was coming God's Holy One who would be raised from the dead. How much of this he understood is not clear. But we read in the NT:

"As to this salvation, the prophets who prophesied of the grace that would come to you made careful searches and inquiries, seeking to know what person or time the Spirit of Christ within them was indicating as He predicted the sufferings of Christ and the glories to follow." (1 Peter 1:10-11).

Lord Jesus, You are God's most Holy One. Therefore, I want to be holy also.

WEEK 18, DAY 3

Holy One of Jacob

But when he sees his children, the work of My hands, in his midst, they will sanctify My name; indeed, they will sanctify the Holy One of Jacob and will stand in awe of the God of Israel. (Isaiah 29:23)

Warning Jerusalem of impending judgment, God sent a message via Isaiah the prophet. The message was like a sealed book that no one could read (Is 29:11-12), indicating that "this people draw near with their words and honor Me with their lip service, but they remove their hearts far from Me, and their reverence for Me consists of tradition learned by rote..." (Is 29:13). But one day, "the deaf will hear words of a book, and out of their gloom and darkness the eyes of the blind will see" (Is 29:18).

Lest God's people are abandoned with no thread of hope, the prophecy of judgment ends with eschatological optimism: "Jacob shall not now be ashamed, nor shall his face now turn pale ..." (Is 29:22). When God refers to Israel as Jacob, He calls to mind the patriarch's original name, which was changed when he became a man of faith who took Abraham and Isaac's God as his God. He did not come by this easily; it took 20 some years of running from his troubles and from God (see Gen 28:20-21; 35:10). Despite all his struggles, Jacob became Israel because he set apart the God of his fathers and put aside all other gods. You could say he sanctified God in his heart.

So now we find in today's verse God juxtaposing the "Holy One of Jacob" and "the God of Israel." The people of God were confronted with judgment because of God's holiness. Therefore they needed to embrace His holiness and live by it. They needed to "sanctify" or set apart God in their hearts with an undivided devotion.

Peter wrote of this concept in his first letter for Christians:

But even if you should suffer for the sake of righteousness, you are blessed. And do not fear their intimidation, and do not be troubled, but sanctify Christ as Lord in your hearts, always being ready to make a defense to everyone who asks you to give an account for the hope that is in you, yet with gentleness and reverence ... (1 Peter 3:14–15).

The words "sanctify" and "holy" are related, thus the connection is clear. We must set apart Christ because He is the Holy God. Can I fill my name into the following blank, God is the "Holy One of _____"?

Holy God, because You are holy and set apart from all other conceptions of deity, I set You apart as Lord in my life, so that I might be holy as You are holy, and ready to defend Your unique existence in this pluralistic, multi-faith world.

WEEK 18, DAY 4

The Lord is My Strength

"I love You, O LORD, my strength." The LORD is my rock and my fortress and my deliverer, My God, my rock, in whom I take refuge; My shield and the horn of my salvation, my stronghold. (Psalm 18:1–2)

The closest to the NT word "agape" that we find in the OT is the Hebrew term "hesed," which refers to God's covenant-keeping love for His people (see Ps 18:50, where it is often translated "loving-kindness"). God loves us as an outworking of His promise to Abraham and His subsequent promises and covenants. This is His commitment to His people.

Psalm 18, which reflects David's deliverance from King Saul (2 Sam 22), uses a Hebrew word that expresses a deep inward feeling for God. When used to describe God's love it carries the connotation of compassion or mercy. Of course, there is little sense in which we can show that kind of feeling for God, so the word's wider field of meaning includes the idea of an inner affection or tenderness toward God for what He has done for us. In David's case, he saw God's deliverance from King Saul as a supremely relational activity. Unlike a pagan's response of fearfulness to an impersonal god, David saw his deliverance as a deeply interpersonal event, between himself and God.

So in Psalm 18:1-2 we see an effluent pouring out of adjectives to describe the God with whom David senses a growing relationship. Notice what follows: "my" rock, "my" fortress, etc. These words reflect a growing bond between Creator and creature, Master and servant, Father and son, Friend and friend, Lover and loved one.

Now the first thing David has to say about God is to call Him "my strength." His life was filled with physical violence, with Saul trying to murder him, and his engagement with the armies of the Philistines, Amalekites and other surrounding people groups. His love of God was rooted very pragmatically, in God's provision of military strength. Some may think this an inferior kind of love: we ought to love God simply because He is beautiful in His being and worthy of love because of His person. Such lofty notions sound spiritual, in a sense similar to those who present legalism as "the appearance of wisdom in self-made religion …" (Col 2:23). So pseudo-spiritualists speak of an esoteric worship of God divorced from the reality of our physical humanity. But God meets us in this physical world where we live. It is His working in our creaturely life (in David's case, giving Him strength), that brings a person deeper into relationship with Himself. So I can love God as "my strength" as I see Him strengthening me for the struggles of life. That is good and acceptable to God.

Lord, You are my strength and song (Ex 15:2), and I love You for that.

WEEK 18, DAY 5

The LORD is My Rock

"I love You, O LORD, my strength." The LORD is my rock and my fortress and my deliverer, My God, my rock, in whom I take refuge; My shield and the horn of my salvation, my stronghold. (Psalm 18:1–2)

While elsewhere the psalmist wrote that God was "the rock of our salvation" (Ps 95:1-2), here he writes more personally and particularly, and more expansively, "The LORD is my rock ...." It is one thing to include oneself in a collective faith, as in, "We the church believe ...." But it is another to write, "I believe." In the end, we will all stand alone before God our Creator when He separates the entire flock, the sheep from the goats–based on our individual responses to Him (Matt 26:31-46).

Here David, the writer, speaks of God as being the rock on which he (David) stands. In battle, rocks can provide many advantages: protection from arrows and spears, hiding places, a way to brace oneself to make one's footing sure—an important facet in hand-to-hand combat. A rock, in a nautical sense, provides a holding point for a boat's anchor in a storm.

For us, God is all of this, metaphorically. He is our rock that gives us a sure footing in the struggles of life. We can brace against Him, so to speak, to keep from slipping in our battle against temptations. We can lean against Him when we are weary; when all else folds or crumbles or gives way, He remains solid. To express it philosophically, He is the immovable reference point for our life, the anchor, the foundation upon which we build.

Jesus contrasted a rock foundation for a house with a sand foundation. Many Christians are raised in believing households but once grown up are confronted with the usual struggles of faith, and give up on a God who does not seem to be real any more. Their feelings and superficial faith render their belief to be like shifting sands. They have not learned to lean on the Rock. He is immovable—how do we know this? "Faith is the assurance of things hoped for, the conviction of things not seen" (Heb 11:1). The greatest challenge of faith is precisely this: we are called upon to be assured of something that is not yet here, to be convinced of something we cannot see in any tangible way. And this is where many Christians stray. They come to rely on their senses, public opinion, humanistic philosophies—all which change with time. We must lean on God our Rock, who never changes. To do otherwise is to assign ourselves to slipping and stumbling through life in the sand and gravel. He is the only Rock that can anchor us to the foundation. Faith is trusting in Him.

Lord, my Rock, I lean against, stand upon, believe in You.

WEEKEND 18 READING
Amos 6-7

PERSONAL REFLECTIONS

WEEK 19, DAY 1

The LORD Is My Fortress

"I love You, O LORD, my strength." The LORD is my rock and my fortress and my deliverer, My God, my rock, in whom I take refuge; My shield and the horn of my salvation, my stronghold. (Psalm 18:1–2)

Fortresses are impregnable by definition. Of course, at a human level no manmade fortress is absolutely impenetrable, for there is always something more powerful than super-thick walls, no matter how deeply buried the building is.

One of the most famous bunkers, called "America's Fortress," is found deep in Cheyenne Mountain, near Colorado Springs in Colorado, a facility of NORAD (North American Aerospace Defense Command). The command complex was built, beginning in 1961, under 2,000 feet of granite covering five acres. Fifteen three-story buildings are protected from earthquakes or explosions by a system of 1,000 giant springs and flexible pipe connectors to limit the operational effect of movement. The bunker is certified to sustain an electro-magnetic pulse and designed to deflect a 30-megaton nuclear explosion as close as 1.2 miles away (www.norad.mil).

But what happens if a 30-megaton nuclear bomb lands half a mile away? What if a meteor hits it dead on? Or an earthquake just beyond the accepted threshold or a cyber-attack or espionage from within? To the designers and military brass, these threats fall into the realm of "tolerable" or "acceptable risk," for assumedly the enormous cost of creating a better, more modern, more technically advanced version of this complex would be prohibitive, plus it would still be vulnerable beyond a certain tolerance of acceptability.

David trusted in God as his fortress, greater than which nothing exists. There is no force, earthquake or nuclear blast that can budge God even one iota.

Though the springs supporting the NORAD command facility may allow movement up to one inch, God is completely immovable. Rather it is He who shakes the earth. Let us not forget "the LORD your maker, who stretched out the heavens and laid the foundations of the earth" (Is 51:13). Remember what David wrote at another time: "The voice of the LORD shakes the wilderness; the LORD shakes the wilderness of Kadesh" (Ps 29:8). People may criticize us or threaten us. Satan may come like a ferocious lion, but we are safely tucked away, protected by Him who is the strongest force in the universe. Nothing gets through Him to us, unless He allows it—and then it is only for our good. The only danger comes if, through unbelief, we do not rest in Him as our fortress.

Lord, I have nothing to fear from anyone, for in You I am completely protected.

WEEK 19, DAY 2

The LORD Is My Deliverer

"I love You, O LORD, my strength." The LORD is my rock and my fortress and my deliverer, My God, my rock, in whom I take refuge; My shield and the horn of my salvation, my stronghold. (Psalm 18:1–2)

The term "deliverance" occurs mostly in the book of Psalms and flows frequently from David's writings. David was a man of action, but he was a wanted man, being number one on King Saul's hit list. His posture was to not raise a finger against "the Lord's anointed," as he referred to Saul. Although David knew he had been anointed to be king in place of his nemesis, he was satisfied to bide his time until God removed him. His honor and respect for the position of kingship as an anointing from God compelled him to suffer many hardships, even fearing for his life.

One might think with super-spiritual thoughts that David lacked faith, for if God had promised him the kingdom, why would he fear for his life? Indeed, he spent much time on the run, even hiding in the caves of Adulum (1 Sam 22:1) and Engedi (1 Sam 23:29). This is similar to the question that if Jesus was truly God, how could the temptation in Gethsemane be a real struggle? Yet how else can we understand Jesus' three-times prayer, "Abba! Father! All things are possible for You; remove this cup from Me; yet not what I will, but what You will" (Mark 14:36)? In the same context, He exhorts His disciples, "Keep watching and praying that you may not come into temptation; the spirit is willing, but the flesh is weak" (Mark 14:38).

So likewise, David believed God's promise and counted on it—and he fled from Saul and sought physical refuge in caves. Yet ultimately, his trust was not in caves, for nothing on earth can keep something hidden forever. Even as Saul inadvertently entered the very cave where David was hiding (1 Sam 24), David was discoverable despite his human efforts. In fact, David's men saw that incident as proof that God had given Saul over to David for victory. However, David "delivered" Saul by sparing him of ambush in the very cave he had accidently stumbled upon. Such was the confidence David had in God his Deliverer, that he could spare the life of the one who was trying to murder him.

Like David, we can find ourselves today hemmed in by circumstances or people who would take advantage of us, walk over us, mistreat us or abuse us. We may feel chained to financial debt, emotional onslaughts, relationship oppressions or failures. But in faith, we can trust in God our Deliverer. He will never fail to deliver!

Lord, I trust You for my deliverance, for nothing can hem You in.

WEEK 19, DAY 3

The LORD Is My Shield

"I love You, O LORD, my strength." The LORD is my rock and my fortress and my deliverer, My God, my rock, in whom I take refuge; My shield and the horn of my salvation, my stronghold. (Psalm 18:1–2)

At the peak of Solomon's reign as Israel's most illustrious king, 22.17 tons of gold flowed into his coffers as gifts of other nations, not including the proceeds from lucrative international trade deals. There was more gold than he knew what to do with (and we are not even talking about silver, which he had in far more abundance). There was no limit to the lavishness: among other things, there were utensils and goblets made of gold and temple furnishings overlaid with gold. He made 200 shields using 15 pounds of hammered gold for each and another 300 shields with up to half that amount of gold each (2 Chron 9:15). Though the exact weights are debated by scholars, the amount of gold used for these shields was nonetheless considerable.

Gold is not known for its hardness, so the shields were most likely ornamental. Solomon of all people knew that shields, gold or otherwise, were not enough to protect him and Israel from defeat and destruction. Just as he understood the "house" he had built for God could not contain the infinite God of the universe, neither could a shield protect Israel from any enemy should God cause defeat.

"Now the LORD has fulfilled His word which He spoke; for I have risen in the place of my father David and sit on the throne of Israel, as the LORD promised, and have built the house for the name of the LORD, the God of Israel. (2 Chron 6:10).

Solomon's reign was characterized as being one of peace—thus he did not actually need battle-ready shields for his army. They were more symbolic, for indeed he knew that God, and God alone, would be their shield.

Solomon learned well the example of David, for in battle the war-hardened veteran had learned that though "He trains my hands for battle" (Ps 18:34), it was the Lord who is "My shield." How often do we find ourselves in the onslaught of the world's attacks against us, or Satan's prowling around ready to pounce on us with temptations of every kind? Like David, we have a shield, and that is the Lord. We can trust in the shield of faith (Eph 6:16) that He will defend us, for He is our advocate on high (Job 16:19). No other defense or shield can do what He can do for us.

Lord, only You know of the many times You have shielded me against dangers of which I am unaware. Thanks that You see everything and defend me.

WEEK 19, DAY 4

The LORD Is the Horn of My Salvation

"I love You, O LORD, my strength." The LORD is my rock and my fortress and my deliverer, My God, my rock, in whom I take refuge; My shield and the horn of my salvation, my stronghold. (Psalm 18:1–2)

God is sufficient in every circumstance. David learned this through many trials and struggles—this is part of his legacy left for the dynasty that began with him. His grandson's great-grandson (i.e. fifth-generation king of Judah), Jehoshaphat, was reminded of this truth about God when faced with overwhelming invaders. The prophet Jahaziel told him, "You need not fight in this battle; station yourselves, stand and see the salvation of the LORD on your behalf ... Do not fear or be dismayed; tomorrow go out to face them, for the LORD is with you" (2 Chron 20:17). Indeed, Jehoshaphat would have had access to David's psalms—for example, "Salvation belongs to the LORD" (Ps 3:8)—and to Solomon's wisdom: "The horse is prepared for the day of battle, but victory belongs to the LORD" (Pr 21:31).

Psalm 18, the litany of epithets with which David describes the Lord, rehearses all he has learned through life experiences, and brings him to praise and worship. In particular, he calls on the Lord who is the "horn of my salvation." Scholars debate the meaning of this, with three possible interpretations. Possibly David sees God protecting him like a bull with horns or equipping David with the weaponry that will be likened to the effectiveness of a bull's horns in a physical battle. Or, he could be referring to the horns of the altar that provide asylum in times of extreme danger (see 1 Kings 1:50, 2:28). Finally, some think this refers to a hill shaped like a horn, being the high ground from which an army makes its stand and can bring about its salvation from enemy oppressors (see Expositor's Bible Commentary). In effect, the natural understanding of this metaphor seems simply to refer to God's incisive and powerful involvement in procuring the salvation of Israel in battle.

We are instructed regarding OT stories, "These things happened to them as an example, and they were written for our instruction, upon whom the ends of the ages have come" (1 Cor 10:11). We learn from David's experience that God can be our horn as well. The horn of our salvation penetrated the gates of hell (Matt 16:18), marched into enemy territory (the world) and saved you and me. Like a bull destroying a roaring lion (1 Pet 5:8), He destroys the work of Satan in our lives. We can run to Him, pleading the blood of Christ, as it were, on the horns of the altar. Yes, He is the "horn of my salvation."

Lord, You are the Horn of my salvation. Thank You for saving and keeping me.

WEEK 19, DAY 5

The LORD Is My Stronghold

"I love You, O LORD, my strength." The LORD is my rock and my fortress and my deliverer, My God, my rock, in whom I take refuge; My shield and the horn of my salvation, my stronghold. (Psalm 18:1–2)

Similar to a fortress, David reflects on God being his "stronghold." A stronghold was a place built up to provide a strong defense and a launching or staging area for military raids. While a fortress offers complete protection, a stronghold is a place of strength. One thinks of the Wild West, when outlaw gangs would set up their strongholds in mountainous regions, high places overlooking canyons and passes, with gunmen at strategic vantage points. The only access was through unprotected, exposed areas, where invaders could be easily picked off.

In the first century, the Jews built just a stronghold on Masada, a large mountaintop plateau southeast of Jerusalem. When the Romans conquered Jerusalem in 70 A.D. it took three years to breach Masada in order to subdue the remaining Jews who had escaped there. The only access to the top was over narrow, openly exposed trails up the steep slopes. Roman attempts to scale the mountain were met with a hail of rocks thrown down from above. Eventually the Romans had Jewish slaves, previously captured in their conquest of Israel, build an enormous ramp to the top. They succeeded because the Jews at the top would not throw down rocks and kill their own. Behind a large battering ram hoisted up the ramp, the Romans were able to break through. That was a stronghold, to withstand the unrelenting, overpowering Roman army for so long.

David's strongholds were not as large or fortified as Masada, but he knew how to make his camps secure. In the same way, he knew how to overcome the strongholds of others. At the beginning of his reign as king over the united tribes of Israel, he captured the Jebusite stronghold of Zion, which became Jerusalem, the central city of Israel (2 Sam 5:6-7). One only needs to see the city today to see how its situation on the highest hill in the area would make for a good stronghold. David (and King Solomon) fortified the city with walls that made it extremely difficult to breach, and the city stood for hundreds of years.

David knew strongholds. So when he says, "The LORD is my stronghold," he knows whereof he speaks. God, Yahweh, is the place where he found protection and from where he could go forth in strength. From there he was able to subdue all the enemies of Israel.

Lord, You are my stronghold. Just like David, I can go forth from Your presence in Your strength to face my life situations.

WEEKEND 19 READING
Amos 8

PERSONAL REFLECTIONS

WEEK 20, DAY 1

Jealous God

"You shall not make for yourself an idol, or any likeness of what is in heaven above or on the earth beneath or in the water under the earth. You shall not worship them or serve them; for I, the LORD your God, am a jealous God, visiting the iniquity of the fathers on the children, on the third and the fourth generations of those who hate Me, but showing lovingkindness to thousands, to those who love Me and keep My commandments." (Exodus 20:4–6)

Uncomfortable as it seems, God's description of Himself as jealous is very clear and unambiguous in the Bible. He so designates Himself at the very beginning of His revelation to Israel, in the giving of the Law. This is not just an incidental thing, a sort of accommodation to ancient sub-Christian thought patterns that can be explained away through clever theological manipulation. This description is repeated at various junctures in the span of OT history (see Ex 34:14, Deut 4:24, Josh 24:19-20, Nah 1:2, Ps 94:1).

What makes this difficult for us today is the association we draw between jealousy and sinful attitudes. We see the problem of jealousy within Jacob's family, first between his wives and then between his sons. The apostle of grace wrote, "Love is ... not jealous" (1 Cor 13:4). So how do we reconcile the truth that "God is love" (1 John 4:8) with God being jealous? It helps to know that Paul used the word jealous (Greek: "zelos") to express an extreme desire. For example, he tells Christians to "desire earnestly" spiritual gifts (1 Cor 12:31, 14:39). Even Paul says, "I am jealous for you with a godly jealousy" (2 Cor 11:2). So we see jealousy is a morally neutral term. The question is what is the jealousy for?

God made it clear that He was jealous for His people. The Theological Wordbook of the OT (TWOT) tells us the Hebrew word "expresses a very strong emotion whereby some quality or passion of the object is desired by the subject." God greatly desires a relationship with His people, Israel. This is not a casual "feeling" but an intense desire. He made humans in His image and chose Abraham and his descendants from among fallen humanity to show to the world what a relationship with the Creator should be like. In the Law, He spells it out. He is jealous for His people and will not share them with other so-called gods that would steal their reciprocal affections away from God. He desires us, our friendship, our worship, our obedience.

Is this not why God sent His Son into this fallen world, because He is jealous to win us over (John 3:16)? He demonstrated His strong desire for us while we were still sinners (Rom 5:8). Praise to Yahweh that He is a jealous God.

Lord, I praise You for being jealous for me. And You continue to be jealous that I would not worship the false gods of today, but You only.

WEEK 20, DAY 2

Judge

But God is the Judge; He puts down one and exalts another. For a cup is in the hand of the LORD, and the wine foams; it is well mixed, and He pours out of this; surely all the wicked of the earth must drain and drink down its dregs. (Psalm 75:7–8)

Most would acknowledge this characteristic of God as Judge. We have an innate sense of justice, that in the end God will impartially and fairly evaluate all that happens on earth. We yearn for the day when abuse, evil and wickedness of every kind will be dealt with finally and completely, especially those violations against us. We are not wanting this so much for our own transgressions; we hope the Lord will concur with our own biased self-justification. But for God to truly be Judge He must be Judge of all—and that is what we fear, or at least, what we should fear. He is not to be trifled with and cannot be fooled. He will not be fooled! "Do not be deceived, God is not mocked; for whatever a man sows, this he will also reap" (Gal 6:7).

While the Old Testament does not give the clarity of imagery of the Great White Throne of God concerning the final judgment over all (Rev 20:11), we do see throne room imagery in the Old Testament where God's judgment is evident (see for example, Is 6:1-7). Certainly, the view of God as Judge is clear in our passage today. He "puts down one and exalts another."

The next metaphor fascinates the student of God's Word. God's judgmental anger is pictured as a cup of wine, foaming and poured out, complete with the "dregs" or settlement of leftover solids from the grapes. Job speaks of the man who sins against God, "Let God repay him so that he may know it. Let his own eyes see his decay, and let him drink of the wrath of the Almighty" (Job 21:19-20). David writes, "Upon the wicked He will rain snares; fire and brimstone and burning wind will be the portion of their cup" (Ps 11:6). Jeremiah is most pointed:

> *For thus the LORD ... says to me, "Take this cup of the wine of wrath from My hand and cause all the nations to whom I send you to drink it. They will drink and stagger and go mad because of the sword that I will send among them." Then I took the cup from the LORD'S hand and made all the nations to whom the LORD sent me drink it ... (Jer 25:15–17).*

Could this be what Jesus had in mind when He prayed three times, "My Father, if it is possible, let this cup pass from Me ..." (Matt 26:39)? On the cross He was about to take on God's wrath because of our sin.

> *Lord, I humbly bow in awe before You for taking on the judgment and wrath of God that was due me.*

WEEK 20, DAY 3

Righteous Mighty One

"But if you have understanding, hear this; listen to the sound of my words. Shall one who hates justice rule? And will you condemn the righteous mighty One…?" (Job 34:16–17)

True words to be sure, but the context reveals their import. The charge is fired against Job's three friends who fancied themselves his counselors. Yet who is talking? The enigmatic Elihu, a young man (see Job 32:1-6) whose anger welled up as he listened to the rhetoric of Job and his three friends, Zophar, Bildad and Eliphaz. Some have suggested Elihu's comments reflect the wisdom of God (the name Elihu means "He is God," and Job makes no retort against him as he did with the three friends). It is possible that the writer of the book represents Elihu's comments as the summation of righteous human reasoning (which in fact, may be right on target), but reserves for God Himself no need of logical defense. When God does speak, He is unambiguous in addressing the insolence of Job. But God does not reduce Himself to a simple defendant in a court case. Instead, He simply pulls back the curtains of the cosmos for a moment to reveal Himself and the huge gulf between Himself and Job.

No theologizing or logical argumentation can adequately address the issues Job raises in his struggle with suffering. The answer God gives is simply Himself in all His righteous, powerful sovereignty. His ways are above our ways, and His thoughts above our thoughts (Is 55:9). That is essentially God's response to Job in Job 38-42: "Who are you, Job, to question Me?"

So Elihu raises the question, which is really a criticism of Job's friends. While Job vigorously questions God's actions in his life, his friends impugn God's character. God later says to Eliphaz, "My wrath is kindled against you and against your two friends, because you have not spoken of Me what is right as My servant Job has" (Job 42:7). In the words of Elihu we see what is wrong with what they had said. Their counsel is an affront to God's righteousness.

Job's counselors criticize him, saying his sufferings are a direct result of God's righteous judgment against Job's secret sins—a logical defense of God's righteousness applied to an unrighteous life. But their conclusion is not just false; it is a condemnation of the true nature of God's righteousness. May we never entertain a hint of reasoning that would attribute another's suffering or misfortune to God's justice against the sufferer. Such is not a defense of God's righteousness, but a condemnation of it.

Lord, I confess to giving in to false reasoning about suffering and Your judgment. Help me be gracious to those who are in the midst of that struggle.

WEEK 20, DAY 4

King

Rejoice greatly, O daughter of Zion! Shout in triumph, O daughter of Jerusalem! Behold, your king is coming to you; He is just and endowed with salvation, humble, and mounted on a donkey, even on a colt, the foal of a donkey. (Zechariah 9:9)

Familiar is this verse from its proclamation at the triumphal entry of Jesus into Jerusalem the week before He was crucified (see Matt 21:5 and John 12:15). It was given at a difficult time in the life of Israel, as was often the case when God sent Messianic messages of hope.

The people of God had just returned to the land after 70 some years of Babylonian captivity. Thoroughly chastised, they had set about readjusting to life back in the Promised Land, but their experience was far from what God had promised Abraham: a blessed life that would in turn be a blessing to the nations. Work on rebuilding the temple lagged, and God needed prophets like Zechariah and Haggai to urge His people on. Zechariah, in particular, had eight visions for the future, one of which is our passage for today, the most notable of all. The Davidic dynasty was in shambles, the glory years of Solomon a faint memory preserved in the ruins of the city. What was to become of the Jews now, still under domination of foreign rulers?

The thread of hope, the ray of God's light, continually shined through by the ministry of the prophets. God's message remained: there is a future for Israel, and there will be a king.

Notice the details of the prophecy. Zechariah speaks poetically of Israel as "O daughter of Zion ... daughter of Jerusalem," conveying an intimacy of familial connection. Second, this prophecy anticipates a time of rejoicing in the dreary, depressing world of post-captivity. A prisoner set free has lost years as well as possessions, 70 years being sufficient to destroy what was left. Jubilation would seem completely misplaced, yet here was the promise that it would come. Third, this prospect is tied in with the promise of a coming King, "your" king. This will not be the king of a nation conquering Israel, but their King, one continuing in the line of David.

Notice the character of the promised, coming King. He will be just and clothed, as it were, with salvation. His victory garb has to do with rescuing His people from all that will keep them from being the blessing to the world as God promised Abraham and his descendants. Finally, notice how the King would arrive: humbly and lowly. Not on a thoroughbred steed, but on a young donkey, indicating victory and peace.

Lord, I need You as King of my life, to rule over my thoughts, fears and doubts.

WEEK 20, DAY 5

Lawgiver

For the LORD is our judge, the LORD is our lawgiver, the LORD is our king; He will save us ... (Isaiah 33:22)

Combining epithets we have written about elsewhere, we focus on the Lord as "our lawgiver." The people of Israel found great delight in the Law of God. They saw Yahweh (to distinguish Him from all false notions of God in currency at the time) as the originator of order in the universe. To be sure, He is the Creator who made everything that exists, and without His involvement nothing has come into existence or continually exists (see Gen 1, John 1:1-3). He has ordered what scientists call the laws of nature. This is simply their way of referring to those fixed operating principles that can be observed in the natural world. These laws include such recognizable forces or principles as gravity, the speed of light, thermodynamics, magnetism, and so on. Try as we might to overcome these things, they are fixed and form the foundation for scientific inquiry and invention. In other words, we can count on them being true, and we build our physical world around their reality. These are God's physical laws of nature.

The Lord also has moral laws of the universe, expected standards of behavior. That He would require these should be no surprise, when we understand that God has made us all in His image (Gen 1:26). Being the Lawgiver simply means He expects His image bearers (that's you and me) to be like Him, to live out the reality of who we are. When Jesus held the Roman coin in His hand and asked whose likeness was on it, the answer was given, "Caesar's." He went on to say, give Caesar that which has his image on it—but also give to God that which has God's image on it. We, being created in God's image, owe our life and behavior to Him. The Law outlines how we are to do that.

For the Jews, the primary audience of Isaiah's writing, that meant the Mosaic Law with all its ritual and behavioral requirements. David saw the Law as his delight and wanted to learn more about it and about God, the Lawgiver:

Your word I have treasured in my heart, that I may not sin against You. ... Open my eyes, that I may behold wonderful things from Your law. (Ps 119:11-18).

Make me understand the way of Your precepts, so I will meditate on Your wonders. (Ps 119:27).

Though the Law cannot save us, it reflects God's wonderful moral order, inner unity and consistency of character. That is what He wants for us.

Lord, help me understand, like David, how wonderful You are as my Lawgiver.

WEEKEND 20 READING
Amos 9

PERSONAL REFLECTIONS

WEEK 21, DAY 1

Leader and Commander

"Incline your ear and come to Me. Listen, that you may live; and I will make an everlasting covenant with you, according to the faithful mercies shown to David. Behold, I have made him a witness to the peoples, a leader and commander for the peoples." (Isaiah 55:3–4)

Messianic overtones drench the context of this passage. The reader will recall chapter 53, where the "tender shoot" who "has no stately form or majesty that we should look upon Him, nor appearance that we should be attracted to Him," portrays in advance the suffering Messiah (Is 53:2, see also Is 11:1-2). This is the One to whom God's people should listen.

To put this passage in its historical context, God gave the people of Israel warning, but also hope. Israel, situated between two "super-powers" (Assyria to the north and Egypt to the south), at times was like a small bit player in worldly affairs. Its armies were overmatched in size, wealth and weaponry. The glory days of King David's military prowess were long past.

In the midst of their spiritual dryness, God, through Isaiah, invites the people back to drink at the eternal cistern of God, so to speak. The chapter begins like this: "Ho! Every one who thirsts, come to the waters; and you who have no money come, buy and eat. Come, buy wine and milk without money and without cost" (Is 55:1). Some commentators hear in this invitation an echo of a water vendor's cry, which was a common part of the ancient world economy. But the promise rings through to us today. God still provides for us a source of "living water." Remember when Jesus spoke to the Samaritan woman, "Everyone who drinks of this water will thirst again; but whoever drinks of the water that I will give him shall never thirst; but the water that I will give him will become in him a well of water springing up to eternal life" (John 4:13–14, see also John 6:35).

According to our passage in Isaiah, God makes "an everlasting covenant" with those who respond to this invitation. One who is associated with David—the Messiah, a descendant in the Davidic dynasty—will be "a leader and commander." What good is it to have water to stave off a drought yet live in a defeated and suppressed nation? The Messiah will not only satisfy His people personally, He will give them victory over all others, including the super-powers of Assyria and Egypt—all the nations of the earth. We are reminded of what the apostle John taught Christians, "Greater is He that is in you, than he that is in the world" (1 John 4:4). He is our Leader and Commander. It is in His army we serve.

My Leader and Commander, I am awaiting Your orders, Sir!

WEEK 21, DAY 2

The Lifter of My Head

Many are saying of my soul, "There is no deliverance for him in God." Selah. But You, O LORD, are a shield about me, my glory, and the One who lifts my head. I was crying to the LORD with my voice, and He answered me from His holy mountain. Selah. (Psalm 3:2–4)

While we see the Lord as a shield in Psalm 18:2 and 2 Sam 22:3, here we see Him as "the One who lifts up my head" or "the Lifter of my head" (ESV, KJV). The background to this psalm gives texture to this cry of the writer's heart. The prescript indicates the writer was David, reflecting his time fleeing from his usurping son, Absolom. If you remember, one of David's sons, Amnon, had raped his half-sister Tamar. When David did nothing about this, Tamar's brother Absalom killed Amnon in revenge. David subsequently banished Absalom for a period of exile. He eventually relented in bringing Absalom back but would have nothing to do with him thereafter. The charismatic Absolom, in bitterness and spite, began to win over the people of Israel, and in time pulled off an insurrection against his father, David (2 Sam 13-14). Such was the dysfunction of David's family, resulting from his earlier sin with Bathsheba. The repercussions of sin propagate through a family.

Rather than fight against his son (2 Sam 15:13-17), David fled Jerusalem and wept bitterly on the Mount of Olives as he went (2 Sam 15:29). This is the time reflected in Psalm 3. Who knows exactly what went through his mind at that time, but in this psalm we can see at least part of his thinking. The word on the street was that David was done for; even God wouldn't be helping him now. Is it not easy to see the sin in others and conclude God is finished with them? Or else when it is us in that position, we believe others are thinking that about us.

David had learned not to put stock in what others thought of him, for even though his family dysfunction was due to his own sin and neglect, he still continued to look to the Lord. This gives us hope today when we feel our sin has marginalized us from usefulness or from God's blessing. No matter where we are or the circumstances in which we find ourselves, God can still be a "shield about me" and "the one who lifts my head." In David's case, that would mean protection from being killed and a restoration to his former position as king. For us today, the protection of God is there for us, if we trust in Him. While He may not restore to us past ministry positions or opportunities, He will take us from where we are to where He wants us to be. He is the "Lifter of my head."

Lord, any of my many sins would disqualify me from service for You. Thank You for continually lifting up my head, giving me a place in Your workforce.

WEEK 21, DAY 3

The Living God

As the deer pants for the water brooks, so my soul pants for You, O God. My soul thirsts for God, for the living God; when shall I come and appear before God? (Psalm 42:1–2)

So begins a heart-wrenching song to the Lord, the expression of a deep desire to quench a spiritually incapacitating drought of the soul. Easily we might assume this was written by David, that sensitive soul who deeply loved the Lord and was devoted wholeheartedly to Him. However, the prescript tells us it was associated with the "sons of Korah." Probably this was part of a collection (note Psalm 42 through 49 are attributed in some way to the "sons of Korah"). If this was the same infamous Korah of Numbers 16, who led an insurrection against Moses and Aaron and was subsequently swallowed up in an ancient form of a sinkhole from God, then it would speak of God's grace that his descendants would have a role in the composition of Scripture. As for who specifically wrote this psalm, we don't know.

Our song today has to do with inner disquiet, what some call spiritual depression. Notice the self-talk in verse 5, "Why are you in despair, O my soul?" (see also vss. 11 and Ps 43:5). We could wish that more would acknowledge parchment of the spirit and long for the "living God." By this description, the psalmist is looking for God's presence in a real way—not just a philosophical tenet of faith, not just a head knowledge. Indeed, all the theological musings in the world will not give one the sense of God's presence. If anything, what marks out the God of Israel is that He is Yahweh, the one who is actively involved in a phenomenal way in their lives. While the name "Yahweh" is not used in this psalm, that is what the writer desires—a real presence of God.

The lack of that real presence of the "living God" precipitates the barrenness of the soul. This is not a unique experience for those of faith in God, for we are called upon to believe in Him whom we cannot see or audibly hear. Some seek after signs and wonders to give that sense of His presence, while others look for a still small voice, a sensation or something. Yet Hebrews 11:1 calls us to a faith that is an "assurance of things hoped for, the conviction of things not seen." Faith itself is the answer to our spiritual thirst. Somehow, in believing in Him, trusting as we would a chair to hold us up, we trust God is present in our lives. We rest on Him. Yes, it is a struggle when God seems to be silent. That makes it all the more important for us to seek Him and believe that He is the living God, who is active in our lives even when we don't sense Him.

Lord, I do believe You are here right now, unseen, but active in ways I will not know until I am with You in glory.

WEEK 21, DAY 4

Living God, the LORD of Hosts

"For you will no longer remember the oracle of the LORD, because every man's own word will become the oracle, and you have perverted the words of the living God, the LORD of hosts, our God." (Jeremiah 23:36)

Weeping prophet, as he was known, Jeremiah was given the unenviable task of being God's mouthpiece against the false prophets of Israel. Many had arisen arrogantly presuming to speak the words of God on His behalf. Hear what God has to say about them:

> *"Behold, I am against the prophets," declares the LORD, "who use their tongues and declare, 'The Lord declares.'" "Behold, I am against those who have prophesied false dreams," declares the LORD, "and related them and led My people astray by their falsehoods and reckless boasting; yet I did not send them or command them, nor do they furnish this people the slightest benefit," declares the LORD. (Jer 23:31–32)*

They use the phrase "the Lord declares" as though saying those words invokes the authority of God. It makes me think of how often Christians so easily say, "The Lord spoke to me" or "The Lord told me to do such and such," when in reality such words are a thin veneer of spirituality to justify one's selfish decisions or human reasoning. We need to be careful about falling into this idle talk, this Christianese use of pseudo-spiritual lingo.

In the midst of the crowded field of "prophecy" Jeremiah's voice rang out clearly with authority when he said "the Lord declares" that those false prophets are leading God's people astray by their falsehoods. What made Jeremiah's declarations more potent than that of the false prophets? Very simply, he truly spoke on God's behalf. He understood that you don't take God lightly, for He is "the living God, the LORD of Hosts, our God." He is alive, not just a concept or a set of phrases and terminology that can be used to manipulate people. He is the commander of hosts, probably a reference to the unseen angelic armies of God. He is Yahweh (LORD); this is the one who makes declaration through Jeremiah. The false prophets make their declarations, but in the original Hebrew, it is clear those declarations are devoid of the command of Yahweh.

So what does this mean for us today? We need to be careful about idly presuming to speak on God's behalf or using spiritual language to give vacuous authority to our assertions. We need to speak the Word of God rightly and know His truth correctly. For He is the living God, the LORD of hosts, our God.

Lord, my living God, I re-commit myself to Your Word, to know it and share it.

WEEK 21, DAY 5

LORD of Hosts, My King and My God

How lovely are Your dwelling places, O LORD of hosts! My soul longed and even yearned for the courts of the LORD; my heart and my flesh sing for joy to the living God. The bird also has found a house, and the swallow a nest for herself, where she may lay her young, even Your altars, O LORD of hosts, My King and my God. How blessed are those who dwell in Your house! They are ever praising You. Selah. (Psalm 84:1–4)

What a contrast with our previous meditation from Jeremiah 23:36, the rebuke to those who speak falsely the words of the Living God (vs. 2), the LORD of Hosts. Here we see a picture of worship as we dwell in His presence. The imagery of birds flying through the temple and making nests in the building is beautiful.

When I walk into our local building supply store, it doesn't take long to notice the chirping birds as they flitter about. Up in the steelwork of the ceiling, evidence of birds' nests abound. If management has made any effort to shoo them out, the feathered creatures of our God are not deterred. Imagine OT Israel in the tabernacle (during King David's time) or in Solomon's temple, the birds flying about, coming and going. I can't imagine Jesus, when walking through the temple during His day, trying to shoo them out. Indeed, He drove out the money changers and their animals, those who were using the temple for their merchandizing, but not the birds freely flying about.

What is interesting about birds like this is that they build their nests as if they own the place. What a comfortable, suitable place for them to make their home and raise their young ones from eggs to hatchlings. How blessed is the believer who can walk, as it were, into the house of the great God of the universe, the LORD of Hosts, and live there in absolute comfort and suitability, feeling right at home there. This is more fantastic than walking into the White House (in the US) or the prime minister's home of Canada or England and making oneself at home.

The LORD of Hosts, King and God, may strike a terrifying note to false prophets and those who presume to speak His word erroneously and arrogantly. But to those who yearn simply to be in His courts, who desire to sing for joy to the living God (vs. 2), dwelling in His presence is sweet. Jesus said, "I am the door; if anyone enters through Me, he will be saved, and will go in and out and find pasture" (John 10:9). Like a child who can freely come and go into his parents' home, so we, being part of the family of God, can enjoy dwelling with the LORD of Hosts, King and God, because He is also our Father.

Lord God, Father, I do long to be home with You forever in Your presence.

WEEKEND 21 READING
Obadiah 1

PERSONAL REFLECTIONS

WEEK 22, DAY 1

LORD of Hosts, God of Israel

"Let Your name be established and magnified forever, saying, 'The LORD of hosts is the God of Israel, even a God to Israel; and the house of David Your servant is established before You.'" (1 Chronicles 17:24)

David has it in his heart to build a house for the Lord to dwell in the midst of Israel. But God turns down his plan and instead promises instead to build a house for David (1 Chron 17:10). David's son Solomon was to be the one who would build the house of God, the temple. Why was this such a significant thing, the building of a house for God?

David had led Israel in recovering from the spiritually impoverished reign of King Saul, the king whom the people wanted so they could be like the other nations. His (Saul's) duplicity was evident and showed in disobeying God at a number of junctures. But, God desired a godly leader who would lead the nation into holiness, that is, to be separated from the practices of the surrounding nations and their false gods. While worship of deity is nearly universal in the world, there are innumerable perspectives of just what that deity or deities are like. They share many similar characteristics, which that makes sense since they are constructs of the imagination of human beings. But, after Saul's weak leadership, David needed to shore up the worship of the true Deity, and it was important to establish beyond all doubt that the true Deity was the God of Israel.

The Deity whom David worshipped was unique. First and foremost, his Deity is the "LORD of Hosts," namely Yahweh Sabbaoth. He is the God of Moses, who was also the God of Abraham, Isaac and Jacob. He is "the God of Israel" and the "God to Israel." Let there be no doubt. This was Israel's God. This might sound repetitive, but the descendants of Abraham, especially from the time of Joshua, struggled for a consistent faith, lapsing frequently into idolatry during the time of the judges. Saul was not much help in refining their understanding of the true God. With David, there would be no ambiguity.

Under David's leadership and influence, Israel attained its highest level of holiness or separateness from the surrounding nations. Indeed, the kings who followed David (in the dynasty of David that continued on down to King Jesus Christ) were often compared to David and his faithfulness to God (see for example 1 Chron 11:33, 38, 1 Kings 15:3-4). Even the Lord Jesus was identified with and compared to David when He was called "the Son of David."

We join with David in exalting and praising the Lord, lifting up our voices to the one and only true God, the God of Israel, Yahweh of Hosts, saying …

"Let Your name be established and magnified forever!"

WEEK 22, DAY 2

LORD My God

"Behold, I am about to build a house for the name of the LORD my God, dedicating it to Him, to burn fragrant incense before Him and to set out the showbread continually, and to offer burnt offerings morning and evening, on sabbaths and on new moons and on the appointed feasts of the LORD our God, this being required forever in Israel." (2 Chronicles 2:4)

Solomon sent word to Hiram, king of Tyre, to contract for cedar lumber for building the temple, the house of the Lord. He carries on in the belief of Yahweh (LORD). But we observe an emphasis on "my." Solomon had embraced faith in Yahweh for himself. Every combination of God's name or epithet we might examine brings out a new or different aspect of God's infinite nature or character.

We could focus on Solomon's journey of faith, where he quickly came to personal belief in God, or how this faith eroded over his lifetime to the point where his many wives turned his heart away from God. In fact, so much of our study of God often falls to the pragmatic, or human focus. Our testimonies too often become more about us than about God. Our study of Scripture becomes more about how we should live than about discovering God, His character and what He is doing in the world. Our worship, therefore, becomes human-centered on our feelings rather than God-centered on His worth.

So in our passage we see God recording this little word "my" in Solomon's declaration as significant in understanding God on a more personal level. The human author, according to Jewish tradition, was Ezra, and the human perspective might see the inclusion of this small word as being somewhat incidental to Ezra's narrative on the life of Solomon. But every word is inspired by God (2 Tim 3:16), so the word may carry more significance in terms of God's character. It is not an unreasonable stretch to say we can see in this word God's desire to be known personally.

God delights in telling us about Solomon, who, like David (see Ps 13:3), worshipped the "LORD my God." Yahweh is the God of the legendary Moses. He is the same God who personally revealed Himself to the great patriarchs Abraham, Isaac and Jacob, giving them the hereditary promise of blessings that would extend to the entire human race. He is the God who created billions of image bearers, beginning with Adam and Eve, to populate this small planet in a universe filled with billions of stars. This omnipresent, omnipotent, omniscient God, without whom nothing would exist, Solomon says is "my God." God desires that each of His image bearers also would know Him as "my God."

Lord, my God – I worship You not because others before have done so, but because You are my God.

WEEK 22, DAY 3

LORD of Kings

The king answered Daniel and said, "Surely your God is a God of gods and a Lord of kings and a revealer of mysteries, since you have been able to reveal this mystery." (Daniel 2:47)

Nebuchadnezzar, king of Babylon, was a man who had an up and down relationship with God, until he was finally humbled. The last words we hear from him are the following:

"Now I, Nebuchadnezzar, praise, exalt and honor the King of heaven, for all His works are true and His ways just, and He is able to humble those who walk in pride." (Dan 4:37)

But he was a deeply flawed man, for his absolute power on the human level kept giving rise to the pride imbedded in the human heart and the attendant arrogance that so easily grips us all. The only difference between us and Nebuchadnezzar is that (on the human level) he had limitless opportunity to live out his self-centeredness. Who of us wouldn't, in all honesty, like to imagine ourselves depicted in a 90-foot-high statue made of gold, for all to see and admire (in fact, to worship), as Nebuchadnezzar had made for himself (Dan 3:1)? While we will probably never have that opportunity, we certainly want to be noticed for our gifts and talents, sometimes blazoning our benevolence for others to see.

Yet even this pagan king, when faced with the real faith of Daniel, admitted that though he himself might be the greatest king on earth at the time, Yahweh, the God of Israel, is the "Lord of kings," as our passage today indicates. The word "Lord" used here is an Aramaic word (used in Daniel 2:4 through 7:28) that carries the normal meaning of our English word "Lord," meaning one having authority to rule over another. We must grant Nebuchadnezzar the honesty to recognize that there was a greater power he could not escape. While many kings through history have chosen to reject completely the notion of anything being greater than themselves, Nebuchadnezzar at least at times humbled himself before this power whom he acknowledged to be the God of Daniel, the God of the Jews.

If, in the words of this king, God is the "Lord of kings," then He is also Lord of all lesser human beings. Whether we are popular, influential, wealthy, politically powerful, highly educated or blessed with good looks, He is Lord over all of us.

Lord, the One who rules over kings, presidents, prime ministers and dictators, I humbly bow to Your lordship over my life.

WEEK 22, DAY 4

LORD of Lords

17 "For the LORD your God is the God of gods and the Lord of lords, the great, the mighty, and the awesome God who does not show partiality nor take a bribe. 18 He executes justice for the orphan and the widow, and shows His love for the alien by giving him food and clothing." (Deuteronomy 10:17–18)

Midst a string of epithets for God, we find the well-known phrase "Lord of lords." Handel's Messiah comes to mind, the great climax reiterating as the Hallelujah chorus crescendos, "King of kings and Lord of lords. And He shall reign forever and ever." It was nothing short of inspired. That chorus is deeply rooted in Scripture as applied to the Lord Jesus:

"These will wage war against the Lamb, and the Lamb will overcome them, because He is Lord of lords and King of kings, and those who are with Him are the called and chosen and faithful." (Rev 17:14)

And on His robe and on His thigh He has a name written, "KING OF KINGS, AND LORD OF LORDS." (Rev 19:16)

Paul writes of Jesus, "…who is the blessed and only Sovereign, the King of kings and Lord of lords" (1 Tim 6:15). The psalmist proclaims, "Give thanks to the Lord of lords, for His lovingkindness is everlasting" (Ps 136:3).

In the second reading of the Law, namely the book of Deuteronomy (the term "deuteronomy" means "second-law"), we see this epithet in connection with God's impartial authority in judgment. Because He is Lord (Heb: Adonai) of lords, He will judge human beings, in particular concerning how we treat the disadvantaged among us. The Lord of lords is concerned about "the orphan and the widow … the alien." In the ancient world, protection and physical security came from one's family relationship. This would leave orphans and widows (which were many because of the continual wars in the ancient world) defenseless and vulnerable to any strong man who came along. The law mandated that God's people take care of, provide for and protect those who were disadvantaged or defenseless.

Even in our world today, with many laws and governmental agencies, many women are abused, harassed, treated unfairly. Children suffer greatly at the hands of merciless, self-centered adults or even bullying by others. The Lord of lords is our judge. Did not even Jesus say that in the last judgment, the sheep would be separated from the goats based on how they treated "the least of these my brothers" (Matt 25:31-46)?

Lord of lords, I confess my neglect of some in my circle of contacts whom I have neglected, who need a defender and protector and a helper.

WEEK 22, DAY 5

LORD Our God

"Hear, O Israel! The LORD is our God, the LORD is one!" (Deuteronomy 6:4)

Called the "Shema," this is considered the central prayer in the Jewish faith. Actually, the Shema is the entire section of Deuteronomy 6:4-9. Embedded in the heart and mind of every Israelite was this statement of allegiance, unity, uniqueness and exclusivity. Here we find monotheism clearly stated: there is one and only one God, and He is Yahweh (LORD) of Israel.

Elsewhere we point out that God desires to be known as "my God" (see 2 Chronicles 2:4). He also wants to be known as "our God." What is the significance of that? While we are to know Him individually and personally, we are also to know Him in community with others who know Him individually and personally. The two are intricately related, like individual branches on a single tree. We are singularly part of a plurality making up a whole.

When God called Abraham, He promised to make a great nation of individual believers in Christ, who corporately would bring a blessing to the world (Gen 12:1-3). God's people are called a nation, a family, a body, and collectively as a wife and bride. In the NT, the people of God are called a church, a household, the body of Christ. We are saved individually, but we are not saved to be isolated. We are saved into the community of believers. God is both "my God" and "our God." Did Jesus not teach us to pray, "Our Father ..."?

The implications of this are huge. Many today claim to be Christians yet have little fellowship with others, remaining aloof or apart from others. They see Him as "my God" but not "our God." They do not see themselves as part of the community of God's people. This is a problem in the eyes of God, who wants to be "our God."

When we see God as "our God" we acknowledge the community focus of faith. This is not just incidental to our lives, along with other compartments into which we divide life. No. Thinking of "our God" leads to our identity not simply as individual believers, but as those who are part of the community of believers. In the NT, our God challenges us through the apostle Paul's writings:

Let us hold fast the confession of our hope without wavering, for He who promised is faithful; and let us consider how to stimulate one another to love and good deeds, not forsaking our own assembling together, as is the habit of some, but encouraging one another; and all the more as you see the day drawing near. (Heb 10:23–25)

"Our Father, who is in heaven ...," along with all other believers, I come to You in community and the humble submission of love for other believers.

WEEKEND 22 READING
Jonah 1-2

PERSONAL REFLECTIONS

WEEK 23, DAY 1

The LORD Our Maker

Come, let us worship and bow down, let us kneel before the LORD our Maker. For He is our God, and we are the people of His pasture and the sheep of His hand. (Psalm 95:6–7a)

Worship, when unhindered by the cares of this world, pours out from the soul that is aligned with God, as the yelps of one who has just discovered himself to be a multi-million-dollar lottery winner. Sure, at times, we discipline ourselves to worship, as we must tame the fleshly pull away from God that continually entices us with the false worship of created things. But the image of God impressed on us from the moment we entered into reality, leads us ultimately back to the One whose image we bear.

At the core, we worship God because He is our Maker, our Creator—we simply cannot escape the connection. We owe our very existence to Him, like a vase owes its existence to the potter, a painting to its artist. It is first and foremost a reality, not an obligation. We ought to worship Him because we were designed to worship Him. And we live and operate best in this world when we align with the purpose for which we were designed.

But what does it mean to worship God? Is this some activity for which we carve out time in our week, a time of giving homage to Him for an hour of worship on a Sunday morning? Some do, in fact, think of worship in that way, fulfilling their obligation by their church attendance. Today we use the term "worship" as synonymous with a certain style of musical expression to God. In fact, in at least one respected seminary, a full length course on worship focuses primarily on church music. To be sure, music can convey worship. And worship can be expressed in many different ways.

Even the architecture of a building in which worship takes place can enhance worship. But Jesus made it clear that worship cannot be restricted to a physical location, for it resides in the attitude of "spirit and truth" (John 4:24). The focus is not on the place, but on the Person. God is the centrality of our worship, we were not made in the image of a building, but in His image. He is our Maker and this cannot be restricted by convention, geography or architecture. Paul preached this clearly:

> *"The God who made the world and all things in it, since He is Lord of heaven and earth, does not dwell in temples made with hands; nor is He served by human hands, as though He needed anything, since He Himself gives to all people life and breath and all things…" (Acts 17:24–25).*

Lord, teach me to worship You rightly, in spirit and truth, because You are my Creator, and in You I live and move and exist.

WEEK 23, DAY 2

The LORD Your God

'The LORD your God who goes before you will Himself fight on your behalf, just as He did for you in Egypt before your eyes, and in the wilderness where you saw how the LORD your God carried you, just as a man carries his son, in all the way which you have walked until you came to this place.' (Deuteronomy 1:30–31)

"Your God" was certainly Moses' God, but he didn't use his words casually. He was preparing the wandering nation of Israel, whom he led out of Egyptian slavery and forged into a nation, having led them for 40 years in the wilderness. It was time they embraced God for themselves, because he was not going in with them.

After Moses died, the Lord spoke to Joshua, "Just as I have been with Moses, I will be with you; I will not fail you or forsake you" (Jos 1:5). God's presence with Moses would now become His presence with Joshua. Then, tellingly, God exhorts Joshua, "Be strong and courageous! Do not tremble or be dismayed, for the LORD your God is with you wherever you go" (Josh 1:9). God essentially was saying, "I am not just Moses' God, but I am now your God."

Now some might mock such fine distinctions as nitpicking, but an important point is to be made here. Everyone must embrace God for him or herself. Each of us needs to be able to say, "He is my God." This is the truth behind the common saying about having a personal relationship with God. We can say, "I know Him. He is not just the God of my church leaders who tell me about Him. He is not just the God of Abraham, Isaac and Jacob. He is my God."

When we don't grasp this, we become like Jacob when he deceived his father, Isaac, in order to steal the blessing that was rightly due his brother, Esau. When his father questioned how swiftly he had prepared the supposed wild game, Jacob revealed he had not yet come to his own relationship with God. He answered, "Because the LORD your God caused it to happen to me" (Gen 27:20).

There is a tremendous leadership lesson here. A Christian leader must never lead people to become dependent upon himself as a conduit to God. They must not rely on our faith. We must ever be training others to go to God for themselves. They must see their own relationship with the One who created them. Their strength and courage to face life's battles can never come from someone else's relationship to God, but through their own embrace of their Lord. Faith cannot be derived or mediated or represented. It must be original and primary with each person.

Lord, You are my God and I worship You; in You I find courage and strength.

WEEK 23, DAY 3

The Loving-Kind God

My God in His lovingkindness will meet me; God will let me look triumphantly upon my foes ... O my strength, I will sing praises to You; for God is my stronghold, the God who shows me lovingkindness. (Psalm 59:10, 17)

Love is from God, we are told in 1 John 4:7. While "agape" love in the NT conveys a self-sacrificing commitment, lovingkindness (Heb: "hesed") in the OT conveys a somewhat different connotation. Scholars used to think the word should be translated mercy, and is so translated in the LXX by the Greek word "eleos" for mercy. However, later studies showed that hesed refers to a loyalty to covenant obligations. So the debate is whether God's lovingkindness (hesed) comes from God's eternal nature and therefore extends to all people, or whether it relates only or primarily to Israel because of the covenant He made with them.

We see in Joshua 2:12 that Rahab's actions in supporting Israel's spies was described as hesed, lovingkindness, so the word itself is not isolated to covenantal use. God describes Himself as "showing lovingkindness to thousands" (Ex 20:6). That is the nature of who He is. Yet the OT clearly presents God's hesed in relationship to the people of the covenant, so we find it difficult to separate God's eternal character from His covenantal obligations.

In what sense is God under obligation? Does that not imply He is accountable to something outside of Himself? Not at all. The best way to look at this is that the covenants God made with Israel, whether we refer to the Abrahamic, Mosaic, Palestinian or Davidic covenants, flow from His eternal character of hesed. He willingly entered into these commitments to show favor to His people. Remember when God had Abraham divide up the animals in the typical form of an ancient covenant, where the two parties would walk through the midst of the cut pieces of the animals, signifying that their individual fates would be like that of those animals should they break covenant (Genesis 15)? In that instance, God put Abraham to sleep and then in the dream passed through the animal pieces by Himself, symbolized by a smoking torch. It was a unilateral agreement, God willingly holding Himself accountable for the promise of land to Abraham's descendants. God holds Himself accountable to Himself.

The Lord has now entered into a new covenant of blood with all who believe, through the perfect sacrifice of Jesus Christ. "As many as received Him, to them He gave the right to become children of God, even to those who believe in His name" (John 1:12). This stems from God's eternal character of loving-kindness. He is committed to loving us, now, as a father loves his children

Lord, unlike human love, You are committed to loving me. Thank You.

WEEK 23, DAY 4

The Merciful God

"For the LORD your God is a compassionate God; He will not fail you nor destroy you nor forget the covenant with your fathers which He swore to them." (Deuteronomy 4:31)

Virtually every other English translation (besides NASB) renders this, "For the Lord your God is a merciful God." The root meaning of the word has to do with a deep love, usually of a "superior" for an "inferior" and can be translated compassion, pity, mercy (Theological Wordbook of the OT). Isaiah 49:15 uses it (in slightly different form) for a mother's love, and Psalm 103:13 uses it for a father's love. Clearly, God looks at His people as a parent who feels for his or her children. Indeed, God extends His compassion (mercy) to whomever He chooses. God proclaimed to Moses, "I Myself will make all My goodness pass before you, and will proclaim the name of the LORD before you; and I will be gracious to whom I will be gracious, and will show compassion on whom I will show compassion." (Ex 33:19).

God's mercy, then, is remarkable—precisely because mercy is not something that can be deserved. This is popularly stated: grace is undeserved favor; mercy is withholding deserved judgment. Nothing we do can invoke any obligation on God's part to show mercy. We commonly use the saying, "throw oneself on the mercy of the court." To accept or appreciate mercy, one must accept one's own guiltiness. In Israel's case, this promise to show compassion follows God's prediction that they will abandon Him:

> *"I call heaven and earth to witness against you today, that you will surely perish quickly from the land where you are going over the Jordan to possess it. You shall not live long on it, but will be utterly destroyed. The LORD will scatter you among the peoples, and you will be left few in number among the nations where the LORD drives you. There you will serve gods, the work of man's hands, wood and stone, which neither see nor hear nor eat nor smell. But from there you will seek the LORD your God, and you will find Him if you search for Him with all your heart and all your soul." (Deut 4:26–29)*

To seek God, then, is to find mercy—and this despite our sin and deserved judgment by God. When a person wholeheartedly seeks God, then His judgment is replaced with mercy. For it is in His eternal character to be compassionate to all who seek Him.

> *Lord, this describes me. I was a sinner, but have sought and found You. Now I enjoy fully the mercy, so undeserved, but appreciated.*

WEEK 23, DAY 5

Messiah the Prince

"So you are to know and discern that from the issuing of a decree to restore and rebuild Jerusalem until Messiah the Prince there will be seven weeks and sixty-two weeks; it will be built again, with plaza and moat, even in times of distress. Then after the sixty-two weeks the Messiah will be cut off and have nothing, and the people of the prince who is to come will destroy the city and the sanctuary. And its end will come with a flood; even to the end there will be war; desolations are determined." (Daniel 9:25–26)

Who can hear the title Messiah without thinking of Handel's oratorio by that name? Covering the central outline of biblical history, Handel focused on the prophecies concerning the coming of God's solution to the sin problem, the unfolding of Christ's redemptive work, and the eschatological culmination of His return for judgment and final resurrection of all. This is the story of Messiah.

The underlying Hebrew word means "the anointed one." The term occurs in the Hebrew OT quite often, but is transliterated as "Messiah" only twice in most English translations. Most notably, though, it is applied to Jesus in the NT gospels. John's account shows the connection clearly, when he adds an editorial comment to Simon Peter's announcement to his brother Andrew, "We have found the Messiah' (which translated means Christ)" (John 1:41, see also John 4:25). The fact that John includes this clarification indicates his audience was probably not well versed in Jewish culture, or they would have known that Christ is the Greek translation of "anointed one" or "Messiah."

Daniel makes clear that the Messiah was the one who is to come, playing a prominent role in the end-time prophecies. The dispensational view interprets this passage as referring to the Messiah being executed at the end of 490 years (69 "weeks" of years), with an ensuing seven years of tribulation. With the rejection of Messiah, though, the prophetic time clock was put on hold until a future date. Dr. Harold Hoehner, in his definitive book "Herod Antipas," includes a timeline showing that the end of the 69 weeks calculates to the very date of the passion week of Christ (precise dating is subject to a margin of error because of difficulty in correlating the various ancient calendar systems.)

The promise of Messiah to the people of Israel was a promise of salvation, as the whole prophecy of Daniel unfolds. The future course of humanity hangs on humanity's treatment of this anointed One. Indeed, what a person does about the life and death of Jesus Christ will determine that person's eternal destiny.

Lord, Messiah, I do believe in You and trust You for my eternal destiny.

WEEKEND 23 READING
Jonah 3-4

PERSONAL REFLECTIONS

WEEK 24, DAY 1

Majestic, Judge, Lawgiver, King

But there the majestic One, the LORD, will be for us a place of rivers and wide canals on which no boat with oars will go, and on which no mighty ship will pass— for the LORD is our judge, the LORD is our lawgiver, the LORD is our king; He will save us ... (Isaiah 33:21–22)

Scripture abounds with epithets for God, sometimes clustered as we find here. Understanding why these four descriptions come together here requires context. The chapter contains judgment against those who "conceived chaff" and who "will give birth to stubble," for God says, "My breath will consume you like a fire, the peoples will be burned to lime, like cut thorns which are burned in the fire" (Is 33:11-12).

Yet there is hope intricately bound up in Yahweh (LORD) as God's divine Name is poignantly connected with all four descriptions. The LORD is the majestic One: "Your eyes will see the King in His beauty" (Is 33:17). Indeed, the adjective "majestic" frequently consorts with kingship, describing a glorious beauty. "Out of Zion, the perfection of beauty, God has shone forth" (Ps 50:2). Or as the Shunamite woman said about her kingly pursuer (if we see this as an allusion to God and His people), "Yes, he is altogether lovely" (S of S 5:16 NKJV). Literally, he is desirable or precious. One lexicon lists "splendid" as the idea behind the Hebrew word translated "majestic."

Not only is the LORD majestic, He is the judge. "Sinners in Zion are terrified; trembling has seized the godless. Who among us can live with the consuming fire? Who among us can live with continual burning?" (Is 33:14). God is not to be trifled with; He is an impartial and fair judge, but His judgment when meted out will be unbending and harsh. He will not let unrighteousness go unpunished—otherwise there would be no hope for a righteous world; in the end there would be no justice.

The LORD is our lawgiver. He gives clear instructions and judges those who violate them. In grace and kindness, He spelled them out in the Law of Moses, which was spoken through the agency of angels and which "proved unalterable, and every transgression and disobedience received a just penalty..." (Heb 2:2). The writer of Hebrews says to us today, "For this reason we must pay much closer attention to what we have heard, so that we do not drift away from it ..." (Heb 2:1), "[f]or indeed we have had good news preached to us, just as they also; but the word they heard did not profit them, because it was not united by faith in those who heard" (Heb 4:2). When the King speaks, we are to obey.

Lord, You are my Majestic King, my Law-giver, my Judge. I humbly bow down before You.

WEEK 24, DAY 2

Most High Over All the Earth

O God, do not remain quiet; do not be silent and, O God, do not be still. For behold, Your enemies make an uproar, and those who hate You have exalted themselves ... That they may know that You alone, whose name is the LORD, are the Most High over all the earth. (Psalm 83:1-2, 18)

People of God have always had their detractors. Whether the OT Jews, the NT Christians, or persecuted Christians around the world today, believers have always faced varying degrees of opposition and oppression. If non-believers mocked Christ on the cross, they will do no less to His followers.

The greatest test of faith is God's silence in the midst of our difficulties, especially when we are persecuted for our faith. Noble, heroic tales of illustrious martyrdoms fascinate us in our youth, inspiring dreams of giving our all for Christ. But when faced with demands to recant our faith, to ease up the pressure, we hear no rousing music in the background, nor flowing oratory of valiant prose describing to an unseen audience our courageous actions. Often there is just silence. Deafening silence. There is no greater screaming silence than the taciturn absence of a response from God.

Great men and women of faith through the millennia have experienced this same thing—even the psalm writers. Even Jesus Christ Himself. On the cross we hear Him cry out the theme verse of Psalm 2, "My God, my God, why have You forsaken me?" (Matt 27:46, Ps 22:1a). The psalm goes on to say, "Far from my deliverance are the words of my groaning. O my God, I cry by day, but You do not answer; and by night, but I have no rest" (Ps 22:1b-2).

We desire more than just an answer to our own personal discomfort. We have dared to believe there is a God, and that He is the Creator over all. So when we see evil seeming to dominate the world, and evildoers arrogantly puffing themselves up in sinfulness and distortions of justice, selfishness and brutal oppressions, we want them and the whole world to know there is accountability to God. No matter what happens on the earth, no matter how powerful any political despot or neighborhood bully, workplace harasser or domestic abuser—there is a God to whom all will answer.

Along with the psalmist we plead with God to speak up, to let all know that He is "the LORD...the Most High over all the earth." He is above presidents, kings, dictators, bosses, manipulators, abusers, bullies, racist bigots, earthquakes, hurricanes or bombs. He is the Most High.

Lord, even when You are silent, I know You are in control. My desire is for You to show Yourself now, plainly, and to put all evildoers in their place now.

WEEK 24, DAY 3

My Confidence

For You are my hope; O Lord GOD, You are my confidence from my youth. By You I have been sustained from my birth; You are He who took me from my mother's womb; my praise is continually of You. (Ps 71:5-6).

"Prayer of an Old Man for Deliverance," as the NASB editors have titled this psalm, summarizes it well. To young ears maybe not so much, but in the hearing that comes from age, the picture is clear:

O God, You have taught me from my youth, and I still declare Your wondrous deeds. And even when I am old and gray, O God, do not forsake me, until I declare Your strength to this generation, Your power to all who are to come. (Ps 71:17–18).

The psalm writer—was it David, proficient as he was with the harp? (Ps 71:22)—is facing a crisis, age not excusing him from life's harshness. Yet with a lifetime of trusting in God, he knows from experience that He will protect him. The first words that drip from his quill resonate a life of trust: "In You, O LORD, I have taken refuge" (Ps 71:1). He has in the past, and he continues into his present circumstance. He has done as Paul in the NT instructs:

Let the word of Christ richly dwell within you ... (Col 3:16)

The Word "richly dwells" in us when we know the Word of God, believe it to be absolutely trustworthy and rest in it during all trials of life. It becomes a life habit. God in His Word has proven reliable, essential and indispensable. Learning from this, we can say God has sustained us from our birth – are we not here and reading these words at this very moment? Despite life circumstances, broken or disappointing relationships, physical difficulties and sickness, failures and sin, we have made it this far. If there is one thing faith teaches us over the years of walking with the Lord, it is that despite our fears and anxieties, He is the God of the ever-present now. And therein is our confidence.

Nothing can shake us: "For I am convinced that neither death, nor life, nor angels, nor principalities, nor things present, nor things to come, nor powers, nor height, nor depth, nor any other created thing, will be able to separate us from the love of God, which is in Christ Jesus our Lord" (Rom 8:38–39).

Because we are loved by God and we have hope in Him, then we can have confidence as we face life's trials. Nothing can get to us, unless God in His divine sovereignty has allowed it to shape us for praising His Son.

Lord, not in fear or anxiety, I choose to walk in confidence, knowing that my trials give me opportunity to praise You before others for the hope You give me.

WEEK 24, DAY 4

My Counselor

I will bless the LORD who has counseled me; indeed, my mind instructs me in the night. (Psalm 16:7).

David learned early in life, on the hillsides of Judea, as he watched over his father's flocks, to order his mind to the Word of God. Being from a faithful family who knew the Law, and judging from his later writing of Psalm 119 and his extended devotion to the Law, he had committed the Word of God to memory. Remember, back in the early part of the first millennium B.C. there were no printing presses, and certainly no pocket Bibles. What could be known or learned about the Word of God was from that recited in the temple or taught in the home, in obedience to Deuteronomy 6:6-9.

So lying under the night-time sky David rolled the Word of God over and over in his mind, and used it to teach himself wisdom. Although alertness to predators or wandering sheep was an ever-present responsibility for a shepherd, there was plenty of time to just think. There are only so many stones one can throw for entertainment. When a young man's mind easily wanders into fleshly thoughts at idle times, David, judging by the place God's Word had in his life, must have spent his "idle time" meditating on what he had been taught. Can we not hear this echo in his later writings? For example,

> *How can a young man keep his way pure? By keeping it according to Your word. With all my heart I have sought You; do not let me wander from Your commandments. Your word I have treasured in my heart, that I may not sin against You. (Ps 119:9–11)*

In the Word of God, he found the Lord as a counselor. Although we don't see many times when the Lord explicitly told David to do something, we see David acting in ways that reflect a man who knew his God and was supremely loyal to Him. He knew what God would want him to do; he didn't often have to stop and ask. That wisdom is often overshadowed by David's selfless commitment, courage, and compelling leadership. Yet it was from the spiritual counsel learned from the Word that he knew God would protect him as he faced the giant whom no one else had the faith to confront, waited patiently for God to take out the king (Saul) who had lost his divine anointing, recovered from his moral failure, and resisted taking revenge on a rebellious son. The key: He instructed himself in the Word of God.

Lord, I bless You for the wisdom You have given in Your Word, as my Counselor. I desire more spiritual wisdom, so I can walk in ways more pleasing to You.

WEEK 24, DAY 5

My Cup

The LORD is the portion of my inheritance and my cup; You support my lot. (Psalm 16:5)

Pleasant or bitter experiences of life fill our cup. In Psalm 23, David's "cup overflows" with "goodness and mercy" (Ps 23:5b-6a). James and John expressed their misguided desire to "drink the cup" that Jesus was about to drink, referring to His suffering (Matt 20:22, Mark 10:39). Jesus Himself prayed three times for the cup to "pass from Me," referring to His coming passion and death on the cross.

The wicked will have their cup filled with "fire and brimstone and burning wind" (Ps 11:6); they will "drink down its dregs," that is, from the cup in the hand of the LORD (Ps 75:8). But of all the possible life experiences that can fill the cup of those who are faithful followers of the Lord, the greatest is our salvation:

What shall I render to the LORD for all His benefits toward me? I shall lift up the cup of salvation and call upon the name of the LORD. (Ps 116:12–13).

So, in the most general way, the psalm writer, David, rejoices that "The LORD is ... my cup." Earlier he said, "You are my Lord; I have no good besides You." There is nothing better with which to fill your life than God Himself. Why? Because the Lord has given you a pleasant heritage (vs. 6, 2), the Lord instructs you, (vs. 7), 3) God's powerful presence is always close by (vs. 8), you have a hope beyond the grave (vs. 10), you have been given the path of life (vs. 11a) and, "In Your presence is fullness of joy; in Your right hand there are pleasures forever" (vs. 11b).

Today life is filled with many superficial things that can populate our hearts and minds with idle and worthless thoughts. People are busier than ever with entertainment, sports, hobbies, money and vacations. Success is too often measured by how many things one has acquired. Many Christians fill their cup with these things to offset the sorrow and difficulty of life that seems to overflow their cup.

The psalm writer chose to focus on the Lord, to let the Lord fill his cup with Himself. In saying "the LORD is my cup," David defines his life experiences by what God is doing in and through him. There is little room for any other contents when life is filled with the Lord.

Lord, I want to fill my cup of life experiences with You, and not waste my life on superficial or worthless things.

WEEKEND 24 READING
Micah 1

PERSONAL REFLECTIONS

WEEK 25, DAY 1

My Exceeding Joy

Then I will go to the altar of God, to God my exceeding joy; and upon the lyre I shall praise You, O God, my God. Why are you in despair, O my soul? And why are you disturbed within me? Hope in God, for I shall again praise Him, the help of my countenance and my God. (Psalm 43:4–5)

Carrying on from Psalm 42, the thirsty soul cries out to God from a spiritually depressed state: "Why are you in despair, O my soul?" – he writes three times in these two psalms (42:5, 11; 43:5). The similar content, wording and style, along with the repeated refrain, lead most commentators to see in these two psalms one original poem. We are unable to identify the specific author, though Psalm 42 is connected to the choir associated with the "sons of Korah" as indicated in the prescript.

Does this not reflect the sometime experience of the conscientious believer during certain spiritual dry spells in life? The inner self-talk often betrays unbelief in the superficial believer, but here it reveals the thoughts of a godly person who wrestles honestly with his own inner struggles of trusting in the Lord. We are reminded of the father of the demon-possessed son. Jesus had responded to the crowd, "O unbelieving generation …" Then He said to the father, "All things are possible to him who believes." The man honestly confessed, "I do believe; help my unbelief." Jesus, seeing the man's integrity and honest struggle with faith (contrary to the scribes and the crowd in general), went on to heal the son (Mark 9:19-24).

This man's struggle reflected the struggle of Psalms 42 and 43. A faithful man believes but struggles with his own unbelief—an admitted oddity or self-contradiction, but nonetheless a reality in the genuine believer's life. In the midst of spiritual depression, the genuine believer counsels himself with the belief that at the end of the day, God is "my exceeding joy." He may not always be experiencing God in that way, but he knows that is the attraction, the draw, the hope that keeps him from giving up in his despair. This is why Paul could say, "We have this treasure in earthen vessels … we are afflicted in every way, but not crushed; perplexed, but not despairing …" (2 Cor 4:7–8).

"For momentary, light affliction is producing for us an eternal weight of glory far beyond all comparison…" (2 Cor 4:17). That glory is to rest in God who is "my exceeding joy." All sorrow, struggle, suffering and pain are eclipsed by the anticipation of exceeding and everlasting joy. A joy that cannot fade away. A joy that we can begin to experience, even in the midst of our trials now.

Lord, in my struggles, I want to believe that You are "my exceeding joy." Sometimes I find that difficult, but I resolve to keep trusting in You.

WEEK 25, DAY 2

My Glory

But You, O LORD, are a shield about me, My glory, and the One who lifts my head. I was crying to the LORD with my voice, and He answered me from His holy mountain. Selah. (Psalm 3:3–4)

There are at least two senses in which this can be taken (discerning minds might see more). The first is that the Lord is glorious and "I" particularly glory in Him. Many people desire to glorify God, but for "me," regardless of what others do, "I" as an individual am focused on glorifying Him personally. Indeed, there are times when we glorify God in a congregation. But other times we glorifying Him individually.

To glorify God is to make Him known and show how great He is, so that others also may glorify Him. The collective whole of God's image bearers were made to reflect God, who created them and in whose image they were fashioned. This is accomplished as individuals reflect that image back to Him, so that He sees Himself in us. I cannot simply assume God receives glory from me because I am connected with a group of believers who give Him glory. It must begin with me; I must be able to say unreservedly that He is "my glory," that is, He is the one I glorify.

The second sense in which we might say He is my glory is that as I reflect His glory, I become glorious with His glory. His glory, as it were, splashes luminescently over me, like a mirror fills with the glory of someone who is beautiful. The light in the reflection is virtually as bright as the actual light. In other words, I become glorious as I more clearly reflect His glory.

Could this be what Paul writes about? "But we all, with unveiled face, beholding as in a mirror the glory of the Lord, are being transformed into the same image from glory to glory, just as from the Lord, the Spirit" (2 Cor 3:18). As the mirror needs buffing to bring out the reflective image, so also God buffs us with the trials of life, a kind of abrasive that smooths us out: "For momentary, light affliction is producing for us an eternal weight of glory far beyond all comparison..." (2 Cor 4:17). The weight of glory refers to a positive, substantive reflection of God in our lives. As the mirror shares in the substantive glory of the object which it reflects, so also we share in the glory of God. We can say, increasingly, He is "my glory."

For the psalmist, in the midst of his difficulty, he calls out to God whom he believes will lift him out of his troubles. In this expression of faith, he glorifies God, and thus we note him for his steadfast faith – which reflects well on God. God is worthy of our trust. Truly, we can say the Lord is "my glory."

Glorious Lord, I desire to live a buffed life so that I can reflect You well.

WEEK 25, DAY 3

My Help

"You, O LORD, be not far off; O You my help, hasten to my assistance" (Psalm 22:19).

We all need help at times, though often we don't admit it. Asking for help admits to neediness. But in this world we sometimes face things much greater than ourselves, and no amount of bolstering our courage will save us from whatever befalls us. David calls out, "You, O LORD, be not far off; O You my help, hasten to my assistance" (Ps 22:19). If we understand this to be part of a Messianic psalm, the first line of which our Lord Jesus quoted on the cross, "My God, my God, why have You forsaken me?" (Ps 22:1), then even He needed help when pinned to the cross for our sins. Repeatedly we see the psalm writers expressing the need for help: "Our soul waits for the LORD; He is our help and our shield" (Ps 33:20). "Behold, God is my helper; the Lord is the sustainer of my soul" (Ps 54:4). Even at the creation of humanity, we see an implicit need for helpers: "Then the LORD God said, 'It is not good for the man to be alone; I will make him a helper suitable for him'" (Gen 2:18). We all need help.

Job suffered greatly, and if anyone needed help, it was he. Yet Job didn't want help; he wanted relief through answers. So he attempted to wrestle with his Creator, who simply refused to engage him in his philosophical, rational, logical reasoning. God's definitive, argument-ending statements shut Job down completely: "Who is this …?" (Job 38:2), "Where were you …?" (Job 38:4), "Have you ever in your life …?" (Job 38:12). God challenged this creature called Job to consider his place in the order of creation. To be sure, as a human Job was created in God's image, and to use theological terms, we humans are charged with being co-regents with God to oversee creation. But that does not give Job or us a special standing to challenge our Creator to a logical duel.

"The LORD said to Job, 'Will the faultfinder contend with the Almighty?'" (Job 40:2). Finally, Job responded, "Behold, I am insignificant; what can I reply to You?" (Job 40:4), and, "Therefore I retract, and I repent in dust and ashes" (Job 42:6). Then God helped Job, relieved his suffering and restored to him all that he had lost and more.

We cannot expect help from God if we are busy trying to create a self-sustainable life. God wants to help us, but only on His terms. He is not obligated or compelled. Rather He does it graciously, even though we deserve none of it. When we believe that and we approach Him humbly, then we don't doubt His care for us, because it doesn't depend on our worthiness.

Father, thank You for being my Help in my times of need.

WEEK 25, DAY 4

My Hope

Rescue me, O my God, out of the hand of the wicked, Out of the grasp of the wrongdoer and ruthless man, For You are my hope; O Lord GOD, You are my confidence from my youth. (Psalm 71:4–5)

One asks for help because one believes that the person being asked can in fact help. Otherwise why ask? A child asks a father to help, implicitly believing the father can in fact help. The only question is whether the father will help. The child believes the answer will be "Yes" – otherwise why ask? These things seem simple, but in a more adult view of things, we are speaking of hope. Someone has defined hope as "desire with expectancy." We want something to happen, and we fully anticipate that it will happen.

The psalm writer was in a predicament, being under siege by an enemy of some sort ("wrongdoer and ruthless man"). We might envision him taking protection in a cave and relating this to the Lord's protection: "In You, O LORD, I have taken refuge ... Be a rock of habitation in which I may continually come ... You are my rock and my fortress" (Ps 71:1-3). We don't know for sure who the author was, but if it was David, then the only person he really feared was Saul, and that only because he refused to fight against "the Lord's anointed" regardless of how much Saul sought to kill him.

In keeping with his integrity, he found himself in a closed-in situation, with no escape presenting itself, so he cried out to the Lord. One might think the Lord's response would be to give him strength and courage to go out and attack his pursuer, but that solution is not prescribed by God – though it may be such an action might be taken. The point is that it is not one's courage or ability that somehow is goal of God's answer to the prayer—the mentality that "if you believe, then you can do it" sort of thing. Rather, the psalm writer believed it was God Himself who would deliver him from this mess. How often do we see God sending a plague on an enemy army, confounding them with rumors that turn them away, or orchestrating various other completely unexpected phenomena or events? Faith does not simply overlay a spiritual worldview of events; faith believes God to be really at work in the world.

To say, "You are my hope" is to believe that God will do what you ask. This is something forged over time as we continually experience God answering our prayers for help. The very next verse testifies that, "By You I have been sustained from my birth ..." (Ps 71:6). This must become our life habit, to give God credit for the work He has done and continues to do in our lives. That is what gives us hope to trust Him in whatever comes our ways.

Lord, when I consider all You have done for me, I praise You as "My Hope."

WEEK 25, DAY 5

My King

... The LORD is King forever and ever; nations have perished from His land. O LORD, You have heard the desire of the humble; You will strengthen their heart, You will incline Your ear (Psalm 10:16–17)

Kingship portrays majesty, highness—being far above the common people. We easily envision crowns, thrones, ornate robes and innumerable attendants. Kings are busy doing, well, kingly things—which are a far cry from the ordinary lives of the "hoi polloi" (a Greek phrase for the common people) or the "am ha'aretz" (a Hebrew phrase meaning the same, literally "people of the land"). The classic tale "The Prince and the Pauper" tells the story a boy raised in royalty wanting to know what life is like for "regular" people, apart from all the privilege and luxury. Some young people born into upper society circles use the slang name "Norm" as a derogatory reference to normal people—those of lower, more common social status. The rich associate with the rich, and even among the upper reaches there is a hierarchy based on status, wealth and prominence. We human beings tend to stratify our social relationships.

But not God! We could use the analogy of the prince becoming a pauper to depict Christ's incarnation. We see many times in the Old Testament both the kingliness of God and His associating with the lower ranks of mankind. He did not keep Himself aloof. In our verse today, He is majestic and powerful and also listens to those of more humble condition. A king, in context of the ancient world, was the top dog, the mightiest warrior who rose to the most prominent of leadership roles. He led in battle, and he had proven himself greater than all other men. His majesty flowed from the accolades and glory attributed to his greatness. He clearly stood out among all men.

Our God is the greatest of all, above all gods. In human terms, He is king forever—He is able to destroy whole nations! Yet it is not beneath Him to hear and respond to the "desires of the humble.... [and] strengthen their heart..." In other words, we have a ready audience with God.

Psalm 84:3 portrays "[t]he swallow [who has] a nest for herself, where she may lay her young, even Your altars, O LORD of hosts, My King and my God" (Ps 84:3). So also God accepts our presence as much as the birds. Once, while I was riding in a taxi cab in Bangkok, Thailand, the driver kept referring to the leader of his country as "my king" with a sense of intimacy, like he knew the monarch personally. Likewise, we can refer to God, the Creator of the universe, as "my King," for not only do we know Him, but He knows us personally.

Lord, You are my King. And I am thankful that You know me.

WEEKEND 25 READING
Micah 2

PERSONAL REFLECTIONS

WEEK 26, DAY 1

My Light

The LORD is my light and my salvation; whom shall I fear? The LORD is the defense of my life; whom shall I dread? (Psalm 27:1)

When Jesus said, "I am the light of the world..." (John 8:12), He was hinting at His identity with the God of the OT. Though the connection might seem rather remote to our non-Jewish ears, it must have been tantalizing—dangerously so—to ears steeped in the Jewish scriptures. Such language was appropriate to God, about whom David said, "The LORD is my light ...." Further, we read:

For You light my lamp; the LORD my God illumines my darkness. (Ps 18:28)

Do not rejoice over me, O my enemy. Though I fall I will rise; though I dwell in darkness, the LORD is a light for me. (Mic 7:8)

Through Isaiah's prophecy, Israel anticipated a coming day when God would fully and tangibly light up the world by His very presence:

"Your sun will no longer set, nor will your moon wane; for you will have the LORD for an everlasting light, and the days of your mourning will be over." (Is 60:20)

As David faced his enemies, who threatened his very life, his first truth to fall back on was that "[t]he LORD is my light." What does this mean? There is nothing special about the word "light" in its basic meaning. But here, in its figurative use, it speaks of how the Lord gives brightness and clarity—not to enable us to see in the dark, but to give us a clear understanding of our situation. David was not content to passively accept what he could not change, pleading ignorance and appealing to God's unknowable reasons for the bad stuff in his life. Rather, in faith, he reminded himself as he wrote that God gives clarity to our perception of what is going on. David could see clearly that God was "my salvation" and "the defense of my life." Therefore, how could he possibly fear anyone or anything?

In the midst of his dark circumstances, threats on his life, his desire was not snuffed out, namely, to clearly "behold the beauty of the LORD and to meditate in His temple" (Ps 27:4b). The Lord gives light to see Him:

When You said, "Seek My face," my heart said to You, "Your face, O LORD, I shall seek. Do not hide Your face from me ...." (Ps 27:8–9)

Lord, help me see the light of Your face and throw away the world's blinders.

WEEK 26, DAY 2

My Portion

The Lord is the portion of my inheritance and my cup; You support my lot. (Psalm 16:5)

When people die, the possessions they leave behind are claimed by their children, near relatives, or those otherwise named, in legal terms, "heirs." What is left behind is called the "inheritance," and it is distributed to the heirs according to the so-called last will and testimony. Everyone related to the deceased person is of course interested in how much was left to him or her. That's the first question. The second is whether they will get their fair share. In other words, how does their portion compare to what other heirs are designated to receive?

We all want what is due to us. We feel we have a right to it; it is ours. But in this fallen world, where we all are infected by sin and self-centeredness (though in varying degrees), none of us can objectively determine what is fair for ourselves, let alone everyone else.

The Lord made this clear when Job felt entitled to an explanation for his suffering. God rebuked him with a review of creation, ending with this biting retort: "Who has given to Me that I should repay him? Whatever is under the whole heaven is Mine" (Job 41:11). We own nothing; we are entitled to nothing. God does not owe answers to any of His creation.

With a legal will, the stuff contested did not belong to us but to the deceased person. He owned it and alone is entitled to disperse it without any obligations. This is not to say we cannot use legal means to gain what is lawfully assigned to us in a will. However, we must remember we are not entitled to anything. If we were entitled, then the thing would not be in the will—it would be represented by some other legal arrangement. But with God there is no arrangement by which we can claim entitlement. He owns everything; He defines the rules. He is under no obligation to us.

However, we do have our portion of an inheritance, one which is far greater than any earthly inheritance of money or property. Our portion is the Lord Himself—not what the He possesses, although that is a side benefit. Through faith we can say He is ours. And there certainly is enough of Him to go around. Far more than we deserve, or could even ask for. We possess Him in a way that far surpasses owning any earthly thing. That is what David meant when he cried out from the bowels of a cave, when he had very little, hiding from his assailant:

"You are my refuge, my portion in the land of the living." (Ps 142:5)

Lord, I am immensely rich, for I already have my portion, which is You!

WEEK 26, DAY 3

My Redeemer

"As for me, I know that my Redeemer lives, and at the last He will take His stand on the earth. Even after my skin is destroyed, yet from my flesh I shall see God; whom I myself shall behold, and whom my eyes will see and not another ...." (Job 19:25–27a)

Job was a man of struggle and loss. His family and his health were taken away from him, and his wife alienated him with her desire for him to curse God and die. Everything was gone. How much worse could life get? The only way to look up would be to wish for death. Yet in the middle of it all, we find this verse of hope. A hope that transcends life.

Job held out no hope for any improvement here on earth, so his thoughts turned to the afterlife. This constituted remarkable faith because the general thinking about the afterlife was encompassed in the words of the psalmist: "For there is no mention of You in death; in Sheol who will give You thanks?" (Ps 6:5). Job seemed to think otherwise; he was confident that after death he would see the Lord, alive and standing over the earth presumably in victory.

Indeed, Job wanted victory over the miserable life he was experiencing. The phrase "[e]ven after my skin is destroyed, yet from my flesh I shall see God" only hinted at resurrection but portrayed a remarkable faith. Though he wrestled severely with God's silence, to the point of frustration and possibly even anger toward God, he never lost faith in God, the one who was inflicting such trials in his life.

Notably he identified God as "my Redeemer." The word means one who delivers, avenges, brings into safety. That was what Job needed, and what he believed God to be. He needed deliverance from his super-overwhelming trials. If not in this life, which seemed to be certain, then in the next life, he was assured. But he didn't just desire the experience of redemption; he desired the Redeemer. There is an old adage that might give us a contrast. "Give a man a fish, and you feed him for a day. But teach him to fish, and you feed him for a life time." Concerning deliverance, we might say, "Give a man deliverance, and you have freed him from his difficulties. Give a man a deliverer, and you have united him with someone who can deliver him from all future difficulties." Job wanted the Redeemer more than he wanted deliverance.

The psalmist framed his worship around this notion: "Let the words of my mouth and the meditation of my heart be acceptable in Your sight, O LORD, my rock and my Redeemer" (Ps 19:14).

Lord, I have many struggles that are beyond me to resolve or conquer, but these only make me desire You more, my Redeemer, my Deliverer.

WEEK 26, DAY 4

My Refuge

He who dwells in the shelter of the Most High will abide in the shadow of the Almighty. I will say to the LORD, "My refuge and my fortress, My God, in whom I trust!" (Psalm 91:1–2)

Sometimes we need the protective confines of a safe place—time to regroup, an anchor point. David sought shelter in caves, particularly those at Adullam (1 Sam 22:1) and Engedi (1 Sam 23:29, 24:1-3). David was unlike those today who think of faith as trusting God and then doing nothing human. He saw faith as a partnership with God, and he never lost sight of the fact that God was the supremely senior partner. In faith, David did his part, which was to hide in caves.

While we do not know the author of Psalm 91, his experience was similar to and could easily reflect what David experienced while hiding in the caves. He was an astute military man, knowing when to fight and when to withhold fighting, when to boldly thrust forward and when to retreat to the caves that so frequently served as a fortress, largely impregnable and safe.

But if he was trusting God, then why hide in a cave? Why not just go boldly forward? That is a reductionist faith, an irresponsible faith. The psalmist saw the cave as God's protection, and he intoned in his prayer that belief. At any time, the cave could be found out and either invaded by a superior army or barricaded to force starvation. In fact, one day David's nemesis, Saul, did wander into the cave where David and his men hid. In that situation, the cave provided the perfect opportunity to pounce on Saul and kill him when he least suspected it (1 Sam 24:3). Not only did God provide a refuge, but God used the cave to give David the upper hand!

Today, when we trust God, we cannot claim faith when we sit back and do nothing. We must act according to that belief. If it means seeking refuge from physical danger, then we need to do that in faith, trusting that God provides the refuge beyond what our efforts alone will provide. The point is, as we go through life, dealing wisely and prudently with the struggles of a fallen world, we don't go about recklessly, but walk in the knowledge that He is oue "refuge." He is our shelter and our fortress. Everywhere we go His shadow of protection will encompass us. Our task as we walk through life on this planet is to "abide in the shadow of the Almighty," for nothing is greater than He; nothing can break through His impenetrable barriers, for He is the Most High (Elyon).

Lord, when I am weak, fearful and feel threatened, I take refuge in You, because that is the safest place in the world. In You, I am secure. Praise God.

WEEK 26, DAY 5

My Salvation

The LORD is my light and my salvation; whom shall I fear? The LORD is the defense of my life; whom shall I dread? (Psalm 27:1)

If there is one thing Christians know about, it is salvation. The word occurs about 400 times in the Bible (either in the form "salvation" or "saved"). It is popularly used today as a catch-all for the entirety of our identity for eternity. A Christian says, "I am saved," making a clear, definitive statement of one's status that separates him or her from those who are not "saved." Some even refer to the lost as those who are "not yet saved" (which might be an inadvertent tip of the hat to universalism). Theologically, related words include redeemed, regenerated, propitiated, forgiven, elect, transformed, made alive, quickened—all in addition to salvation. We are all of these things.

When David used the term "salvation" he was thinking in more practical terms. A good interpretative practice when coming across the word "salvation" or "saved" in the Bible is to ask, "Saved from what?" At times, it means to be spiritually saved from condemnation for our sins, from an eternity in hell. But at other times, like in our passage above, it refers to physical salvation.

Just as God as our refuge, He is our salvation. That means no matter what situation in which I find myself, I am in good hands with God. While the particular circumstances may obscure the promise implied in this verse, faith leads us to believe it completely, without needing to dictate to God the nature of our salvation in the situation. His salvation might be keeping me from falling into ungodly responses to those who would oppose or harm me, or enabling me to love my enemies while they are persecuting me. It may mean He holds us up so that we would endure the struggle in Christ's name.

There are many ways God can defend us. The greatest is found in the New Testament: "My little children, I am writing these things to you so that you may not sin. And if anyone sins, we have an Advocate with the Father, Jesus Christ the righteous ..." (1 John 2:1). We can have confidence that our trust in God as our salvation may not save us from every earthly difficulty, but we believe and count on Jesus' advocacy to the Father on our behalf. Though we still sin, we are saved from the accusation of the enemy of our soul. I have absolutely nothing to fear. If God is for me, who can be against me?!

It was because he knew God as "my salvation" that David could counsel his own soul: "Wait for the LORD; be strong and let your heart take courage; yes, wait for the LORD" (Ps 27:14).

Lord, I pray that You will save me in the midst of the difficulty I am facing right now. Whether that is saving me out of it or raising me above it, I trust in You.

WEEKEND 26 READING
Micah 3

PERSONAL REFLECTIONS

WEEK 27, DAY 1

My Song

The LORD is my strength and song, and He has become my salvation. (Psalm 118:14)

Figures of speech abound in Scripture, especially the OT poetic literature, like the book of Psalms. Here we find what E.W. Bullinger calls a metonymy, where one thing is put or given for another ("Figures of Speech Used in the Bible"). In this case, an action (singing to the Lord) is depicted by an object related to it (a song). The phrase "The LORD is my ... song" conveys the sense that the Lord causes me or gives me reason to sing. Indeed, notice the next two verses:

The sound of joyful shouting and salvation is in the tents of the righteous; the right hand of the LORD does valiantly. The right hand of the LORD is exalted; the right hand of the LORD does valiantly. (Psalm 118:15–16)

Because of the Lord, the psalm writer has much to sing about. Have you ever noticed how many songs are contained in Scripture? Not only do we have the book of Psalms, which were all meant to be sung either individually or in a group, but we find them sprinkled throughout the rest of the Bible (among many examples we cite Deuteronomy 33 in the OT, Philippians 2:5-11 in the NT). Psalm 100 calls us to sing with spiritual gusto: "Shout joyfully to the LORD, all the earth. Serve the LORD with gladness; Come before Him with joyful singing" (Psalm 100:1–2). While some singing is somber, reflecting the laments frequently found in the psalms, other singing is lively and emotionally joyful.

We have much to joyfully sing about, for the Lord has "become my salvation." We sing because we are saved, rescued, redeemed—even though we live in this fallen, sin-cursed world, constantly fighting off attacks of Satan, challenges to our security, hits against our faith, temptations to sin and doubt. We who believe God's message are saved! That is more than enough to elicit us to sing lustily in praise of God.

This verse is poignantly nuanced: it is not our salvation per se that causes us to sing. Rather, it is God, who is our salvation, who causes us to sing. To be sure, the two are intricately connected, like a potter, the process of sculpting a pot, and the result, the pot itself. Salvation is the process of God retrieving us from our sin and judgment; being saved is the result, but God is the one to be praised, not the process or even the fact of our salvation. We sing because of our salvation, because we are joyful over the One who saved us.

Lord, I look not to the gift, but to You as the Giver. You are my song, for You put a melody in my heart. You give me reason to sing.

WEEK 27, DAY 2

The One Enthroned in Heaven

He who sits in the heavens laughs, the Lord scoffs at them. (Psalm 2:4)

The NIV renders this verse, "The One enthroned in heaven laughs...." The Lord is pictured as one who rules (see NLT), as echoed in what is called the Lord's Prayer: "Our Father, who is in heaven ...." This psalm speaks of earthly kings rising up against God, a laughable thought if it weren't so tragic. Words come to mind: foolish, absurd. One wants to say to those kings, "What in the world were you thinking?!"

The context of Psalm 2 has to do with surrounding nations that have come up against the kingdom of Israel. While Messianic in nature, this psalm also reflects on the anointed king of Israel:

But as for Me, I have installed My King upon Zion, My holy mountain. (Ps 2:6)

I will surely tell of the decree of the LORD: He said to Me, "You are My Son, today I have begotten You." (Ps 2:7)

The kings of the earth take their stand and the rulers take counsel together against the LORD and against His Anointed... (Ps 2:2)

God's biting sarcasm reflects His incredulity at their foolish audacity:

He who sits in the heavens laughs, the Lord scoffs at them. Then He will speak to them in His anger and terrify them in His fury .... (Ps 2:4–5)

It is like God says, "I can't believe what I am seeing. You actually think you can stand up against Me!" This is the One who is seated in heaven, enthroned and ruling over all creation, the One who created these very kings that are rising up against Him. He who spoke all things into existence by simply speaking forth His word, "Let there be ...," could snuff out these puny kings, small men among the millions and billions of human image bearers He placed on earth. They are smaller than even ants compared to an elephant.

The entire psalm is given for us, not because we all rise up audaciously against God and against His anointed the way those kings did but because we are like them when we knowingly sin, for then we reject God's sovereign rule over our lives. We "forget" that He is seated in heaven, enthroned. And from that vantage point, He not only sees what we do, but has authority over what we do. We ought not make Him laugh with incredulity at the our willful sinning.

Lord, I must admit that I sometimes spurn Your authority over me when I knowingly sin. Thank You for the grace that is greater than all my sin.

WEEK 27, DAY 3

The One of Sinai

O God, when you went out before your people, when you marched through the wilderness, Selah the earth quaked, the heavens poured down rain, before God, the One of Sinai, before God, the God of Israel. (Psalm 68:7–8 ESV)

The Hebrew phrasing is a bit complicated, as reflected in the differing English translations. The NASB, which we normally use here, renders the phrase "Sinai itself quaked," and the NKJV is similar, but the NIV, NET and NLT agree with the ESV, "the One of Sinai." Translations aren't always an exact science, so we praise God for being alerted by the variety of renderings among modern versions.

God is forever associated with Sinai, the place where He met Moses and gave what has come to be called "the Law of Moses." Psalm 68:7-8 provides a brief synopsis of God's phenomenal show of power leading up to and including that giving of the Law. The people of Israel had "marched through the wilderness" for 40 years after the exodus from Egypt. During that time they experienced earthquakes and all kinds of weather phenomena.

Early in that time period, Moses went up Mt. Sinai to meet God (Ex 20-23). The abbreviated version, what might be called the prologue to the Law, is found in the well-known "Ten Commandments" (Ex 20:2-17). After this, "All the people perceived the thunder and the lightning flashes and the sound of the trumpet and the mountain smoking; and when the people saw it, they trembled and stood at a distance" (Ex 20:18). This volcanic-like activity put the fear of God in His people, to be sure.

Today, some attempt to tame God, limiting Him to the NT, as being a God of love and grace only, not a God who invokes fear and law. The God of the NT, they say, is different from the God of the OT. But God doesn't change. The notion that He has fundamentally changed in His character and is no longer the God of Sinai denies His eternal, unchanging nature. If God's character changes then all hope is gone, for we cannot be assured that He will not also change in the future? What if we were to arrive at the judgment of believers, and He announces that He has changed His mind about righteousness and will evaluate our eternal destiny of heaven or hell based on our deeds?

No, God is still the God of Sinai. We need to know Him as the Lawgiver first so that we can understand His love and grace in forgiving us. We were truly guilty—not because of culturally induced shame feelings or religious oppression, as society would have us believe, but because we had sinned against the God of the Law, the One of Sinai.

Lord, thank You for sending Your Son as a sacrifice to take away my guilt.

WEEK 27, DAY 4

The One to Be Feared

Make vows to the LORD your God and fulfill them; let all who are around Him bring gifts to Him who is to be feared. He will cut off the spirit of princes; He is feared by the kings of the earth. (Psalm 76:11–12)

We tend to distance ourselves from thinking of God as a wrathful deity, with visions of hellfire-and-brimstone preaching echo embarrassingly in our collective consciences. Yet we cherish the psalms as providing comfort to hurting, struggling Christians without appreciating the frequently sobering words found in Psalm 76: "You, even You, are to be feared; and who may stand in Your presence when once You are angry?" (Ps 76:7). Can we find anything here useful for us who have experienced the loving grace of God and don't want to portray to the world a medieval sort of deity that instills fear in order to manipulate people into behavioral conformity.

We must remember that the NT contains this assertion:

All Scripture is inspired by God and profitable for teaching, for reproof, for correction, for training in righteousness; so that the man of God may be adequate, equipped for every good work. (2 Tim 3:16–17)

The Apostle Paul, the great communicator of God's grace and love, could not be any clearer. Psalm 76:11-12 is inspired and profitable for us today. So then, how can we see this in a way that is not just palatable, but also profitable for training in righteousness?

Taking vows, although minimized in the NT, was a common practice in the OT. When performing religious activity such as vows, God's people need to fulfill what they promise to do, what they say they are going to do. Jesus taught, "I say to you, make no oath at all … but let your statement be, 'Yes, yes' or 'No, no'; anything beyond these is of evil" (Matt 5:34, 37). James, the half-brother of Jesus, who wrote the book by the same name, emphasized this same thing and added a warning, "so that you may not fall under judgment" (James 5:12). God doesn't take duplicity or lip-service lightly.

Christians should be people of their word; they should say what they mean and mean what they say, and act consistently with their words. Did not Jesus reserve His harshest rebuke for hypocrites? "This people honors Me with their lips, but their heart is far away from Me" (Is 29:13). Yes, a person should fear God if he or she approaches God hypocritically. He is not a deity to be trifled with, presumed upon, mocked or patronized.

Search me, O God, and know my heart; try me and know my anxious thoughts; and see if there be any hurtful way in me, and lead me in the everlasting way (Ps 139:23–24).

WEEK 27, DAY 5

The One Who Goes With You

"Hear, O Israel, you are approaching the battle against your enemies today. Do not be fainthearted. Do not be afraid, or panic, or tremble before them, for the LORD your God is the one who goes with you, to fight for you against your enemies, to save you." (Deuteronomy 20:3–4)

Life is filled with battles. Children fight over toys; adolescents compete over athletics, appearances, popularity, gaming skills. Families battle over slights, selfishness, arrogance—the list goes go on. There are workplace power struggles and neighborhood fights over noisy parties, unkempt lawns, parking encroachments and boundary lines—all added to private battles against failing health, financial problems and personal demons. Yes, life is filled with battles.

This passage is a help to all who are "fainthearted," who are "afraid, or panic, or tremble" in the face of adversity. That means all of us at one time or another. Those who claim never to experience these kinds of reactions have a faux self-competence and would do well to learn from Israel, who went into battle without seeking the Lord's guidance or help, resulting in complete disaster and overwhelming hardship.

In today's passage, Israel—preparing to enter the Promised Land after 40 years in the desert—was being instructed on how to ready themselves for the expected battles. The conflicts would be intense, for the land was filled with extremely immoral, decadent people who had been settled there for centuries. God warned Israel, "... every abominable act which the LORD hates they have done for their gods; for they even burn their sons and daughters in the fire to their gods" (Deut 12:31). The people of Canaan would not go down easily.

Israel was not to fear or shrink back or try to avoid the conflict. They were rather to face up to it, for they were on a mission from God to take the land. They were to be on the offensive, not the defensive. They did not need to fear the battle because "the LORD your God is the one who goes with you, to fight for you against your enemies, to save you." They were to be certain of their mission and who was going with them: the Lord.

So also today, Christians have been commissioned to go out into the world to make disciples and have received the same promise from Jesus, " ... and lo, I am with you always, even to the end of the age" (Matt 28:18-20). No personal or interpersonal conflict can halt the progress of the Great Commission—nothing but fear of the battle. So let us not fear, for God is with us. Let us boldly move out into the world on our assignment from God.

Lord, I have nothing to fear, for You are with me. No battle can stop me.

WEEKEND 27 READING
Micah 4

PERSONAL REFLECTIONS

WEEK 28, DAY 1

The One Who Remembers

[God] remembered us in our low estate, for His lovingkindness is everlasting… (Psalm 136:23)

So glad God has a good memory. By good, I mean He remembers well according to His goodness. After all, Scripture does speak of His forgetfulness, in the sense that He chooses not to remember. "I, even I, am the one who wipes out your transgressions for My own sake, and I will not remember your sins" (Is 43:25, see also Jer 31:34).

But there are times when God's judgment is compared with human forgetfulness: "Why do You forget us forever? Why do You forsake us so long?" (Lam 5:20). His forgetting is not a case of cosmic amnesia, like someone forgetting where the car keys got left. This is, rather, a choice by God to treat people in a way that looks very much like God has forgotten them. Israel's sin had become so bad, and had tested God's patience to such a degree, that He treated them in a way that made them think He had forgotten them, as though He just didn't care enough about them to even think about them.

The psalm writer wrestles with this: "Why do You hide Your face and forget our affliction and our oppression?" (Ps 44:24). "How long, O LORD? Will You forget me forever? How long will You hide Your face from me?" (Ps 13:1). Nothing can be worse in a relationship than to feel marginalized, ignored, forgotten.

However, God, being gracious and merciful, will not maintain that posture forever, for His "knee-jerk" reaction is always to hear any human cry to Him for help. "For He who requires blood remembers them; He does not forget the cry of the afflicted" (Ps 9:12). "He remembered His covenant for their sake, and relented according to the greatness of His lovingkindness" (Ps 106:45).

We sometimes pray, "Lord, remember me …." We are not asking God to tie a string on His finger as a way to remind Himself at the appropriate time. We are asking God to make His presence active and come to help us. In reality, we don't need to tell God what to do; He is infinitely wise and gracious—we can be assured that He "is able to do far more abundantly beyond all that we ask or think, according to the power that works within us…" (Eph 3:20). We approach Him because He is "Our Father, who is in heaven," who from His perspective oversees all things. Therefore, our most simple prayer to Him is this: "Lord, remember me," just like the thief on the cross petitioned the Savior in anticipation of the kingdom (Luke 23:42). We may qualify this in various ways, but ultimately, we simply want Yahweh to remember us, as He promised.

Lord, remember me, that I might continue to live in Your blessing.

WEEK 28, DAY 2

The One Enthroned on High

From the rising of the sun to its setting the name of the LORD is to be praised. The LORD is high above all nations; His glory is above the heavens. Who is like the LORD our God, who is enthroned on high ... (Psalm 113:3–5)

God is up—we perceive this physically when we look up toward the sky in prayer or call out for help. The ancients tended to build their altars on mountain tops, giving the sense of being closer to deity. Abraham ascended Mt. Moriah to offer up Isaac, this place also being associated with the Jewish temple later built in Jerusalem. Moses went up to the top of Mt. Sinai to meet God for the giving of the Law. Isaiah's classic imagery conveys this as well: "In the year that King Uzziah died I saw the Lord sitting upon a throne, high and lifted up; and the train of His robe filled the temple" (Is 6:1 ESV, also NIV, NKJV). Yes, we are given to picture God as being "high."

Obviously, this "high" terminology is not meant to be directional, since that would change depending on one's geographical coordinates of observation. "High" means conceptually above the one contemplating God. He is superior to all human activity and thought, in every way:

> "For My thoughts are not your thoughts, nor are your ways My ways," declares the Lord. "For as the heavens are higher than the earth, so are My ways higher than your ways and My thoughts than your thoughts." (Is 55:8–9)

So we can understand in our passage today that "the LORD is high above all nations." No country on earth can thwart His sovereign plans or intentions. He is in absolute control. Solomon inferred this when he wrote, "The king's heart is like channels of water in the hand of the Lord; He turns it wherever He wishes" (Pr 21:1). So the inspired NT writer James instructs us to plan our lives this way, "If the Lord wills, we will live and also do this or that" (James 4:15).

God is not only sovereign above all, but He is also "above the heavens." No spiritual being is above Him to whom He is answerable. There is nothing greater than God. From an apologetic point of view, if there were an entity greater and higher than God, then that entity would be God. The only thing that has changed is our conception of God. As theologians have said, God is that which nothing is greater than. By definition, God, then, is greater than all else.

And finally, God is "enthroned on high." Therefore, we praise Him, the King of all creation, who is completely and perfectly worthy of our worship.

Lord, I worship You with all of my being as my exalted and lofty King.

WEEK 28, DAY 3

Priest

The LORD has sworn and will not change His mind, "You are a priest forever according to the order of Melchizedek." (Psalm 110:4)

This Melchizedek is an enigmatic character to most Bible readers. He is first mentioned in Genesis 14 as part of the biography of Abraham the patriarch, but interpreted and related to Jesus Christ in Hebrews 5:9-10 and chapter 7. Who exactly is he anyway? Long story short, we believe the best understanding is that Melchizedek was a preincarnate manifestation of Christ.

The story as originally told is rather non-descript in its original context. Melchizedek was a king in the ancient land of Canaan, whose possessions Abraham recovered along with Lot and his entourage. The king, whose name literally means "King of Righteousness," was the monarch of Salem. He was a priest, but obviously not part of the Levitical priesthood that came over 400 years later. What is noteworthy was that Abraham gave 10 percent of his spoils to Melchizedek—an odd thing, it would seem, for the man to whom God had given the pivotal promise of blessing that would affect the whole world.

Psalm 110 is the next time we see a reference in Scripture to Melchizedek, and it is one of the more well-quoted OT verses in the NT. It begins, "The LORD says to my Lord: 'Sit at My right hand until I make Your enemies a footstool for Your feet'" (Ps 110:1). Jesus Himself, in confounding the Pharisees who believed that the Messiah would be the son of David (Matt 22:42), asks, "If David [the writer of Psalm 110] then calls Him 'Lord,' how is He his son?" (Matt 22:45). Clearly, Jesus was inferring that the Messiah is Lord over David. For the Pharisees this was a dilemma, but the solution—which blind eyes cannot see, but is now revealed to those of faith—is that the Messiah is greater than David and is, in fact, David's Lord. That refers ultimately to Jesus Himself.

The writer to the Hebrews elucidates this very clearly, that this Melchizedek was:

Without father, without mother, without genealogy, having neither beginning of days nor end of life, but made like the Son of God, he remains a priest perpetually. (Heb 7:3)

He is able also to save forever those who draw near to God through Him, since He always lives to make intercession for them. (Heb 7:25).

In summary, Jesus Christ, our Messiah, was appointed to be our Priest, our one and only Intercessor. And this appointment came long before His earthly birth.

Lord, as Priest, You are my only mediator with God (1 Tim 2:5). Thank You.

WEEK 28, DAY 4

God of My Righteousness

Answer me when I call, O God of my righteousness! You have relieved me in my distress; be gracious to me and hear my prayer. (Psalm 4:1)

Calling out to a righteous God is a dangerous thing. Why would He want to help us who are sinners? We are not even in the same category of moral character. To be sure, we mere humans, being made in His image, can and do act at times benevolently and do the right things. But God's righteousness dwells in a category of an infinitely greater magnitude. He is not just more righteous than we are. Though the word "righteousness" is used in reference to both God and man, His righteousness is a quantum shift beyond ours. The prophet Habakkuk's fundamental miscalculation was this: he considered the Jews to be more righteous than the Chaldeans, the invaders whom God was planning to use to punish Israel (Hab 1:13) and considered himself to have a higher moral compass than God Himself:

> *Are You not from everlasting, O LORD, my God, my Holy One? We will not die. You, O LORD, have appointed them to judge; and You, O Rock, have established them to correct. Your eyes are too pure to approve evil, and You can not look on wickedness with favor. Why do You look with favor on those who deal treacherously? Why are You silent when the wicked swallow up those more righteous than they? (Hab 1:12–13)*

In our passage today, we find the psalm writer, David, calling out to "God of my righteousness." Certainly God is righteous, but the passage is not making that point. Nor is David saying, "The God who recognizes that I am righteous." For he knew that he was a sinner, falling far short of God's righteous standard. No, what he is saying is this: "I come to You, God, because You are the one who has made me righteous, the one who gives me righteousness." Anything David did that was righteous was because he served a righteous God. It is God who justifies, that is, who makes people righteous. What is obliquely seen in an OT passage like this is made clear in the NT. The apostle Paul wrote that God "demonstrate[d] … His righteousness at the present time, so that He would be just and the justifier of the one who has faith in Jesus" (Rom 3:26).

That is the kind of God we believe in, One who makes us righteous. No other conceptions of deity portray God in this way, and thus they consign people to the treadmill of trying to gain righteousness through their own good deeds. But as believers in the God of the Bible, we can approach Him as "God of my righteousness." We are confident that He has made us righteous.

Lord, God of my righteousness, I rest secure in being made right by You.

WEEK 28, DAY 5

Righteous God

"Declare and set forth your case; indeed, let them consult together. Who has announced this from of old? Who has long since declared it? Is it not I, the LORD? And there is no other God besides Me, a righteous God and a Savior; there is none except Me." (Is 45:21)

Righteousness is the goal of human religion: telling people how to be right with their deity. This rightness, or righteousness, comes through human effort to better oneself, to do what is right toward others. That concept is universal—that somehow a person's destiny and value relates to how he or she treats others. The so-called "Golden Rule" that Jesus spoke of in Luke 6:31, "Do to others what you would have them do for you," was not uncommon among ancient religions, though worded in different ways.

But with the God of the Bible we find a different kind of righteousness—one that is given, not earned. True, Jesus spoke of treating others well as a general life principle given by God. But He never spoke of righteousness as something we can earn through righteous efforts. He died on the cross because we all have failed in our standing before the Lord. That is why "God so loved the world that He gave His only begotten Son …" (John 3:16). The whole world needs God's salvation, because we are all failures in trying to gain it on our own. Our lives only prove that we are unrighteous.

What we need is a righteousness that comes to us from a perfectly righteous God. Pagan gods, so-called, had their foibles and portrayed very human tendencies, capable of capricious or revengeful behaviors. But the God of the Bible is perfect, high above human ways. His righteousness is perfect, absolute and never failing. Our only hope is found in this. For what would it mean to be righteous if God were not perfectly righteous? If there were any unrighteousness in Him, then we could never be sure that our sin would be done away with for eternity, that our "eternal life" was really eternal in length.

But He is righteous and never deals with us in an unrighteous way. We saw in Psalm 41:1 that He is "the God of my righteousness." Therefore, my righteousness is perfect also, because He is perfectly righteous. That does not mean that I walk perfectly or that I always the way God desires. But it means that God accepts me as perfectly right with Him. Sit back and think about that for a moment. What other god among the many religions in the world is like that, who gives us righteousness and before whom we can continually stand as righteous? God Himself says, "There is no other God besides Me, a righteous God and a Savior; there is none except Me."

Righteous Lord, I stand before You only because You have made me righteous.

WEEKEND 28 READING
Micah 5

PERSONAL REFLECTIONS

WEEK 29, DAY 1

Savior

Wondrously show Your lovingkindness, O Savior of those who take refuge at Your right hand from those who rise up against them. (Psalm 17:7)

How could one do a study of the names and epithets of God without commenting on one of the most frequently used terms for God as Savior? Often Christians refer to Jesus Christ in this way, but this was not an uncommonly used nom de deguerre (i.e. name or alias) for God in the OT as well. The term itself can be translated as "One who saves" (as in the NIV), but also as a noun (Savior).

Most often we tend to think of the word "save," from which the term Savior is derived, in terms of spiritual salvation, that is, an equivalent to redemption. We are saved from an eternity in hell. However, in the OT use of the concept, salvation can take on earthly connotations, as is the case of our passage today. God is the one whom His people trust to save them from particular difficulties, for example, physical harm from those who would oppress them.

In fact, God is referred to no fewer than 13 times in the OT as Savior. A simple concordance search reveals that title is reserved for Him only. God even asserts this about Himself: "I, even I, am the LORD, and there is no savior besides Me" (Is 43:11). "And there is no other God besides Me, a righteous God and a Savior; there is none except Me. (Is 45:21b). God saved them from bondage in Egypt (Ps 106:21, Hos 13:4), and He promised to save them from further captivity (Is 60:16).

So in his prayer to God, King David has absolute trust in the "Savior" of Israel and confidence that He will defend Israel against their enemies. Even more so, David could trust that God would be his personal savior against "my deadly enemies who surround me" (Ps 17:9). We can spiritualize this to refer to spiritual foes, but David lived in a rough-and-tumble tangible world. At times he feared for his life, and his prayers were down-to-earth cries for literal, physical salvation from the iminent threats against his life.

As Christians, certainly we are saved from the greatest threat to our lives: the eternal judgment of hell. But God is also interested in our earthly, physical lives. Do not our lives fill up with concerns about physical health, personal oppositions and threats to our financial well-being? God is the Savior in all these things as well. While He may not remove these difficulties, He saves us from being consumed by them and being knocked off our path of righteousness. We are secure in Him, because He is our Savior who loves us.

Lord, thank You for saving me from being overwhelmed by my circumstances.

WEEK 29, DAY 2

Shiloh

"The scepter shall not depart from Judah, nor the ruler's staff from between his feet, until Shiloh comes, and to him shall be the obedience of the peoples." (Genesis 49:10)

Located about 20 miles north of Jerusalem, the town of Shiloh was the place where the tabernacle and Ark of the Covenant were kept in the early days of the judges. It became the center of Jewish worship in the pre-Jerusalem days (Josh 18:1; 1 Sam 1:3, 3:3, 4:11). In Genesis 49:10, the underlying Hebrew word translated here as "Shiloh" can be translated "one who goes in to whom it belongs" (see NIV, ESV, NET). As usual, due to linguistic technicalities, deriving exact translations word for word into English can be challenging. Other translations, NASB and NKJV, take the term as a name, not to be confused with the city of the same name, soon to be discovered and occupied in the Promised Land.

In our passage today, the verse is found in the patriarch Jacob's blessing on his children, who were to become the heads of the 12 tribes of Israel. In particular, Judah was promised that one of his descendants would become king over all the tribes, the Jewish people, the nation that would one day be called Israel. This "Shiloh" (or "the one who comes") will "[tie] his foal to the vine, and his donkey's colt to the choice vine; He washes his garments in wine, and his robes in the blood of grapes" (Gen 49:11). At the same time, this coming One whom, with the NASB and NKJV, we may call Shiloh, would be a man of peace and man of war. The imagery is effusive. One cannot miss the echo years later in Zechariah's prophecy of the Messiah:

Rejoice greatly, O daughter of Zion! Shout in triumph, O daughter of Jerusalem! Behold, your king is coming to you; He is just and endowed with salvation, humble, and mounted on a donkey, even on a colt, the foal of a donkey. (Zec 9:9)

The Messiah will also come as a warrior:

"The scepter shall not depart from Judah, nor the ruler's staff from between his feet, until Shiloh comes, and to him shall be the obedience of the peoples." (Gen 49:10)

So, whether Shiloh is a name or not, there is One coming, promised from the time of the Patriarchs, who will bring peace and victory. That One will prove to be King Jesus, to whom all will someday bow (Matt 21:2, Phil 2:9-11).

Lord, my life is rooted in the belief that You are coming back for Your own.

WEEK 29, DAY 3

Sun

Behold our shield, O God, and look upon the face of Your anointed. For a day in Your courts is better than a thousand outside. I would rather stand at the threshold of the house of my God than dwell in the tents of wickedness. For the LORD God is a sun and shield; the LORD gives grace and glory; no good thing does He withhold from those who walk uprightly. (Psalm 84:9–11)

Discovering the meaning of a word is part etymology (the study of the way word meanings change over time) and part usage. In Psalm 84:9-11, the basic meaning of the word "sun" is that yellow ball in the sky. In context, the word is obviously being used metaphorically.

We can easily jump to the idea that the LORD God brings brightness to our lives. But it is more than that, when we consider the rich context. We must remember that light and dark are a common antithesis in Scripture. From the first days of creation, God separated out the light from the dark (Gen 1:1-4). In the Gospel According to John, this dichotomy is seen in John 8:12, 12:35, 12:46. So the contrast in Scripture is stark.

Paul writes of this most notably: "Do not be bound together with unbelievers; for what partnership have righteousness and lawlessness, or what fellowship has light with darkness?" (2 Cor 6:14). In this sense, the psalmist writes, "I would rather stand at the threshold of the house of my God than dwell in the tents of wickedness." He would rather "look upon the face of Your anointed" than to see in the darkness. There is absolutely no comparison with being in God's presence ("courts"); it's a thousand times better than anything else. To be in God's presence is to bask in His "grace and glory."

Why, knowing all this, would anyone want to live any other lifestyle than one that God would describe as "walk[ing] uprightly"? Why would one want to live in the darkness, where things are difficult to see, when one can live in the bright sunlight, with clear sight? Why would anyone desire to grope through life, stumbling over worldly enchantments and sins that feed the dark side of the soul, when one could dance along with clear purpose and perspective?

We believe, with the psalm writer, that "no good thing does He withhold from those who walk uprightly." When life gets difficult, when God seems to be silent, when He appears to be AWOL, faith means continuing to believe He will still reward us with "good thing[s]." We believe He is good when our circumstances would whisper to us that He is not. Why? Because by faith we choose to see as clearly as the noonday sun Him who will guide our footsteps and continue to infuse us with His purpose for us.

Lord, You are the Sun of my life, and through You I can see more clearly.

WEEK 29, DAY 4

Sun of Righteousness

"But for you who fear My name, the sun of righteousness will rise with healing in its wings; and you will go forth and skip about like calves from the stall." (Malachi 4:2)

Contrasted with the previous verse, we who believe have a spring in our step, so to speak, causing us to "skip" through life. For the unbeliever, the Scripture is stark:

"For behold, the day is coming, burning like a furnace; and all the arrogant and every evildoer will be chaff; and the day that is coming will set them ablaze," says the LORD of hosts, "so that it will leave them neither root nor branch." (Mal 4:1)

Whereas those without faith have no good prospect, believers have everything to look forward to. The imagery is that of a new morning portraying a healing from yesterday's pain. We are reminded of another passage:

"For His anger is but for a moment, His favor is for a lifetime; weeping may last for the night, but a shout of joy comes in the morning." (Ps 30:5)

There is much in this world to get us down: personal illness and pain, relationship struggles, financial stress, internal conflicts, painful memories, personal or sexual abuse, and the list goes on. We could include those difficulties that result from our personal failings. Possibly the greatest character pain is found in the proverb, "Pride goes before destruction, and a haughty spirit before stumbling" (Pr 16:18). All these weigh down the soul; no amount of worldly soothing or anesthetics of alcohol or drugs can dull the soul pain that all these things bring. Apart from God, these things all continue every day with no relief.

But for those "who fear My name," who trust in God, they "will rise with healing" because God is their "sun of righteousness." Morning will bring joy, not just another day. The skeptical Christian, tired of the so-called "clichés," sometimes times throws out God's promises onto the trash heap of "well-intentioned, but misguided" advice. "Give up, and curse God, for He obviously has it in for you," suggested Job's wife (Job 2:9). His judgment is severe.

But for those who "fear" the Lord, who live according to God's righteousness, the Lord infuses life in their steps. Despite the most miserable gloom around them, their reason to get up in the morning is to bask in the Sun, the God who will not condemn them.

Lord, I throw back the curtains of unbelief and rest in Your warm acceptance.

WEEK 29, DAY 5

Sustainer of My Soul

Behold, God is my helper; the Lord is the sustainer of my soul. (Psalm 54:4)

Just when difficulties calm down, tragedy strikes unexpectedly and sometimes repeatedly. Many people can handle one or two difficulties in life, but at times it seems the enemy of our souls relentlessly assaults and abuses, like he did Job. It is clear that Job saw his divine Maker not as his helper or the sustainer of his soul, but rather as a silent adversary. This mere man wanted God to present Himself like a man so that Job (or we) could have it out with Him. But instead, God resorted to tactics in His dealing with Job that can only be described as unfair. After all, what chance did Job or anyone have when contending with God, since He is God and we are not?

The psalmist, David, was no stranger to difficulties. To some, his life may seem charmed: at an early age he was recognized for his handsome looks and prowess in battle, whether with a lion or with Goliath (1 Sam 17:37, 50), and he was tabbed for his musical ability to serve King Saul of Israel. Yet he was the youngest of eight sons, demeaned by his older brothers, falsely accused by Saul, and even physically threatened by that insecure and possibly mentally deranged monarch who threw spears at him in unfounded rage. David fled to a cave from Saul, fearing for his life.

No, David's life was not charmed—he had more than his share of difficulties. But he was a man who was striving after God's heart. He learned at an early age that his Lord was trustworthy and would not fail him. Lean, lay, rest, – these are alternative suggestions for the response of one who is sustained (as inferred from the root of the Hebrew word here rendered "sustainer"). He is the One who will not only help us in a given instances of need, but sustain us for the long haul. We can lean on Him. He will support us unshakably. When He sustains us, we shall be unmovable.

Back in the day, we used to hear people say Christianity is a crutch for people who can't make it in the world. Rather than cower before such insults to our faith, someone devised a witty response: "If faith is a crutch, then I will have as many crutches as I can get." Only the supremely arrogant think they do not need supernatural help from Him. It is an amazingly foolish thing to say—on the order of an atheist who asserts, "There is no God" (Ps 14:1, 53:1).

But for us who believe, we do not have to face life's difficulties alone or battle the enemy from a weak position. We have One who sustains us when we are down, tired, discouraged and ready to give up. All we need is to believe God and take Him at His Word. He is my helper and the sustainer of my soul.

Lord, sustain me now and in the coming time, for the battle is hard and long.

WEEKEND 29 READING
Micah 6

PERSONAL REFLECTIONS

WEEK 30, DAY 1

God of Retribution

For the destroyer is coming against her, against Babylon, and her mighty men will be captured, their bows are shattered; for the LORD is a God of recompense, He will fully repay. (Jeremiah 51:56)

Trifling with God is not a good thing. In fact, it is quite dangerous to treat God in any way except with fear. By fear, I don't mean frightfulness, but a full appreciation that God is a loving Father who will not hesitate to react strongly to sin, injustice and distortion of the truth. The word used here in the NASB and most other English translations is "recompense" and is translated "retribution" in the NIV. It can mean either "reward" or "punishment" based on what a person deserves. In this case, Jeremiah warns of the divine consequences against Babylon for its violence against Israel. There will be a just payback—God will see to that!

In today's popular Christian culture, God is seen in one dimension as loving. But He is also just. The Law wasn't just an arbitrary standard—it reflects His holiness. To oppose God's people or His Law was tantamount to going against God Himself. And He is no pushover.

The nations and rulers of Psalm 2 who "take counsel together against the LORD and against His Anointed ..." are faced with this terse retort: "He who sits in the heavens laughs, the Lord scoffs at them. Then He will speak to them in His anger and terrify them in His fury..." (Ps 2:2, 4-5). Lest we think this is only for kings of nations, we read, "He who mocks the poor taunts his Maker; he who rejoices at calamity will not go unpunished" (Pr 17:5).

Lest we also think this is just an OT portrayal of God and the NT has a more kindly, gentle depiction, the letter of Paul that exalts the Gospel of grace puts it this way: "Do not be deceived, God is not mocked; for whatever a man sows, this he will also reap" (Gal 6:7).

Hinduism's karma views one's life as forming the basis of future consequences, either good or bad. In one sense, the Bible says something similar: there are consequences for your actions. However, the difference is this: in Hinduism, the connection is based simply on an impersonal principle. In the Bible, the connection is based on a personal, divine causation. When we reap what we sow, it is because God has intended this to be, and He is personally involved in causing the consequences to happen. That is why God sometimes withholds those just consequences. That is called mercy. However, we dare not presume upon God's mercy, for He can be a terrifying force in our lives when we push against Him.

Lord, thanks for Your overwhelming mercy; without it, I would be destroyed.

WEEK 30, DAY 2

The Lord Who Heals

And [God] said, "If you will give earnest heed to the voice of the LORD your God, and do what is right in His sight, and give ear to His commandments, and keep all His statutes, I will put none of the diseases on you which I have put on the Egyptians; for I, the LORD, am your healer." (Exodus 15:26)

This was an ancient promise to the people of Israel as they were being led out of the land of Egypt on their way to the Promised Land. Healing is a big subject in the Bible, as anyone with even a cursory familiarity with it will know. It is something we all desire for ourselves and those we love; we pray for it and even beg God for it. Yet here, God promises it before or apart from anyone asking for it. We might be tempted to interpret this to mean that God may be more interested in healing us than we are ourselves!

God's greater concern, though, is our obedience. Healing is secondary to Him. Our priorities should be the same. Why do we not passionately desire obedience as much as we desire health, physical comfort, financial prosperity, prideful recognition, revenge or self-sufficiency?

The people of Israel had front row seats to God's amazing power to inflict what we have called "plagues" on Egypt, 10 in all. There were boils, infestations, various "natural" phenomena and even death. Those must have been amazing times. We wonder how the Israelites could hesitate to obey the God who caused all that to happen and protected Israel from it all. But God knew that His people would continually turn away. So they were not free from the diseases that Egypt experienced.

Still, we must not forget that God defines Himself as Yahweh the Healer. Think about that for a moment. Sin is the greatest sickness, for it leads to spiritual death. Humankind contracted it when Adam and Eve ate from the tree against God's explicit command (Gen 2:17). This genetic illness of sinful rebellion against God has been passed down to all people, for we all have descended from that first couple. We are all guilty of the same problem. Yet God did not abandon us. He has offered healing to all who "obey" Him—healing from our greatest illness.

So we pray to God for healing today, and rightly so. We find great hope in "The LORD who heals." Why He doesn't always heal is a great mystery. Maybe it is our disobedience, or maybe it's a timing issue, a "not yet" sort of thing. Or possibly we must patiently wait for the ultimate healing when we graduate to glory. However, our greater concern should be why we don't always obey now.

Lord, I set as my priority to obey You, more so than seeking healing.

WEEK 30, DAY 3

My Tower of Strength

For You have been a refuge for me, a tower of strength against the enemy. (Psalm 61:3)

God is our strength and stronghold (Ps 18:1-2). He is, further, our Tower of Strength. We can't get enough of this truth that God is strong for us and will make us strong. Technically, we might observe that a tower is a structure taller than its diameter or width, and God is without dimension. But the term tower here suggests an imposing, impregnable building in a fortified enclosure. This is a defensive construction that provides security—both from its sheer height, which makes is virtually unscalable, and from its lofty vantage point from which to launch a counterattack on approaching enemies.

Today in our western world, enemies come in many forms. There are physical threats like a home invasion, road rage or even a physical confrontation of some sort. God is a tower of strength in those situations, to allow the believer to react calmly and with strength. While the Lord can certainly provide physical, superhuman strength, as some Christian legends convey, most often He provides an inner strength to enable us to respond wisely to those threats against our person.

But bullying, which is at the fore of our societal consciousness today, can be a real threat. The old childhood jingle, "Sticks and stones may break my bones, but words will never harm me," doesn't quite ring true anymore. Words can be like daggers that drive deep to our insecurities, inciting our fears. Could this be what David meant when he wrote, "My soul is among lions; I must lie among those who breathe forth fire, even the sons of men, whose teeth are spears and arrows and their tongue a sharp sword" (Ps 57:4, see also Ps 22:12-13)? Against this, we have a God who is our Tower of Strength.

The devil also is our enemy, along with his minions, constantly prowling around like a roaring lion looking to destroy God's people (1 Peter 5:8). How does he do this? By tempting us to sin, by leading us to question God's sovereignty or goodness. "Did God really say …?" (Gen 3:1 NIV). He tempts us with lies: Maybe God is not sovereign and we don't really need to obey Him, or maybe He is not able to do what He says He will do. Maybe He is sovereign, but He is not so good after all. Maybe He is out to get me for no reason at all.

But to use the illustration in our passage, a lion cannot jump the height of our Tower of Strength. How high is that? Did not Jesus tell us to pray like this: "Our Father, who is in heaven…"? That's a tall tower! Satan is like an ant in comparison.

Lord, I look to You for protection against all that I fear, especially today.

WEEK 30, DAY 4

My Witness

Then Jonathan said to David, "The LORD, the God of Israel, be witness! When I have sounded out my father about this time tomorrow, or the third day, behold, if there is good feeling toward David, shall I not then send to you and make it known to you?" (1 Samuel 20:12)

Jonathan wanted to assure his friend David about what he was going to do. So to emphasize the certainty of his plan, that David could bet his life on it, he said, "The LORD, the God of Israel, be witness!" Today in the United States, in a court of law, a witness takes an oath that traditionally goes like this: "Do you swear to tell the truth, the whole truth, and nothing but the truth, so help you God?" This comes from the biblical concept of calling on God as witness to the truth of a statement, as Jonathan does in our passage.

A person of faith should not need any oaths (Matt 5:37) but should be one "who walks with integrity … and speaks truth in his heart" (Ps 15:2). The seventh commandment says, "You shall not bear false witness" (Ex 20:16). But Jonathan wanted David to know the depth of his commitment to David's safety.

The knowledge that God is a witness to all that we do provides a strong motivation in our behavior.

> *"For the eyes of the LORD move to and fro throughout the earth that He may strongly support those whose heart is completely His." (2 Chron 16:9)*

He is always watching; He knows our hearts and thoughts:

> *"O LORD, You have searched me and known me. You know when I sit down and when I rise up; You understand my thought from afar. You scrutinize my path and my lying down, and are intimately acquainted with all my ways." (Ps 139:1–3)*

There is no escaping the all-present God; He is our constant witness, watching everything we do and think. This can strike fear in the hearts of those who sin, but for those who rest in His love, this truth provides comfort and encouragement. We are not forgotten or unseen. Even when no one else is around, in the quiet of our home or even in the solitude of our minds, God is still there. Our character and integrity still matter, even when no other human can see us. God can. He is a witness to our entire life.

So yes, the whole world is a stage—not for others to watch us perform for them, but for God to watch us live for Him and reflect His glory. His eyes are intently watching the play called "This is My Life."

Lord, I live and perform only for You, my one and most important audience.

WEEK 30, DAY 5

My Keeper

The LORD is your keeper; the LORD is your shade on your right hand. The sun will not smite you by day, nor the moon by night. The LORD will protect you from all evil; He will keep your soul. (Psalm 121:5–7)

Cain's angry retort to God reflected his contempt of Abel and his sacrifice. And God's answer was that yes, he was in fact his brother's keeper—at least at the horizontal level, human to human, sibling to sibling. That was implied in the time of Adam and Eve's sons (Cain should have known), and it was explicitly stated in Jesus' teaching much later: "You shall love your neighbor as yourself" (Matt 22:39).

But this harmonious, self-giving concern for others, being our "brother's keeper," goes against our self-centered nature as fallen sinners. That is God's design—He commanded it—but it has been problematic since the days of Eden.

The good news is that God's commands reflect His character. In this case, we are to be one another's keepers because God is our ultimate keeper. According to the standard Hebrew lexicons, the word "keeper" used here means "one who keeps, watches, preserves us from injury, harm or danger." Now God does not protect us from everything. Standing out in the summer sun too long can bring a sunburn. Faithful Christians do get into accidents. God-honoring Christians do sometimes experience abuse.

But note that "He will keep your soul," using the same root word as "keeper." No matter the external difficulties, God will keep our souls. This is not so much a statement of eternal security (although we believe that promise from the Lord is taught elsewhere in Scripture), but a statement of preservation of our soul's wellbeing.

What do we mean by that? The apostle Paul put it this way: "Therefore we do not lose heart, but though our outer man is decaying, yet our inner man is being renewed day by day" (2 Cor 4:16). Despite our circumstances, whatever difficulty we encounter, no matter how long our trial lasts, we can maintain our spiritual equilibrium with the comforting truth that God is our Keeper. People will fail us, friends forsake us, but He will never leave nor forsake us (Heb 13:5). He is the Keeper who never fails.

When we are down, He picks us up. When we feel left out, He includes us. When we are discouraged, He encourages us through the ministering work of His Holy Spirit. When no human way out seems possible, He sustains us. "If God is for us, who is against us?" (Rom 8:31). In the midst of our trials, we can rest in God, for He is our Keeper.

Lord, my wonderful Keeper, I rest in You and will not be afraid.

WEEKEND 30 READING
Micah 7

PERSONAL REFLECTIONS

WEEK 31, DAY 1

My Shade

The LORD is your keeper; the LORD is your shade on your right hand. The sun will not smite you by day, nor the moon by night. The LORD will protect you from all evil; He will keep your soul. (Psalm 121:5–7)

Related to the Lord being our keeper, He is also our Shade. We take this as a metaphor to convey that God protects us from that which is normally good for us, but can destroy us if we get too much. This probably does not refer to the Lord providing an atmosphere around the earth that protects us from harmful radiation—that would be beyond the scope of understanding for the ancient pre-scientific people of Israel. Rather, a shade is that which protects against light that is unwanted or, in this case, harmful.

We take for granted that the sun is needed for a comfortable life. Plants use the sun for a biological process called photosynthesis to produce plant growth for food, which is crucial to the entire earthly ecosystem. Exposure to the sun increases vitamin D in the human blood stream (Webmed.com). Of course, the sun provides warmth so that we humans can live comfortably.

However, the sun is dangerous, and our placement in the solar system must be precise or else we would burn up or die of the cold. Mars and Venus, our closest planetary neighbors, are too cold or too hot respectively for human life. On earth, with too much unprotected exposure, the sun can not only burn human skin, but also cause dehydration, heatstroke and sun stroke – all of which can be deadly if not treated. The sun can cause blindness, as every child is reminded when a solar eclipse comes around. Life is tolerable on this planet because there is shade to moderate the sun's effects. Shade comes in the form of clouds, sunglasses, sunscreen, umbrellas, tinted windows, curtains, and opaque objects of all sorts. The most notable shade in the Bible is probably the one provided by God for Jonah when he was angry with God for forgiving the Ninevites (Jonah 4:6-8). When God removed the shade of the tree, "the sun beat down on Jonah's head so that he became faint and begged with all his soul to die, saying, 'Death is better to me than life'" (Jonah 4:6–8).

God provides shade from many good things that would otherwise destroy us in their overabundance. For example, God provides us with encouragement from others but protects us from too much that would feed our pride. When others fail to encourage us as we think we might need, this causes us to look to God for our encouragement. His shading reminds us that only He can ultimately encourage us enough to sustain our souls, for He is our Keeper and our Shade.

Lord, I praise You for protecting me from things that would burn my soul.

WEEK 31, DAY 2

God ("Theos")

In the beginning was the Word, and the Word was with God, and the Word was God. (John 1:1)

New Testament references to God in general use the generic Greek term for deity, "Theos." Employed some 1,400 times in the Bible (give or take depending on the English translation), the term predominantly (with few exceptions, such as Acts 17:23 and 19:26) points to the same deity as that of the Old Testament. It is the default term used for God in the standard Scripture of Jesus' day, the Greek translation of the OT, which today we call the Septuagint or LXX. In Genesis 1 ("In the beginning God created …"), God shows in the Hebrew text as "Elohim" and in the Septuagint as "Theos." This is the case throughout the OT. So when Jesus and the gospel writers used the term "Theos" they were not referring to a new God, but to Elohim, whose name is Yahweh. All the names, epithets and name combinations of the OT carry over to "Theos" of the NT.

So when the apostle John begins his gospel account, he poignantly and succinctly packs great truth into one sentence. He speaks of "the Word" as being "in the beginning." One is hard pressed not to see the allusion to Genesis 1:1, the start of the entire Bible: "In the beginning God created the heavens and the earth." To Jewish minds this was startling—such a bold proclamation. Granted, at the time of John's writing this near the close of the first century, Christian teaching had become fairly widespread, and the shock effect of this teaching may have been tempered a bit. But the scandal of it would not have diminished. Whatever John was about to write in his account of the Gospel of Jesus Christ was irrevocably connected to and identified with Elohim, the one and only sovereign God of the universe, who became known as Yahweh—the One who would phenomenally and actively be present for His people in the way they would need Him to be.

This was the God (Theos) over all people, not just the Jews. In Athens, Paul debated the Greek philosophers and staked out the divine turf:

For while I was passing through and examining the objects of your worship, I also found an altar with this inscription, 'TO AN UNKNOWN GOD.' Therefore what you worship in ignorance, this I proclaim to you. The God who made the world and all things in it … (Acts 17:23–24)

As NT believers we hold that the One we worship is the supreme Creator God over everything, the absolute Theos, above whom there is no other.

Lord, I worship You as the one and only true God. There is no other.

WEEK 31, DAY 3

God the Word ("Logos")

In the beginning was the Word, and the Word was with God, and the Word was God. (John 1:1)

Pivotal between the OT and NT, this verse packs a huge punch, being significant on several levels. While the Gospel According to John holds fourth place in the standard arrangement of the NT canon, it presents the story from John's perspective in continuity with the OT.

The term "gospel" does not technically refer to the book, as people today popularly refer to the first four books of the NT (e.g. "There are four gospels: Matthew, Mark, Luke and John.") There is one, and only one, Gospel: the story of the good news of Jesus Christ. The earliest titles of the four books were "According to Matthew," "According to Mark," etc. Each one starts at the beginning. Matthew, Mark and Luke are often referred to as the "synoptics" because they cover many of the same incidents of Jesus' life and ministry and have a great many similarities in presentation. They all begin with the start of Jesus' earthly life. But the Gospel According to John is different in many ways, and begins at the beginning of all things, similar to Genesis 1:1.

The central figure of the story is, of course, Jesus. The writer of our passage today, John, focuses in his account on only seven of the miracle stories but provides a great amount of commentary for each. He writes with simple Greek grammatical construction and vocabulary but conveys lofty concepts. Most likely, he wrote many years after the three other accounts were penned, and being aware of their writings, he wanted to give not just a different emphasis but a much deeper understanding of Christ in His divinity.

So he begins with an identity statement. Now it is clear that "the Word" refers to Jesus Christ: "The Word became flesh, and dwelt among us, and we saw His glory, glory as of the only begotten from the Father, full of grace and truth" (John 1:14). But why describe Him as "the Word" ("logos")? Much has been written on this subject. A common understanding comes from the Greek philosophical context that sees "logos" as the ultimate controlling principle that animates all living things. While there may be some hints of this usage in John's writings, he himself was not educated in the philosophic writings of the secular thinkers of the ancient world. Remember, he was a simple fisherman by trade. While Greek philosophy had indeed saturated Roman culture during John's day, he was more a child of Hebrew thought. And together with the many parallels in his gospel account with the OT stories, it is best to understand the meaning of Christ being "the Word" in the Jewish context.

Lord, thank You for preserving the written Word, the four gospel accounts.

WEEK 31, DAY 2

The Word in the Beginning

In the beginning was the Word, and the Word was with God, and the Word was God. (John 1:1)

Eternality is the first of three assertions made about "the Word," which as we see from John 1:14 is Jesus Christ, who is the "Word became flesh." In the beginning Jesus Christ existed. A whole volume could be written on this, but we are limited to this short space. Whenever "the beginning" took place, Christ was there in existence. Philosophers wrestle with the concept of time. A common understanding is that time is simply a measure of change. If there were no change then there would be no time. Albert Einstein introduced the concept of time being relative, depending on speed and mass of an object. Interestingly, the Bible presents God as unchanging (therefore, time is not a category by which to define God), and He is not relative to anything else, being the one supreme constant in existence.

So what then is meant by "in the beginning"? This could only mean that at the point of creation, when things came into existence, Christ already existed. Further, Christ must have always existed, for if there was a point when He came into existence, then He could not have existed at the beginning, but He would have come into existence at the beginning. So He must have existed before the beginning. At this point, being constrained by our place in time, we stretch beyond all logic the use of the time words to describe the existence of Christ. Therefore, we conclude that Christ is ever-existing, eternal in His very nature. He exists apart from or outside of time.

We can see this truth of the eternality of Christ in various places in Scripture. Probably this is what the writer of Hebrews meant when addressing the enigmatic character Melchizedek, "Without father, without mother, without genealogy, having neither beginning of days nor end of life, but made like the Son of God, he remains a priest perpetually" (Heb 7:3). Paul appealed to Christ's timelessness when he wrote, "[God] chose us in Him [Christ] before the foundation of the world ..." (Eph 1:4).

Further, when God created the universe, take note—He spoke it into existence. The mean use of words began the sequence of change in the universe that we call time. The Word was His means for doing it. To monotheistic minds, this was huge. There is no question, John's gospel account presents Jesus as God, Elohim of the OT, the Creator God of the universe. No wonder they repeatedly tried to kill Him with the charge, "You, being a man, make Yourself out to be God" (John 10:33).

Lord Jesus Christ, I believe You are the Creator of all; I humbly submit to You.

WEEK 31, DAY 5

The Word with God

In the beginning was the Word, and the Word was with God, and the Word was God. (John 1:1)

Not only was the Word in the beginning, but more precisely, the Word was "with God." There was never a time when Christ, who is the Word, was not with God. Here is the first use of the Greek word "Theos" in John's gospel account. One of the last times John uses this word is in recording Thomas' acknowledging Jesus as "[m]y Lord and my God!" (John 20:28). John himself explains why he wrote his account the way he did, "so that you may believe that Jesus is the Christ, the Son of God; and that believing you may have life in His name" (John 20:31).

To be "with God" implies both proximity and purpose. When we say, "I'm with you on that," we mean, "I agree fully." Christ was and is in perfect alignment with God. He said, "I and the Father are one" (John 10:30). Christ was not just a bystander from eternity past while God was doing His thing. He was involved; He was unified with God in all those activities.

This unity involves more than just activities; there is complete harmony of purpose and intention. Jesus said, "My food is to do the will of Him who sent Me and to accomplish His work" (John 4:34). Further, "I can do nothing on My own initiative. As I hear, I judge; and My judgment is just, because I do not seek My own will, but the will of Him who sent Me" (John 5:30).

But this unity goes back all the way to the beginning. It wasn't just God's plan that He then delegated to Christ. As long as there has been time, Christ was in league with God, fully participating in the inner counsels and recesses of the Godhead. In no way was or is He inferior to God in His essence. Certainly, we may see role differentiation in what we have come to call the Trinity, but in the essential nature of God, Christ is indistinguishable. He was "with God." While we may be tempted to see in this an implication of separation, the thrust of these simple words has more to do with concord and harmony. Any doubt about this is removed in the next phrase (which we will address shortly).

The picture at this point is that the Word, namely Jesus Christ, is eternally existent, and His existence relates closely to God in His eternity and purposes. Even at this point, we find it incredulous that anyone could deny the implications that Jesus Christ, the Word, is in fact, fully divine, fully God—that is, not only was the Word with God, but "the Word was God." Next we shall examine this final statement in John 1:1.

Lord, I want to be unified with Your purposes, just like You are unified with God's purposes.

WEEKEND 31 READING
Nahum 1

PERSONAL REFLECTIONS

WEEK 32, DAY 1

The Word Was God

In the beginning was the Word, and the Word was with God, and the Word was God. (John 1:1)

One of the clearest statements on the deity of Jesus Christ is found in this simple statement, "and the Word was God." It is entirely clear and without any confusion that "the Word" refers to Jesus Christ (John 1:14), and the word "God" comes from the Greek word "Theos," the standard word for deity in the NT. Yet some deny the deity of Christ, or at least deny identifying Christ as the incarnate Elohim of the OT. They appeal to the Greek language behind the English text. A certain translation in a cultic version of the Bible reads, "The Word was a god." To a beginning Greek student or uninformed Greek reader, this might seem convincing. However, no reputable Greek scholar would agree. Even non-Christian Greek scholars looking at this objectively would agree that "the Word was God" is the proper translation.

In the interest of apologetics, we can admit that the statement "the Word was a god" is true, even if it is not a correct translation. Jesus was, in fact, a god. This begs the question, then, if He was a god ("theos"), but not the God of the OT (who presumably still existed in the NT times), then there must be more than one god. A certain cult today is quick to point out where Jesus quoted Psalm 82:6, "Has it not been written in your Law, 'I said, you are gods'?" (John 10:34). Jesus was attempting (quite successfully) to trip up the Jewish leaders who were trying to condemn Him for blasphemy. A full exegesis of that interaction goes beyond the scope of our purposes here, but suffice it to say, the interchange was going far deeper than meets the eye. The Jewish leaders had been putting themselves on the level of God, and thus over the Word of God, and ultimately over Christ, who, as John makes clear, was God.

John 1:1, in its fullest meaning, would be preposterous if Jesus were not the God of the Bible, if He were some lesser divine being. He was there at the beginning, He was with God, and He was divine. He is therefore in the same category of existence as the Creator God of the universe, Elohim of the OT. If He were just a man or a lesser divine being, this claim would be absurd. Either John would be assaulting the strict monotheism that was endemic to the Jewish faith, or he would be committing a gross blasphemy by claiming Christ, a mere man, was on the same level as God. The only reasonable and consistent interpretation of this beginning of John's gospel account is that Jesus is fully God, and He was in the beginning with God—for He was, in fact, God Himself.

Lord, I fully embrace that Jesus my Lord is God in the flesh!

WEEK 32, DAY 2

The Word Was [the only] God

In the beginning was the Word, and the Word was with God, and the Word was God. (John 1:1)

Further supporting the full and unique deity of Christ, we simply observe other Scripture that consistently upholds this idea:

Before Me there was no God formed, and there will be none after Me. I, even I, am the LORD, And there is no savior besides Me. (Is 43:10–11)

Thus says the LORD, the King of Israel and his Redeemer, the LORD of hosts: 'I am the first and I am the last, and there is no God besides Me.' (Is 44:6)

I am the LORD, and there is no other; besides Me there is no God. I will gird you, though you have not known Me; that men may know from the rising to the setting of the sun that there is no one besides Me. I am the LORD, and there is no other. (Is 45:6)

I am the LORD, and there is none else. (Is 45:18)

Remember the former things long past, for I am God, and there is no other; I am God, and there is no one like Me. (Is 46:9)

Listen to Me, O Jacob, even Israel whom I called; I am He, I am the first, I am also the last. Surely My hand founded the earth, and My right hand spread out the heavens; when I call to them, they stand together. (Is 48:12–13)

Behold, I [Jesus] am coming quickly, and My reward is with Me, to render to every man according to what he has done. I am the Alpha and the Omega, the first and the last, the beginning and the end. (Rev 22:12–13)

For it was the Father's good pleasure for all the fullness to dwell in Him [Christ]. (Col 1:19)

For in Him [Christ] all the fullness of Deity dwells in bodily form. (Col 2:9)

Thomas answered and said to Him, "My Lord and my God!" (John 20:28)

And He [Christ] is the radiance of His [God's] glory and the exact representation of His nature ... (Heb 1:3)

> Lord Jesus, You are my Lord and my God. I worship You as the supreme Creator of the universe. Let all the angels witness my testimony.

WEEK 32, DAY 3

The LORD God, the Almighty

And the four living creatures, each one of them having six wings, are full of eyes around and within; and day and night they do not cease to say, "HOLY, HOLY, HOLY is THE LORD GOD, THE ALMIGHTY, WHO WAS AND WHO IS AND WHO IS TO COME." (Revelation 4:8)

Mysterious as the book of Revelation is, some things are quite evident. The book depicts the end times and focuses on Christ's return for the cosmic battle against the forces of evil, culminating in the ushering in of the new heaven and earth. The theme: Christ will be completely victorious, and God will reign forever and ever.

In this great apocalyptic prophecy, "Christ" and "God" are both distinguished and identified indistinguishably—not surprising given the nature of the Trinity and incarnation. For our purposes here, the names of God, we see one sitting on a throne, "The LORD God, the Almighty" (repeated at least seven other times in Revelation). The angels echo the praises of their counterparts in Isaiah 6:3, where clearly Yahweh is in view. The angels continue to "give glory and honor and thanks to Him who sits on the throne, to Him who lives forever and ever…"

At the same time, we find "the Lamb in the center of the throne" (Rev 7:17) and repeated phrases like "a river of the water of life, clear as crystal, coming from the throne of God and of the Lamb" (Rev 22:1). Considering the sharing of other epithets such as "the beginning and the end" and the "alpha and omega" (Rev 1:8, 21:6, 22:13), we can see that the Lamb, Jesus Christ, is clearly being presented as God, and in particular, the Lord God, the Almighty.

Some might quibble theologically that the distinction between the Lamb and God is more dominant than the identification of the two. Relative dominance is really a side issue, but is only important to those who struggle with the concept of the Trinity. But the Bible teaches that Jesus Christ, the Son of God, is clearly God. He is the Lord God, the Almighty. He may distinguish His roles and His place in the Trinity, but there is one God, not three. And He exists in three persons. Church councils wrestled with this concept, but Christians through the centuries have accepted and believed it as a settled matter, and the deity of Christ is central to Christian theology and thinking.

To our point, the Lord Jesus Christ is the Lord (Yahweh) God of the Bible. If He were not, then the book of Revelation would be grossly blasphemous in exalting Christ to God's throne and extolling Him as worthy of the praise that is only due to Yahweh, God of Israel.

Lord Jesus, mysterious as it seems, I worship You as my Lord and my God.

WEEK 32, DAY 4

The Lord Jesus Christ

Since we have heard that some of our number to whom we gave no instruction have disturbed you with their words, unsettling your souls, it seemed good to us, having become of one mind, to select men to send to you with our beloved Barnabas and Paul, men who have risked their lives for the name of our Lord Jesus Christ. (Acts 15:24–26)

The name and full title of the one we believe in, follow and worship is "the Lord Jesus Christ." This exact phrasing in the original language occurs 33 times in the NT, and in modified form "the name of the Lord Jesus" many more times. But the full version includes three terms of significance.

First, He is Lord. That means He is the supreme authority over our lives. Paul counsels Timothy to "keep the commandment without stain or reproach until the appearing of our Lord Jesus Christ, which He will bring about at the proper time— He who is the blessed and only Sovereign, the King of kings and Lord of lords" (1 Tim 6:14–15). He is the one who will return on a white horse for the battle against the forces of Satan:

> *"His eyes are a flame of fire, and on His head are many diadems…clothed with a robe dipped in blood, and His name is called The Word of God … and on His robe and on His thigh He has a name written, 'King of kings, and Lord of lords." (Rev 19:12-16)*

He is the one who must be confessed as Lord for salvation (Rom 10:9), which in reality is a recognition of Him as God.

Second, He is Jesus, emphasizing His historical incarnation. He was the man who was born in Bethlehem and raised in Nazareth, and who lived and walked throughout the provinces of Galilee and Judea in first-century Israel. He was human with a human name, and people called Him Jesus of Nazareth, a carpenter's son (albeit adopted son). He died a physical death and was physically raised. We continue to worship an incarnate God, who continues with His humanity along with His deity forever (notice the post-resurrection depiction of Jesus' wounds in His hands and side in John 20:27).

Finally, He is Christ. The apostle John informs us that "Christ" is the translation of "Messiah" (John 1:41). The Messiah is "the anointed one" the Jews were seeking to deliver them from all oppression. Sometimes the Scripture refers to Him as "the" Christ, for it is a description rather than a name. We do well to address Him and refer to Him by His full title: our Lord Jesus Christ.

Father, I praise You for Your Son, the Lord Jesus Christ, whom I follow.

WEEK 32, DAY 5

God of All Comfort - 1

Blessed be the God and Father of our Lord Jesus Christ, the Father of mercies and God of all comfort ... (2 Corinthians 1:3)

Since we believe the Scripture teaches Jesus is God, then what is true of God is true of Jesus. Often, in looking at individual passages, the distinction between God the Father and God the Son is clear, but sometimes there is overlap or lack of a clear line of demarcation. In our passage today, we need to peel back the layers carefully.

First, the reference to God and Father is not contemplating two separate entities, but rather one. This is what linguists call a hendiadys, where two words connected by "and" refer to the same thing. For example, we might say, "I am good and ready" or "I am husband and father." Paul, the inspired author, calls for a blessing to the one who is both God and Father. The latter term refers to His relationship with the "Lord Jesus Christ." And it is in His fatherly relationship to Christ, that He is the Father of mercies and the God of all comfort.

Notice the interesting chiasm (the reversal of order):

Blessed be the God
    Father of our Lord Jesus Christ
    Father of mercies
God of all comfort

Writers of Scripture often use a poetic style to convey profound truth. Our verse today possibly reflects early church hymnody, with its metric flow and rhythm. This comforting God is reminiscent of the many psalms that convey God's protection, such as the classic shepherd's psalm, "Your rod and Your staff, they comfort me" (Ps 23:4).

Father God's comfort for us emanates from His relationship with His Son, the perfect love that existed between them from eternity past. We are now brothers of Christ: "For both He who sanctifies and those who are sanctified are all from one Father; for which reason He is not ashamed to call them brethren" (Heb 2:11). We are now children of God: "See how great a love the Father has bestowed on us, that we would be called children of God" (1 John 3:1). And "if children, heirs also, heirs of God and fellow heirs with Christ" (Rom 8:17).

As members of God's family, sharing with Christ in all things, we have access to His Father, the God of all comfort. No matter what difficult times we may go through, we trust that He will comfort us with His eternal love.

Lord, I ask for Your comfort in my life and in the life of that person You are bringing to my mind right now.

WEEKEND 32 READING
Nahum 2

PERSONAL REFLECTIONS

WEEK 33, DAY 1

God of All Comfort - 2

Blessed be the God and Father of our Lord Jesus Christ, the Father of mercies and God of all comfort ... (2 Corinthians 1:3)

Someone once said, somewhat skeptically, "Yes, I believe God will help us Christians when we need Him, but I still need someone to help me take out the trash and fix things around the house." She was a widow struggling through everyday living. In essence, she was asking, "Where is the tangibility of God's comfort and help?" That is an excellent question. What do we mean when we refer to God being the Father of comfort?

For some, the expectation is a euphoric or esoteric spiritual feeling that sweeps over a person. I purposely use those fancy, "obscure" words to convey that this feeling some are looking for is little understood and usually just beyond reach. They imagine they will know it when they see it. However, life is filled with all kinds of feelings, and we simply cannot judge God's involvement in our lives based on the feelings we experience. This is a surefire path toward doubt.

Rather, faith is looking for God's comfort as He brings it to us, accepting it in whatever way He provides. The smallest act of kindness can be seen as God's reminder that He is present. Unfaith is oblivious to these small events; it demands and will only be satisfied with its preconceived acts on God's part. It is a requirement that God must work in a certain way that in reality would not require faith on our part; by making something happen that would completely overwhelm us and be absolutely clear without any doubt that God is in my life comforting me.

The irony is that faith, unleashed from narrow expectations and demands on God, does provide the path to the overwhelming comfort of God. While He may not provide someone to fix my house appliance, He may provide help in another, different way, by another avenue of kindness or comfort. By faith, we may see a flower in an unexpected place, hear a kind word spoken in just the right way or have an offer to help in a different area. Above all, God wants us to go beyond our own need and simply trust in Him "who comforts us in all our affliction so that we will be able to comfort those who are in any affliction with the comfort with which we ourselves are comforted by God" (2 Cor 1:4). What a privilege that He still wants to use us even when we are so focused on our own need of comfort! In fact, out of our need of and faith in His comfort, we become God's comfort to someone else in need of the same comfort. If in the church we all did this, there would be more than enough of God's comfort to go around!

Lord, let me be used by You to comfort others.

WEEK 33, DAY 2

God of All Grace

After you have suffered for a little while, the God of all grace, who called you to His eternal glory in Christ, will Himself perfect, confirm, strengthen and establish you. (1 Peter 5:10)

Grace is one of the most important words in the NT, used in Paul's writings 83 times and Peter's 10 times. It is an action word, as in God acts graciously towards us, and it is a "thing," a noun, something given: "May grace and peace be yours in the fullest measure" (1 Peter 1:2). In our context today, God is defined as the God of all grace—that is, He acts towards us in all graciousness, and He abundantly gives us all grace.

God's grace was foretold in the OT: "The prophets who prophesied of the grace that would come to you made careful searches and inquiries" (1 Peter 1:10).

God's grace sustains us in suffering: "Fix your hope completely on the grace to be brought to you at the revelation of Jesus Christ" (1 Peter 1:13).

God's grace crosses gender lines: "Show her [your wife] honor as a fellow heir of the grace of life" (1 Peter 3:7).

God shows His grace often through human means: "As each one has received a special gift, employ it in serving one another as good stewards of the manifold grace of God" (1 Peter 4:10).

Grace is selectively experienced: "God is opposed to the proud, but gives grace to the humble" (1 Peter 5:5).

We must respond to God's grace with resolved faith: "I have written to you … that this is the true grace of God. Stand firm in it!" (1 Peter 5:12).

God desires for us the full grace experience: "Grace and peace be multiplied to you in the knowledge of God and of Jesus our Lord" (2 Peter 1:2).

Peter's final word on this subject is that we should never stop maturing in grace: "Grow in the grace and knowledge of our Lord and Savior Jesus Christ. To Him be the glory, both now and to the day of eternity. Amen" (2 Peter 3:18).

Yes, God is the God of all grace. He is graciously at work in us, not because we deserve any of it. He graciously has called us "to His eternal glory in Christ!" How good is that?! If that were not enough, He has committed Himself to making us perfect. To the scattered believers who were living as "aliens" in the eastern Mediterranean area of the ancient world, God would also confirm them in their faith, strengthen them and establish them. In other words, persecution would not get the better of them, because God is the God of all grace. And He continues to be the God of all grace to us, as well.

Dear Lord, I am so thankful that You graciously work in my life in every way.

WEEK 33, DAY 3

God of Love

Finally, brethren, rejoice, be made complete, be comforted, be like-minded, live in peace; and the God of love and peace will be with you. (2 Corinthians 13:11)

While the exact phrase, "the God of love," only occurs here in the NT (NASB), His character as loving saturates the NT. According to Jesus, love summarizes the entire Law of Moses, namely, loving God and loving your neighbor (Luke 10:27). Who of us cannot quote John 3:16? Who has not come across John's assessment: "The one who does not love does not know God, for God is love" (1 John 4:8)? Or, "God is love, and the one who abides in love abides in God, and God abides in him" (1 John 4:16)?

Yes, God is the God of love. Did you notice how much of the NT talk about God's love is connected with our love for each other? The apostle John reflects, "Beloved, if God so loved us, we also ought to love one another" (1 John 4:11).

What is poignant about the phrase "the God of love" in our passage today is that it comes at the end of Paul's writings to a selfish, divisive bunch of believers who could be described in many ways, except loving! They even used the Lord's Supper, communion, for their own selfish purposes. Paul thoroughly rebukes them for this: "Therefore when you meet together, it is not to eat the Lord's Supper, for in your eating each one takes his own supper first; and one is hungry and another is drunk" (1 Cor 11:20–21). Hard to believe the level of self-interest that existed there in that worldly church!

The great irony is this: If the Corinthians had truly understood that He is the God of love, then they would have been the disciples of love. Remember what Jesus taught His closest followers in the Upper Room: "By this all men will know that you are My disciples, if you have love for one another" (John 13:35). Love begets love. That will be the evidence of our faith, of our connection with Christ. Love for others will be the substantiation of our testimony that God loves the whole world (John 3:16).

This is how we know God is love: One, the Bible says so. Two, Christ in love died for us (Rom 5:8). Three, God loves us through the loving actions of other Christians toward us. Four, God loves others through our loving acts toward them. All because He is the "God of love."

This concept is not a club to use against other Christians when they mis-treat us. Rather it is a clarion call for each of us to reflect God's image, showing others so that they can know Him as the God of love, working through us toward them.

Lord, use me to love others, the way You love me.

WEEK 33, DAY 4

God of Peace

Finally, brethren, rejoice, be made complete, be comforted, be like-minded, live in peace; and the God of love and peace will be with you. (2 Corinthians 13:11)

Universal in its desire, peace appears to be a rare commodity. In the ancient world, brute force and violence were the primary tools for establishing peace. Among the ancient Sumerians, Egyptians, Assyrians, Babylonians, Greeks and Romans, war dominated at every level of society. People became adept at defending their property and their relations. Laws came into being in recognition of this basic human tendency at the interpersonal and societal level: The strongest and smartest win, and everyone else suffers.

The Pax Romana—that is, the Roman peace—was remarkable for its longevity. By various estimates, Rome's dominance in the ancient world extended upwards of seven centuries. Its remains are still visible today in the Roman ruins around the Mediterranean and as far as the British Isles. Great structures, like the Coliseum in Rome, still stand—albeit in ruins—an ever-present reminder of the supremacy of the empire's might. The peace extended to its citizenry, but not to the millions of conquered people who became slaves to the highest bidders.

At the time of Paul's writings, in the first century, the Christians had marginal political freedom. But life for most was miserable. On top of the physical stresses of life, social and interpersonal tensions existed back then as they do now. The church at Corinth was a prime example, rife with divisions, conflicts, selfishness and immorality of the worst kind. The city had a reputation throughout the empire of being a grossly immoral place, so that a common slur used to describe a sexually loose or immoral woman was this: "She is a Corinthian woman." The Corinthian believers seem to have brought much of their pre-conversion lifestyle into the church with them. If any gathering of believers needed peace among themselves and with God, it was the Corinthians!

It was to this people that Paul wrote, "Live in peace." A life of peace displays evidence of having been imbued with the God of love and peace. That is His nature. He desires to bring peace between man and Himself, overcoming the alienation between humankind and God that began in the Garden of Eden. Paul writes similarly to another group, "Now may the God of peace Himself sanctify you entirely; and may your spirit and soul and body be preserved complete, without blame at the coming of our Lord Jesus Christ" (1 Thess 5:23). God brings peace among Christians through our sanctification.

Lord, help me to live in peace with that brother or sister who comes to mind right now.

WEEK 33, DAY 5

God of the Living

But Jesus answered and said to [the Sadducees], "You are mistaken, not understanding the Scriptures nor the power of God ... regarding the resurrection of the dead, have you not read what was spoken to you by God: 'I AM THE GOD OF ABRAHAM, AND THE GOD OF ISAAC, AND THE GOD OF JACOB'? He is not the God of the dead but of the living." (Matthew 22:29–32)

Sadducees were those comprising a religio-political group of Jews that opposed the Pharisees on many levels, especially the resurrection. The former simply did not believe there would be one, whereas the latter believed all people would one day be raised from the dead.

Rarely did Jesus wade into the debates of these two groups, but this one is an exception; Jesus takes the Sadducees to task. Why this time? Because the resurrection debate reflects on a fundamental truth of the One whom all Jews, both fishermen and high priest, called "the living God" (Matt 16:16, 26:63). So Jesus begins with a clear rebuke to the Sadducees, "You are mistaken," and challenges their faulty understanding of both the written Scriptures (what we call the OT) and of God's power to raise the dead. In other words, the Scripture teaches about a God who is powerful enough even to raise the dead.

For Scripture, Jesus appeals to God's message to Moses in the wilderness in preparation for the Exodus. The voice out of the burning bush self-identified as "I am the God ...of Abraham, the God of Isaac, and the God of Jacob." From the forming of Israel as a nation, the God they (including the Sadducees of Jesus' day) worshipped was the God of the patriarchs and of Moses. Nothing could be more fundamental than this. Jesus uses the "I am" phrasing similar to John 8:58 ("Truly, truly, I say to you, before Abraham was born, I am") with an emphasis on the currency of the reality. God is not simply a God who "was" (past tense), but a God who "is" (present tense). According to standard Greek convention, the present tense at times conveys an ongoing or progressive sense. Jesus is saying that God continues to be a God who is there. In an interesting turn of words, we might say God continues to be the God of the patriarchs.

Jesus takes from this "God of the living" idea to infer there will be resurrection. In fact, He presents that as convincing support. If God is (presently) the God of Abraham who long ago died, then Abraham must in some sense still be living. Otherwise, God was (previously) the God of Abraham, but no longer is. The solution to the dilemma is that our Lord is, in fact, the God of the living and will raise up to eternal life all those who have believed in Him.

Lord, You are ever present in my life, and even after I die, because I will be resurrected to be with You forever.

WEEKEND 33 READING
Nahum 3

PERSONAL REFLECTIONS

WEEK 34, DAY 1

God of the Spirits of the Prophets

And he said to me, "These words are faithful and true"; and the Lord, the God of the spirits of the prophets, sent His angel to show to His bond-servants the things which must soon take place." (Revelation 22:6)

Fascinating descriptions of God abound in Scripture, of which this is one. A few observations will highlight the significance of referring to the Lord as "the God of the spirits of the prophets." First, the book of Revelation is a prophecy, and thus John writes as a prophet. From an earthly viewpoint, prophets are to be highly honored, but they are simply a tool, often without any significant qualifications. John had been a businessman carrying on the family trade (fishing). Yet God raised him up to be a divine mouthpiece to convey the great picture story of end-times prophecy. The honor, therefore, goes to the God of the prophet, rather than the human instrument. Remember, God can speak through a donkey (Num 22:27); He can bring praise out of rocks (Luke 19:40). So He can use any human as a prophet. The point is that the focus is on God, the author of the prophecy.

Further, He is the God of not only the prophets, but also "the spirits of the prophets." Paul uses that phrase in speaking of order in the church: "The spirits of prophets are subject to prophets; for God is not a God of confusion but of peace, as in all the churches of the saints" (1 Cor 14:32–33). He controls and directs His prophets. In the worship service of the church, there should be order and control in how things play out; those speaking on behalf of God are under both God's control and self-control. In other words, worship is not a completely unleashed experience where a prophet loses all control of his utterances, as some in certain factions of Christendom believe. Prophetic utterances don't require the prophet to go into a hypnotic or even a completely passive mode. His conscious awareness and self-control work together with and are brought under the control of God, who is the "God of the spirits of the prophets."

Too often today Christians seek an instantaneous and overwhelming emotional experience of God's presence in their lives, some sort of spiritual manifestation to prove God is real in this physical, tangible world. We believe God is at work, but most often we see His work in His orderly communication through those who speak on His behalf. He speaks to us through preaching, Sunday school or small group teaching, books, and even our brothers and sisters who speak life and grace into our lives.

Lord, I believe You speak to me through many different mouthpieces. Because it is You who speaks, I am listening.

WEEK 34, DAY 2

I Am

Jesus said to them, "Truly, truly, I say to you, before Abraham was born, I am." Therefore they picked up stones to throw at Him, but Jesus hid Himself and went out of the temple. (John 8:58)

We have seen elsewhere in this study the connection of John 8:58 with Exodus 3:14 and the prophecies of Isaiah (see "Lord Jesus Who Acts"). He is Yahweh of the OT, incarnate. While we recognize the Greek influence on the life and times of Jesus, the Hebrew influence is much greater. Therefore, we don't see this statement—"before Abraham was, I am"—as a declaration of Jesus' eternal existence. While certainly that can be implied, we see here rather the identification with Yahweh, who happens to also be eternal. Jesus is playing on both concepts, to be sure, but the reaction of the crowd to attempt to stone Him shows they clearly understood the Hebrew connection with Yahweh. Just as in the OT God acts towards His people as they need, so Jesus came to be whatever we need Him to be. Notice, this does not mean that God will be whatever we want Him to be, but what we need Him to be. He is far better at determining what we need, which is not always apparent to us.

The phrase "I am," though brief to the point of being mysterious, occupies a place among the most profound of statements. In normal language, the phrase "I am" begs the question, "What is he?" As it stands, it is an incomplete sentence. Language experts tell us that a predicate nominative is needed to finish the sentence, that is, a word on the other side of the "am" that completes the thought or description about the subject of the sentence, "I." In other portions of Scripture, we do find complete sentences, like "I am the light" or "I am the door." But here in John 8:5, there is simply "I am." From a literary point of view, Jesus is the one who is without any limiting or defining traits. "I am" stands on it own! His is unqualified, active existence, and by connection with the Hebrew mindset, He is Yahweh of the OT.

The force of the apparent grammatical incompleteness of the sentence compels English translators to supply "he" earlier in the chapter, when in fact the Greek is identical to that of 8:59: "Unless you believe that I am He, you will die in your sins" (John 8:24, see also 8:28). At the most fundamental level, Jesus is "I am." His active, unqualified, unmitigated existence is the basis for all that He is and shows Himself to be. So when we see phrases like "I am the light," we are seeing one aspect of who He is, the One who actively shines His light into this world and into our lives, because He is the one who said, "I am."

Lord, "Such knowledge is too wonderful for me ..." (Psalm 139:6).

WEEK 34, DAY 3

I Am the ...

There was the true Light which, coming into the world, enlightens every man. (John 1:9)

Then Jesus again spoke to them, saying, "I am the Light of the world; he who follows Me will not walk in the darkness, but will have the Light of life." (John 8:12)

The Gospel According to John records the well-known "I am" statements of Jesus. We list them here for the broad survey of Jesus' own self-definition: He said "I am…"

The Bread of Life

I am the bread of life; he who comes to Me will not hunger, and he who believes in Me will never thirst. (John 6:35)

The Light

I am the Light of the world; he who follows Me will not walk in the darkness, but will have the Light of life. (John 8:12)

The Door

I am the door; if anyone enters through Me, he will be saved, and will go in and out and find pasture. (John 10:9)

The Good Shepherd

I am the good shepherd; the good shepherd lays down His life for the sheep … I am the good shepherd, and I know My own and My own know Me … (John 10:11, 14)

The Resurrection

I am the resurrection and the life; he who believes in Me will live even if he dies … (John 11:25)

The True Vine

I am the true vine, and My Father is the vinedresser. (John 15:1)

The Way, Truth, Life

I am the way, and the truth, and the life; no one comes to the Father but through Me. (John 14:6)

Lord, You are my all in all. Every single description of You thrills my soul!

WEEK 34, DAY 4

I Am the Light

Then Jesus again spoke to them, saying, "I am the Light of the world; he who follows Me will not walk in the darkness, but will have the Light of life." (John 8:12)

Darkness engulfs the world—spiritual darkness. Apart from God, His image bearers walk around blind, unable to see the glory of God that fills all the earth (Is 6:3). A picturesque sunset might tantalize the faint echo of God, but there is simply too much evil for such occasional glimpses to reside for any length of time. The connectedness with their Maker is a distant hope, hidden by layers of superficial satisfactions that don't really bring peace or purpose to a person.

But when Jesus came, brilliance broke onto the scene. The apostle John in his preamble to his biography of Jesus wrote: "There was the true Light which, coming into the world, enlightens every man" (John 1:9). He is the solution to the darkness of our souls that Jeremiah wrote about long before: "The heart is more deceitful than all else and is desperately sick; Who can understand it?" (Jer 17:9). Jesus came as the light of the world. "And He is the radiance of His glory and the exact representation of His nature, and upholds all things by the word of His power …" (Heb 1:3). How good is that?!

However, there is a problem. Light demands a response, and the response is somewhat checkered; the assessment of Jeremiah is a formidable obstacle:

This is the judgment, that the Light has come into the world, and men loved the darkness rather than the Light, for their deeds were evil. For everyone who does evil hates the Light, and does not come to the Light for fear that his deeds will be exposed. But he who practices the truth comes to the Light, so that his deeds may be manifested as having been wrought in God." (John 3:19–21)

Just like in the creation account—when the creation of light divided the day from the night, the light from the dark (Gen 1:3-4)—so also Christ came as the light to separate out those who love the light from those who do not.

Praise God, those who believe in the Lord Jesus Christ "were formerly darkness, but now you are Light in the Lord; walk as children of Light" (Eph 5:8). Because He is the Light of the World, we as God's children now also become lights to those around us, pointing the way to the Light of the World" who has enabled us to see more clearly His glory in all the earth.

Lord, I once was blind but now I see (John 9:25). Thank You a thousand times!

WEEK 34, DAY 5

I Am the Bread of Life

Jesus said to them, "I am the bread of life; he who comes to Me will not hunger, and he who believes in Me will never thirst." (John 6:35)

Hunger is an epidemic in our world today. Almost 780 million people suffer from chronic undernourishment (worldhunger.org); that's about one in nine worldwide! Spiritual hunger, on the other hand, is probably much more prevalent. Statistics on religious adherents are not helpful, even when counting those who identify as Christian. For who can know for sure the reality of the redeemed life in those who identify themselves as members of a Christian religion or denomination? Jesus made it clear the vast majority would not gain eternal life: "The way is broad that leads to destruction, and there are many who enter through it. For the gate is small and the way is narrow that leads to life, and there are few who find it" (Matt 7:13–14).

Therefore, there is great spiritual undernourishment in the world. The un-saved, unredeemed, unregenerate children of darkness—those who do not believe in the Lord Jesus Christ—are not receiving spiritual food. Either they are uninterested, being dead in their sins and satiated by the junk satisfactions of the world, or they are unable to find spiritual food because of their ignorance of Jesus Christ.

Spiritual hunger manifests itself in different ways and is not satisfied with substitutes. Our souls hunger after God and His righteousness. "Blessed are those who hunger and thirst for righteousness, for they shall be satisfied" (Matt 5:6). Apart from Him, people seek justice through the legal system, cultural pressure and other means, even war. Liberation theology of an earlier time sought to bring about political and legal righteousness as a means to alleviate the suffering of the oppressed. While the goal is admirable, the means are skewed. For the hunger for true righteousness can only be satisfied in Christ, who brings righteousness even in the midst of injustices. What good is it to bring about political, cultural and legal justice, if a person suffers a lost eternity apart from the God of righteousness? Our hunger for righteousness can only be found in Christ!

Just like the people who followed Jesus during His earthly life had their physical hunger satisfied when He multiplied the loaves and fishes to feed the thousands, so He fulfills all our hunger and longings. He is the nourishment for our souls. Is it not wonderful that we who believe "are invited to the marriage supper of the Lamb" (Rev 19:9)?

Lord, while You satisfy me now, I look forward to being fully satiated in Your presence.

WEEKEND 34 READING
Habakkuk 1-2

PERSONAL REFLECTIONS

WEEK 35, DAY 1

I Am the Door

I am the door; if anyone enters through Me, he will be saved, and will go in and out and find pasture. The thief comes only to steal and kill and destroy; I came that they may have life, and have it abundantly. (John 10:9–10)

Doors are for entering into places, for walking through to another location. They are the transition from here to there. Doors open to a new experience, a new existence. Jesus is the door to life, and that life is abundant. Anything else, by comparison, leads not to life but to something else, an alternative existence.

Nothing is more central to Christian faith than this truth. While popular philosophy tells us there are many paths that lead to God, the Bible is clear when it quotes Jesus' own words, "no one comes to the Father but through Me" (John 14:6). He is the only door, the only path. Peter was not cowed by the "religiously-correct police" of his day when he proclaimed, "There is salvation in no one else; for there is no other name under heaven that has been given among men by which we must be saved" (Acts 4:12). There are not many doors that lead to God; there is only one and that is Christ. All others result in eternal destruction. If some think Christianity is narrow-minded, it is only because Jesus spoke the truth, and the truth is by definition narrow-minded.

Jesus in His upper room prayer said, "This is eternal life, that they may know You, the only true God, and Jesus Christ whom You have sent" (John 17:3). The abundant life of John 10:10 is the eternal life of John 17:3. And both come through Jesus Christ, who is the doorway to that life.

Notice, first of all, that entering the door leads to salvation. In context, the analogy Jesus relates is confusing to the Jews, but to us who know the whole story, this salvation refers to being rescued from separation from God and the death it leads to, and the restoration of relationship with Him—in other words, spiritual salvation. Notice also, this is connected with entering through a door into life. What was left behind was death, and what lies ahead is life. As if that did not communicate enough, Jesus clarifies, this will be abundant life. This is life now and anticipates life to come. In other words, we now begin the abundant life we will live to the fullest in the future.

Of all people, we believers have a reason to wake up in the morning, to live another day of abundant life. We can go "in and out and find pasture." There are times of rest in the sheepfold away from the world, and there are times of heading back into the world full of spiritual life. And this aliveness can't help but communicate to those around that Christ is alive and living in us.

Lord, I want to live more of the abundant life by trusting continually in Christ.

WEEK 35, DAY 2

I Am the Good Shepherd

"I am the good shepherd; the good shepherd lays down His life for the sheep." (John 10:11)

"I am the good shepherd, and I know My own and My own know Me." (John 10:14)

Probably the best-known metaphor describing Christ is that of a shepherd. Who hasn't see a picture of the Savior standing on a hillside with a shepherd's staff in His hand and sheep at His feet? Or the classic depiction of a lamb draped over His shoulders, imaging for us the rescue of the one lost sheep out of 100?

We dare not let the shepherd imagery languish as part of antiquated, old-time religion. The imagery takes a remarkable turn from normal animal husbandry. A shepherd normally raises sheep for his own financial livelihood, for wool and meat. Ultimately, the sheep will be killed in order to feed people. But Christ is like a shepherd who would die for his sheep. That is a startling twist to what one would expect, like saying I would be willing to die for my pet parakeet. Absurd—or remarkable. Jesus is no ordinary shepherd, and His sheep are not like ordinary sheep.

"We are His people and the sheep of His pasture" (Ps 100:3b). Christ died for us, like a shepherd dying for his sheep. The consummate irony of this is that the religious leaders of the people in Jesus' day were like shepherds who would see the sheep as existing only for their benefit. The idea of dying for them would seem absolutely absurd. Jesus said in His immediately preceding breath, "The thief comes only to steal and kill and destroy; I came that they may have life, and have it abundantly" (John 10:10). In the same way that Jesus was not like the earthly religious leaders, He was not like an earthly shepherd.

Jesus is the one who cares for our souls, our entire well-being. When we go astray, He searches for us and finds us. No matter how far away we go, we recognize His voice, at times still and quiet. We stray because we fall into the temptation of thinking the world, the flesh or the devil has something better to offer us. When Jesus brings us back, His grace overflows and He continues to shepherd us, guiding, protecting, feeding and nurturing us. Peter writes: "For you were continually straying like sheep, but now you have returned to the Shepherd and Guardian of your souls" (1 Peter 2:25).

Lord Jesus, the Shepherd of my soul, I continually return to You and confess my frequently wandering away. Your gracious voice never ceases to call out to me. Thank You.

WEEK 35, DAY 3

I Am the Resurrection

Jesus said to [Martha], "I am the resurrection and the life; he who believes in Me will live even if he dies, and everyone who lives and believes in Me will never die. Do you believe this?" (John 11:25–26)

The family trio who were part of Jesus' intimate circle—Mary, Martha and Lazarus, who had just died—discovered this truth about Jesus. Jesus was and is the resurrection! In other places He uses concrete objects (e.g. door, shepherd, bread) to describe Himself, but here He uses an event. In what sense is He an event?

Lazarus' death was confirmed by his being entombed for four days already (John 11:39). Jesus had purposely delayed showing up at the scene, but once there, He did not waste any time raising the brother back to life—but not without teaching a lesson related to what He was about to do. Jesus said to Martha, "I am the resurrection," and He explained what He meant by it, relating it to life. Whoever believes in Him will live, even though he will physically die. To prove that He had the authority to say this—that is, to validate the truth of the statement—Jesus did something remarkable by anyone's standards: He raised Lazarus back to life from the dead. He performed a resurrection.

This action begs the conclusion: If Jesus has the authority and ability to raise a dead person back to life, then He has the authority and ability to raise anyone back to life. He has complete mastery over death, not just preventing it but reversing its effects. Clearly, the latter is more impressive than the former. Every day doctors prevent people from dying, firemen rescue people from burning buildings and good Samaritans rescue people from all kinds of terminal situations. But resurrection involves bringing people back from the dead! Jesus can do this.

Therefore, when He says people who believe in Him will never die, He means death will not have the permanent final say. The world may say death and taxes are permanent and unchanging. But because Jesus said, "I am the resurrection," death is reversible for those who believe (plus there is nothing in Scripture about taxation in heaven!). The best non-believers can do is to garner a hope that is baseless, or at best fixed on shaky ground. But for believers in Jesus Christ, we have a sure foundation, a promise, the truth of resurrection, because we have trusted in the very One who, by definition, is the resurrection. He proved the truth of this further and ultimately by His own resurrection from the dead. "Death is swallowed up in victory... thanks be to God, who gives us the victory through our Lord Jesus Christ. (1 Cor 15:54, 57).

Lord, I believe for sure that You are my resurrection; I have no fear of death.

WEEK 35, DAY 4

I Am the True Vine

"I am the true vine, and My Father is the vinedresser." (John 15:1)

"I am the vine, you are the branches; he who abides in Me and I in him, he bears much fruit, for apart from Me you can do nothing." (John 15:5)

The popular Christian chorus from back in the day goes like this: "Abiding in the Vine, abiding in the Vine, peace, love, joy and happiness are mine." Indeed, the fruitfulness of the Spirit involves that and more (Gal 5:22-24). But it all requires abiding in the Vine, the Lord Jesus.

For us today, the metaphor stands on its own as we can easily picture the truth portrayed. We, like branches, must stay connected and keep drawing our sustenance (sap) from Jesus Christ (the vine/plant). Actually, the vine in Jesus' telling is the entire plant, including all its branches, though one might conceive the reference is to the trunk of the vine. Nevertheless, we must stay vitally connected to the entire plant as a whole. This harkens to the later teaching by the apostle Paul that we are all the body of Christ, each of us members of the whole (Eph 1:23, 4:12-16; 1 Cor 12:27).

In the Jewish culture, Jesus' comment would have been met with mixed reactions. In the book of Isaiah, God says:

> *Let me sing now for my well-beloved a song of my beloved concerning His vineyard. My well-beloved had a vineyard on a fertile hill. He dug it all around, removed its stones, and planted it with the choicest vine. And He built a tower in the middle of it and also hewed out a wine vat in it; then He expected it to produce good grapes, but it produced only worthless ones ... For the vineyard of the Lord of hosts is the house of Israel and the men of Judah His delightful plant. Thus He looked for justice, but behold, bloodshed; for righteousness, but behold, a cry of distress. (Is 5:1-2, 7)*

So for Jesus to co-opt the metaphor and use it in reference to Himself would have been startling. He was saying that rather than being connected to God through the people of Israel (either genetically or by conversion to Judaism as a proselyte), one must instead be connected to God through Jesus Christ. That is the vine that Jesus' "Father" is tending. Clearly, Jesus was inaugurating a change of significant proportions. The life God requires is the life connected to the Lord Jesus Christ. He does not replace the vine of Israel, but rather brings the vine imagery into focus—onto Himself. Our spiritual life comes from Him, not from ecclesiastical associations, helpful as they may be. We must abide in Him in order to be fruitful for God's good pleasure and enjoyment.

Lord, thank You for providing all the sustenance I need, as I abide in You.

WEEK 35, DAY 5

I Am the True Vine (continued)

"I am the true vine, and My Father is the vinedresser." (John 15:1)

"I am the vine, you are the branches; he who abides in Me and I in him, he bears much fruit, for apart from Me you can do nothing." (John 15:5)

Abiding in the vine is the dynamic of spiritual life, without which nothing can be accomplished in the believer's life. No abiding means no growth, no fruitfulness, no joy for the Lord through a life well-lived for His glory. Nothing could be more fundamentally important for a Christian than abiding in Christ. Jesus said in our passage, "Apart from Me you can do nothing."

An exhaustive study of the original Greek language, searching the lexicons of the ancient Greek and the cognate languages of that day, results in this conclusion: The word "nothing" does in fact mean "nothing"! All the major English translations render the Greek word as "nothing." There is absolutely nothing that anyone can do apart from Christ.

We must take careful and serious note of this seemingly benign observation. How much of the so-called Christian life is caught up in the superficial, non-essential things? The apostle Paul writes of "matters which have, to be sure, the appearance of wisdom in self-made religion and self-abasement and severe treatment of the body, but are of no value against fleshly indulgence" (Col 2:23). Focusing on such matters is not abiding in Christ.

One can go through the motions of the spiritual disciplines without abiding in Christ, and a superficial congregation of believers would never know the difference. Imagine drawing a picture of grapes on a sheet of paper with crayons, then going into an orchard and taping it onto a grapevine. Even if a Rembrandt or Michelangelo were commissioned to create a magnificent painting on canvas of a cluster of grapes, hanging that picture on a vine would not bring fruitfulness. Neither you nor those Renaissance masters could generate anything compared to the genuine fruitfulness that God produces on branches that are connected to (abiding in) the vine. The first drop of rain would mock the fake fruit.

So too, with the Christian life, fruitfulness can be contrived through our own human efforts and disciplines. But only the nourishment of being vitally connected to Christ, through drawing life through Him, will produce real fruit in our lives. There are no substitutes or quick growth schemes. We are fruitful as believers when we continue to trust in Christ in every aspect of our lives.

Lord, where You are is where I want to be, connected to You in every way.

WEEKEND 35 READING
Habakkuk 3

PERSONAL REFLECTIONS

WEEK 36, DAY 1

I Am the Way

Jesus said to him, "I am the way, and the truth, and the life; no one comes to the Father but through Me." (John 14:6)

One verse, three metaphors; John with simple words conveys profound truths. With a soaring prologue (John 1:1-18) to begin this biography of Christ, one should expect nothing less from this simple fisherman turned philosopher-theologian. Though John would blanch at such accolades, his use of imagery throughout the book to convey ideas of faith, life and love are the hallmarks not only of good story telling, but of vividly portraying the truth about who Christ is. If God can use an uneducated peasant of little training as the pen of divine writing, could He not use you and me? Is it any wonder many evangelists recommend this book as the place to begin for seeking sinners?

John alone of all the gospel writers captures Jesus' words here, and conveys them in three "I am" words. These work together to bring us to the climactic truth: The path to God is absolutely unique, exclusive and intolerant. "No one" can go to God in any other way. This begs of no exceptions. Each of the words is qualified by the word "the." The Bible is very clear at this juncture. Jesus is "the" way, "the" truth and "the" life. He is not "a" way, "a" truth or "a" life. He is not one particular path to God, should you want to choose it. He is "the" path to God. One cannot be more absolute than this. Jesus is the complete package for access to God!

He is also the exclusive path to God. All other paths are not "the" way, "the" truth" and "the" life." Nothing qualifies for either of the three, let alone all three. There are not many ways to God that are true and life-giving. There is no other path that has even just two of these. For example, what good would it be to have a way to God that is true, but does not involve life eternal? Paul assesses the situation: "If we have hoped in Christ in this life only, we are of all men most to be pitied" (1 Cor 15:19). Or what good is it to have the truth if it does not give access to God? Adam and Eve gained the truth, their eyes were opened to know good and evil, but it drove them out of the presence of God.

This verse is intolerant of other attempted paths to God. Christians are accused of being narrow-minded, saying there is only way to God. But this is the teaching of the One whom we follow. If an accusation of intolerance is to be made, it must go against the greatest moral and spiritual teacher ever. We do Him a disservice by watering down His statement in any way.

Lord, I will not be embarrassed about what You said, for I believe it to be true – You are the absolute, exclusive and intolerant way to the Father.

WEEK 36, DAY 2

I Am the Truth

Jesus said to him, "I am the way, and the truth, and the life; no one comes to the Father but through Me." (John 14:6)

Second of the three metaphors captured in this verse is Jesus' assertion, "I am the truth." Popular post-modern thinking would have us believe there are many truths, alternative truths, relative truths, but above all, no absolute truth. This is popularly regurgitated in our ecumenical culture.

Yet against all this, Jesus makes the astounding assertion that He is the truth. He didn't say that He was a teacher of the truth, though He certainly spoke truth (John 8:45-46). He didn't say He was the pointer to the truth, though again, He certainly did that (John 1:17). In fact, He didn't say that the truth was in Him, though He certainly was full of truth (John 1:14). We must not assign to poetic license or marginalize the most alarming but straightfor-ward impact of this. Jesus said He was the complete embodiment of truth.

If Pilate had asked his oft-quoted question—"What is truth?" (John 18:38)—at this juncture instead of later during Jesus' trial, the Lord's answer would have been, "I am the truth." He didn't respond later to Pilate's query, because He knew that "[e]veryone who is of the truth hears My voice" (John 18:37), and presumably Pilate was not open to hearing a truthful answer to His question. Just like many today. But, praise God, we who are believers have embraced Jesus as the truth.

This is absolute, exclusive and intolerant of all that is untrue. The world thinks this is an intolerable position to hold, that Jesus is "the truth," exclusive of all other ways to God. But truth by its very nature is intolerant of what is not true. For example, 1 plus 1 equals 2. If someone told us, "That may be true to you, but I like to think of 1 plus 1 equaling 3," we would say that's absurd. Passengers on airplanes are thankful that pilots confine themselves to landing on straight and narrow runways, and doing it the long way. Imagine a pilot trying to land a plane perpendicular to the runway, thinking that all approaches to landing are equally valid. Such nonsense is like the modern notion that all approaches to God are equally valid—that we all are free to choose the path we would like to think of as being best for us.

The world's rejection of the idea of absolute truth is like thumbing one's nose to existence itself. It is man's effort to ascend above the very throne of the Creator God and proclaim himself as the lord of creation, to be hindered by no one else's truth but his own. However, Jesus was clear, "I am the truth," and that is the truth that sets people free (John 8:32).

Lord, I am so thankful that my life is anchored in You, the Truth.

WEEK 36, DAY 3

I Am the Life

Jesus said to him, "I am the way, and the truth, and the life; no one comes to the Father but through Me." (John 14:6)

"Life," the word, occurs 47 times in the Gospel According to John, more than the other three gospel accounts combined. When John (quoting Jesus) uses that term, he is not just thinking of the animation of moving, biological entities. Rather, he conveys the sense of aliveness with the Spirit of God animating us fully to be what God has created us to be, namely, His image bearers. On the sixth day of creation, "The LORD God formed man of dust from the ground, and breathed into his nostrils the breath of life; and man became a living being" (Gen 2:7). That is life, the energizing of a biological entity with the Spirit of God.

Enter sin through disobedience in the Garden, and our first fore-parents died (Gen 1:17). Satan would have us to believe otherwise (Gen 3:4), but the human race died spiritually, being separated from the life of and relationship with God. Physically, they continued on until their earthly death (separation from physical life), but they lived a life of death from their disobedience on.

Enter Jesus Christ, who came as "the Life." John prologues this to us, when he writes, "In Him was life, and the life was the Light of men" (John 1:4). He quotes Jesus Himself, saying, "The thief comes only to steal and kill and destroy; I came that they may have life, and have it abundantly" (John 10:10). What a contrast with the religious leaders of that day, whose influence toward godliness was motivated by self-interest and disregard for the true needs of others. Jesus spoke in extremely harsh but poignant terms.

Yet, He offered life to all who would believe in Him. At the death of her brother Lazarus, Jesus said to Martha: "I am the resurrection and the life; he who believes in Me will live even if he dies, and everyone who lives and believes in Me will never die. Do you believe this?" (John 11:25–26). This remains the question today: Do we believe this? As believers, we trust what Jesus said in the Upper Room, "This is eternal life, that they may know You, the only true God, and Jesus Christ whom You have sent" (John 17:3).

And we need to trust Him continuously as our life, and not fall back into thinking that we need what the world offers in order to experience life. He is the only life we need, because He is life. Knowing Him is life. Knowing eternal life is knowing Him. That is why Christians through the ages have been willing to die for Christ, because He is greater than our life.

Lord, as an ancient poet wrote, I confess that in You, I "live and move and have [my] being" (Acts 17:28). I can do nothing apart from You, Lord.

WEEK 36, DAY 4

The Last Adam

So also it is written, "The first MAN, Adam, BECAME A LIVING SOUL." The last Adam became a life-giving spirit. (1 Corinthians 15:45)

The name "Adam" represents not only the first individual created by God, but also the entire human race. In the Hebrew OT, the underlying word, transliterated as the name, can also be rendered "man." Adam was the first man, as our passage today concurs. Theologians speak of him being the federal head, in that he represents the entire human race.

The NT clearly connects Jesus with Adam. In his letter to the Romans, the apostle Paul wrote:

Just as through one man sin entered into the world, and death through sin, and so death spread to all men, because all sinned ... Nevertheless death reigned from Adam until Moses, even over those who had not sinned in the likeness of the offense of Adam, who is a type of Him who was to come. (Rom 5:12, 14)

Adam pre-figured Christ. Like a shadow, the first man gave a broad outline of what Christ was all about, even though many thousands of years before. Similar to how a photograph shows what a person looks like, so Adam gave a sense of what Christ would be like, ahead of Christ's actual coming.

The apostle points out that the human race was defined by sin from the time of Adam until the giving of the Law of Moses. And of course, the Law dominated since then until the time of Christ. So Paul went on to write:

If by the transgression of the one [Adam], death reigned through the one, much more those who receive the abundance of grace and of the gift of righteousness will reign in life through the One, Jesus Christ. (Rom 5:17).

In our verse today, we see that Jesus is like Adam in His headship role. But more to the point, Christ was like Adam seminally. That is, Adam is the seminal beginning of the human race, and all humanity descended from him physically. Christ is the spiritual beginning of the new humanity. Physically we were "in" Adam, but we who are believers are now "in" Christ, and we now inherit not guilt or sin, but the "abundance of grace and ... the gift of righteousness." Christ is the "last" Adam. There are only two humans who have had such a pivotal role in setting the course of human history. We find it supremely appropriate to divide history based on the birth of the last Adam, B.C. and A.D!

Lord, when You gave me new life by Your grace, my personal history became divided into two sections: before Christ and now in Christ. Praise God.

WEEK 36, DAY 5

Advocate

My little children, I am writing these things to you so that you may not sin. And if anyone sins, we have an Advocate with the Father, Jesus Christ the righteous ... (1 John 2:1)

Plan A – don't sin; Plan B – and God provides an advocate. John's simplicity has confounded theologians. Was the work of Christ on the cross (here, His advocacy) an afterthought, the result in God's mind of sin coming into the world? In other words, did God's original plan not work out because His image bearers thwarted God's glory, so He is going with a secondary plan to redeem His image bearers? Or was the work of Christ part of God's plan from the very beginning, a plan for His creation in which His glory could best be seen through redemption? We leave these debates to the theologians and academics.

John keeps things simple. At the end of the day we must become like children in our faith. Did not Jesus say this was how following Him begins? "Truly I say to you, unless you are converted and become like children, you will not enter the kingdom of heaven" (Matt 18:3). John preserves that notion as he addresses his readers 14 times as "children." In particular he writes, "See how great a love the Father has bestowed on us, that we would be called children of God; and such we are" (1 John 3:1).

This is not meant to minimize deep, reflective theological thinking, for some things taught in Scripture are in fact difficult to understand (2 Peter 3:15-16). John brings us to a faith we need in our daily, spiritual realities. We should not sin! Let no one ever say that salvation means we no longer need to obey God's commands. Nor does it mean we will never sin again. "If we say that we have no sin, we are deceiving ourselves and the truth is not in us" (1 John 1:8). The phrase "if anyone sins" must be understood as "when anyone sins."

The point is this: we have an Advocate to come alongside and defend us. The Greek term for "Advocate" is the same word used in John 14:15 for the Holy Spirit as our "Helper" (NASB, ESV, NKJV). Here our defender is "Jesus Christ the righteous." If He who is the perfectly righteous one is our Helper, our

Advocate, then we have nothing to fear from the discovery of sin in our lives. But on what basis can this be? The next verse answers this: "He Himself is the propitiation for our sins ..." (1 John 2:2). Christ has satisfied the wrath of God, the judicial guilt based on the Law, so that we are no longer declared unrighteous – and this despite that, as Christians, we still do sin at times.

Lord, You know I want to avoid sin, but I fail constantly. Thank You for Your eternal advocacy on my behalf, that I will never have to face the wrath of God.

WEEKEND 36 READING
Zephaniah 1-2

PERSONAL REFLECTIONS

WEEK 37, DAY 1

The Almighty

"I am the Alpha and the Omega," says the Lord God, "who is and who was and who is to come, the Almighty." (Revelation 1:8)

Of the many descriptions of God in the Bible, "Almighty" is very common, reflecting the One who is more powerful than anything or anyone else. He is the Almighty. In ancient Greek and Roman thought—in fact, in all ancient religion—the various so-called gods were ranked according to their power. The nations that gained victory in war would consider their gods greater than the gods of the defeated armies. There were conceived gods of the harvest who had the power to bring about good crops. The gods of thunder and mountains and plains all had their respective authority.

Christians inherited the knowledge of the one and only true God (monotheism) from the Jews, the God whose power was greater than any and all notions of pagan gods. He is "the Lord God" of Israel.

Yet commentators seem divided on whether the speaker in today's passage is the Lord Jesus Christ. First, in the immediate context, John's attention (and ours) is turned to Jesus (verses 4-6, but especially 7): "Behold, He is coming with the clouds, and every eye will see Him, even those who pierced Him; and all the tribes of the earth will mourn over Him. So it is to be. Amen" (Rev 1:7). The natural reading is that the speaker in verse 8 would be that same one, Jesus.

Second, the use of "I am" (Greek: ego eimi) harkens back to John's gospel account of the "I am" statements of Jesus. John, of all the evangelists, focuses in on that phrase in presenting the deity of Christ. Paul asserts that salvation for the Jews requires that "you confess with your mouth Jesus as Lord" in order to be saved (Rom 10:9). In context of Paul's statements in Romans, "Lord" refers there to the God of the prophets, none other than Yahweh of the Jews. At the very least, we can infer that if Jesus were not God incarnate, the close connection in this passage between the Lord Jesus Christ and the Lord God, the Almighty would be idolatrous.

As God begins to unfold to John (and to us) His end-game strategy for the future, He assures us that He possesses unequaled, unlimited strength and power. What He decides to do cannot be limited or contained in any way by anything outside of Himself. Therefore, we can be certain things will happen just as He describes in the book of Revelation. There is no question about the outcome! We can't help but join with the great multitude, who "like the voice of a great multitude and like the sound of many waters and like the sound of mighty peals of thunder" sang:

"Hallelujah! For the Lord our God, the Almighty, reigns." (Rev 19:6)

WEEK 37, DAY 2

The Alpha and Omega

"I am the Alpha and the Omega," says the Lord God, "who is and who was and who is to come, the Almighty." (Revelation 1:8)

Then He said to me, "It is done. I am the Alpha and the Omega, the beginning and the end. I will give to the one who thirsts from the spring of the water of life without cost." (Revelation 21:6)

"I am the Alpha and the Omega, the first and the last, the beginning and the end." (Revelation 22:13)

First and last letters of the Greek alphabet, Alpha and Omega, form a descriptive title for the Lord, picturing Christ as the sum total of all the letters, or the embodiment of language. Taken together with the first words John wrote, "In the beginning was the Word, and the Word was with God, and the Word was God," we see the metaphor taking shape. Jesus Christ is the complete package, the all-embracing Word of God. He was there at creation, and He will be there at the end of history.

When God spoke, the world came into existence; the sheer intonation of His voice created that which was not there. Theologians call this "ex nihilo," out of nothing. God expressed Himself into nothingness and history began, as recorded in Genesis, which we refer to as "the beginning." That is the Alpha of God's movement into this world.

His Omega, the final word, fittingly portrayed in the last book of the Bible, depicts the end times and the eternal state. In the book of Revelation itself, the title Alpha and Omega occurs at the beginning in chapter 1 and the ending in chapter 22, forming an inclusion, or bookends, for the apocalyptic message. This is the same God, start to finish, from beginning to end, with His all-encompassing message.

Hidden (though not very deeply) is an affirmation of the deity of Jesus Christ. The first use of Alpha and Omega as a title is attached to "The Lord God," where it clearly alludes to the LORD God of the Old Testament, the common English rendition of Yahweh Adonai. The same title is used of Christ, Alpha and Omega, in Revelation 21:6 and 22:13. Such titular equivalence would be nothing short of blasphemous if Christ were not identified as the Lord God of Israel! But Jesus is the one seated on the throne of God (Rev 21:5). He is none other than God.

Our Lord Jesus Christ is the all-encompassing expression of Yahweh to us, speaking into our lives in all wisdom and knowledge and understanding and insight. We do well to study Him and believe in Him and follow Him.

Lord, You are the beginning and completion of life for me, and I praise You.

WEEK 37, DAY 3

The Amen

"To the angel of the church in Laodicea write: The Amen, the faithful and true Witness, the Beginning of the creation of God, says this ..." (Revelation 3:14)

"For as many as are the promises of God, in Him they are yes; therefore also through Him is our Amen to the glory of God through us." (2 Corinthians 1:20)

Ubiquitous in the language of Christianity, the word "Amen" is one we say without thinking but conclude virtually all our prayers with. It is one of those words transliterated from its Greek counterpart, "amen." This means the English word is taken directly from the original language and pronounced virtually the same.

Interestingly, the word is used to introduce important lessons with an emphasis. For example, when Jesus emphasized the enduring validity of the Law of Moses, He put it this way: "For truly (literally: "amen") I say to you, until heaven and earth pass away, not the smallest letter or stroke shall pass from the Law until all is accomplished" (Matt 5:18). The NKJV renders this, "For assuredly, I say to you ..."

In the Gospel According to John, every time Jesus uses the word, He doubles it up. For example, "Truly, truly, I say to you, he who hears My word, and believes Him who sent Me, has eternal life, and does not come into judgment, but has passed out of death into life" (John 5:24). Twenty-five times He begins a statement in this demonstrative way. While everything Jesus taught was true, regardless of whether He began it that way, He certainly wanted to draw special attention at certain junctures to pivotal teachings.

In the epistles, unlike the gospel accounts, we find the word amen being used almost exclusively at the end of a prayer or benediction. In that sense, it means, "We affirm what has just been said as being true and complete; we are in full agreement." It is like a verbal signature affixed to our solemn statement. And so we do well to continue the long tradition of using amen to conclude our prayers or as an expression of agreement with others.

But in two passages, the word is used as a name of Jesus; He is "the Amen" or "our Amen." He is God's signature, the divine affirmation of all God has done and is doing in this world, in our lives. When we walk in accord with the Lord, we can have the assurance we mesh with His will. As we become "one with Him" and as a church we grow up into the fullness of Christ, God speaks His Amen to us through the Lord Jesus. And when we present Christ to others, we have the privilege of conveying God's signature message that is faithful and true.

Lord, thank You for being my Amen. Amen!

WEEK 37, DAY 4

Apostle of Our Confession

Therefore, holy brethren, partakers of a heavenly calling, consider Jesus, the Apostle and High Priest of our confession… (Hebrews 3:1)

Normally we think of apostles as the original twelve disciples identified in the gospel accounts (Matt 10:2, Mark 6:30, Luke 6:13). But the term "apostle" came to be used of a wider circle of disciples in the early church with the inclusion of Barnabas and Paul (Acts 14:14, Rom 1:1), James the half-brother of Jesus (Gal 1:19), Apollos (1 Cor 4:6-9) and Epaphroditus (Phil 2:25), among others.

The word "apostle" does not seem to be used as a title but as a description. Certainly, the Scripture speaks of the gift of apostle (Eph 4:11). In its most basic meaning, an apostle is a "sent one," an ambassador who represents and carries the authority of the One who sent him. Clearly, the original twelve were called and sent by Christ. Paul understood clearly that he was appointed by God to be His representative to the Gentiles (read Galatians 1-2). And the church was built on the foundation of the apostles and prophets (Eph 2:20).

As with many truths of the Christian faith, whatever God has called any of us to, He embodies to the fullest. Jesus Christ is "the Apostle" of our confession. Never is anyone else referred to as "the" apostle. Paul always referred to himself as "an" apostle. Peter the same. John simply never referred to himself with that term, although we read frequently in the Gospel According to John that Jesus was the sent One from God. Jesus is the sent one, who in turn sent out others to spread His message. He is the Apostle, par excellence!

John writes: "For He whom God has sent speaks the words of God" (John 3:34). And continually we read Jesus testifying about His apostleship, that is, His being sent from God:

> *"Truly, truly, I say to you, he who hears My word, and believes Him who sent Me, has eternal life, and does not come into judgment, but has passed out of death into life." (John 5:24)*

> *Jesus answered and said to them, "This is the work of God, that you believe in Him whom He has sent." (John 6:29)*

Our confession is this: We believe that Jesus is the sent One from God, who came into this world to save sinners. This is absolutely central to our faith for salvation. There is no other way of salvation. He is the Apostle, the sent One of our confession. And believing this we have been saved.

*Lord, I believe the Father has sent You specifically to me,
for You are the Apostle of my confession.*

WEEK 37, DAY 5

Beginning of God's Creation

"To the angel of the church in Laodicea write: The Amen, the faithful and true Witness, the Beginning of the creation of God, says this…" (Revelation 3:14)

Christ was not a created being, period. The Scripture is clear about that in many convincing passages. Yet false religions focus on these kinds of verses to assert that Jesus was only human, or a semi-god, a created being lower than the Creator God of the universe. What do we make of this?

First, we must examine the passage carefully. The passage does not say "the first created being." It is better understood as Christ being the beginning agent of creation, the one who kicked it all off, so to speak. He inaugurated it. Second, we must review the Scriptures that are clear in relationship to the beginning of creation:

For by Him all things were created, both in the heavens and on earth, visible and invisible, whether thrones or dominions or rulers or authorities—all things have been created through Him and for Him. (Col 1:16)

This statement would essentially be falsified if there were an exception, if Christ Himself were a created being. How could He create Himself?

For from Him and through Him and to Him are all things. To Him be the glory forever. Amen. (Rom 11:36)

[F]or us there is but one God, the Father, from whom are all things and we exist for Him; and one Lord, Jesus Christ, by whom are all things, and we exist through Him. (1 Cor 8:6)

He is before all things, and in Him all things hold together. (Col 1:17)

These statements would be utter nonsense if Jesus Christ were a created being. Such could only be said of God, the Creator.

In the beginning was the Word, and the Word was with God, and the Word was God. He was in the beginning with God. All things came into being through Him, and apart from Him nothing came into being that has come into being. (John 1:1–3).

Jesus Christ did not come into being; He already existed when creation began. If something has come into being (that is, was created), then it was created through Him. If not, then it simply would not exist. We can only make sense of this if we understand Jesus Christ to be the Beginning of Creation.

Lord, creation owes its existence to You, for You began it all. All praise to You.

WEEKEND 37 READING
Zephaniah 3

PERSONAL REFLECTIONS

WEEK 38, DAY 1

Beloved Son

[B]ehold, a voice out of the heavens said, "This is My beloved Son, in whom I am well-pleased." (Matthew 3:17)

In a world of broken relationships and unrequited love, where animosity, mistrust and hatred so often reign, God is love. Before creation, after creation and in creation, God loved, loves and will love. What a relief, what a hope! God in His essence is love (1 John 4:8).

But who does God love? His love cannot depend on having us humans to love; before creation God was complete in Himself. He is perfect—always was and always will be. The concept that He is love, if indeed it is an eternal attribute, requires a Trinitarian understanding of God—or that there are at least two persons of the Godhead. Why is this? Love requires an object of like kind. And if God was complete in Himself, without any lack, then before creation He must have had an object of His affections. Further, it would seem that for God to be pure love, the object of His love must be something greater than His creation. For a potter to love the pottery he created by his own hand is not the same as a potter loving his wife. Perfect love requires an object of like kind.

In Christ we find the perfect object of God's love. God makes this clear during Jesus' tenure on earth. Yet this love the Father had for His Son didn't begin there. We find the first mention of this eternal love affair in the book of Psalms:

"I will surely tell of the decree of the Lord: He said to Me, 'You are My Son, Today I have begotten You'" (Ps 2:7).

Further, He delights in His Son:

"Behold, My Servant, whom I uphold; My chosen one in whom My soul delights. I have put My Spirit upon Him; He will bring forth justice to the nations. (Is 42:1).

The Father then shows His love to His Son by populating the Son's kingdom with us, His image bearers:

For He rescued us from the domain of darkness, and transferred us to the kingdom of His beloved Son" (Col 1:13).

Because of the Father's eternal and passionate love for His Son, we who are saved are the eternal beneficiaries, for we have been brought into the love circle of the Godhead. Indeed, that is our hope! That is real love!

Lord, I am privileged to experience Your love because You first loved Your Son.

WEEK 38, DAY 2

Beloved Son (cont.)

[B]ehold, a voice out of the heavens said, "This is My beloved Son, in whom I am well-pleased." (Matthew 3:17)

"Beloved" by His Father, what a description of Jesus Christ! Religionists and legalists have a difficult time understanding this, for to them spirituality has to do with laws and rituals, things one does to gain God's favor. But genuine love is core to who God is.

Notice, this voice from heaven (which is clearly the Father's) proclaimed Jesus as His beloved before He went to the cross! While His obedience (Heb 5:8) was exemplary, and there was joy in it (Heb 12:2), the Father's love preceded all that. These were the outcomes of His love, not the cause.

The Father was "well-pleased" with His Son. Often Christians will know theologically that God loves them, but whether God is pleased with them is a different question, and somewhat unsettling. In Christ, God's love and pleasure go hand in hand; there is no division between the two. To be sure, Jesus did not sin, in contrast to we who do sin (1 John 1:8). But if we are in Christ, and Christ is beloved and God is "well-pleased" with Him, then we must conclude by faith and by reason that we are, too. God is well-pleased with us.

God is not pleased with lack of faith or blatant sin. But our sin doesn't mean God stops loving us, for our sins do not remove us from being "in Christ." Interestingly, Paul writes to the carnal Christians in Corinth,

[Y]ou are not lacking in any gift, awaiting eagerly the revelation of our Lord Jesus Christ, who will also confirm you to the end, blameless in the day of our Lord Jesus Christ. God is faithful, through whom you were called into fellowship with His Son, Jesus Christ our Lord. (1 Cor 1:7–9)

Yet Paul also wrote, "Therefore we also have as our ambition, whether at home or absent, to be pleasing to Him" (2 Cor 5:9). He wanted to be like Christ, and that meant becoming well-pleasing to God. The important thing here is that this is only possible because we have been called into fellowship (that is, to the sharing of all things) with Christ. In other words, as believers, we are invited into the full pleasure of God that Jesus Christ enjoys. Why? Because He is beloved by God. And therefore so are we.

Beloved, now we are children of God, and it has not appeared as yet what we will be. We know that when He appears, we will be like Him, because we will see Him just as He is. (1 John 3:2)

Lord, let my life be pleasing to You, for I am beloved by You.

WEEK 38, DAY 3

Beloved Son (cont.)

[B]ehold, a voice out of the heavens said, "This is My beloved Son, in whom I am well-pleased." (Matthew 3:17)

The concept of Sonship has tripped up many. How could Jesus Christ be God if He is God's Son? The mystery of the incarnation by its nature challenges our mental capabilities. How could the Creator God of the universe become part of His creation, while remaining fully God? Then, to express the relationship between God incarnate and God who is not incarnate using Father-Son terminology stretches things further.

On the surface, one assumes it is certainly within the power of the Creator God of the universe to enter into His own creation. And it would naturally follow that this would be incomprehensible for us who are finite, created beings. Additionally, the Sonship relationship that the incarnate God (Jesus Christ) has with the non-incarnate God (the Father) existed long before the creaturely birth of Christ (the incarnation). In the Upper Room Jesus prayed, "Now, Father, glorify Me together with Yourself, with the glory which I had with You before the world was" (John 17:5). The Father-Son relationship existed before creation, that is, eternally.

When confronting the mystery of God becoming man, we must rely on God's revelation, for there is no other way that finite creatures can bridge the gap, unless it is revealed by the infinite Creator. And God tells us to think of this in one of the most intimate of human relationships, that of a Father and Son. This goes beyond the incarnation, but exists in the Godhead from all eternity past and into eternity future.

God the Father was pleased with God the Son. What a beautiful picture: the proud Papa and the Son who lives to please His Father. Like Father, like Son. We can use all the proverbial sayings to help us appreciate this imagery that God gives us. Yet, we dare say, the reality is even greater than that. Since God is perfect in all He is and all He does, then this pleasure in His Son is absolutely perfect and complete. There is nothing the Lord Jesus Christ does that displeases the Father—even during His questioning in Gethsemane, where He prayed three times, "My Father, if it is possible, let this cup pass from Me; yet not as I will, but as You will" (Matt 26:39). Asking three times pleased God because three times the Son refused to turn away from "the joy set before Him" (Heb 12:2a), and He "endured the cross, despising the shame, and has sat down at the right hand of the throne of God" (Heb 12:2b). Before and after the cross, Father and Son have immensely enjoyed their relationship.

Lord, I want to enjoy my relationship with You as Your Son does.

WEEK 38, DAY 4

Blessed God

... according to the glorious gospel of the blessed God, with which I have been entrusted. (1 Timothy 1:11)

How can God be blessed? Isn't that something He does to us, the greater bestowing upon the lesser? Yet we see that:

Lord Jesus Christ ... is the blessed and only Sovereign, the King of kings and Lord of lords, who alone possesses immortality and dwells in unapproachable light, whom no man has seen or can see. To Him be honor and eternal dominion! Amen. (1 Tim 6:14–16)

Christ [is] ... God blessed forever. Amen. (Rom 9:5)

God is blessed, yes. But who blesses Him? We must state that either He blesses Himself or that being blessed is an eternal, self-existing part of God's nature. Understanding the word "blessed" in a passive sense would require a certain plurality in the Godhead—for there must be a blesser if one is blessed. Of course, God in His perfection could be both in a singular reflexive sense, but at the least this would fit with the concept of Trinity, in the same way as does the terminology of Genesis 1:26 ("Let Us make man in Our image ...").

However, the word blessed carries the meaning of "happy" or "fortunate." This is the word used in the beatitudes, where nine times a person is declared blessed if they live out one of the characteristics there listed. It is a state of being that is more than an emotion of happiness. Rather it is a deep-seated and joyful contentedness, a consummately appropriate satisfaction and pleasure. In this sense of the word, we can see that God is completely fulfilled in Himself. He needs nothing else to give Him joy, nothing else to add to His contentment. There are no goals, no accomplishments that could add to His being blessed. He owns everything by virtue of His creation; everything He does is perfect, so there are no surprises to Him that add to His pleasure.

We finite humans have difficulty understanding this state of being that is so foreign to us. Yet we long for it and believe it will be our experience when we graduate to glory and enter that state of eternal blessedness. God is already there.

So why then, if God is completely blessed just as He is, did He create anything? He certainly didn't need to in order to fulfill any need He had within Himself. The answer is this: He created because that is the natural expression of His blessedness; He is intrinsically blessed. Just as a happy person smiles, so in creation the blessed God blesses. And we are the beneficiaries.

Lord, how fortunate I am to know You, the blessed God who blesses.

WEEK 38, DAY 5

Author of Salvation

For it was fitting for Him, for whom are all things, and through whom are all things, in bringing many sons to glory, to perfect the author of their salvation through sufferings. (Hebrews 2:10)

The goal of many communicators, whether journalists, theologians or preachers, is to author a book. In some sense, being an author immortalizes a writer, even the most obscure, with the hope that some future generation will discover his or her piece and be blessed by the written ministry. In so doing the author has etched him or herself into written history. To be sure, vanity is something an author (and everyone) struggles with.

Jesus Christ (while not wrestling with vanity in the least) was an author, did you know? Not the writing kind, for the only record we have of anything Jesus wrote was His fingering the dirt in front of the Pharisees who attempted to trip Him up with the case of the adulterous woman (John 8:10-11). What we wouldn't give to know what He wrote, but the Bible has not revealed that to us. The imprint of that on the woman's soul, let alone on the consciences of the Pharisees, had a long-lasting effect.

But His authorship extended beyond that. Our Scripture today says that for Christians—that means you and me—He is the "author of their salvation." Our Christian lives are recorded in His book of our lives, beginning with salvation. We wonder if this is related to the Lamb's book of life that is written about in Revelation (e.g. Rev 4:3, 21:27, etc.). For those who reject Christ, the writing is completely erased (Rev 3:5), as though they were never recorded there in the first place (Rev 13:8, 17:8).

The phrase "author of their salvation" could also be translated as Christ being the "founder" (ESV), "pioneer" (NIV), "leader" (NLT) or "captain" (NKJV). Like a novelist who brings his characters to life, Christ has brought us who believe into eternal life. He pioneered our new life in Himself, because He was raised from the dead.

Sit back and let this sink in. God is creating His story through you. You are one of the lead characters, being woven together into a grand theme that brings glory to our spiritual progenitor. In a sense, we could say Jesus writes His autobiography in and through our lives. It is truly not ultimately about us, but about Him. Like a wonderful, intricately woven plot, where even the smallest of details find meaning in the unfolding of the plot, you and I are part of God's masterpiece, truly His magnum opus! What a tremendous Author!

Lord, I am amazed at how You weave together the intricate details of our lives into the glorious story of You!

WEEKEND 38 READING
Haggai 1-2

PERSONAL REFLECTIONS

WEEK 39, DAY 1

Chief Shepherd

And when the Chief Shepherd appears, you will receive the unfading crown of glory. (1 Peter 5:4)

The Lord is a Shepherd (1 Peter 2:25), my Shepherd (Ps 23:1) and the Good Shepherd (John 10:11). He is also the Chief Shepherd. No priest, pastor or elder can take on that role. In contemporary terms, the Lord Jesus is Senior Pastor of the Church universal and also of the church local.

It is important to notice that our verse occurs in a passage addressed to the elders of the church, beginning with:

Therefore, I exhort the elders among you, as your fellow elder and witness of the sufferings of Christ ... (1 Peter 5:1)

Peter, whom some in so-called Christendom think of as the shepherd of the church, is very terse in his instructions:

Shepherd the flock of God among you, exercising oversight not under compulsion, but voluntarily, according to the will of God; and not for sordid gain, but with eagerness; nor yet as lording it over those allotted to your charge, but proving to be examples to the flock. (1 Peter 5:2–3)

Then he finishes with an appeal to the "Chief Shepherd" so as to make it clear that elders (or for that matter any other church leader, regardless of title or name) are not the chief or senior shepherds. Christ is! Much emphasis is given today to who the "pastor" of the church is, with distinctions in "Father," "Senior," "Monsignor," "associate," "youth," "executive," "children's" or "worship" pastors. The hierarchy would repulse the apostle Peter. Shepherding is a function of spiritual leadership. Peter does not speak of positions or jobs, but of character and function. Primarily the role is voluntary, not a financially compensated career path. It must be according to God's will, that is, done in God's way. The role of elder/shepherd is not simply a position of authority to get one's way, but an opportunity to model the Christian life and ministry so that others will have an example to follow.

Christ is the Chief Shepherd. That means He is the first, He is the best, He is the priority, He is at the head. He is the ultimate overseer. Elders are simply, as some have aptly put it, "undershepherds." We do well to remember this, both those who are elders and those who are not. We must look to God as our ultimate Shepherd, not to men. And elders must look to the Chief Shepherd for their guidance in being undershepherds of the flock of God.

Lord, I am glad that You and not just mere men are watching over Your church.

WEEK 39, DAY 2

Christ of God

[Jesus] said to them, "But who do you say that I am?" Simon Peter answered, "You are the Christ, the Son of the living God." And Jesus said to him, "Blessed are you, Simon Barjona, because flesh and blood did not reveal this to you, but My Father who is in heaven." (Matthew 16:15–17)

"Christ" is not the last name of Jesus despite the fact that we normally put the term in the "last name" or "surname" position. Such naming conventions are more modern than we realize, but in ancient times, a person would often be referred to by his given name—in this case, "Jesus"—followed by the phrase "son of …" In Jesus' case that presumably should have been "son of Joseph."

While it is true that Jesus would have been the adoptive son of Joseph, the husband of His mother Mary, He was not the biological son of Joseph. We say adoptive because His right to the throne of David came through the kingly line, which was Joseph's, not the biological line, which was Mary's.

Interestingly, one of Jesus' favorite self-references was "Son of Man," a phrase exclusively used by Christ 84 times in the gospel accounts. Yet He was also called "the son of David" 18 times by others. Only three times do we see in the gospels the combination "Jesus Christ." That terminology is used, though, 132 times in the rest of the NT, along with 91 instances of other forms like "Christ Jesus." Thus, the Savior came to be known as Jesus Christ.

But where did "Christ" come from? The word is a transliteration of the Greek term "Christos," which translates the Hebrew word Messiah. The apostle John makes this clear as he recorded Peter's (Simon's) exclamation:

He found first his own brother Simon and said to him, "We have found the Messiah" (which translated means Christ). (John 1:41)

Messiah means "anointed one," the long-awaited deliverer of Israel.

Some have tried to divide the historic Jesus of Nazareth of first-century Palestine from the divine Christ who existed from eternity. The idea is that Jesus was just a man, but the concept of Christ was much larger, splashing over into the general concept of the divine that somehow influenced the early centuries of the Christian movement and morphed into an incarnation myth.

This theory, however, does not line up with the historical record. The earliest Christian records show that Jesus was identified as the Christ from the beginning. Peter confessed Him as "the Christ," the Messiah, the coming One of God. Jesus Himself affirmed this as a truth coming from God.

Lord Jesus, I too believe You are the Christ, the Son of the living God.

WEEK 39, DAY 3

Consolation of Israel

And there was a man in Jerusalem whose name was Simeon; and this man was righteous and devout, looking for the consolation of Israel; and the Holy Spirit was upon him. (Luke 2:25)

Little is known about this man Simeon, but that he is mentioned is remarkable. Either he is to be taken as a representative sample of a certain category of Jews of similar characteristics or he was an exemplary case of one who stood out. It is noteworthy that a bit-role individual is mentioned at all—except when we consider his description and his reaction to the Christ Child when Mary and Joseph brought Him to the temple for the infant's dedication.

Luke's account of Simeon mentions no religio-political affiliation (in contrast with Niocodemus, who is noted in John 3:1 as a Pharisee, a ruler) and no family connections. Simeon is described as "righteous and just." One thinks of Job, who was "blameless, upright, fearing God and turning away from evil" (Job 1:1). There are believers in every generation, in almost every dispensation, who get it right! They understand who God is and believe what He says.

Simeon was "looking for the consolation of Israel." The word "consolation" (Greek: "paraclesis") means encouragement, the act of giving relief or comfort in affliction. In the Greek OT in common use in that day, we find the verb form of the word (translated "comfort") used to introduce the "suffering servant" section of Isaiah:

"Comfort, O comfort My people," says your God. "Speak kindly to Jerusalem; and call out to her, that her warfare has ended, that her iniquity has been removed ...." (Isaiah 40:1–2)

Then in that great passage that Jesus quoted in His first sermon:

The Spirit of the Lord GOD is upon me, because the LORD has anointed me to bring good news to the afflicted; He has sent me to bind up the brokenhearted, to proclaim liberty to captives and freedom to prisoners; to proclaim the favorable year of the LORD ... (Isaiah 61:1, cp. Luke 4:18)

Simeon was a genuine OT believer. He looked forward to the fulfillment of God's promised paraclesis, who would provide a solution to the difficulties of the Jews. As Luke further writes, "the Holy Spirit was upon him," the Spirit who in John 14:16, 15:26, 6:7 is called the "paraclete," a related word translated "helper" or "advocate." Jesus Himself, and later the Holy Spirit, is God's answer of "comfort and consolation" to all Israel's problems.

Lord, I look to You as my comfort and consolation in time of need.

WEEK 39, DAY 4

Creator

All things came into being through Him, and apart from Him nothing came into being that has come into being. (John 1:3)

For they exchanged the truth of God for a lie, and worshiped and served the creature rather than the Creator, who is blessed forever. Amen. (Romans 1:25)

Nothing could be more obvious than God being described as the Creator. That He is by definition. Yet one cannot prove this to be true by the very nature of the statement, for we as created beings have no objective position for asserting this claim. We cannot know independently whether there is another creator besides God. We only have His Word for this.

The challenge of apologetics—the defense of the Christian faith—is that the fundamental core of what we believe cannot be proved in an empirical, scientific sense. A microbe under a microscope cannot prove the eye looking at it exists. So we as created beings cannot prove that God exists. We can certainly deduce His existence, and we can argue that postulating His existence best explains what we see in the world. But prove it we cannot.

At its core, Christianity is a "revealed" religion; we believe what God has revealed to us, for the meaning behind everything can only be known if God tells it to us. Some may think this to be circular philosophy or reasoning—that is, we are relying on belief to substantiate our belief. However, if one begins with the belief in a Creator God (and there are ample evidences for doing so), then it makes sense that the Creator God would communicate with His creation. He would, among other things, be a communicating God, for how could He be any less if He created communicating beings like us?

So we have a record of communication that we call the Bible, where God does in fact reveal to us things we could not possibly know otherwise. That communication says that if anything exists, it was created by God (John 1:3). Therefore, He is the one and only Creator, the originator of everything. He is the first cause from which all effects ultimately come. He is over all because He made all—and therefore we all have a responsibility to Him.

As Creator, Romans 1:25 says, He is blessed forever. In other words, no matter how creation turns out (from our perspective), including the coming of sin, rebellion, idolatry of false gods, conflicts and suffering, God's equilibrium is unaffected. He remains blessed forever. He has created excellently, and evil somehow plays into His tapestry of creation, if only in relief to see more clearly His character and glory, things we cannot understand apart from His revealing it to us.

Lord, I don't understand everything about Your creation but I believe in You.

WEEK 39, DAY 5

Deliverer

... and so all Israel will be saved; just as it is written, "THE DELIVERER WILL COME FROM ZION, HE WILL REMOVE UNGODLINESS FROM JACOB." (Romans 11:26)

Another common description of Jesus Christ is that of "deliverer." We should note that Stephen, one of the first seven "proto-deacons" of the early church, in his sweeping pre-martyr sermon, speaks of Joseph among the 12 sons of Jacob as a "deliverer" (Acts 7:25) and of Moses as a "deliverer" (Acts 7:35). In each case, he points out, the people resisted the deliverer. Then as his message reaches its zenith, he acerbically proclaims:

"You men who are stiff-necked and uncircumcised in heart and ears are always resisting the Holy Spirit; you are doing just as your fathers did. Which one of the prophets did your fathers not persecute? They killed those who had previously announced the coming of the Righteous One, whose betrayers and murderers you have now become; you who received the law as ordained by angels, and yet did not keep it." (Acts 7:51–53).

Though the word "deliverer" is not used here of Christ, the implication is clear. Like previous deliverers for Israel, Christ was resisted, even rejected. He came to rescue His people not only from their political woes, but also from their guilt of sin. Yet as the apostle John writes: "He came to His own, and those who were His own did not receive Him" (John 1:11).

Today, Jesus continues His ministry of deliverance—first in saving people from their sin, and then in saving people from sin. Salvation, in the sense of deliverance, is an ongoing thing, not a once-for-all event. To be sure, salvation has a beginning: the moment when a person is forgiven and cleansed from all unrighteousness (1 John 1:9) and made alive spiritually, having been delivered from the eternal consequences of sin. But Christians continue to need a deliverer. Think, for example, of the deliverance God provides from temptation (1 Cor 10:13) or from pride (2 Cor 12:7).

We must learn from the failure of God's people in the OT so we do not resist God's deliverance for us in the face of those things that would enslave us today. We do well to heed the warning of Hebrews:

For indeed we have had good news preached to us, just as they [OT Israel] also; but the word they heard did not profit them, because it was not united by faith in those who heard. (Heb 4:1–2)

Lord, help me believe in Your deliverance in the daily struggles of life. I want to give up my struggle to solve my own problems, and trust You more.

WEEKEND 39 READING
Zechariah 1-2

PERSONAL REFLECTIONS

WEEK 40, DAY 1

Chosen One

"Behold, My Servant, whom I uphold; My chosen one in whom My soul delights. I have put My Spirit upon Him; He will bring forth justice to the nations." (Isaiah 42:1)

Chosen One, or as the NKJV renders it, Elect One—what a beautiful description of Christ in the OT. Clearly Messianic, this passage shows that God has a favorite! And that one, as it turns out, is Christ. The term carries the connotation of "choice" or "best." The focus is not so much on a theological concept of election as on the valuation God places on the one called "chosen." Of course, God's choosing Christ has eternal relevance to us believers in view of the fact that "He chose us in Him before the foundation of the world, that we would be holy and blameless before Him" (Eph 1:4). We are His choice possessions, and therefore we individually are God's favorites. Is that not a beautiful thought?!

One remembers the psalmist's exultation while contemplating God's omniscience and omnipresence: "How precious also are Your thoughts to me, O God! How vast is the sum of them!" (Ps 139:17). He was completely contented, even overwhelmed with amazement in contemplating that God had good thoughts about him. That goes for you and me as well. And it is not dependent on any moral superiority we fancy for ourselves, but rather on the grace of God!

How different this is than the person who, through unbelief, sees God only in judgmental terms and fears that God's thoughts are primarily harsh and negative toward him. God's proclamation to Jesus, "You are My beloved Son, in You I am well-pleased" (Mark 1:11), is true now for believers in Christ, for we have been "blessed ... with every spiritual blessing in the heavenly places in Christ" (Eph 1:3). In fact, our being "in Christ" means we are adopted as sons, "according to the kind intention of His will" (Eph 1:5); we have been lavished with forgiveness "according to the riches of His grace" (Eph 1:7-8). That sounds like we are now God's "choice" possessions, does it not?

Because Christ is God's chosen one, we too, in Him, are likewise chosen. He was the first, but we also are included. We must remember that when we are feeling alone or abandoned, rejected or unloved. Our Savior is God's choice, and so are we. We are His first round draft pick, to use a sports illustration. Because we are in Christ, the Chosen One, we are like the number one pick, along with Christ. God wants us, and His thoughts about us are fantastically good; we can be assured that He not only likes us, but deeply loves us.

Lord, "How precious also are Your thoughts to me, O God! How vast is the sum of them!" (Ps 139:17). You really do love me!

WEEK 40, DAY 2

Wonderful Counselor

For a child will be born to us, a son will be given to us; and the government will rest on His shoulders; and His name will be called Wonderful Counselor, Mighty God, Eternal Father, Prince of Peace. (Isaiah 9:6)

Four magnificent names of Christ! Musically rendered by Handel in his classic oratorio "Messiah," this passage has thrilled many with its lofty exaltation of the promised Savior. It was written during Israel's dark days of sin, amid prophecy of God's impending judgment—first by the Babylonians and then the Assyrians, first against the northern kingdom of Israel (the rebel tribes led by Ephraim) and then the southern kingdom (of Judah and Benjamin). There is always a ray of hope, a lifeline to the believing remnant.

One would suspect that expectations and hopes would have been slim or completely absent upon hearing the Babylonians would completely ransack Israel and take the people away as slaves. But God always gives the faithful His promises to which they can anchor their faith, so that they might not descend into the vortex of unbelief when the chaotic world spins around them. In the midst of foreboding prophecies is this gem, this description of the longer-term picture: One is coming who would will exceed all their hopes and expectations.

By seeing the coming one referred to as a "child" and a "son," the faithful should understand that God's salvation would come from among their own people, born a Jew. In fulfillment, Jesus was born as a Jew. It would not be a military intervention and rescue by another nation. It would be a solution "given" by God. He would be a governing person, and as such, Jesus was a descendent of the kingly throne of David.

He would first of all be a "Wonderful Counselor." "For by wise guidance you will wage war, and in abundance of counselors there is victory" (Pr 24:6, see also 20:18, Luke 14:31). The conquering Messiah will wage an excellent war against all of God's enemies, whether physical or spiritual. He will not need an abundance of military advisors, for His counsel will be "wonderful" (in the sense of miraculous, unusually good). It has been described as "of an extraordinary nature making it mysterious or difficult to comprehend" (Logos.com). In the end, everyone will be in a state of "shock and awe" at how He carries it out!

While we rightly interpret this prophecy as the Messiah coming in military and political victory over the political forces of this world (Is 9:7), Christians have long understood that He is also a victor over the spiritual forces of darkness. And if He is a wonderful counselor at war, then we can go to Him in His Word and in prayer for wonderful counsel for all of life.

Lord, thank You that I am not left alone to my own understanding (Pr 3:5-6).

WEEK 40, DAY 3

Mighty God

For a child will be born to us, a son will be given to us; and the government will rest on His shoulders; and His name will be called Wonderful Counselor, Mighty God, Eternal Father, Prince of Peace. (Isaiah 9:6)

Many times in the Bible we see the mightiness of God, so the phrase in itself is not unusual. But this appellation is given to the child who would be born; He would be called "Mighty God." From our Christian, Trinitarian perspective, the implications are enormous: The coming of Jesus into the world would be the incarnation, God in the flesh, becoming part of His creation. Nothing could be more fundamental to orthodox, historic Christianity.

Consider this from the Jewish perspective, though. When did Jesus ever run the government of Israel? When was Jesus ever called any of these names? Other names in the OT often carry meanings about God; for example, Elihu means "He is God." That doesn't mean that the man Elihu was God incarnate, so why think "Mighty God" in Isaiah 9:6 is a reference to God coming in the flesh? Further, how could Jesus be a "Father" when in the Trinity He is the Son? Therefore, Jewish interpreters see this verse as referring to Hezekiah, whose name in meaning is similar to the phrase "Mighty God." Some today interpret this verse as giving prophetic names to King Hezekiah, who serves as testimony to God's greatness. Even referring to a Jewish king as "son of God" was not unheard of among the Jews (see Psalm 2:7).

Left without the NT, one might be sympathetic to such a Jewish understanding, for the idea of this verse saying that God would become a man is preposterous. In fact, the idea of an incarnation did not "catch on" until the Jews came face to face with the evidence. Jesus Himself claimed for Himself the OT prophecies about the Messiah. For example, in quoting Isaiah 61:1, he stated, "Today this Scripture has been fulfilled in your hearing" (Luke 4:17-21). In connection with this, the Jews tried to stone Him. At another time, they concluded that Jesus claimed to be God when He said, "Before Abraham was, I am" followed by their trying to stone Him (John 8:58-49).

Jesus' followers certainly came to the conclusion He was God, there being no greater witness than a former doubter who changed his mind, namely Thomas, who confessed before Christ, "My Lord and my God" (John 20:28). There is no question, Jesus did many things only God Almighty could do: He healed the sick, stilled the storms and raised the dead. Therefore, without blasphemy or idolatry we worship Jesus Christ as the mighty God in the flesh.

Lord Jesus Christ, I believe and worship You as my Lord and my God.

WEEK 40, DAY 4

Eternal Father

For a child will be born to us, a son will be given to us; and the government will rest on His shoulders; and His name will be called Wonderful Counselor, Mighty God, Eternal Father, Prince of Peace. (Isaiah 9:6)

Odd as it sounds, the coming Messiah, Jesus Christ, would be "called .. Eternal Father." But when we use the term "father" we must ask "father of what?" His being called "Father" is not to be put in relationship to the other members of the Trinity, where Messiah is actually the second person, the Son. Rather, the term "Father" used here has to do with His relationship to eternity. He is the Father of Eternity, as the Hebrew literally puts it. Daniel writes that He is "the Ancient of Days" (Dan 7:9). As the Bible Knowledge Commentary says, "The Messiah will be a "fatherly' ruler."

Another commentator suggests that this title implies that, like an earthly father will not abandon his children, so Messiah will not, after securing the victory of Israel, abandon His people (Barnes Notes). Indeed, it is not all too infrequent that earthly rulers abandon what is good and right for their people and live for themselves. Saul, the first king of Israel, was concerned more about his reputation than with doing right in leading the people in obedience to God. Solomon spent copious amounts of time in pursuit of pleasure and self-aggrandizing public works, even the pleasure of any woman he wanted. In the end, the people of Israel suffered because his failed earthly fatherhood was remiss in training up his son, Rehoboam, to be a righteous king to carry on the godly dynasty of His father, David. History is replete with examples of pagan and even so-called "Christian" rulers who put themselves before their people. Messiah would not be like that. He would be the Father of Eternity, who would always care for His people.

It could also convey the sense that was common in Hebrew culture that the person who possesses a thing is called the father of it (see Barnes Notes again). So the father of strength means the person is strong, the father of knowledge is intelligent, etc. So the Father of Eternity is everlasting. Abraham is inferred to be the father of all who believe. He was the original believer, and is the "federal" head of all who believe, that is, the one who set faith as the standard. He was faithful, par excellence.

Finally, did not Jesus often refer to His followers as "children" (see John 13:33)? Yes, Messiah would be Father of Eternity, who would lead those who follow Him by faith into eternity.

Lord, I have come to know true life by faith in You for eternity (John 17:3).

WEEK 40, DAY 5

Prince of Peace

For a child will be born to us, a son will be given to us; and the government will rest on His shoulders; and His name will be called Wonderful Counselor, Mighty God, Eternal Father, Prince of Peace. (Isaiah 9:6)

At the birth of Christ the Messiah, the angels heralded, "Glory to God in the highest, and on earth peace among men with whom He is pleased." (Luke 2:14). To be sure, at His second coming He will come like a warrior, as John's prophecy depicts Him in the final days:

> *And I saw heaven opened, and behold, a white horse, and He [Jesus Christ] who sat on it is called Faithful and True, and in righteousness He judges and wages war. His eyes are a flame of fire ... From His mouth comes a sharp sword, so that with it He may strike down the nations, and He will rule them with a rod of iron; and He treads the wine press of the fierce wrath of God, the Almighty. (Rev. 19:11-15)*

In other words, Jesus Christ is no pushover. Being the Prince of Peace implies no weakness. Rather, He is like a conquering hero who symbolically and triumphantly rides on a colt of a donkey into a war-torn city and conveys the end of war and a new and better regime to come. He comes as a prince of peace. Only in Messiah's case, He entered the world as Prince of Peace before the final battle is won! Now that is some confidence! That can only come from one who is eternal by nature (Eternal Father), who knows the outcome before it happens.

So Isaiah's proclamation in today's verse and the angelic announcement at His birth form the ultimate statement of God's purposes in Christ. That is what the Scripture says: "For God did not send the Son into the world to judge the world, but that the world might be saved through Him" (John 3:17). For this is His ultimate purpose in the incarnation, "namely, that God was in Christ reconciling the world to Himself, not counting their trespasses against them, and He has committed to us the word of reconciliation" (2 Cor 5:19).

Peace with God—this is what we need more than anything else, that we would be made right with the One whose image we bear. Unless He makes this happen, there is no hope that we can reconcile ourselves to Him. There is nothing we can do to procure peace with Him—we simply have nothing to give Him that is not His already, nothing that would motivate Him to accept our offerings of peace. But on His side, He is the Prince of Peace, and He demonstrated this by giving us the ultimate peace offering, the sacrifice of Himself (Eph 2:15).

> *Lord, I am completely contented and at rest with You. You have freed me up to live for You without any fear of judgment. You are my Prince of Peace!*

WEEKEND 40 READING
Zechariah 3-4

PERSONAL REFLECTIONS

WEEK 41, DAY 1

Heir of All Things

[God]... in these last days has spoken to us in His Son, whom He appointed heir of all things, through whom also He made the world. And He is the radiance of His glory and the exact representation of His nature, and upholds all things by the word of His power. When He had made purification of sins, He sat down at the right hand of the Majesty on high... (Hebrews 1:2–3)

Analogies abound in Scripture, comparing spiritual truth to common things of life to help us understand God. A simile is when a writer says, "God is like a father who has appointed His son as an heir." A metaphor is when a writer says, "God has appointed His Son as an heir." Both are essentially analogies, comparing one thing with another. How else can God describe Himself to human beings? The apostle Paul, when he was "caught up into Paradise ... heard inexpressible words" (2 Cor 12:4). The description of the New Jerusalem stretches our imagination, with each of the city gates described as a single pearl (Rev 21:21)—how is that? I can imagine God saying, "I know this doesn't make complete sense now, but that is the best way to explain it. When you see it you will then understand why I described it that way."

So Jesus has been appointed by the Father as the heir of all things. The analogy is based on our understanding of inheritance of a father to a son. What makes this interesting is that Christ is the originator of everything, yet He is also the one "through whom [God] made the world." Or as Paul wrote:

For by [Christ] all things were created, both in the heavens and on earth, visible and invisible, whether thrones or dominions or rulers or authorities—all things have been created through Him and for Him. He is before all things, and in Him all things hold together. (Col 1:16–17)

So God the Son was involved in the creation of everything, and everything was made for Him. Think of an earthly father who owns a construction company and who desires to build a house for himself. So he engages his son to be the project manager to do the actual building. The son, in honor and respect for the father, does in fact build the house for his father, according to the father's specifications, knowing that the father has written in his will that the son will inherit the house. Can you imagine how well that house would be built? God the Father appointed the Son of God to create all things, and then bequeathed it all to the Son.

So all creation is Jesus' inheritance. It all stays in the family, and we have become part of the family of God by adoption as sons (Eph 1:5, 3:1).

Lord, thank You for making me a fellow heir with Christ Jesus (Rom 8:17).

WEEK 41, DAY 2

Radiance of God's Glory

[God]... in these last days has spoken to us in His Son, whom He appointed heir of all things, through whom also He made the world. And He is the radiance of His glory and the exact representation of His nature, and upholds all things by the word of His power. When He had made purification of sins, He sat down at the right hand of the Majesty on high ... (Hebrews 1:2–3)

Unique word that it is, "radiance," found only here in the NT, is an apt description of the unique Son of God. The NKJV renders the word here in Hebrews 1:3 as "brightness" of His glory. In Mark 9:30, Jesus' garments on the Mount of Transfiguration are described as "radiant" in English (NASB), but that translates a different Greek word. There, radiance seems to be symbolic of the glory of the person so clothed.

Artists often depict the glory of God as a bright radiance emanating out from God, like sun rays in the sky, possibly drawing from this very passage. Michelangelo, the Italian Renaissance artist, in his celebrated fresco, "The Last Judgment," depicted the second coming of Christ as the central figure with an illuminated halo around His body. The empty tomb is often pictured with rays of light coming from the opening.

But Christ's radiance must be more than a physical, optical manifestation. The writer of Hebrews himself had never seen the physical Christ (inferred from Hebrews 2-4), nor had his readers. Yet he portrays Christ as the continual radiance of God's glory. Clearly this speaks of spiritual radiance. In Christ, we spiritually see the manifestation of God in all His glory. He does not show us just part of God's glory as a little bit of radiance. He is the radiance. There is no part of the radiance of God's glory that we do not see in Christ. That is why Jesus said to the apostle Philip, "He who has seen Me has seen the Father" (John 14:9). Earlier Jesus had told the disciples that He Himself was the only source of direct, firsthand information about God: "Not that anyone has seen the Father, except the One who is from God; He has seen the Father" (John 6:46).

Further, as John the apostle wrote, "No one has seen God at any time; the only begotten God who is in the bosom of the Father, He has explained Him" (John 1:18). The word "explained" comes from a Greek word that means to exegete, or to draw out the full meaning and understanding.

So in order to know God in all His glory, we must know Christ (see John 17:3). Jesus is like a prism, through whom we see God in all His many facets. He is like a magnifying glass so we see the magnitude of God's character. And no place do we see God's glory more clearly than when we contemplate Jesus on the cross, where God and every aspect of His character is on full display!

Lord, as the visitors to Jerusalem said, "We wish to see Jesus." (John 12:21)

WEEK 41, DAY 3

Radiance of God's Glory (cont.)

[God]... in these last days has spoken to us in His Son, whom He appointed heir of all things, through whom also He made the world. And He is the radiance of His glory and the exact representation of His nature, and upholds all things by the word of His power. When He had made purification of sins, He sat down at the right hand of the Majesty on high ... (Hebrews 1:2–3)

To see Jesus is to see God and to see Him in all His glory. It is not just that Jesus is God; He is the excellent radiance of God, the full manifestation of God. As the apostle Paul wrote, "For it was the Father's good pleasure for all the fullness to dwell in Him" (Col 1:19).

To be sure, during His incarnation on the earth, before His resurrection, He modulated the manifestation of God's glory. As Scripture says,

"But we do see Him who was made for a little while lower than the angels, namely, Jesus, because of the suffering of death crowned with glory and honor, so that by the grace of God He might taste death for everyone." (Heb 2:9)

But there is coming a time when the glory of God will be on full display through Christ:

God highly exalted Him, and bestowed on Him the name which is above every name, so that at the name of Jesus every knee will bow, of those who are in heaven and on earth and under the earth, and that every tongue will confess that Jesus Christ is Lord, to the glory of God the Father. (Phil 2:9–11)

In Christ we find the glory of God. So what do we do about this testimony of the apostles about God's glory in Christ? What is our application? We can do no better than the application the Bible gives:

Therefore, since we have so great a cloud of witnesses surrounding us, let us also lay aside every encumbrance and the sin which so easily entangles us, and let us run with endurance the race that is set before us, fixing our eyes on Jesus, the author and perfecter of faith, who for the joy set before Him endured the cross, despising the shame, and has sat down at the right hand of the throne of God. (Heb 12:1–2)

Therefore, holy brethren, partakers of a heavenly calling, consider Jesus, the Apostle and High Priest of our confession... (Heb 3:1)

Lord Jesus, I worship and glorify God through You for You magnify His glory. I commit to meditating on all You are and all You have done.

WEEK 41, DAY 4

Exact Representation of His Nature

[God]... in these last days has spoken to us in His Son, whom He appointed heir of all things, through whom also He made the world. And He is the radiance of His glory and the exact representation of His nature, and upholds all things by the word of His power. When He had made purification of sins, He sat down at the right hand of the Majesty on high ... (Hebrews 1:2–3)

One would be hard pressed to find a clearer statement of the deity of Christ. If Jesus was just a man, then the writers of Scripture foisted on us a monstrously false teaching, deceiving millions of people through the centuries. But the writers really did believe and teach that Jesus was more than just a man. He was absolutely unique in both the earthly realm (God in the flesh) and the spiritual realm (the only God, Elohim Yahweh of eternity).

Here we see Christ depicted as the "exact representation of [God's] nature." That God is in view is evident from verse one, where the term is the standard Greek word, "theos," and is so used throughout the book of Hebrews. "Theos" is exactly represented to humans through and as the Lord Jesus Christ, depicted here as "His Son."

Some might quibble that to say Jesus represents God does not equate Him with God. But the underlying words carry a richness of meaning that defies singular translation into English. Read how the various English versions render this phrase:

ESV: "the exact imprint of his nature"
NIV: "the exact representation of his being"
NET: "the representation of his essence"
NLT: "expresses the very character of God"
NKJV: "the express image of His person"

The word "image" used in the NKJV, while not the best translation here in Hebrews 1, is certainly the most accurate rendering of Colossians 1:15, where Christ is "the image of the invisible God," where the underlying Greek word is "eikon," from which we get our English word "icon." The point is that Christ is the best picture given to us of what God is like.

Certainly, we see God in nature, as Paul writes: "[God's] invisible attributes, His eternal power and divine nature, have been clearly seen, being understood through what has been made" (Rom 1:20). But the full picture of God's character, essence or being is much more accurately seen in Jesus Christ.

Lord Jesus, You are my Lord and my God. I worship the Lord God, Elohim, of the universe through You, for You are His exact representation.

WEEK 41, DAY 5

The Magnifier of God

[God]... in these last days has spoken to us in His Son, whom He appointed heir of all things, through whom also He made the world. And He is the radiance of His glory and the exact representation of His nature, and upholds all things by the word of His power. When He had made purification of sins, He sat down at the right hand of the Majesty on high ... (Hebrews 1:2–3)

In Christ, we see God magnified perfectly and accurately. He is the Son, and by that we mean He is of the same nature as God Himself. He is the Creator as we see also in John 1:1-2. He is the radiance of God's glory. And He is the exact representation of God's nature. We conclude that if we want to grow in our knowledge and understanding of God, we need to study the representation of Himself that He has given to us, namely the Lord Jesus Christ.

The world's artists, poets and orators craft God in various images and depictions. Huge murals, frescoes, church architectures, literary tomes and grand sermons have been created. But nothing can improve on the picture God has given us in Scripture. That is why Peter says in his final writing, "Grow in grace and in the knowledge of our Lord and Savior Jesus Christ" (2 Peter 3:18).

How do we see God's character in Christ? We can study the gospel accounts of what Jesus taught about God, the miracles He performed and His compassion for the sick, poor and outcast. We can read descriptions in the apostles' letters of what they saw or what was revealed to them for us. But the greatest magnifying glass that helps us see God's character best is the person of Jesus Christ on the cross, bar none! Like a perfect telescope or microscope, Christ shows us God in both His largeness and His detail.

Think of any characteristic of God, and you will see it in amplified form on the cross. Certainly we see his love: "Greater love has no one than this, that one lay down his life for his friends" (John 15:13). The greatest demonstration of God's ability to love His creation is giving us that which was most dear to Him, His Son "in whom [He is] well-pleased" (Mark 1:11). On the other end of the character spectrum, we see God's severe anger and justice in pouring out his judgment for our sin on Christ. We say "severe anger and justice," for why else would Christ plead with His Father three times (Matt 26:39, see also Jer 25:25)? He alone would know the horror of His father's judgment. On the cross, we see the patience of God, for He is "not wishing for any to perish but for all to come to repentance" (2 Peter 3:9). We see God's reconciliation, forgiveness, redemption, grace, mercy, longsuffering and the list goes on. In His agony He provided for His mother to be looked after by John (John 19:26). Everything about God is seen and magnified in Christ on the cross.

"O magnify the LORD with me, and let us exalt His name together." (Ps 34:3)

WEEKEND 41 READING
Zechariah 5-6

PERSONAL REFLECTIONS

WEEK 42, DAY 1

Faithful and True Witness

"To the angel of the church in Laodicea write: The Amen, the faithful and true Witness, the Beginning of the creation of God ..." (Revelation 3:14).

Eyewitness accounts can differ, whether in the minor details of an event or in the major elements. Juries in court are often called on to determine who is recounting the scene accurately. Depending on the witness, the account can be skewed toward one perspective at the expense of another. One person, in protecting himself or herself or someone else, may shade the facts. Scripture warns against believing the first rendition of a story without cross-examination: "The first to plead his case seems right, until another comes and examines him" (Pr 18:17). How often do we believe what a person says, only to later hear the "other side of the story"? Who can you believe without question? Whose word settles any matter without even the slightest fear of disputation? There is only one: Jesus Christ, the "faithful and true Witness."

If Jesus were just a man and not God, then at some point fallen human nature would render Him unfaithful to His own words. If He were not God in the flesh, then He would be subject to the same truism mouthed of every other human being: "No one is perfect." Everyone is flawed at some level. At the level of His flaw, if He were not God, He would become a hypocrite and couldn't be trusted. Moreover, since He is considered the greatest teacher and moral revolutionary who ever existed, how could we possibly know which of His words could be trusted as a faithful witness of God and His truth, and which of His words reflected some moral deficit at some level, no matter how miniscule it might seem in view of His otherwise greatness? In truth, we would simply not know, and would need, for our own integrity's sake, to cross-examine the teachings of Christ with the philosophies and teachings of other so-called great teachers of morality and spirituality.

Against all this, the apostle Paul proclaims (if we might adapt his apt words), "May it never be! Rather, let God be found true, though every man be found a liar, as it is written" (Rom 3:4). Because Jesus is God, then any cross-examination is preempted with the truth that Jesus is the Word of God, the Logos (John 1:1, 14). He is truth defined (John 14:6). Therefore, whatever the Lord Jesus Christ says about God is faithful and true. He does not spin things, but speaks of God straightforwardly. Jesus asserted confidently to Pilate, "For this I have been born, and for this I have come into the world, to testify to the truth. Everyone who is of the truth hears My voice" (John 18:37). We can trust every word Christ says without ever fearing He will lead us astray.

Lord, I believe You even when tempted by the misleading voices of this world.

WEEK 42, DAY 2

Image of God

He is the image of the invisible God, the firstborn of all creation. (Colossians 1:15)

Many are the descriptions, titles and epithets of the Lord Jesus Christ. One of the most interesting is that He is the "image of the invisible God." To Moses, God said, "My face shall not be seen" (Ex 33:23). In the Law of Moses, God commands, "You shall make for yourself an idol, or any likeness of what is in heaven above ..." (Ex 20:4). Some English translations use the word "image" for "idol." God was not to be seen or represented in any way that would provide visual imagery or effigy. Regardless of the reason (and clearly, God warns against pagan idolatry—the worship of lifeless statues depicting divine beings), the command against imagery of God stands at the head of the commandments. The downward spiral away from God always results in people foolishly embracing false imagery of their Creator: "Professing to be wise, they became fools, and exchanged the glory of the incorruptible God for an image in the form of corruptible man and of birds and four-footed animals and crawling creatures" (Rom 1:22–23).

So against all this, the New Testament declares that Jesus is "the image of the invisible God." The only way this could not be a violation of the first commandment is if Jesus were Himself God. Otherwise, He would be a false image, misrepresenting God.

Paul's declaration that Jesus is the image of God is not the same as what God said at the creation: "God created man in His own image, in the image of God He created him; male and female He created them" (Gen 1:27). Humans were created, and were patterned in God's image. But the text does not say that humans "are" the image of God. They are facsimiles, replicas, copies, but they are not the originals. To be sure, we should live our lives like fine reproductions that are hard to distinguish from the original, but we are not the original. Christ is the original. He was not "created" in the image of God; He "is" the image of God, the original.

This is what Jesus was getting at when He said to Thomas, "He who has seen Me has seen the Father..." (John 14:9). God in His unmitigated glory cannot be seen by human eyes (Ex 33:20). But God incarnate can be seen "a little lower than the angels" (Ps 8:5-6, Heb 2:7). "No one has seen God at any time; the only begotten God who is in the bosom of the Father, He has explained Him" (John 1:18). If a picture is better than a thousand words, than Christ as the image of God is the perfect explanation of who God is!

Lord Jesus, I look to no other imagination of what God is like, but only to You.

WEEK 42, DAY 3

Firstborn of Creation

He is the image of the invisible God, the firstborn of all creation. (Colossians 1:15)

God incarnate, of course, takes the most preeminent position in creation. But we must not confuse this fact with the false notion that Christ was a created being. He took up a place in creation with a created human body, but nowhere does the Bible indicate or even imply that He was created. He existed before the day of His birth 2,000 years ago.

The book of Hebrews identifies Him as the OT character Melchizedek and says that He was "[w]ithout father, without mother, without genealogy, having neither beginning of days nor end of life…" (Heb 7:3). He is the One who said, "Before Abraham was, I am" (John 8:58). No, Jesus Christ was not created at His birth, nor was He created at all. In the beginning, Christ was already there (John 1:1).

So when we read that He is the firstborn of all creation, we do not read that He is the first-created of all creation. So what, then, does "firstborn" mean? It can mean the first in a series. This is the sense in Revelation where we read, "Jesus Christ, the faithful witness, the firstborn of the dead" (Rev 1:5). He led the way of resurrection into new life.

Yet the term "firstborn" also carries the sense of priority or prominence. In Jewish history and culture, the oldest male child had special privileges and prerogatives. All the firstborn sons were originally dedicated to God ("The firstborn of your sons you shall give to Me" (Ex 22:29). But in time this changed: "Now, behold, I have taken the Levites from among the sons of Israel instead of every firstborn, the first issue of the womb among the sons of Israel. So the Levites shall be Mine" (Num 3:12). As a nation, God spoke of Israel holding a primary status apart from all other nations: "Israel is My son, My firstborn" (Ex 4:22). God affirmed this much later when He said of His people, "I am a father to Israel, and Ephraim is My firstborn" (Jer 31:9).

We see that the concept of firstborn, while rooted in the first to be born in a family, came to refer to priority or preference, and could be assigned in a non-literal sense (see 1 Chronicles 26:10). Jesus as God's designated firstborn of all creation is the most important entity in existence: He is most important to God, as He should also be to us. As God in the flesh, He is pre-eminent over all: "He is before all things, and in Him all things hold together. He is the beginning, the firstborn from the dead, so that He Himself will come to have first place in everything" (Col 1:17-18).

Lord Jesus, I worship You as the central focus, first and priority of everything.

WEEK 42, DAY 4

Forerunner

Jesus has entered as a forerunner for us, having become a high priest forever according to the order of Melchizedek. (Hebrews 6:20)

In a time before modern communications technology, long before the internet, telephone or telegraph, long distance communication was done by sending out runners, advance men. A forerunner was an individual who went before and on behalf of another, to prepare for or to announce the arrival of another. The OT is filled with examples of those assigned to run ahead with news, whether good or bad, to announce the coming of someone else. Of course the most well-known forerunner for Christians was John the Baptist, of whom it was written, "The voice of one crying in the wilderness, 'Make ready the way of the Lord, make His paths straight!'" (Matt 3:3).

Surprising at first, but the Lord Jesus Christ is called our forerunner! But this designation makes sense in light of things Jesus Himself said: "In My Father's house are many dwelling places ... I go to prepare a place for you" (John 14:2). He is getting things ready for our grand "entrance into the eternal kingdom of our Lord and Savior Jesus Christ [that] will be abundantly supplied to [us]" (2 Pet 1:11). "Since we have a great high priest who has passed through the heavens, Jesus the Son of God, let us hold fast our confession" (Heb 4:14). Unlike the earthly priests, Jesus is an eternal high priest and has a permanent residence in that celestial Holy of Holies, and we shall follow Him there. So we read that until we get there, He has entered heaven "to appear in the presence of God for us" (Heb 9:24). We are coming too, because He has gone ahead of us and gone in for us and entered on our behalf.

He has taken His seat next to the Father in advance of us: "Now the main point in what has been said is this: we have such a high priest, who has taken His seat at the right hand of the throne of the Majesty in the heavens" (Heb 8:1). That seating is ours as well, as though we were now seated with Him: "[E]ven when we were dead in our transgressions, [He] made us alive together with Christ (by grace you have been saved), and raised us up with Him, and seated us with Him in the heavenly places in Christ Jesus" (Eph 2:5–6).

As William MacDonald has put it, "It is no exaggeration to say that the simplest believer on earth is as certain of heaven as the saints who are already there." How can we be sure? Our forerunner, our high priest, has gone before us, to secure our place there with the Father and announce our coming.

Lord Jesus Christ, the victory over sin and judgment has already been won, and You have gone ahead and announced that to all heaven, in the very presence of Your Father. You have secured me a seat there in His presence. Thank You!

WEEK 42, DAY 5

Great High Priest

Therefore, holy brethren, partakers of a heavenly calling, consider Jesus, the Apostle and High Priest of our confession … (Hebrews 3:1)

Therefore, since we have a great high priest who has passed through the heavens, Jesus the Son of God, let us hold fast our confession. (Hebrews 4:14)

The book of Hebrews presents Jesus as a priest, in contrast to the OT priesthood. We have seen elsewhere that His priesthood preceded and supersedes the Levitical priesthood, for He belonged to the Melchizedekian priesthood (Ps 110:4, Heb 7:11-17). But He is likened in the book of Hebrews to the OT priesthood as the High Priest. Why is this significant?

Our passage today asserts that as high priest He has "passed through the heavens." One cannot help but envision the Jewish high priest on the Day of Atonement, entering through the massive curtains into the Most Holy Place of the tabernacle (later the temple). The curtains separated everything else from God's symbolic presence. In the Most Holy Place resided the Ark of the Covenant, topped with what was called the mercy seat. Here was the Shekina glory of God representing God's glorious presence. Only once a year could anyone enter into that place, under penalty of death. And then only the High Priest, a direct descendant of Aaron, Moses' brother, was permitted to humbly enter with the atonement offering to present to God. The atonement represented God's prescribed method for dealing with all the sin the people committed through the year. When the high priest died, a new one would take his place.

Now with Christ, we have a permanent high priest, who has gone into God's very presence. Not the symbolic presence of the earthly Most Holy Place, but into the actual presence of God. Not through physical curtains, but celestial and spiritual spaces. The distance, the separation between us and God, is now removed. Note well the symbolism at the time of Jesus' death: "the veil [curtain] of the temple was torn in two from top to bottom" (Matt 27:51).

As high priest, Jesus has the permission, the right and the access to go before God on our behalf. Instead of an animal sacrifice, which was symbolic of something better, He as High Priest offered Himself as the sacrifice:

[He] does not need daily, like those high priests, to offer up sacrifices, first for His own sins and then for the sins of the people, because this He did once for all when He offered up Himself. (Heb 7:27).

We need no other mediator: "For there is one God, *and* one mediator also between God and men, *the* man Christ Jesus" (1 Tim 2:5).

Lord, with You as my High Priest I have no fear of judgment in God's presence.

WEEKEND 42 READING
Zechariah 7

PERSONAL REFLECTIONS

WEEK 43, DAY 1

Guardian of our Souls

For you were continually straying like sheep, but now you have returned to the Shepherd and Guardian of your souls. (1 Peter 2:25)

We have seen in other places that the Lord is our Shepherd (Ps 23:1, 80:1), our Good Shepherd (John 10:11, 14) and our Chief Shepherd (1 Peter 5:4). Here we see that as our Shepherd, He guards our souls. What an assuring thought!

While sometimes the term "soul" refers to a person or people in general, in Peter's writings it refers to the inner man, the moral center of his life, the essence of who he is as a moral entity before God. This is where the battle for Christian morality is waged with the world system. "Beloved, I urge you as aliens and strangers to abstain from fleshly lusts which wage war against the soul" (1 Peter 2:11).

Theologians struggle to distinguish between the physical, moral and spiritual aspects of us humans who are made in the image of God. Certainly the apostle Paul, writing under the inspiration of the Holy Spirit, envisioned a tripartite view of humanity when he wrote, "May the God of peace Himself sanctify you entirely; and may your spirit and soul and body be preserved complete, without blame at the coming of our Lord Jesus Christ" (1 Thess 5:23). But the overlap and interrelationship between the three aspects of our humanity defy precise explanation. Suffice it to say each affects the others.

Peter focuses on the soul, but what happens in our soul also affects the spirit in us, and is acted out in our physical bodies and minds. Some have suggested the body is the physical entry point of temptation to the soul, as the physical brain is the window to the soul. Be that as it may, our souls, whatever the means of temptation, are the target for the world's temptation. And for this we need protection.

To be sure, believers have already "obtain[ed] as the outcome of your faith the salvation of your souls" (1 Peter 1:9). And it is their responsibility to "entrust their souls to a faithful Creator in doing what is right" (1 Peter 4:19). The example of OT Lot should be instructive, "for by what he saw and heard that righteous man, while living among them, felt his righteous soul tormented day after day by their lawless deeds" (2 Peter 2:8). This is serious business, and righteousness does not preclude overwhelming temptations. The crucial promise of 1 Corinthians 10:13 is rooted in God being the Guardian of our souls. He is constantly at work protecting us from the satanic, roaring lion (1 Peter 5:8) whose goal is to consume God's sheep. Our Guardian is our protector.

Lord, knowing You are my Guardian gives me confidence to resist temptation.

WEEK 43, DAY 2

Head of the Church

And He put all things in subjection under His feet, and gave Him as head over all things to the church ... (Ephesians 1:22)

Often Christians don't pay attention to the significance of Christ being the head of the church—that is, He is the ultimate authority of the church, not an ecclesiastical headquarters, bishop, pope or pastor. Not even the elders of the church are the head—for though elders are to shepherd God's people (1 Peter 5:2) and are to guard the flock (Acts 20:28), Jesus is the Chief Shepherd (1 Peter 5:4). To say that the pope is Christ's vicar or any human man is His representative is to go beyond Scriptural warrant. "For there is one God, and one mediator also between God and men, the man Christ Jesus, who gave Himself as a ransom for all, the testimony given at the proper time. (1 Tim 2:5–6). Christ is our Priest, our one and only intercessor (see the entire book of Hebrews). To be sure, we are to obey our earthly leaders (Heb 13:17) and follow them insofar as they are following Christ (1 Cor 11:1), but our ultimate accountability is to the Head of the church, the Lord Jesus Christ.

Have a problem with your local church leaders or elders? Your responsibility is to respect them and care for them, for they are Christ's undershepherds. Pray for them. When they are in error, you have the prerogative to appeal to the Head of the church, through prayer. Do we not believe that the Chief Shepherd can override the faulty leadership of the undershepherds? Cannot the Head of the church bypass the prescribed body functioning of the church and directly provide nurture and help through other means? We can never expect to justify our harsh criticisms of church leaders without in some way impugning Christ Himself as the Head.

If we really believe that He is the Head, then we have two responsibilities. First, we are to be "speaking the truth in love" so that we "grow up in all aspects into Him who is the head, even Christ" (Eph 4:15). Love covers a multitude of sins (1 Peter 4:8). Speaking truth is relatively easy; many fancy themselves experts at this. Some even boast having the gift of "prophecy," but often that is a fleshly justification for being opinionated and critical. Aside from the difficulty of this faulty (and abusive) understanding of that spiritual gift, love is completely left out of the equation. To speak the truth in love is extremely difficult. Our motive should be one of genuine concern for people, not the self-satisfaction of "speaking my mind."

Our second responsibility is to so live our lives in the church that Christ "Himself will come to have first place in everything" (Col 1:18).

Lord, I confess that too often I have acted like I want first place in the church!

WEEK 43, DAY 3

Holy One of God

As a result of this many of His disciples withdrew and were not walking with Him anymore. So Jesus said to the twelve, "You do not want to go away also, do you?" Simon Peter answered Him, "Lord, to whom shall we go? You have words of eternal life. "We have believed and have come to know that You are the Holy One of God." (John 6:66–69)

Most people would say Jesus is holy, for after all, that is a common religious descriptor. Those called saints are said to be holy. Certain articles and implements are said to be holy. The term "sanctuary," although a different English word, comes from the Greek concept of holy, meaning "a holy place." But what exactly does the word mean?

Jesus' closest disciples, in the most critical moment of following Him, declared their belief in His holiness, as seen in the words of Peter. God Himself, through prophecy, calls Jesus "Holy" (Ps 16:10, Acts 2:27). The demons ceded ground to Jesus by also calling Him "the Holy One of God." What did God, His disciples and demons see in Him that would cause them to call Him holy?

In its most basic concept, the word "holy" means to be set apart or dedicated for a purpose, and as a result to be treated differently. In relationship to God, it came to be a designation of something for which He has declared a special use. By way of analogy, a person might serve food to their guests on paper plates, but for a birthday party use decorated paper plates in honor of a special occasion. For extra special occasions, fine china might be used. One does not crumble up fine china like a paper plate and throw it in the garbage after one use. It is treated carefully and stored carefully. It is, to use our word, holy—set apart and treated differently than common things.

So far, so good. But is Jesus holy in the same sense as holy objects and holy places or holy people? Yes and no. He was certainly set apart from all other human beings as different. Humans who have come to faith in Christ are set apart for God's purpose, but Christ is set apart as a whole other category. It's like the difference between paper plates and fine china.

Paul was set apart "from [his] mother's womb" to be an apostle (Gal 1:15-16), but Jesus was set apart from eternity. He was with God in eternity past (John 1:1) and sent into this world to die as the Lamb of God to take away our sins. Indeed, Jesus came into this world set apart in His unique, virgin birth. He was the "only begotten of the Father" (John 1:14). He is as set apart and separate from the world as God the Father is. Faith includes seeing Christ as absolutely holy.

Lord, along with Peter I believe You are the Holy One of God. Help me live a holy life, just as You are holy.

WEEK 43, DAY 4

Holy One of God (cont.)

As a result of this many of His disciples withdrew and were not walking with Him anymore. So Jesus said to the twelve, "You do not want to go away also, do you?" Simon Peter answered Him, "Lord, to whom shall we go? You have words of eternal life. We have believed and have come to know that You are the Holy One of God." (John 6:66–69)

The holiness of Christ brings implications. What we know and believe about God affects life. He didn't intend theology ("knowledge about God") to reside in the mind or in ivory towers. Certainly He does not find it entertaining to listen to our esoteric and erudite debates or discourse about Him using big fancy words. Theology is meant to give knowledge that straightens out distorted thinking about life and how to live it.

At the most fundamental level, we are commanded, "[L]ike the Holy One who called you, be holy yourselves also in all your behavior; because it is written, 'You shall be holy, for I am holy'" (1 Peter 1:15–16). The apostle draws on at least three times in the OT where God commands this kind of holiness from His people (Lev 11:44, 19:2, 20:7). Peter applies this to the holiness of Jesus Christ. We as His followers need to act on this:

> *Therefore, prepare your minds for action, keep sober in spirit, fix your hope completely on the grace to be brought to you at the revelation of Jesus Christ. As obedient children, do not be conformed to the former lusts which were yours in your ignorance... (1 Peter 1:13–14).*

The Christian is never satisfied with worldliness or even a moderate holiness, but should always be striving for complete and perfect holiness. This is the standard, and it's a lifelong pursuit. Peter himself, writing in his later years, shared his passion when he instructs us, "Grow in the grace and knowledge of our Lord and Savior Jesus Christ" (2 Peter 3:18). We must grow in our knowledge and practice of holiness—to be separated from the lusts of the world, the spirit of this secular, immoral age, the false thinking of today's philosophies.

A second implication of the holiness of Jesus Christ, whom even the demons respected, is how we treat His name. The use of the phrase "Jesus Christ" by itself as an exclamation entails using His name as a common swear word, and shows huge disrespect to the holder of that name, the Holy One of God. How dare anyone treat His name is such a way! How dare Christians entertain themselves with movies where the characters blatantly disrespect their Holy One, whom they love and worship! Yes, the holiness of Jesus Christ must affect our everyday life and decisions, even to the point of walking out of a movie.

Lord, I want to be holy just as Your Son, the Lord Jesus Christ, is Holy.

WEEK 43, DAY 5

Horn of Salvation

And has raised up a horn of salvation for us in the house of David His servant ... (Luke 1:69)

To non-Jewish ears, "Horn of Salvation" is an odd description of Christ. Interestingly, this phrase was uttered by the father of John the Baptist, who had been struck speechless during his wife's pregnancy because of his unbelief (Luke 1:20). When his son was born, speech returned to him, and he used this descriptor of the coming Savior, of whom his son John would be the forerunner, the announcer.

A horn obviously comes from the bony protrusion from an animal's head. Horns were used to fashion sound-making instruments for worship (2 Chron 15:14) and for signaling during war (Josh 6:5, 13). The altar in Jewish liturgy was made with protrusions at the four corners (Ex 27:2) on which the priests were to sprinkle blood (Lev 4:7). While the significance of this is unclear, we do see people taking hold of these horns for protection when accused of capital wrongdoings (1 King 1:50-51). One can possibly imagine the reference to Christ as the horn of salvation, referring to the call to repent, or the place where one can find refuge from the judgment of God:

> *"The Lord is my rock and my fortress and my deliverer, my God, my rock, in whom I take refuge; my shield and the horn of my salvation, my stronghold." (Ps 18:2)*

However, the most prominent use of the word "horn" seems to symbolize power. Psalm 18 pictures the power of God being our shield—the believer finds confidence and security in the powerful fortress and shield of God, whose strength is likened to the power of an ox, symbolized by its horns. During the exodus, the Word says, "God brings them out of Egypt, He is for them like the horns of the wild ox" (Num 23:22). In the NT, the only other use of the word "horn" has to do with the powerful rulers in the end-time depicted in the book of the Revelation (envisioned as the ten horns of the beast in Rev 13:1, etc.).

Christ, then, is our Horn of Salvation, or as Paul writes about the good news of the gospel, "it is the power of God for salvation to everyone who believes, to the Jew first and also to the Greek" (Rom 1:16). Christ is the announcement of the Gospel, He is the strong security of the Gospel and He is the power of the Gospel to all who believe. He is the Horn of our Salvation. We are secure in Him, our Horn!

Lord I am overwhelmed to have heard Your call to salvation. Nothing can separate me from Your love. I rest in that truth and am secure in You.

WEEKEND 43 READING
Zechariah 8

PERSONAL REFLECTIONS

WEEK 44, DAY 1

Immanuel

"Behold, the virgin shall be with child and shall bear a Son, and they shall call His name Immanuel," which translated means, "God with us." (Matthew 1:23)

Normally we don't think of this name of Christ except around the Christmas season—probably because it has to do with His birth. But in light of Jesus' promise at the end of His earthly life, "Lo, I am with you always, even to the end of the age" (Matt 28:20), we do well to contemplate this name more frequently than once a year.

Let this sink in—God with us. The Creator of the cosmos, Maker of billions of galaxies, each containing billions of stars, scattered throughout the universe. In a more relatable picture, this is the One who has "… measured the waters in the hollow of His hand, and marked off the heavens by the span [of His hand], and calculated the dust of the earth by the measure, and weighed the mountains in a balance and the hills in a pair of scales…" (Is 40:12–13). This God of infinite proportions, whose power is exceeded by nothing else, whose personal space is not exceeded by the extremities of everything that exists, has taken up residence in this small speck of a planet, among His image bearers. The infinite has come personally; that which knows no limits has condescended to the finite. He who is super-personal has connected with the human-personal, God fellowshipping with that which was made in His image. That's Immanuel.

Uncovering the meaning of this name is not rocket science, for the Scripture tells us plainly what it means. But the wonder of it all was how it came to be that God is "with us." The virgin birth shatters our categories of comprehension, for the most basic, self-evident facts of life would contradict such an event. Yet it should not surprise us that God's coming to be with us would be marked by an extraordinary event. For after all, the tangible intersection of the Creator with His creation would be a singularity on a similar order as the original creation of the world. Cosmologists today speak of the beginning of the universe as a Big Bang, where all matter existing in a super-compressed form exploded into the expansive universe we see today. This is what they call the singularity. Certainly, creation was a big bang, no matter how you look at it. But for the Creator to become part of His creation, to become Immanuel, would involve an event much greater than any nuclear fission or fusion. Were it not for the fact that "in Him all things hold together" (Col 1:17), the universe at the point of incarnation would have exploded into infinite chaos. A virgin birth, in that perspective, would seem like an understated event. Yet, in that small act, God became Immanuel!

Lord, I commit to walk in a way that reflects Your presence in my life.

WEEK 44, DAY 2

Immortal God

Professing to be wise, they became fools, and exchanged the glory of the incorruptible God for an image in the form of corruptible man and of birds and four-footed animals and crawling creatures. (Romans 1:22–23)

Nothing bodes worse for anyone than to exchange that which is infinitely better for that which is finitely worse. Always pulled to idolatry, the fallen human heart craves earthly, limited wisdom. While libraries on many campuses may anonymously quote Jesus' words, "The truth shall set you free" (John 8:32, out of context I might add), secularism has blinded that noble quest, turning attention to that which is reduced to and by human reason. Indeed, the apostle Paul wrote 2,000 years ago as modern a criticism as could be laid today: "Professing to be wise, they became fools." Higher education, when not preparing people to make money, finds superficial meaning in the pursuit of truth while denying the goal of that pursuit, objective reality. Truth has become super-personal, whatever one fashions it to be for oneself—it's all relative.

Today's idolatry is the fluidity of self-discovery and self-identity. These are the graven images that replace the religious statuary of past generations and time periods. The results are the same: absolute foolishness. Because the cause is the same. And the exchange is extremely costly. Many satisfy themselves with that which is temporal, shifting, faddish and foolishly dangerous as a basis for life.

In its most essential form, sin can be described as moving away from the immortal God and taking up with and resting one's life on the shifting sand of anything substituted in God's place. It is one thing to blind oneself to the truth by denying God, but it is another to think oneself wise for doing so, totally unaware that one is thereby rendered a complete fool. Imagine a person with a pompous sense of pride and sophistication looking at the moon and proclaiming it with great self-assurance to be the sun!

God, on the other hand, is immortal (NIV, ESV), or as the NASB translates it, incorruptible. The word can also be translated imperishable (see 1 Cor 9:25 NASB). He is truth defined, forever, never changing, never fading, never going out of style, so to speak. Statues made from wood or metals or anything else will eventually rot or rust. If our culture thinks of belief in an immortal God as unfashionable and unsophisticated, then it is the world culture that is out of step with God. Philosophies change, religious thought and theories come and go. But believers echo the refrain: "Now to the King eternal, immortal, invisible, the only God, be honor and glory forever and ever. Amen" (1 Tim 1:17).

Lord, I trust You as my immortal foundation, for You are unchanged forever.

WEEK 44, DAY 3

Invisible God

He is the image of the invisible God, the firstborn of all creation. (Colossians 1:15)

Simply put, God is invisible; we can't physically see Him the way we would see another person. He is beyond our five senses. Yet God at times, straining language conventions, does seem to appear to people in some fashion.

On the one hand, we read that He told Moses, "You cannot see My face, for no man can see Me and live!" (Ex 33:20). God's invisibility to fallen humanity protects us all from being blown away by the unfiltered radiance of His glory. Just as He prevented the first couple from eating from the tree of life lest they live forever in a fallen state, so too, His cloak of invisibility protects us from immediate annihilation. If one glimpse at a solar eclipse can leave a person blind, one look at God could rip a person apart atom by atom in his own personal nuclear explosion.

Yet Jacob, after wrestling with the Angel of the Lord, said, "I have seen God face to face, yet my life has been preserved" (Gen 32:30). It appears God at times does reveal His awesome glory, but it must be dialed down for human consumption. How else could it be? In fact, how could God possibly reveal anything about Himself in a way that is humanly perceivable? Simply putting anything about God into words is a reductionist exercise. Like trying to proverbially describe an elephant to an ant, it's virtually impossible.

Yet God, in the ultimate cosmic condescension, shows His glory in a way that we can comprehend: He sent Jesus to explain Him fully to us. As the apostle John write, "No one has seen God at any time; the only begotten God who is in the bosom of the Father, He has explained Him" (John 1:18). God in the flesh, Immanuel, can now be seen.

Today, we can't physically see Jesus. We see Him through reading the Word and contemplating what has been written about Him. The Spirit of God in us resonates these truths deeply so that we can say, "Yes, once I was blind, but now I can see." The words Jesus spoke to Philip are profound: "He who has seen Me has seen the Father" (John 14:9).

What does all this mean for us? Some day we shall literally and physically see Him in all His glory, unmitigated, unfiltered. Not just an earthly Jesus, but a resurrected Jesus. And then we will not be blown away, but instantly changed. John writes, "We know that when He appears, we will be like Him, because we will see Him just as He is" (1 John 3:2). What glory that will be!

Lord, I eagerly await the first thing I shall see in heaven: You.

WEEK 44, DAY 4

Invisible God (cont.)

He is the image of the invisible God, the firstborn of all creation. (Colossians 1:15)

So what do we do with a God we cannot see? Are we guilty of resorting to the God of the gaps as a way of explaining things that seem to have no scientific basis? We must beg the question, though, what would constitute evidentiary proof that God exists? What would convince us that we have seen God? If, for the sake of argument, we begin with the belief in the existence of God, and reason from there, the process is not really much different from beginning with the belief in the non-existence of God. One cannot simply begin with non-belief. Even the scientific method begins with a postulate and then sets about to prove or disprove the postulate. In other words, thinking about the ultimate existence of everything must begin with a belief of some kind.

If we begin with the belief in God, then it follows that the lack of empirical proof would be expected, because the creator would be very difficult to perceive and understand. Younger cosmologists who hold to the Big Bang theory of the beginning of the universe are finally addressing the question of where that original Big Bang (called the singularity event) came from. Some are postulating a "multiverse," out of which our present universe originated. But that solves nothing; it simply moves the problem of origins farther back.

But if we begin with God, think in spatial proportions for a minute. He must be larger than that which He created. We live on planet earth, which is part of a solar system circulating around an average star. As a recent Scientific American journal article explains, our sun is one of some 200 billion stars in the Milky Way galaxy. "Our galaxy is but one of an estimated several hundred billion structures in the observable universe" (Fall 2017). So we have a case far more extreme than an ant trying to see an elephant. All he sees is a long snake, flappy flesh, thick tree trunks, a rope or a big wall – depending on where on the elephant he stands. But he doesn't know that he is seeing an elephant.

Our inability to "see" God doesn't mean He does not exist. We may be seeing Him and not realizing it. In fact, Christians have long maintained that the evidence is there, when pieced together. When we overlay what we do physically see and perceive with the belief in God, we see a creation that wonderfully reflects God's glory. And we praise Him as "the blessed and only Sovereign, the King of kings and Lord of lords, who alone possesses immortality and dwells in unapproachable light, whom no man has seen or can see. To Him be honor and eternal dominion! Amen" (1 Tim 6:15–16).

Lord, I see You in the ebb and flow of my life, everywhere I turn. Amen.

WEEK 44, DAY 5

Jesus

"She will bear a Son; and you shall call His name Jesus, for He will save His people from their sins." (Matthew 1:21)

37 And above His head they put up the charge against Him which read, "This is Jesus the King of the Jews." (Matthew 27:37)

At His birth and at His death, His birth certificate (as it were) and His death certificate – His given name is listed as Jesus. Because it is the most common name by which He is known, we can easily forget its significance. His name was not just a casual assignment given by Joseph; it was assigned by God and announced through an angel. God wanted Him called Jesus! But why?

The name is related to the mission: Jesus would save His people from their sins. He was marked from birth. Every time someone spoke His name, the Word of God was on their lips, God's plan of salvation. How ironically poignant that the sign above His head on the cross pointed clearly to the identity of the One hanging there: "This is Jesus." He is the Savior. That's what made Him King of the Jews; he came to deliver His people from their sins.

The early Christians took the name of Jesus quite seriously, for we read they:

> Were baptized "in the name of Jesus Christ" (Acts 2:38, 10:48)
> Healed "in the name of Jesus Christ" (Acts 3:6)
> Preached "the name of Jesus" (Acts 8:12)
> Preached "*in* the name of Jesus" (Acts 4:18, 9:27)
> Performed exorcisms "in the name of Jesus Christ" (Acts 16:18)
> Were persecuted because of "the name of Jesus of Nazareth" (Acts 26:9)

His name is central to conversion:

> *"There is salvation in no one else; for there is no other name under heaven that has been given among men by which we must be saved." (Acts 4:12)*

His name is the focus for the ultimate submission of all creation and worship:

> *For this reason also, God highly exalted Him, and bestowed on Him the name which is above every name, so that at the name of Jesus EVERY KNEE WILL BOW, of those who are in heaven and on earth and under the earth, and that every tongue will confess that Jesus Christ is Lord, to the glory of God the Father. (Phil 2:9–11)*

Lord, at the sound of Your name I bow down, honor and worship You.

WEEKEND 44 READING
Zechariah 9

PERSONAL REFLECTIONS

King of Kings and Lord of Lords

... the appearing of our Lord Jesus Christ, ... who is the blessed and only Sovereign, the King of kings and Lord of lords, who alone possesses immortality and dwells in unapproachable light, whom no man has seen or can see. To Him be honor and eternal dominion! Amen. (1 Timothy 6:14–16)

Doxologies, words of praise for God, are abundant in Scripture. The Bible is not just a theological textbook intended for ivory towers and academic dissection. True, it can be studied in great detail, and the making of commentaries expounding its meaning proliferate without end. It seems like in every generation Christian scholars feel compelled to add to the already overwhelming plethora of books on seminary and Bible school shelves, not to mention the personal libraries of students of the Word around the world.

But the study of God's Word should always lead us to doxology, the praise of God. No more clearly is this seen than in Paul's instructions to Timothy regarding order in the church. While great debates occur about church polity, Paul, who wrote the original inspired texts that we wrestle with concerning these things, can't contain his gleeful heart. In fact, it comes in the middle of his solemn charge to Timothy, "I charge you in the presence of God ... that you keep the commandment without stain ..." (1 Tim 6:13). He urges the young disciple to keep this instruction with the view of Christ's return – and the thought of Christ's return sets off Paul's praise!

What has triggered Paul's exclamation? The absolute sovereignty of Christ. While that term has a broad field of meaning, the focus seems to be on His authority, for He is the King of kings and Lord of lords. Whatever those concepts mean, Jesus excels to the max in both. There are earthly kings and lords, those in authority over us by right of political ascension or some other earthly, cultural or worldly means. Jesus Himself recognized human authority when He said, "Render to Caesar what is Caesar's" (Matt 22:21). He is the King par excellence (that is, the perfect example and in a class by Himself). And He is the Lord, par excellence. And He is King and Lord in authority over all kings and lords.

The winds obey Him (Matt 8:27). The demons bow before Him (Mark 5:4-7, 6:7, Luke 4:36). Jesus has the authority to judge all people (John 5:27). He has the authority to take His own life and to rise again from the dead (John 19:10-11, 10:18). He has authority to give eternal life (John 17:2). Yes, Jesus is sovereign as King of kings and Lord of Lords. Nothing is beyond His authority and all authorities here are accountable to Him (Rom 13:1-4). He is in control!

Lord, I declare with Moses,"For the LORD [our] God is the God of gods and the Lord of lords, the great, the mighty, and the awesome God..." (Deut 10:17).

WEEK 45, DAY 2

King of the Jews

"Where is He who has been born King of the Jews? For we saw His star in the east and have come to worship Him." (Matthew 2:2)

And above His head they put up the charge against Him which read, "This is Jesus the King of the Jews." (Matthew 27:37)

The book of Matthew presents Jesus as the long-awaited King, the coming Messiah. Yet a conundrum faces us: If Jesus was the King of the Jews, why did He not go down as the great national leader like King David, the illustrious and revered king who led Israel to be the dominant super-power of the ancient world? Or why does He not hold the same status as David Ben-gurion, the primary founder of the present-day Israeli state and first prime minister?

To say He was king does not mean the nation accepted Him as king. In fact, the charge against Him was nailed to the cross above His head, as was typical to name the crime in that time period. He was being killed because He was the King of the Jews. Although the politico-religious leaders wanted Pilate to change that (John 19:21), the verdict stood, and is recorded for us in all four gospel accounts. The Jews may have provoked this death penalty because of jealousy, charges of blasphemy or breaking Sabbath (a plethora of offenses against the status-quo and rabbinical authorities), but God's assessment was that Jesus came to be the King of Israel but was rejected as the King of Israel.

When He rode on the donkey into Jerusalem on what we call His triumphal entry (also called Palm Sunday in the liturgical calendar), He was clearly signaling His arrival to take up His position as King. But a few days later the religious leaders, speaking as the leaders of the people, wanted His death even though Pilate gave them a chance to change their minds.

So [the Jews] cried out, "Away with Him, away with Him, crucify Him!" Pilate said to them, "Shall I crucify your King?" The chief priests answered, "We have no king but Caesar" (John 19:15).

But the rejected King of Israel will return, the great hope of all believers. He will come as the "King of the nations" (Rev 15:3). He will engage in the war to end all wars and will prevail (Rev 17:14). His robe will be emblazoned with this title: "King of kings, and Lord of lords" (Rev 19:16). There will be no rejecting of His reign, for it will be firmly established. The angels say it well: "The kingdom of the world has become the kingdom of our Lord and of His Christ; and He will reign forever and ever" (Rev 11:15).

Lord Jesus, You are still King of the Jews and You are the King of my life.

WEEK 45, DAY 3

Lamb of God

The next day [John the Baptist] saw Jesus coming to him and said, "Behold, the Lamb of God who takes away the sin of the world!" (John 1:29)

The greatest presentation the world has ever heard. Such a simple little sentence in an obscure part of the world, during the height of the greatest super-power nation the world has ever seen. The extensive and hugely dominant Roman Empire would fade away in 400-500 years, with its architectural ruins and cultural remnants remaining as proof of its decline. Many Caesars (the title taken from Julius Caesar and applied to all emperors of Rome) and subsequent world leaders have come and gone. In contrast, the one introduced by John near a small, dirty river in the valley between ancient Israel and Moab (present-day country of Jordan) lived a rather short life of 33 some odd years (although precise dating is difficult to establish). Although the ancient Roman writings do mention Jesus Christ in passing, the references are scant, and are found almost entirely in the Christian records of the first century.

Yet, to use today's vernacular, we hear John bellowing across the ages, "Ladies and gentlemen, may I introduce to you, the one, the only, Lamb of God!" Many respond with a shrug of the shoulders, but many others respond with wonderment and faith. Those with a Jewish background or familiarity with the OT would immediately see the reference to the liturgical sacrificial system instituted by God, which caused His people to anticipate the perfect sacrifice, the final dealing with sin.

Yes, this was a human sacrifice, as horrible as that may sound. Of course, for any human to commit human sacrifice would be an abomination, because it is not our right to take life, since we are not the giver of life. To heighten the horribleness, it was a divine sacrifice – the putting to death of the God-man, the Messiah, the One God sent to set His people finally free. Their bondage was not primarily to their Roman overlords (although the Jews have certainly had their share of oppression, from the Egyptian to the Babylonian and Assyrian enslavements). Their real bondage was to sin, just as it is for people today.

We may think of ourselves as obscure, small individuals in the mass of humanity. We may not be famous or great, or have a large "platform" like professional athletes or celebrities. But we have been given the privilege of echoing John's proclamation, introducing the Lamb of God who takes away sin. "[W]e are ambassadors for Christ, as though God were making an appeal through us; we beg you on behalf of Christ, be reconciled to God" (2 Cor 5:20). And what a privilege that is! All the kings of the earth will bow before Him.

Lord, help me have the courage and compassion to introduce Jesus to others.

WEEK 45, DAY 4

Lion of Judah

...one of the elders said to me, "Stop weeping; behold, the Lion that is from the tribe of Judah, the Root of David, has overcome so as to open the book and its seven seals." (Revelation 5:5)

This title or description of our Lord sounds manly and strong. King Richard I of 12th-century England was called "lion-hearted" because of his renown as a military leader since the age of 16. Historically, he was preceded by another, and greater, leader—King David of Israel—about 1,000 years before Christ. As a young lad, David killed a lion with his bare hands, grabbing the animal by its chin whiskers (1 Sam 17:34-36). If that wasn't enough to prove his emerging manhood, he also took down a bear single-handed. When all others cowered in fear at the Philistine giant, David, still a youth, ran to engage Goliath without any armor, equipped with only a sling and five stones. It didn't matter the foe, he was ready to take on whatever stood in his way. Why five stones? It was known that Goliath had four brothers (2 Sam 21:19-22), so young David was readying himself to take them all on, one at a time – one stone is all that was needed for each! Surely he had a lion's heart.

How fitting that the iconic king of Israel should come from the Jewish tribe of patriarch Judah, of whom Jacob said, "Judah is a lion's whelp; from the prey, my son, you have gone up. He crouches, he lies down as a lion, and as a lion, who dares rouse him up?" (Gen 49:9).

Interestingly, the book of the Revelation pictures a book of prophecy that was secured with seven seals. As John writes it,

"And I saw a strong angel proclaiming with a loud voice, 'Who is worthy to open the book and to break its seals?' And no one in heaven or on the earth or under the earth was able to open the book or to look into it." (Rev 5:2–3)

But, there is one, pictured as "the Lion that is from the tribe of Judah," a descendant of David, as seen in our verse for today, Rev 5:5. This is the same individual described in the next few verses as the "Lamb" (Rev 5:6). In John's vision, those present worshipped Him:

"Worthy are You to take the book and to break its seals; for You were slain, and purchased for God with Your blood men from every tribe and tongue and people and nation" (Rev 5:9)

Lord, You powerfully procured our salvation through Your humility and weakness as a Lamb. You defeated the enemy of our souls by sacrificing Yourself.

WEEK 45, DAY 5

Living and True God

... "For while I was passing through and examining the objects of your worship, I also found an altar with this inscription, 'TO AN UNKNOWN GOD.' Therefore what you worship in ignorance, this I proclaim to you." (Acts 17:23)

"... for in Him we live and move and exist, as even some of your own poets have said, 'For we also are His children.'" (Acts 17:28)

For they themselves report about us what kind of a reception we had with you, and how you turned to God from idols to serve a living and true God (1 Thessalonians 1:9)

Athens was the intellectual and philosophical center of the ancient world during the first century, when the NT was written. Rome was the political center, but the Greek way of thought and life carried over from the preceding empire of Alexander the Great. Paul found himself on his second missionary tour traveling through what we would call modern-day Greece. First he entered in the north and travelled through towns like Philippi, Berea and Thessalonica, and then down to Athens (and eventually to Corinth). If there was a church established in the preeminent Greek city, it is not mentioned in the NT. But its significance lay in being the thought center that would have a far-reaching influence, not the least of which is for the example this story in Acts 17 provides for today's apologists in defending the Christian faith.

Paul fearlessly takes on the intellectual elite of the day, and essentially calls them ignorant. In fact, any worship of any so-called god, apart from the "living and true God," is uninformed. The Athenians portrayed a surprisingly superficial sophistication, similar to atheistic or agnostic religionists and philosophers today. Paul breaks all norms of the day and proposes an informed view to stem their ignorance. Imagine those learned scholars upon hearing Paul's comments. They were looking for something on which to pounce, and they found it when he brought up the resurrection (Acts 17:32). But Paul didn't hold back; he proclaimed it anyway.

Why? Because the true God is the One in whom "we live and move and exist." The Athenian poets wrote about this, and their country cousins to the north, in Thessalonica, heard and believed, rejecting their idols and turning "to serve a living and true God." God is not something a person carves out of wood. There is a true and living God. He was (and is) alive, not just an object of our imagination, or philosophical reasoning. And He is tangibly active in this world—and in our lives. Our very lives have meaning because of Him.

*Lord, I have turned my back on everything because I believe
You are the one and only true and living God.*

WEEKEND 45 READING
Zechariah 10

PERSONAL REFLECTIONS

WEEK 46, DAY 1

Lord

[If] you confess with your mouth Jesus as Lord, and believe in your heart that God raised Him from the dead, you will be saved; for with the heart a person believes, resulting in righteousness, and with the mouth he confesses, resulting in salvation ... for "WHOEVER WILL CALL ON THE NAME OF THE LORD WILL BE SAVED." (Romans 10:9-10, 13)

To confess Jesus as Lord in contemporary Christian thinking has come up for debate, particularly in the area of soteriology, the study of how one is saved. Must a person submit himself to Christ's lordship or simply believe Him to be Savior? The debate is not new. As early as the fourth and fifth centuries, scholar/churchman Augustine, who was saved from a decadent life, emphatically taught that no amount of good works or promises of such could save a person; it was all of God's grace. His theological foe Pelagius, raised in a Christian home, championed the view that one needs to turn from sin and obey Christ in order to be saved—grace is seen as giving humans free will, and they must then choose to submit that free will to God. Variations of this debate have emerged throughout the history of Christianity. Today, the issue can be seen in the Calvinism/Arminianism debates or in the "Lordship salvation" debates.

It is common in popular presentations of the Gospel to use Romans 10:9-10 as a succinct explanation of what is required to be saved: confess Jesus as Lord and believe in His resurrection (usually termed as His death and resurrection). Does this mean a person needs to submit and change his or her life? Does it mean human effort is partly responsible or merit-worthy of salvation? What does it mean to confess Jesus as Lord?

First of all, Jesus is Lord, whether we acknowledge it or not. Second, no Christian ever perfectly submits to Christ's Lordship (1 John 1:10). It is true that Paul deals with Jewish issues in this section of Romans, and that for a Jew to be saved, He must acknowledge that Jesus is the Lord of the OT, the God of Israel. In fact, Romans 9:13, which says, "Whoever calls on the name of the Lord will be saved," is a quote from Joel 2:32, where "Lord" translates Yahweh! But this does not mean these verses do not apply to all who would come to salvation. The book of Romans has to do with becoming right with God, first for the Jews, but also for the Gentiles (Rom 1:16). And it makes sense that all people must confess Jesus as God, which is the essence of the meaning. So salvation, based on this verse, does not mean a believer needs to take steps to change his life in order to be saved. But he must believe that Jesus, as God, died and was raised again for him, and call upon the name of the Lord.

Lord, I could do nothing to add to or help with my salvation. All I did was confess Your Son Jesus as God and believe in what He did for me on the cross.

WEEK 46, DAY 2

Lord Almighty

"And I will be a father to you, and you shall be sons and daughters to Me," says the Lord Almighty. (2 Corinthians 6:18)

To Christians ears, calling Jesus "Lord" does not sound strange or earthshaking. Even in our post-Christian Western society, Christian terminology endures, and most can easily slip into using the term "Lord" in reference to Christ. However, the implications are huge.

The term can harken to medieval Europe to refer to a certain level of nobility or even to the present-day "House of Lords" in parliament of the United Kingdom. In the first century, however, "Lord" was used to address someone in authority or simply as a formal term of respect. It was not limited to and did not always imply divine authority.

However, Jesus is frequently called Lord, and often in contexts where the word "Lord" is used to translate the divine name of God in the OT. Remember that the Jews bordered on superstition in not ever verbalizing God's name, Yahweh. In written form (throughout the OT), the consonants of Yahweh were present, but the vowels were not (as with all Hebrew writing). English translations routinely indicate the divine name as "LORD" in what we call small caps. When the ancient Jews read their scriptures, when they came across the divine name, they would say "The Name" or similar. It is critically important to understand that when the Greek translation (called the Septuagint or LXX for short) was produced, the word "Lord" was routinely used to render the divine name of God. That Greek translation was the text normally in use during the first century, not the Hebrew text.

So when the NT quotes from the OT, we often see the form recorded in the Greek version of the OT. Thus, our passage today, 2 Corinthians 6:18, loosely quotes and adapts 2 Samuel 7:14 or 1 Chronicles 17:13 and attributes this quote to the "Lord Almighty," using language that was familiar to Jewish ears as a clear reference to God Almighty. In this letter to the Corinthians, Paul has been using the term "Lord" regularly to refer to the "Lord" Jesus Christ, no less than three times in the opening chapter of the letter alone! He says, "We do not preach ourselves but Christ Jesus as Lord" (2 Cor 4:5). He closes his letter with the benediction: "The grace of the Lord Jesus Christ … be with you all" (2 Cor 13:14). Clearly, Paul teaches that Jesus Christ is the Lord Almighty! He is God! If Jesus was and is not God, then Paul committed a faux pas of blasphemous proportions, by referring to Him in the way He did as "Lord."

Lord Jesus Christ, I am overwhelmed that You have made me to be Your child, a child of the Lord Almighty.

WEEK 46, DAY 3

Lord of All

"The word which He sent to the sons of Israel, preaching peace through Jesus Christ (He is Lord of all) …" (Acts 10:36)

Peter had become accustomed to calling Jesus "Lord." One of his more iconic responses to Jesus' teaching came when Jesus intensified His teaching of discipleship to demand complete commitment to follow Him. Most of the massive crowd following Christ abandoned Him, revealing their motives were nothing more than enjoying the benefits of His miraculous activities. Jesus turned to the twelve (what was left of the 5,000 men plus women and children – see John 6:10) and asked, "You do not want to go away also, do you?" A time of testing had arrived. Was Jesus Christ truly their Lord or not? Were they willing to commit all to follow Him, or would they, like the crowds, hang around only while the tangible benefits of miraculously provided food were abundant, and healings were taking place—when the going was good? To this, Peter, speaking on behalf of the twelve, responded, "Lord, to whom shall we go? You have words of eternal life" (John 6:68).

Jesus was Peter's Lord. He was the disciples' Lord. And as he preached that great Pentecostal sermon, the first Gospel message of the first evangelistic campaign of the first believers after the resurrection, in speaking of Jesus Christ he quoted Joel 2:32, "Everyone who calls on the name of the LORD will be saved" (Acts 2:21). His sermon finished with this: "Therefore let all the house of Israel know for certain that God has made Him both Lord and Christ—this Jesus whom you crucified" (Acts 2:36). Jesus was Lord, not just over the twelve apostles and the early believers but He was Lord over all Israel.

However, this was not to be just a Jewish acknowledgment of Jesus as Lord. Peter was sent by God also to bring the message of Jesus' Lordship to the non-Jews. For as Paul writes, "[T]he gospel … is the power of God for salvation to everyone who believes, to the Jew first and also to the Greek [that is, the non-Jews]" (Rom 1:16). Peter discovered this when he was sent to a Roman centurion named Cornelius. When he finally understood it, Peter proclaimed to Cornelius that Jesus Christ is "Lord of all" (Acts 10:36).

He is the God Almighty, the sovereign over all people—not just the Christians, not just the Jews, but all people. We cannot forget to remind ourselves or fail to inform non-believers that "God highly exalted Him … that at the name of Jesus every knee will bow … every tongue will confess that Jesus Christ is Lord, to the glory of God the Father" (Phil 2:9–11).

Lord Jesus Christ, I humbly bow before You now, willingly and gladly. You are sovereign in my life, and I want to live worshipfully and obediently to You.

WEEK 46, DAY 4

Lord of Glory

... we speak God's wisdom in a mystery, the hidden wisdom which God predestined before the ages to our glory; the wisdom which none of the rulers of this age has understood; for if they had understood it they would not have crucified the Lord of glory... (1 Corinthians 2:7–8)

Each title, description or epithet of God helps us focus on one aspect of His character and being, like a prism separates out the various colors that make up the light spectrum. At times God is revealed in all His glory, like a blinding light. When God represented His presence entering the tabernacle and later the temple, the phenomenon is called the Shekinah glory. In the wilderness travels of the exodus, Israel saw the glory of God as a bright cloud by day and a flaming fire by night (Num 9:15-23). Isaiah saw the glory of God in His heavenly temple, as the angels called out, "Heaven and earth are filled with His glory" (Is 6:3). But Ezekiel depicts the glory of the Lord this way:

> *As the appearance of the rainbow in the clouds on a rainy day, so was the appearance of the surrounding radiance. Such was the appearance of the likeness of the glory of the LORD ... (Ezek 1:28)*

One wonders if Ezekiel, for a very brief moment, could see the many characteristics of God all differentiated, yet blending together in a continuous whole. Indeed, God, though complex in the extension of His many different aspects and attributes, is at the same time simple in His unity. But unlike a rainbow, whose colors show seamless connections with adjacent colors and hues, all of God's attributes and characteristics seamlessly flow with every other attribute and characteristic. None are contrasting to any other, but all fit perfectly together, with no gradients, blending smoothly. While we may differentiate them so as to focus on each, in reality, He is one whole entity. Theologians call this the simplicity of God. He is the ultimate "integer," the ultimate whole.

To all this, the apostle Paul, with inspired wisdom, identifies Christ as the Lord of Glory. If Jesus were not God, Paul would be guilty of blasphemy, for God clearly said, "I am the Lord, that is My name; I will not give My glory to another..." (Is 42:8). But Jesus is God in the flesh, and glory is His. True, He "... was made for a little while lower than the angels ... because of the suffering of death," yet now He is "crowned with glory and honor ..." (Heb 2:9). All glory is His, in all its facets, perfectly as one whole.

Lord, as Moses desired (Ex 33:18), I am looking forward to seeing You in all Your glory.

WEEK 46, DAY 5

Lord of Glory (cont.)

... we speak God's wisdom in a mystery, the hidden wisdom which God predestined before the ages to our glory; the wisdom which none of the rulers of this age has understood; for if they had understood it they would not have crucified the Lord of glory... (1 Corinthians 2:7–8)

The glory of God cannot be understood apart from supernatural revelation. True, there are some things about God that we can know from the natural creation (Rom 1:20), but the specifics are not humanly discerned. We may see echoes of His glory in the actions of others, since we humans were created in His image, but that image is clouded by our earthiness, by our sin. The "fine print" of Scripture is where God's glory comes into focus. Only with God's help can we understand it. Why is that? Because His glory is that large, that extensive, that other-worldly. Yet when understood, God's glory superimposes over all this world.

In the Upper Room the night before He died, the first thoughts in His prayer to the Father show what was preeminently on Jesus' mind:

"Father, the hour has come; glorify Your Son, that the Son may glorify You ... Now, Father, glorify Me together with Yourself, with the glory which I had with You before the world was." (John 17:1, 5)

He had temporarily set aside His glory, or as Paul says, He "emptied Himself, taking the form of a bond-servant and being made in the likeness of men" (Phil 2:7). He was assigned to be "a little while lower than the angels" (Heb 2:9), but now no longer. We can't physically see Him now, but in order to seek God, we focus our attention on Jesus. While some may explain this is exercising our imagination, we insist that our imagination is guided by scriptural teaching. Hebrews 12:1 teaches us to "consider," "fix our thoughts on" Jesus, "fixing our eyes on," "looking to" Jesus. Why Jesus and not God the Father? Because Scripture says Jesus, the Son of God, is "the radiance of [the Father's] glory and the exact representation of His nature" (Heb 1:3). The Word of God teaches that if we want to really know God in His glory, we need to look to Jesus.

How exactly do we do this? By spending time reading what God says about Him in the Bible, meditating on what we learn, contemplating Christ's glory on the cross, looking for Him working in our lives and talking with others about how great He is. Then will we begin to understand what Paul wrote:

But we all ... beholding as in a mirror the glory of the Lord, are being transformed into the same image from glory to glory (2 Cor 3:18).

Lord, until I see You in heaven I will look for Your glory now in Christ Jesus.

WEEKEND 46 READING
Zechariah 11

PERSONAL REFLECTIONS

WEEK 47, DAY 1

Lord of Heaven and Earth

"For while I was passing through and examining the objects of your worship, I also found an altar with this inscription, 'To an unknown god.' Therefore what you worship in ignorance, this I proclaim to you. "The God who made the world and all things in it, since He is Lord of heaven and earth, does not dwell in temples made with hands ... (Acts 17:23–24)

Christian apologetics is the discipline of defending what we believe to show that it will stand up against other belief systems. A polemic is the term given to the effort of taking the offensive in showing that those other belief systems are wrong. Basically these are two sides of one coin, and the apostle Paul used both on Mars Hill in Athens as he engages the philosophers. It was different with those who had a Judaic understanding of the world and of God. With them the text characterizes him as "reasoning in the synagogue with the Jews and the God-fearing Gentiles, and in the market place every day with those who happened to be present" (Acts 17:17). Paul had much common ground from which to reason.

With the intellects of the Athenian academy, things were different. Their orientation to the world and life were completely different. Paul went in search of common ground on which to build his reasoning with them. How do you do that with people who are described like this: "[A]ll the Athenians and the strangers visiting there used to spend their time in nothing other than telling or hearing something new" (Acts 17:21)? To them theological/philosophical debates were nothing more than a pastime with which to entertain themselves. The chance to hear Paul would be amusing—so Paul got his audience.

The apostle found something good about them to compliment them: that they were "very religious in all respects" (Acts 17:22). Religiousness was certainly commendable. It's always good to start on the positive! He pointed out their own acknowledged limitations in their beliefs—in this case, an altar "to an unknown God." He filled in the blanks: they needed to know the Creator God who is "Lord of heaven and earth." That is their unknown God. He is not just one of a pantheon of the Greek or Roman deities, one among many to choose from. He is the ultimate God over all. There is none greater than He. Everything is under His Lordship. If the Greeks believed Zeus was the most powerful of the gods, then Paul's God is greater. Christians have one God, who is supreme over all who live in heaven or on earth. This is the one who will judge us all, who raised Jesus Christ from the dead (Acts 17:31).

Lord, help me to remember in my evangelism not to shy away from talking about the Creator God who is the supreme authority over all.

WEEK 47, DAY 2

Lord of the Harvest

Then He said to His disciples, "The harvest is plentiful, but the workers are few. Therefore beseech the Lord of the harvest to send out workers into His harvest." (Matthew 9:37–38)

Salvation belongs to the Lord; winning lost sinners to Himself is His responsibility. The apostle Paul recognized this when he wrote, "I planted, Apollos watered, but God was causing the growth. So then neither the one who plants nor the one who waters is anything, but God who causes the growth" (1 Cor 3:6–7). Praise God He has given gifted evangelists like the apostle Paul, and down through the ages, men like D.L. Moody and Billy Graham. And pioneer missionaries like David Livingstone and Hudson Taylor. Which of us could possibly write the "Who's Who" of gifted evangelists who have served unheralded, reaching out to the lost in every conceivable corner of the world, workplaces, neighborhoods and families? The Lord of the Harvest notices, for He has sent out the army of Good News proclaimers:

How then will they call on Him in whom they have not believed? How will they believe in Him whom they have not heard? And how will they hear without a preacher? How will they preach unless they are sent? Just as it is written, "HOW BEAUTIFUL ARE THE FEET OF THOSE WHO BRING GOOD NEWS OF GOOD THINGS!". (Rom 10:14–15, quoting Is 52:7)

One can imagine the Lord watching as each one goes out, yet in unison through the ages, saying to Himself, "What a beautiful sight!" He rejoices as Lord of the Harvest to see all His obedient messengers spreading out across the globe, across the centuries, with the same message, that of reconciliation between God and His image bearers who have been fallen since that fateful day in the Garden of Eden.

Such a beautiful thing for the Lord, but a source of anxiety for many Christians. The gifted evangelist (Eph 4:11) is like an Alaskan husky dog that was made for running and pulling: harness it to a sled and it is in its glory; that is what it was made for. But for us who are not gifted evangelists, Paul's challenge to Timothy is our motivation: "But you, be sober in all things, endure hardship, do the work of an evangelist, fulfill your ministry" (2 Tim 4:5). Why should we do it? Because the Lord of the Harvest wants to join our feet to the beauty of those feet who are marching out to bring in His harvest. When we join in the effort to reach the lost, we become qualified to rejoice in the harvest and to sit at the table of Thanksgiving of eternity.

Lord, help me overcome my fear of sharing the Good News with others.

WEEK 47, DAY 3

Majestic Glory

For when He received honor and glory from God the Father, such an utterance as this was made to Him by the Majestic Glory, "This is My beloved Son with whom I am well-pleased ..." (2 Peter 1:17)

Hymn writer Jack Hayford captures it well: "Majesty, worship His majesty. Unto Jesus be all glory, honor and praise." The ultimate picture of God, a supreme epithet—God is "the Majestic Glory"!

The writer to the Hebrews conveys this ultimate sentiment as well:

"And [the Son] is the radiance of His glory and the exact representation of His nature, and upholds all things by the word of His power. When He had made purification of sins, He sat down at the right hand of the Majesty on high ..." (Heb 1:3)

Artists have rendered this with bright shining light coming from the throne of God Almighty. Lexicographers, those experts who study and lay out for us the meaning of words, define the term "majestic" as "inspiring awe or reverence in the beholder; it can be related to size, strength, power or authority." Further elucidation of its meaning includes "magnificent, sublime, impressive, very wonderful." Add that to the term "glory," which means "brightness, splendor, radiance, greatness," and we find it hard to imagine a more illustrious description of God.

Is it any wonder that Isaiah fell distraught before the Lord on His throne and cried out, "Woe is me, for I am ruined! Because I am a man of unclean lips..." (Is 6:1)? To be in the presence of the Majestic Glory as a mere mortal would be an overwhelming experience.

The disciples saw a preview of this at the Mount of Transfiguration, when "He was transfigured before them, and His face shone like the sun, and His garments became as white as light" (Matt 17:2). Could it have been a flash of this Majestic Glory that overcame the arresting mob (a mix of Roman soldiers and religious leaders) in Gethsemane on the fateful night before Jesus died? The gospel writer describes their reaction to His self-identification: "[W]hen He said to them, 'I am He,' they drew back and fell to the ground" (John 18:6).

What does this mean for us? Christ has "taken His seat at the right hand of the throne of the Majesty in the heavens" (Heb 8:1). God has "raised us up with Him, and seated us with Him in the heavenly places in Christ Jesus" (Eph 2:6). Now the "Majestic Glory" shares His pleasure with us believers, because we are seated with His "Beloved son," with whom He is well-pleased.

Lord, in Your presence, I am not terrified but I bask in all Your majesty and glory. What a wonderful experience that will be to enjoy You for eternity!

WEEK 47, DAY 4

Man of Sorrows

He was despised and forsaken of men, a man of sorrows and acquainted with grief; and like one from whom men hide their face He was despised, and we did not esteem Him. (Isaiah 53:3)

From majesty and glory in eternity past (John 17:5), the Son of God entered time and space and became a man. Though He came in the "fullness of time" (Gal 4:4), He did not come in the fullness of glory. To be sure, at times His magnificence shone through His humanness, but He "emptied Himself" (Phil 2:7a) of outward glory, "taking the form of a bond-servant, and being made in the likeness of men" (Phil 2:7b-8a). Not as an illustrious man, like King Solomon, the richest and most glorious man on earth in his day. No, the Son of God came into the world as "a man of sorrows."

Who would have ever written the story like that? No novelist could have ever thought up this plot, this story line, especially in the ancient world. The entire earthly life of Jesus Christ was one of humbleness. He commanded no armies, held no public or royal office. No religious leadership fell on Him.

Jesus' teachings attracted a crowd, but mostly because He spoke up for the religiously oppressed in Israel who felt beaten down by the spiritual requirements imposed by religious elite (namely, the Pharisees and Sadducees). One would think His miraculous powers would have paved the way for a new exodus out from under Roman domination for the people of God.

To be sure, His birth was heralded by angels, but only a few were in audience for that proclamation. While today, nativity scenes with wise men and shepherds are found in abundance, a relative few took note of His birth. His three short years of public ministry, though beginning with crowds mesmerized by His seemingly unorthodox and fresh teachings, ended with few followers when His teaching moved to a call for commitment (John 6:66). Opposition followed Him to the point of complete rejection by the populace, betrayal by a friend and abandonment by His closest followers. We see His wrestling even with His own Father in Gethsemane, where He prayed three times to avoid the ultimate task for which He came into this world. Even today, millions upon millions continue to reject Jesus Christ and His death on the cross for their sins.

The Lord Jesus Christ endured as the Man of Sorrows, praise God, so that we might be saved. We echo the words of the hymn writer A.P. Bliss:

"Man of Sorrows, what a name, for the Son of God who came. Ruined sinners to reclaim. Hallelujah, what a Savior! Bearing shame and scoffing rude, in my place condemned he stood, sealed my pardon with his blood: Hallelujah, what a Savior."

WEEK 47, DAY 5

Mediator

For there is one God, and one mediator also between God and men, the man Christ Jesus ... (1 Timothy 2:5)

The Majestic, Glorious God (2 Peter 1:17) became the Man of Sorrows (Is 53:3), so that He would become the Mediator between God and man. That in brief captures the true plan of redemption. Religions of the world have concocted all sorts of "paths" to Nirvana, Enlightenment, at-oneness-with-the-Absolute, and intricate sets of rules and regulations for appeasing the deity (whomever or whatever that may be). The Bible cuts through the muck with the simplest, yet most profound truth. The apostle Paul personalized this when he wrote:

> *It is a trustworthy statement, deserving full acceptance, that Christ Jesus came into the world to save sinners, among whom I am foremost of all. (1 Tim 1:15)*

A number of implications come to the fore upon closer examination. First, salvation must come from God, initiated by Him. We are sinners, and precisely so because we have not gone to God. "There is none righteous, not even one ... there is none who seeks for God; all have turned aside ..." (Rom 3:10-12). If salvation is going to happen, it won't begin with us. God must take the initiative—and He did!

Second, His way of saving us was by sending a mediator. In one sense the idea of a mediator was not new, for that was the core role of a priest. And virtually every religion of the world has its priests, those who go between mere humans and the ultimate object of their worship. But in the Bible's message, the intermediary God accepts, as our verse today points out, is "the man Christ Jesus." The book of Hebrews speaks to this extensively. The OT had its Levitical priesthood, men who temporarily mediated between man and God, but Jesus has replaced them all.

Now there is one and only one priest, one mediator between God and men. Any religious system that subscribes to human priests is a false religion, for it embraces false mediators. Believers in Christ can go directly to God through Jesus Christ. We do not need any other priest. In fact, to attempt to go to God through an earthly priest would be a huge affront to the Lord Jesus Christ and a denial of God's written Word that never changes. We have been invited to directly "draw near with confidence to the throne of grace" (Heb 4:16).

Lord, I am humbled by the invitation and the privilege to enter directly into Your presence, the place of grace, without the need of a human priesthood.

WEEKEND 47 READING
Zechariah 12

PERSONAL REFLECTIONS

WEEK 48, DAY 1

Melchizedek

And having been made perfect, He became to all those who obey Him the source of eternal salvation, being designated by God as a high priest according to the order of Melchizedek. Concerning him we have much to say, and it is hard to explain, since you have become dull of hearing. (Hebrews 5:9–11)

Some passages in Scripture are difficult to understand. Peter admits this about some of Paul's writings (2 Peter 3:14-16). One may think of Romans 9-11 as a candidate for this assessment, where the subject matter of election has challenged believers for centuries. In today's passage, the problem lies in the readers' limitations. They ought to be able to understand the connection between the Son of God and the seemingly obscure OT person of Melchizedek (Gen 14:17-24). The charge might also apply to us present-day readers, for our initial experience with this issue of Melchizedek can reveal us also to be "dull of hearing" when we ought to be able to understand.

At this juncture in the book of Hebrews, the writer takes an excurses from Hebrews 5:12-6:20 and picks up the subject of Melchizedek in chapter 7. The details require much more space than we have here, but the important thing for our study is that Jesus is likened to a king by that name, to whom Abraham offered a tenth of what he had. Though not a name technically for Jesus, the identification is so close that many scholars conclude Melchizedek was a preincarnate appearance of the second person of the Trinity, the Son of God.

The book of Hebrews identifies Jesus Christ as a priest in the Melchizedekian order. But that person is described in an unusual way, "Without father, without mother, without genealogy, having neither beginning of days nor end of life, but made like the Son of God, he remains a priest perpetually" (Heb 7:3). Jesus was "according to the likeness of Melchizedek" (Heb 7:15). And apparently that likeness included "an indestructible life ... a priest forever" (Heb 7:16). If, as the writer of Hebrews points out, the Son's priesthood is unique— that is, He is the only one and it is perpetual—then He must be one and the same with Melchizedek. So what is the significance of this?

The name Melchizedek, as Hebrews 7:2 points out, means "king of righteousness." Thus we have in Christ both king and priest. We have absolute and perfect righteousness. As the king-priest, His work on the cross perfectly satisfies the righteous requirements of God. His work of making us right before God is permanent and cannot ever be lost or nullified. He truly is Melchizedek, the King of Righteousness, our High Priest.

Lord, I have no righteousness of my own. But You have made me righteous permanently. Your righteousness is mine forever. I will never stop thanking You!

WEEK 48, DAY 2

Morning Star

"I, Jesus, have sent My angel to testify to you these things for the churches. I am the root and the descendant of David, the bright morning star." (Revelation 22:16)

In today's vernacular, we sometimes refer to an exceptionally gifted youth as a "rising young star." Christ as a child certainly was that, but He was much more. Speaking in this revelation to the apostle John, Jesus is the exalted Christ, who is now seated at the throne of the Majestic Glory. He is no longer a child, yet He calls Himself the "bright morning star." What do we make of this?

First of all, we notice that he is speaking to "you," which in the original language is plural, indicating that the message is to all the churches of Revelation, and by extension to all Christians today. Whatever we say about the book of the Revelation with all its prophecy, we must acknowledge it is written to all churches, not just to a future people for a future time. He is now the bright morning star, not just in the future to someone else.

The second thing we notice is the distinctive use of "I am" to identify Himself. In his account of the gospel, the apostle John used that phrase very specifically to reflect on the divine name Yahweh of the OT. In the book of Revelation, he uses the phrase three times: in Revelation 1:8, 1:17 and here in 22:16. (While in our English versions, "I am," occurs also in Revelation 22:13, the underlying Greek phrase is different than the idiosyncratic Johannine phrase "ego eimi," translated "I am"). Divine implications are unmistakable.

The title "bright morning star" is coupled with the description "the root and descendant of David." This is a Messianic title with militaristic overtones, alluding to Isaiah 11:1 and 10. Most telling, though, is the description during Moses' time of the future deliverer of Israel:

"I see him, but not now; I behold him, but not near; a star shall come forth from Jacob, a scepter shall rise from Israel, and shall crush through the forehead of Moab, and tear down all the sons of Sheth. (Num 24:17).

Jesus Christ is the "star" who will lead me over the enemy of my soul. He is the one of whom Peter wrote:

So we have the prophetic word made more sure, to which you do well to pay attention as to a lamp shining in a dark place, until the day dawns and the morning star arises in your hearts. (2 Peter 1:19)

Lord, You have arisen in my heart as the Bright Morning Star, for the Light of the World has shone into my life – and now I can see!

WEEK 48, DAY 3

The Most High

"He will be great and will be called the Son of the Most High; and the Lord God will give Him the throne of His father David …" (Luke 1:32)

Luke, the third Gospel chronicler and author also of the book of Acts, stands alone in his reference to God with the standalone title "the Most High." Mark 5:7 shows a demon referring to "the Most High God," and Hebrews 7:1 depicts Melchizedek as having been a priest of "the Most High God." But Luke leaves off the term "God" and simply puts it "the Most High"—a seemingly small distinction, perhaps, but notable for our meditation.

This reference to God frequently (though not exclusively) is found in the Greek OT (the Septuagint in common use in the first century) where non-Jews are involved. Balaam, the pagan prophet, for example, when he was forbidden by God from cursing Israel, referred to Him as "the Most High" (Num 24:16). Moses, in reference to God's sovereignty over all the nations, referred to Him as "the Most High" (Deut 32:8). In the NT, Luke is the only Gentile writer of the four gospel accounts, so it may not be surprising that he records this reference to God as "the Most High." He is using the broadest concept of God that would communicate to his audience. Appealing primarily to a Greek audience, he communicates that the God about whom he writes is the highest of all concepts of God.

The Greek pantheon was filled with so-called gods, all ranked in order of power and influence. The one considered the highest changed from time to time, and the top spot depended on the attribute in consideration. Zeus was often considered the highest overall, but the other deities could overthrow him if he crossed them too much. Others had greater control in different areas. Roman gods were plentiful as well, with Apollo, Jupiter, Athena, etc. The Hindus have Vishnu, Devi, Shiva and multitudes of others. Islam has Allah (although many missionaries would say the term "Allah" simply means God, and was in use before Islam was born). Mormons have the plethora of gods, with ultimately all followers becoming gods of their own worlds.

Against all this, Luke writes of "the Most High." Whatever the concept anyone has of deity or spiritual powers or the ultimate forces of the universe, the one Luke writes about is "the Most High." There is nothing and no one higher that He. There is no force greater than this God. In fact, there is no other god. Christianity is all about Jesus Christ, the Son of the "Most High." This is reality, this is the truth. Narrow-minded? Yes. Because it allows for no falseness. All other concepts of God are false. Only the Bible presents the "Most High."

Lord, because You are the Most High, I humble myself before You as my Lord.

WEEK 48, DAY 4

Nazarene

[Joseph, Mary and Jesus] came and lived in a city called Nazareth. This was to fulfill what was spoken through the prophets: "He shall be called a Nazarene." (Matthew 2:23)

In studying God through His names and epithets, when looked at closely we discover nuances like the subtle hues of the rainbow. On the surface, calling Jesus a Nazarene is about as significant as saying I am a Rochesterian because I live in Rochester. But there is more to the story. First, we must correct a common misunderstanding: Jesus was not a "Nazarite," that is, an OT individual who took the Nazarite vow involving certain asceticisms. A "Nazarene" (different word) is a person who hails from the village of Nazareth.

Second, there is no prophecy recorded in the OT that specifically says Jesus would be called a Nazarene, yet on the surface that is what Matthew seems to be saying. This has created a wide variety of explanations through the years. An in-depth study of the alternatives is beyond the scope of this essay, but suffice it to say that Matthew is probably alluding to an OT prediction in a general way (we might even say an applicational sort of way). Jesus as the Messiah came from an obscure, humble origin, which was predicted in the OT. Remember Nathanael's response to Philip telling him about Jesus: "Can anything good come out of Nazareth?" (John 1:46). Such identification of Jesus' origin would not bode well with those who had expected a more lofty start for the One who would deliver Israel from its Roman oppressors. To call Jesus a Nazarene would be a slight, a sneer.

This reaction of insinuation fits well with the suffering servant passage of Isaiah in particular: "He was despised ... and we did not esteem Him." First-century readers would understand Matthew to be saying that Jesus had an ignoble beginning, not being attractive in the usual way that humans are impressed with people—just as the OT prophets foresaw.

Jesus didn't have a privileged start, riding on the coattails of an illustrious father, from a well-to-do city, with the finest human pedigree. Rather, He "emptied Himself, taking the form of a bond-servant, and being made in the likeness of men. Being found in appearance as a man, He humbled Himself ..." (Phil 2:7–8). He was not known as a Bethlehemite, which would have looked much better on His resume, being from the city of great King David, the greatest, most iconic king in Israel's history. Jesus' earthly beginning was inauspicious, from the backwoods (so to speak) village of Nazareth.

> *Lord, I now understand that You can do great things through me even though I do not have an advantageous or privileged upbringing.*

WEEK 48, DAY 5

Only Begotten Son

No one has seen God at any time; the only begotten God who is in the bosom of the Father, He has explained Him. (John 1:18)

We include "Son" in this epithet because of the NKJV translation (and the KJV before it), although the inclusion of the word is disputed. Most modern translations do not include it. Some blame this on a modern drift from the so-called "authorized" version of the Word of God. But that is not the case; there is actually a legitimate disagreement on the form of the original Greek text behind our English translations.

The conflicting issue has to do with how we determine among the over 5,000 extant (currently existing) ancient Greek manuscripts which ones reflect the original documents. Of course, we do not have the original, physical writings of the NT authors; we have copies made from copies in a long line of textual iterations. Until the late 1400s all copies were created by hand, as scribes meticulously created faithful facsimiles of previous copies. In time minor discrepancies crept in, with copies in certain geographical areas showing signs of identifiable characteristics. None of these differences in the copies affect major doctrines, but at times they must be dealt with, as in our passage today.

In the fourth century, the Emperor Constantine, ostensibly professing Christian faith, authorized 50 copies to be made from one copy in common use in the eastern part of the Roman Empire. That "edition" became the standard which was copiously copied, resulting in what is now called the "Byzantine" family of manuscripts. This played significantly into what is popularly called the "Majority Text," since it represents the overwhelming preponderance of ancient texts that exist today. These date primarily to the 9th through 11th centuries and form the textual family upon which the KJV and NKJV rely.

Modern archeological discoveries have uncovered manuscripts dating back much earlier than the Middle Ages, as early as the second through fourth centuries. These older texts differ in places from the Majority Text tradition and collectively are sometimes called the "Western" text. Many feel this textual tradition needs to be considered in all discussions concerning the original text. While this has been a cursory overview of what is called "textual criticism," suffice it to say that some of the earliest manuscripts do not include "son" in our verse for today, rendering it similarly to the NASB: "the only begotten God." In our next essay, we will contemplate the significance of both versions' renderings.

Lord, whether this verse says Jesus is the only begotten Son of God, or the only begotten God, Your Word makes it clear that He is the Son and He is God.

WEEKEND 48 READING
Zechariah 13

PERSONAL REFLECTIONS

WEEK 49, DAY 1

Only Begotten Son (cont.)

No one has seen God at any time; the only begotten God who is in the bosom of the Father, He has explained Him. (John 1:18)

While the inclusion of "Son" in John 1:18 ("only begotten Son of God" NKJV) is questionable in the ancient manuscripts, the phrase "the only begotten Son" is indisputably included elsewhere in the apostle John's writings. The most well-known is:

> *"For God so loved the world, that He gave His only begotten Son, that whoever believes in Him shall not perish, but have eternal life." (John 3:16, see also John 3:18, 1 John 4:9)*

So what exactly does it mean that He is the "only begotten"? First, it sets Jesus apart from all others who are called "sons." On the one hand, we believers are often called "sons of God." We became "sons of God" through faith (Gal 3:26). We are often called "children" of God, using a different word than "sons," for example:

> *"But as many as received Him, to them He gave the right to become children of God, even to those who believe in His name ..." (John 1:12)*

Yet our sonship comes through adoption (Rom 8:23, Gal 4:6, Eph 1:5). Scripture never says that we as believers are "begotten" sons of God. Even the angels, who are sometimes referred to as "sons of God" in the OT (see Gen 6:2, Job 1:6, 2:1), are not begotten of God:

> *"For to which of the angels did He ever say, 'You are My Son, Today I have begotten You'? And again, 'I will be a Father to Him and He shall be a Son to Me'?" (Heb 1:5)*

English translations render the single Greek word "monogenes" as two words. The first, "only," stresses uniqueness; the second, "begotten," emphasizes origin. The focus is on the incomparable nature of Christ. The word is used to point to an only child of a mother or father (Luke 7:12, 8:42). God had only one child who originated from Him "organically," we might say. Christ "issued" from God, as theologians put it, as the incomparable Son of His father.

In John 1:18, while the word "Son" may not be original in the text, sonship is implied. If Jesus is the "only begotten" Son (John 3:16), then He must be the "only begotten" God. That is because He is of the same nature as the Father, just as we are of the same nature as our earthly parents. Therefore, Jesus is in the best position to reveal to us the true nature of God the Father.

Lord, thank You for bringing me into Your family as an adopted child.

WEEK 49, DAY 2

Our Passover

Clean out the old leaven so that you may be a new lump, just as you are in fact unleavened. For Christ our Passover also has been sacrificed. (1 Corinthians 5:7)

What a beautiful word picture of Christ this places before us! He is "our Passover." What unique light of the glory of Christ does this reveal to us? In context, the apostle Paul, writing under the inspiration of the Holy Spirit, is dealing with unrepentant immorality in the church at Corinth. The believers there were tolerant of illicit sexual activity (1 Cor 5:1). Interestingly, since only the sinning "brother" is mentioned for discipline, it may even have been a case of sexual abuse. The church had become "arrogant (1 Cor 5:2) and "boasting" about their tolerance, like those today who look down their long pseudo-sophisticated noses on Christians who hold to a high standard of morality. The snide labels of "Victorian" or "Puritan" have become pejorative swipes at biblical teachings.

The apostle Paul thoroughly chastises such attitudes and counsels the church to deal definitively with the sinning individual. Non-judgmentalism ("live and let live" philosophy or "boys will be boys" dismissal) will not work in the church. He reasons this way: If you allow sin, it will affect the whole church. In fact, the whole church there was permeated with sin, as we can see from the plethora of problems Paul addresses in this letter. The Corinthians were a prime example of the truth, "a little leaven [yeast] leavens the whole lump of dough" (1 Cor 5:6). Anyone who has baked bread knows that adding a little yeast permeates an entire batch of dough. In the same way, sin by someone in the church can affect the entire church. In the body metaphor of 1 Corinthians 12, bacteria entering one part of the body makes the whole body sick.

Paul's Passover metaphor points to the time of Israel's birth as a nation, when God liberated them from Egypt and gave them a Passover celebration where a lamb was killed to remind them of their redemption. They were to eat unleavened bread, reminding them of their new, different life—a life based on God's Word, not Egyptian ways. Unfortunately, the Jews kept returning to Egyptian ways and also to their gods. The Corinthians were doing essentially the same thing.

The same truths apply now. Christ is our Passover, in that He provided eternal redemption. We need to leave the old ways of the world behind and conduct ourselves with the highest Christian standards.

Lord, the world has such a strong pull. Please help me resist and to continually leave those things behind.

WEEK 49, DAY 3

Ruler of Kings

... Jesus Christ, the faithful witness, the firstborn of the dead, and the ruler of the kings of the earth ... (Revelation 1:5)

Authority comes intrinsic to life—we all have those to whom we answer. Of course our ultimate authority or ruler is the Creator God, who was manifest in the flesh. But we also have earthly rulers we must obey, like our government, our local police and our bosses at work:

Every person is to be in subjection to the governing authorities. For there is no authority except from God, and those which exist are established by God. Therefore whoever resists authority has opposed the ordinance of God; and they who have opposed will receive condemnation upon themselves. (Rom 13:1–2)

Young Christians get caught in endless debates about what to do when the laws of man conflict with the laws of God. For example, should Christians smuggle Bibles into countries where that is forbidden? Should we lie when asked, "Are you smuggling Bibles into our country?" We must remember when interpreting Scripture that general principles are often presented without addressing every possible application. That is why each believer must be "diligent to present [himself] approved to God as a workman who does not need to be ashamed, accurately handling the word of truth" (2 Tim 2:15). If God had explained every single application and interaction of His Word in complete detail, it would have created a book so large no library on earth would be big enough to hold it. But He has given us His Spirit and wisdom to study the Word when tension exists in applying seemingly conflicting Biblical teachings.

What to us might be a dilemma, to the apostles was a no-brainer. When the commands of earthly authority conflicted with the clear command of God, they would always go with God. When forbidden by the religious authorities to preach the Gospel, Peter and John responded, "Whether it is right in the sight of God to give heed to you rather than to God, you be the judge" (Acts 4:19). Later, after continuing to preach Christ, the command to stop was repeated to them. This time Peter, with the complete agreement of all the other apostles, confidently and tersely said, "We must obey God rather than men" (Acts 5:29).

We should obey the authorities of this earth because the ruler of all authorities has commanded us to do so. But when they contravene God's higher commands, we must remember our higher allegiance, to the Ruler of Kings.

Lord, I am willing to suffer the consequences when I refuse to obey an authority in my life that requires me to be disloyal to Christ.

WEEK 49, DAY 4

Prince of Life

"But you disowned the Holy and Righteous One and asked for a murderer to be granted to you, but put to death the Prince of life, the one whom God raised from the dead, a fact to which we are witnesses." (Acts 3:14–15)

Second sermons often build on the first sermons, and this one proves that true. In Peter's first, he blasts his countrymen for their rejection of Christ:

"Men of Israel, listen to these words: Jesus the Nazarene, a man attested to you by God with miracles and wonders and signs which God performed through Him in your midst, just as you yourselves know— this Man, delivered over by the predetermined plan and foreknowledge of God, you nailed to a cross by the hands of godless men and put Him to death. (Acts 2:22–23)

Now, he further describes this "attested one" as "Holy," "Righteous" and "Prince of life." Given just one of these, their rejection of Christ was shocking. The last, our focus today, is additionally ironic: They put to death the Prince of life. How could they do such a thing? Further, how is such an action even possible?

The word translated "prince" comes from the root Greek word that carries the connotation of "primacy" and is related to the word in Revelation 1:5, where Jesus is the "ruler of kings." Here the specific word refers to primacy by authorship. That is why many English versions render this as Jesus being the "Author of life." So we have here the idea of someone writing a book, and then the very characters of that book he created conspiring to put him to death! Such things have the makings of a good sci-fi movie. But that is essentially the nature of humanity's rejection of their Creator, the one who authored us all into existence, in the grand story of life. His rejection is the penultimate chapter of the book.

As the story unfolds, the Father of the Author of Life writes the final chapter, after the one about the Author's death, where all the various threads of the story come to a perfect resolution: The Author is raised back to life! The story leaps, as it were, off the pages, a depressing, fatalistic ending being wonderfully transformed into the most fantastic story ever. The Author became part of his own novel, died in the story (a very real death) and was raised again. What an Author! What a story! He is the Prince, the Author of Life. We are His created characters in the story, created for a real life of communion with the One who Authored us into existence!

Lord, thank You for writing Your life into mine, that I might really live!

WEEK 49, DAY 5

Prophet

"Moses said, 'THE LORD GOD WILL RAISE UP FOR YOU A PROPHET LIKE ME FROM YOUR BRETHREN; TO HIM YOU SHALL GIVE HEED to everything He says to you.'" (Acts 3:22).

Peter's sermon shortly after Pentecost identifies Jesus as a prophet just like Moses, a statement which bordered on treason to the Jewish people. Moses was so highly revered that to put anyone in the same category would be tantamount to diminishing Moses. The Law of Moses was at the very core of Jewish life. Every child began memorizing it from an early age. The issue for most was not what the Law of Moses said, but how to apply it in the details of life. The knowledge of it permeated all of their lives.

The people of Israel should have expected another one like Moses, but like so many prophecies, they rejected the message God had spoken directly to their hypocrisy and self-righteousness. The one Moses prophesied about was One whom they should obey just as though His teachings came from Moses himself! In other words, Christ's teachings had the same authority as the Law of Moses!

To us today, what's the big deal? To us it would be more important that Jesus was identified as God. But to Jews, that meant Jesus was to be obeyed just like Moses himself! To further stress the matter, Peter goes on: "And it will be that every soul that does not heed that prophet shall be utterly destroyed from among the people" (Acts 3:23). This reminds us of what Jesus said:

> *"Everyone who hears these words of Mine and does not act on them, will be like a foolish man who built his house on the sand. The rain fell, and the floods came, and the winds blew and slammed against that house; and it fell—and great was its fall." (Matt 7:26–27)*

Such statements were unthinkable and unacceptable to the Jews, who for their whole lives gave complete, exclusive allegiance to the Law of Moses.

Some today have fallen into the misconception that since we are saved by grace apart from the law (Rom 3:21, 28), we do not therefore need to obey God. But that simply is not so. It is true that obedience does not save us; in fact, our inability to perfectly obey God was the cause of our need for grace. But God did not save us to "enjoy" a lawless life. Sin may not bring us eternal judgment, but it can certainly put our lives here in shambles with much heartache, like a house fallen in the midst of life's difficulties. Christ is the new prophet that replaces Moses. And we need to obey His commands for an abundant life.

Lord, thank You for reminding me that You are the prophet of God speaking truth into my life. It is You whom I exclusively obey. Help me in my disobedience!

WEEKEND 49 READING
Zechariah 14

PERSONAL REFLECTIONS

WEEK 50, DAY 1

Spiritual Rock

For I do not want you to be unaware, brethren, that our fathers ... all drank the same spiritual drink, for they were drinking from a spiritual rock which followed them; and the rock was Christ. (1 Corinthians 10:1–4)

We often proclaim, "Jesus is our Rock," extolling His solidness, unchangeableness—and rightly so. We can depend on Him, and when we set our lives on His teachings we are on a solid foundation (Matt 7:25). Peter's declaration of faith was said to be rock solid when Jesus said, "[U]pon this rock I will build my church" (Matt 16:18). God is an "everlasting Rock" (Is 26:4, Hab 1:12) whose truth and judgment will not change. God Himself says, "Is there any God besides Me, or is there any other Rock? I know of none" (Is 44:8). The Psalms are full of references to God as a Rock in whom I find deliverance and protection (Ps 18:2), strength (Ps 31:2) and sure-footedness in life (Ps 40:2) and eternity (Ps 62:2, 6).

However, in 1 Corinthians 10:1-4, the metaphor takes on a different connotation. The backstory comes from Exodus 17, where the Lord addressed Israel's complaining about being thirsty during the exodus travel from Egypt in the desert of Sinai. It got so bad that Moses feared they would kill him. So God told Moses to hit a specific rock at Horeb in plain sight before the people to result in a flow of water more than enough to meet their need. Moses was to use the same rod he had used to strike the Nile River during the ten plagues on Egypt before they left the land. Those plagues were judgment for repressing the Israelite people.

Paul refers to this incident, which apparently was not a one-off occurrence during the Exodus. The point, though, is that Christ is likened to that Rock. That was a picture of the coming Messiah. Paul, a few verses later, cites these kinds of OT stories as "examples" (1 Cor 10:6, 11). The Greek word he uses is "tupos" from which we get our English word "type." Some, then, have seen in this story a "type" of Christ, an OT event that specifically pre-figured Christ in a particular way, like a mold whose shape gives a preview of that which it is used to form. Perhaps this would be reasonable to suggest: Just as the rod Moses used to strike the Rock was also the instrument of judgment to bring on the plagues of Egypt (Ex 17:5), so also the "rod" of God's judgment—the cross—was brought to Jesus so that it can be said of each follower of Christ, "From his innermost being will flow rivers of living water" (John 7:38).

Lord, in every way You are my Spiritual Rock. And the judgment for my sin laid on You proved that You are the unmovable Rock of my salvation.

WEEK 50, DAY 2

Root and Descendant of David

"I, Jesus, have sent My angel to testify to you these things for the churches. I am the root and the descendant of David, the bright morning star." (Revelation 22:16)

Understanding the connection between Jesus and the beloved David is crucial to fully grasping the whole redemption story. Like a perfect novel, the divine plan of the ages is more than a simple message of God rescuing us from sin. The way He did it brings Him amazing glory! Reading the entire Bible reveals the grand themes that sometimes seem vague in the details but in the end prove to be woven together in intricate detail. Repeated readings, continually bring out the details that wonderfully fill out the whole.

When we read a classic literary novel for the first time, we enjoy the story line, often with the various sub-plots finally coming to resolution at the end. The better stories beg to be re-read, but now with a picture of the whole, in order to re-examine and appreciate how the author has brought in the individual details. Sometimes we overlook a detail in the prose upon first reading, but appreciate it for its surprising significance during subsequent readings.

So it is with the Word of God, only infinitely more so. The more we study it, the more we see the details portraying the magnificent glory of God. And that is what the story is ultimately all about. As wonderful as salvation is to us, the greater message of the Bible is God's glory as the Author of Life.

So here we find at the very end of the Bible, the last chapter of the Book of the Revelation, a swing back to the historical person of King David, the man whom God called "a man after My own heart" (1 Sam 13:14, Acts 13:22). As interesting as that insight is, we could extol David as an example of the kind of character to which we should aspire. True as the application of the story may be, David is far more than just as an example to us. In the larger story line, as God brings together all the strands of the many biblical stories, we hear Jesus identifying with David. God's work in and through the life of David did not end when David died but was fulfilled in Christ, who said, "I am the root and descendant of David." We see what God really meant when He told David, "I will establish the throne of his kingdom forever" (2 Sam 7:13). A promise made around 3,000 years ago is the beginning of a golden thread, so to speak, that weaves through biblical history and finds its ultimate fulfillment in Christ. He will return as the "Root and descendant of David"!

Lord, I rest in the trustworthiness of Your promises. And I look forward to the ultimate King David to come, the Lord Jesus Christ.

WEEK 50, DAY 3

Ruler

"And you, Bethlehem, land of Judah, are by no means least among the leaders of Judah; for out of you shall come forth a Ruler who will shepherd My people Israel." (Matthew 2:6)

From earliest times, God's image bearers have desired to follow a leader. We were created to follow God's lead by innately reflecting His image back to Him. But the first humans (and every one after) responded to a different ruler than God—and that has been our downfall ever since. Ultimately Satan made his move against the pinnacle of humanity in the temptation of Jesus (Matthew 4), in order to obtain worship from the incarnate Son of God. This fulfilled Isaiah's prophesy:

"But you said in your heart, 'I will ascend to heaven; I will raise my throne above the stars of God, and I will sit on the mount of assembly in the recesses of the north. 'I will ascend above the heights of the clouds; I will make myself like the Most High.'" (Is 14:13–14, where the speaker is identified in the NKJV as Lucifer in Is 14:12).

Every country or people group has its kings, presidents, governors, mayors, chiefs, generals, bosses or authorities. But God is king over all of them. The biblical story has this issue woven throughout as a central theme. Think of God's people in their formative years as a nation. When they saw that all the other nations had their kings and leaders, they wanted to imitate them. God anticipated this when He spoke through Moses during the Exodus:

"When you enter the land which the LORD your God gives you, and you possess it and live in it, and you say, 'I will set a king over me like all the nations who are around me,' you shall surely set a king over you whom the LORD your God chooses, one from among your countrymen you shall set as king over yourselves; you may not put a foreigner over yourselves who is not your countryman. (Deut 17:14–15)

As the story unfolded, the people rejected God's rule over them and chose their own idea for a ruler, King Saul, who turned out to be a complete failure. But if it was a man they wanted, then God raised up David, the man of His own choice. Yet David was simply a picture of a much greater ruler, namely the One born in Bethlehem, the hometown of David, the Lord Jesus Christ. He is the Ruler of God's choice. He, as the God-man, now perfectly shepherds His people! And there are no scandals, no faults, no shortcomings in Him.

Lord, I re-commit myself every day to following Your leadership in my life.

WEEK 50, DAY 4

Ruler (cont.)

"And you, Bethlehem, land of Judah, are by no means least among the leaders of Judah; for out of you shall come forth a Ruler who will shepherd My people Israel." (Matthew 2:6)

The idea of Jesus being a ruler of His people is multi-faceted. In context, Micah's prophesy (quoted in Matthew 2:6) was intended for the Jews. A ruling king in the dynasty of King David would come, and in the gospel accounts this points to Jesus Christ. Christians debate, though, how this applies to us today, whether the kingdom of God (or "kingdom of heaven") is now or future. Is Jesus reigning over the earth now or does this refer to the millennial reign of Revelation 20:4? While resolving this issue goes beyond these meditations, we can all agree God still reigns over all the earth, both now and into eternity future. He was, is and always will be the Ruler.

The actual Greek word ("hegeomai") used in Matthew 2:6 to describe Jesus has a broad field of meaning, but all major English translations translate it as "ruler." It is where we get our English word "hegemony." Webster defines this as "influence or authority over others." Further, it conveys this sense: "the social, cultural, ideological, or economic influence exerted by a dominant group." While we don't want to read the English meaning of hegemony back into the Greek word, we can agree that the definition of that English word captures the truth of Christ's rule over us.

Following Christ should affect our social interactions. His listing of the second greatest commandment (after loving God) is a foundational statement on social interactions: "You shall love your neighbor as yourself'" (Mark 12:31).

Are not disciples of Christ to influence the surrounding culture?

> *"You are the salt of the earth; but if the salt has become tasteless, how can it be made salty again? It is no longer good for anything, except to be thrown out and trampled under foot by men. "You are the light of the world. A city set on a hill cannot be hidden." (Matt 5:13–14)*

Does not Christ's hegemony extend to the ideological areas of our lives?

> *"We are destroying speculations and every lofty thing raised up against the knowledge of God, and we are taking every thought captive to the obedience of Christ ..." (2 Cor 10:5)*

Finally, are our financial lives not shaped by the truth that "God will supply all [our] needs according to His riches in glory in Christ Jesus" (Phil 4:19)?

> *Lord, You are the ruler over every area of my life, I humbly submit to You.*

WEEK 50, DAY 5

Savior

"... for today in the city of David there has been born for you a Savior, who is Christ the Lord." (Luke 2:11)

The descriptor "Savior" is actually used in the gospel accounts only three times: once by Mary the mother of the earthly Jesus, once in the angelic announcement to the Bethlehem shepherds at the birth of Christ, and one other time by the Samaritans. To be sure, we see the verbal form of that description applied to Christ: "For the Son of Man has come to seek and to save that which was lost" (Luke 19:10). So the title is His because that is what He does—He saves.

The concept of salvation immediately invokes in Christians a reference to eternal salvation. And that is the most wonderful and ultimate sense of the word. However, when we shine the truth of salvation through the prism of the whole counsel of God, we discover a richness of our Savior that we dare not miss. For example (and we cannot come even close to exhausting all the hues of what it means), we are saved from the wrath of God that we justly deserved. We are saved from eternal damnation in hell, where the "worm does not die, and the fire is not quenched" (Mark 9:48). Also, Scripture tells us, Christ saves us from being "cast out into the outer darkness; in that place there will be weeping and gnashing of teeth" (Matt 8:12). We are saved from an eternity apart from His presence, apart from His love, grace and mercy. We are spared from eternal hopelessness. Rightly did Dante post on the sign at hell's entrance, "Abandon all hope, ye who enter" (Dante's Inferno).

But Christ also saves us from a meaningless existence. He saves us from the strictures of the Law. He released us from bondage to sin and the tentacles of Satan. He rescued us from the sting of death and from the enslavement of empty human philosophies about life after death. He liberates us from bondage to other people's opinions of us.

A great and precious perspective of Christ as our Savior overwhelms us when we realize that if God is for us, who can be against us (Rom 8:31)? As such, He frees us from guilt, the self-destructive thinking associated with lack of assurance. We are saved to live without turmoil, anxiety, worry, self-doubts, insecurities or anything else that would separate us from the love of Christ.

Yes, Christ is our Savior. While our eternal salvation is secure forever, we often don't experience salvation from the daily things that oppose us. God calls us to believe this great truth: "In all these things we are more than conquerors through Him who loved us" (Rom 8:37 ESV).

Lord, I trust You as my Savior both for eternity and for right now!

WEEKEND 50 READING
Malachi 1

PERSONAL REFLECTIONS

WEEK 51, DAY 1

Son of David

The record of the genealogy of Jesus the Messiah, the son of David, the son of Abraham … (Matthew 1:1)

"What do you think about the Christ, whose son is He?" [The Pharisees] said to Him, "The son of David." He said to them, "Then how does David in the Spirit call Him 'Lord,' saying, 'THE LORD SAID TO MY LORD, "SIT AT MY RIGHT HAND, UNTIL I PUT YOUR ENEMIES BENEATH YOUR FEET"' ? (Matthew 22:42–44)

To say someone is "the son of …" often meant a simple genealogical connection. Jesus was identified with His physical ancestor, King David, through both His mother's side (Luke 3:31) and His adoptive father's side (Matt 1:1). Or the phrase could mean that someone takes the characteristics of another. In this sense, Jesus was like King David in certain ways. David was not only the greatest military leader of Israel, but also the iconic ideal of a godly leader. All kings after David, including his illustrious son Solomon, were compared to David! Of all the Jewish kings in Jesus' lineage, David was the only one with whom Jesus was identified.

Yet our Lord never referred to Himself as the Son of David. We find the two blind men at Jericho calling Him that (Matt 9:27) and also the Canaanite woman with a demon-possessed daughter (Matt 15:22). The crowds at first wondered about the miracle-working preacher (Matt 12:23) but eventually exalted Him as "Son of David" (Matt 21:9). His silence at this praise suggests that Jesus accepted the appellation.

Most poignant was Jesus' challenging the Pharisees' understanding of the "son of David" as the "nom deguerre," or code name for Messiah. He centers on Psalm 110 (the most quoted OT chapter in the NT which was generally understood to be written by David and referring to Messiah). If, as the Pharisees admit, "Christ" (which is synonymous with "Messiah") was the "son of David" then they have a problem with David referring to Messiah as "my Lord." In other words, the Messiah who is David's son is also David's Lord. The point Jesus makes is that the Son of David was and is none other than Yahweh, the God of Israel. So those referring to Him as "Son of David" would be essentially acclaiming Him as Messiah, which in Jesus' intimation means divinity!

The full understanding of Psalm 110 would require more space than this essay affords, but suffice it to say that Jesus = "Son of David" = "Messiah" = "Yahweh." In Jesus, the Davidic promise of an eternal throne would find its fulfillment in that Jesus will reign forever and ever.

Lord Jesus, I join with the triumphal chorus, "Hosanna to the Son of David."

WEEK 51, DAY 2

Son of Man

"For the Son of Man has come to save that which was lost." (Matthew 18:11).

A favorite way Jesus referred to Himself was as "Son of Man" in contrast to "Son of David," which He was reticent to use. Used primarily in the gospel accounts in the NT, it finds common use in the OT as a simple reference to an individual as a human being or an offspring of a human being. For example, "God is not a man, that He should lie, nor a son of man, that He should repent" (Num 23:19). This could be seen in contrast to the phrase "sons of God" used in Job 6:1-3, where many commentators see a reference to angels, or super-humans, as opposed to the offspring of humans, in that case, "daughters of men." Essentially, the phrase emphasizes the humanness of the individual(s).

The writer of Hebrews, though, quotes Psalm 8:4 and applies it to Jesus:

But one has testified somewhere, saying, "What is man, that You remember him? Or the son of man, that You are concerned about him? You have made him for a little while lower than the angels; You have crowned him with glory and honor, and have appointed him over the works of Your hands; You have put all things in subjection under his feet." (Heb 2:6–8a)

Jesus was made human, and indeed, in referring to Himself as the Son of Man identified with His fellow human beings.

Most poignant is the Messianic background of the phrase, found in Daniel's prophecy: "I kept looking in the night visions, and behold, with the clouds of heaven One like a Son of Man was coming, and He came up to the Ancient of Days and was presented before Him" (Dan 7:13). Obscure in Daniel, yet clearly seen in Jesus, the Son of Man came from heaven and would return to the Father's presence ("the Ancient of Days") at His ascension. As Daniel goes on to say, "And to Him was given dominion, glory and a kingdom, that all the peoples, nations and men of every language might serve Him. His dominion is an everlasting dominion which will not pass away; and His kingdom is one which will not be destroyed" (Dan 7:14).

Jesus, as Son of Man, presented Himself as fully human, yet also as the promised Messiah who would one day rule the world. To use Mark Twain's novel "The Prince and the Pauper" as an analogy, the second person of the Trinity, "the Prince," became a human being, "the Pauper," and dwelt among fellow human beings, only to reassume His royal position in the end. But in the process, as we stray from Twain's novel, this Pauper became the Savior.

Lord, I praise You for becoming human like me so that You could be my Savior.

WEEK 51, DAY 3

Son of Man (cont.)

"For the Son of Man has come to save that which was lost." (Matthew 18:11).

As Son of Man, Jesus showed not only His humanness, but also what true humanity looks like. We humans were created in God's image, have fallen, but are now restored through the perfect image of God:

He is the image of the invisible God... (Col 1:15)

And He is the radiance of His glory and the exact representation of His nature, and upholds all things by the word of His power ... (Heb 1:3a)

[Christians] have put on the new self who is being renewed to a true knowledge according to the image of the One who created him ... (Col 3:10)

But we all, with unveiled face, beholding as in a mirror the glory of the Lord, are being transformed into the same image from glory to glory, just as from the Lord, the Spirit. (2 Cor 3:18)

So as the "Son of Man" was raised from the dead (Matt 12:40), we also as fellow humans, with the restored image of God in us, will also be raised from the dead. As the image of God in "the Son of Man" is seen in the parable of the sower and the seed (Matt 13:37), so we too, as fellow image bearers, should sow the seed of evangelism. Just as angels served the Son of Man (Matt 13:41), so also angels serve us as ministering spirits. Just as the Son of Man will come in His glorious kingdom, we also will see and join in with Him in His glory, as fellow humans, when He comes. "Just as the Son of Man did not come to be served, but to serve ..." (Matt 20:28), so we also should follow His example.

Some assert that Jesus became human like us in every way except for sin. Such a statement assumes sin to be intrinsic to humanity. But that could not be possible since we were created in God's image, and that could not possibly have included sin. It is better to think of sin as completely unnatural, anti-human in every sense of the word. Sin goes completely contrary to the way God created us. We were made for something intrinsically better: to reflect God's glory. Sin came into our human world, not because of our humanity but in spite of our humanity, to make us less than human. Jesus restores to us the true sense of what it means to be human. So yes, the Son of Man was an exception in that He did not sin, but that is not an exception to humanity per se. He refused to do that which is anti-human.

Lord, I praise You for changing me daily into true humanity, that is more like the image of God.

WEEK 51, DAY 4

Son of the Living God

Now when Jesus came into the district of Caesarea Philippi, He was asking His disciples, "Who do people say that the Son of Man is?" And they said, "Some say John the Baptist; and others, Elijah; but still others, Jeremiah, or one of the prophets." He said to them, "But who do you say that I am?" Simon Peter answered, "You are the Christ, the Son of the living God." (Matthew 16:13–16)

Defining juncture in the training of the twelve—that's what this is! The first moment of a risk: blasphemous if they were wrong, eternally life-changing if they were right. Some even go so far as to say this was the point where they entered into eternal salvation. Jesus later said, "This is eternal life, that they may know You, the only true God, and Jesus Christ whom You have sent" (John 17:3). They had truly come to know who Jesus was, He was and is the Son of the living God.

Why is this so pivotal? Because as Master Teacher He pulled back the curtains, He gave the twelve a back-stage pass, so to speak. Another time was the extended dissertation in the Upper Room the night before He was crucified, when Jesus took them into His most private counsel, preparing them for life without His physical presence. Here the Lord takes dead aim at their understanding of who He is. It was sort of an identity crisis, but not for Jesus. It was a moment of crisis for the twelve – what is the identity of this individual they were following? Who is He really?

This query appears somewhat mid-ministry for the mission of Christ. Right after Peter's response of faith, the confession of His conviction, Jesus begins talking about the church's foundation of faith (Matt 16:17-20), His death (Matt 16:21-23) and the cost of discipleship (Matt 16:24-28). Then comes the Mount of Transfiguration (Matt 17:1-13), where they see His glory. None of this could happen until they confessed their faith in the Son of the Living God!

Enough time had passed, enough miracles and teaching had taken place to provide evidence of Jesus' true identity. So no time is wasted with oblique or obfuscated debates, as so often happens today. Believing is an action word, a binary risk of everything because of the identity of Jesus Christ. He is either the Son of the Living God, or He is not. This is not dead orthodoxy open for debate, against the philosophical-religious sophistry of modern "spirituality" that relegates such propositional assertions to oppressive religion. No, Peter believed in the "Living" God, who was active in the world. And He believed that Jesus was His Son. That settled it for Peter and the others. Does that settle it for you?

Lord, I pray that all who read this would be able to confess that Jesus is the Christ, the Son of the Living God—and have life everlasting.

WEEK 51, DAY 5

Son of the Blessed

The high priest stood up and came forward and questioned Jesus, saying, "Do You not answer? What is it that these men are testifying against You?" But He kept silent and did not answer. Again the high priest was questioning Him, and saying to Him, "Are You the Christ, the Son of the Blessed One?" And Jesus said, "I am ..." Tearing his clothes, the high priest said, "What further need do we have of witnesses? You have heard the blasphemy; how does it seem to you?" And they all condemned Him to be deserving of death. (Mark 14:60–64)

His faithful disciples did not demand of Jesus an explicit statement of His true identity. But to the unbelieving religious leaders, an explicit acknowledgement only served to inflame their anger against Him. They knew who He was, at least in part, and what they knew they rejected. Remember when Nicodemus came to Jesus? He was a "man of the Pharisees" and a "ruler of the Jews" (John 3:1). Speaking on behalf of the other religious leaders, he said, "Rabbi, we know that You have come from God as a teacher; for no one can do these signs that You do unless God is with him" (John 3:2). They knew at the very least that Jesus was a prophet of God, and on that basis they should have accepted His teachings and repented of their sins.

The multitude followed Jesus because of His miracles, but abandoned Him when He began speaking of total commitment to His teachings (John 6:66). Only the few, the twelve, kept following:

Jesus said to the twelve, "You do not want to go away also, do you?" Simon Peter answered Him, "Lord, to whom shall we go? You have words of eternal life. "We have believed and have come to know that You are the Holy One of God." (John 6:67–69)

Not so the religious leaders! Of all people, one would think they would have been the ones most in tune with God to recognize and submit to the teachings of one whom they knew to be a prophet. However, they rejected Jesus from early on. They saw the same miraculous signs and heard the same teaching. What the writer of Hebrews wrote applies to them:

[T]he word they heard did not profit them, because it was not united by faith in those who heard. (Heb 4:2).

Poignant was the question demanded of Him, "Are you the Christ, the son of the Blessed One?" That is code for, "Are you on the level of Yahweh?" To be "the son of" meant to share in all the characteristics and nature of Yahweh. Jesus, the Master Teacher and prophet sent from God, said, "I am"!

Lord, I join with the twelve disciples and acknowledge You as Yahweh, my God.

WEEKEND 51 READING
Malachi 2

PERSONAL REFLECTIONS

WEEK 52, DAY 1

Son of the Highest

"He will be great and will be called the Son of the Most High; and the Lord God will give Him the throne of His father David ..." (Luke 1:32)

Superlatives convey absolutes, beyond which nothing else compares. Jesus Christ, as told by the tongue of an angel, would be the Son of God (as we are intended to understand "the Most High"). Calling Jesus "Son of the Most High" means that He would share in the characteristics and attributes of "the Most High." He would be, as theologians say, of the substance of God, who is Yahweh. If anything is clear in Scripture, Yahweh is the Most High God:

> *Abram said to the king of Sodom, "I have sworn to the LORD God Most High [Yahweh El Elyon], possessor of heaven and earth ..." (Gen 14:22)*

It seems odd to us today that such an appellation as "most high" God is needed since we are so inculcated in our Western world with monotheism, the belief in the existence of one and only one God, and that all others so-called "gods" are simply figments of human inventiveness. We must remember though, in ancient times, God's people lived in a predominantly pagan world, where other people worshiped "other" gods and often many "gods." Such beliefs were rampant, as one might expect from those who reject their divine Maker. So the emphasis in those kinds of cultures must be noted, that the One who sent Gabriel to Mary was, just to make it absolutely clear, the God of Abraham. In other words, his message comes from the highest authority!

But more to the point, as the Son of the Most High, Jesus Christ takes a back seat to absolutely no one. For us today, as believers in the Son of the Most High, that means we should set as our goal what the apostle Paul wrote to the small-minded, self-centered Corinthians: "We are destroying speculations and every lofty thing raised up against the knowledge of God, and we are taking every thought captive to the obedience of Christ" (2 Cor 10:5).

In other words, we do not think of Christianity as one of many viable worldviews. It is not just one of many historical movements to capture the esoteric but nebulous spirituality that we humans just can't seem to avoid. Nor is Christianity a way of life that is simply "better" than non-Christianity, whose evangelism consists of showing that superiority. It is not that what we believe is the "best" way of thinking and living. It is whom we believe in that is the best. Or rather, He is the highest object of our worship and allegiance, because He is the Son of the Most High!

Lord, I confess falling often into the idolatry of using Your Word as a self-help manual, rather than seeing in Your Word the exaltation of Christ to the Highest.

WEEK 52, DAY 2

Source of Eternal Salvation

Although He was a Son, He learned obedience from the things which He suffered. And having been made perfect, He became to all those who obey Him the source of eternal salvation ... (Hebrews 5:8–9)

Eternal security is a wonderful doctrine! Although the precise English phrase is not actually used in Scripture, the concept is clearly present as in our verse today. First, perfection in this passage applies to Christ, and to Him alone. Whatever "obedience" means, only Christ was perfectly obedient. Second, if perfect obedience was required of us, then who of us could be saved? James adroitly recorded, "For whoever keeps the whole law and yet stumbles in one point, he has become guilty of all" (James 2:10). Furthermore, eternal salvation involves a quality component, an eternal quality of spiritual life, but also a "quantity" component. In other words, salvation that is sourced in Christ is never ending and thus cannot ever be lost, or it would not be eternal.

Notice the tenses of the verbs. Christ is our source of eternal salvation, because He "learned obedience" (past tense), "He became (past tense) the source of eternal salvation," and this "to all those who obey Him" (present tense, implying an ongoing activity). All major English translations render these tenses the same. So we have two things happening in the past and one happening in the present. For those who wrongly believe a person can lose salvation through disobedience or falling away from the faith, that means something they do now (i.e. stop obeying) would change something that took place in the past (i.e. Christ became for them the source of eternal salvation)—an absurd idea.

Did Christ then give eternal salvation only to those whom He foreknew would perfectly obey? We have already seen that no one can perfectly obey. And the idea of God applying obedience on a sliding scale smacks of human religion, for the Bible says, "All have sinned and come short of the glory of God" (Rom 3:23). Even as Spirit-indwelt Christians we could never obey well enough to keep our salvation. Yet the verse emphasizes that Christ alone was "perfect"! While the word "obey" is used only sparsely in Hebrews, we see a major theme of the book is that Israel did not benefit from the "good news" of God because "it was not united by faith in those who heard" but "we who have believed enter that rest ..." (Heb 4:2-3). So the Jews were to obey the command to "enter that rest," which they refused to do because of unbelief. Therefore, in our passage today, "those who obey Him" are those who have put their faith in Christ, the promise and source of eternal salvation (see Acts 6:7, Rom 1:5, 16:26).

Lord, by Your grace I obeyed when You commanded that all should believe. And in You I rest secure and call on You as the source of my eternal salvation.

WEEK 52, DAY 3

Sovereign Lord

... they cried out with a loud voice, saying, "How long, O Lord, holy and true, will You refrain from judging and avenging our blood on those who dwell on the earth?" (Revelation 6:10)

The cry of the heart reverberates through the heavens to the Sovereign Master of the Universe: "How long, O Lord ..." The underlying Greek word, "despotes," often used for the master in a slave relationship, is not used of God very often in the Bible. In modern parlance, the familiar-sounding English word, "despot," commonly refers to a ruler with absolute power and authority, often exercised in a brutal or oppressive way. However, the Greek word does not imply that negative connotation; it simply conveys the idea of absolute authority without reference to intent or character.

Simeon used this word when he first laid eyes on the Christ child, in his prayer to God at Jesus' dedication: "Now Lord ["despotes"], You are releasing Your bond-servant to depart in peace ..." (Luke 2:29). What faith he had to see in this child the act of the all-powerful, absolutely ruling potentate of the universe!

Peter and John, after the Jewish council's menacing inquisition over the first miraculous healing in the early church, "lifted their voice to God with one accord and said, "O Lord ["despotes"], it is You who made the heaven and the earth ..." (Acts 4:24). They recognized that God was indeed able "to do whatever Your hand and Your purpose predestined to occur" (Acts 4:28). Their prayer for protection came from their confidence in God's absolute sovereignty.

So also in our passage today, we see an appeal to the absolute Sovereign of the universe from "... the souls of those who had been slain because of the word of God, and because of the testimony which they had maintained..." (Rev 6:9). During the future tribulation period, when untold destruction is poured out, the tribulation martyrs echo the pleading of persecuted believers through the ages: "How long ...?" At times like these, nothing other than a confidence in the God whose authority and power is unchallenged will do. When persecution is unremitting, suffering unending and hope stretched to the breaking point, faith calls out to the sovereignty of the God who is the ultimate master, controller and potentate of all that exists. The other major English translations render the word as "Sovereign Lord." He is the One who made the heavens and the earth, and "apart from Him nothing came into being that has come into being" (John 1:3). He is the One for whom all His enemies will become His footstool (Heb 1:13).

Sovereign Lord, I come with all my struggles knowing that nothing escapes Your authority and nothing is greater than Your power.

WEEK 52, DAY 4

The Sunrise from on High

"Because of the tender mercy of our God, with which the Sunrise from on high will visit us …" (Luke 1:78)

This final epithet of God we are considering reflects on the newness, the freshness of God's coming into the world in the fullness of re-creation. The dawn conjures a new start, with new potential of things to be accomplished and experienced. The night is past and the new day has arrived.

One thinks of the dawn of human creation, where we read of "the LORD God walking in the garden in the cool of the day…" (Gen 3:8). He was on His way, so to speak, to fellowship with His image bearers—perhaps like someone going to look at Himself in a mirror. Though the day began with a good start, it did not end well, for Adam and Eve resisted that fellowship because of their sin and hid from God. It was like they wanted to cover over the image of God so that God could not see Himself reflected in them, and they could not see Him in person the way He really was.

All through biblical history, the image of God has been veiled. Moses could only see the "backside of God" (Ex 33:22-23). The sunrise was obscured. When Moses came down from the mountain the reflection of the brilliance of God's glory was shrouded with a covering over his head (2 Cor 3:7), fading as that reflected glory was.

Glimpses of the brilliance of the sunrise can be seen when Jesus "was transfigured before them; and His face shone like the sun, and His garments became as white as light…" (Matt 17:2). And when the empty tomb was discovered on Easter morning, the whiteness of the attending angel's garments lit up the darkened cave. How could one not have sensed the atmosphere brighten in the Upper Room when Jesus appeared to all His disciples after His resurrection and when He said to Thomas, "Reach out your hand …"?

However, the glory of Christ as the Sunrise from on high is best seen arising from the darkness of our sinful souls. Peter put it this way: "So we have the prophetic word made more sure, to which you do well to pay attention as to a lamp shining in a dark place, until the day dawns and the morning star arises in your hearts" (2 Peter 1:19). As believers we rejoice and celebrate that Jesus has arisen in our lives, as an eternal sunrise, a newness of soul that will never become old. An eternal new life in Him. "Therefore if anyone is in Christ, he is a new creature; the old things passed away; behold, new things have come" (2 Cor 5:17). Now that is a Sunrise!

Praise God! I have a new, fresh day to experience for eternity because Christ has arisen in my life.

WEEK 52, DAY 5

Names and Epithets of God

"I AM WHO I AM"; and He said, "Thus you shall say to the sons of Israel, 'I AM has sent me to you.'" God, furthermore, said to Moses, "Thus you shall say to the sons of Israel, 'The LORD [YAHWEH], the God of your fathers, the God of Abraham, the God of Isaac, and the God of Jacob, has sent me to you.' This is My name forever, and this is My memorial-name to all generations." (Ex 3:14–15)

The popular reference app Wikipedia defines "name" in this way: "A name is a term used for identification. Names can identify a class or category of things, or a single thing, either uniquely, or within a given context. A personal name identifies, not necessarily uniquely, a specific individual human."

An epithet is a "byname, or a descriptive term (word or phrase), accompanying or occurring in place of a name." How do you label God, except in extremely limited ways? Hopefully these meditations on His names and epithets across the books and chapters of Scripture have grown our understanding of God.

God's given name, however—the name He has given Himself to be known to us—is foundational to everything else we know about Him. That is why we began this study at and end with Exodus 3:14.

He is the eternally, actively present One, who shows Himself in the ways suitable and needful for us, His image bearers. He truly, to use a modern phrase, "is there for us." While we humans toss that phrase about, such promises are inherently limited by time, circumstances and abilities. But God is without limit, so when He says His Name is "I am" and gives us the label that is a play on that word, "Yahweh," we can rest assured that He truly is there for us—without limit, without restriction and without hindrances. His time is eternal, His circumstances are under His sovereign control, and His abilities extend to His omnipotence.

We have seen the descriptors like "Elohim," "Adonai" and "Shaddai." We have noted adjectival constructs (like eternal, holy, etc.) and verbal combinations ("Yahweh Jireh," "Yahweh who provides"). In Jesus, metaphors abound with the profound self-descriptors formed on His "I am ..." statements. But at the most fundamental, self-identifying level, made absolutely clear, "Before Abraham was, I am" (John 8:58). The one named the Lord Jesus Christ is the one named Yahweh, El Shaddai. He is our God!

Lord, thank You for revealing something of Yourself to us in Your Word! I will praise You with all of my being for all of eternity.

WEEKEND 52 READING
Malachi 3-4

PERSONAL REFLECTIONS

The Names of God
An Index

Notes: 1) The following is an index of names and epithets of God and the passages used in the book. 2) A thorough study of each of these names would require an in-depth analysis of every occurrence in Scripture, many of which are not included in this index. 3) The distinction between the terms LORD (Yahweh) and Lord (Elohim) are consistent with the convention used in the book.

Hebrew Names of God

The following are the primary Hebrew names and combinations, along with the page numbers where they are found in this book.

Adonai - 45	Elohim - 8-9	Yahweh Elohim - 10
Adonai Yahweh - 46	Elohim Abraham - 67	Yahweh Elohim Mispat - 80
Adonai Yahweh Sabbaoth - 47	Elohim El Han-Emen - 62	Yahweh Elohim Sabaoth - 27
El Elohe Yisrael - 15	Elohim Ibbriyyim - 83	Yahweh Elyon - 28
El Elohim Yahweh - 16	Elohim Nahor - 71	Yahweh Jireh - 32
El Elyon - 13	Elohim Olam Yahweh Bara - 61	Yahweh Macaddeshkem - 33
El Gibor - 17	Elohim Sabbaoth - 11	Yahweh Nissi - 34
El Hayyay - 82	Elohim Yaaqob - 69–70	Yahweh Ra'ah - 35
El Roi - 19	Elohim Yishaq - 68	Yahweh Rapha - 37
El Shaddai - 20	Elyon - 14	Yahweh Sabbaoth - 29, 38–39
El Yisrael - 79	Pahad Yishaq - 63	Yahweh Samah - 31
Elah - 21	Yah - 44	Yahweh Shalom - 40
Elah Illai - 22	Yahweh - 1–7	Yahweh Shammah - 41
Eloah - 23	Yahweh El Elyon - 25	Yahweh Sur Yisrael - 81
Eloah Selihah - 64	Yahweh El Olam - 26	Yahweh Tsidkenu – 43

English Names of God

The following is not an exhaustive list, for these can be delineated in various ways. Included here are those identified in the book, along with the page numbers where they are found in this book.

Abounding in Love and Truth - 53
Advocate - 215
Almighty - 217
Alpha and Omega - 218
Amen - 219
Ancient of Days - 49
Apostle of Our Confession - 220
Author of Salvation - 227
Beginning of God's Creation - 221
Beloved Son - 223–25
Blessed God - 226
Calling on the Lord - 7
Chief Shepherd - 229
Chosen One - 235
Christ of God - 230
Compassionate, Gracious - 50–51
Consolation of Israel - 231
Cornerstone - 57–58
Creator - 232
Defense of My Life - 59
Deliverer - 233
Eternal Father - 238
Everlasting God, LORD - 61
Exact Rep. of His Nature - 244
Faithful and True Witness - 247
Fear of Isaac - 63
Firstborn of Creation - 249
Forerunner - 250
Forgiving God - 55, 64

God ("Theos") - 21, 23, 182
God Almighty - 20
God in the Beginning - 8–9
God Most High - 13, 22
God of Abraham - 67
God of All Comfort - 191, 193
God of All Grace - 194
God of Bethel - 75
God of Gods, Lord of Lords - 77
God of Hosts - 11
God of Isaac - 68
God of Israel - 79
God of Jacob - 69, 70
God of Love - 195
God of My Life - 82
God of My Righteousness - 166
God of Nahor - 71
God of Peace - 196
God of Retribution - 175
God of Spirits of All Flesh - 85
God of Spirits of Prophets - 199
God of the Hebrews - 83
God of the Living - 197
God of the Patriarchs - 65
God of Their Fathers - 86
God of Truth - 91
God of Your Father - 87
God the Word ("Logos") - 183
God Who Avenges - 92

God Who Punishes Wicked - 56
God Who Sees - 19
God, the Faithful God - 62
God's Holy One - 104
God's Son - 93
Gracious, Compass., God - 94–95
Great God and King - 99
Great High Priest - 251
Great, Awesome God - 98
Guardian of our Souls - 253
Head of the Church - 254
Heir of All Things - 241
Holy One of God - 255–56
Holy One of Israel - 103
Holy One of Jacob - 105
Horn of Salvation - 257
I Am - 1–2, 200
I Am the Bread of Life - 203
I Am the Door - 205
I Am the Good Shepherd - 206
I Am the Life - 213
I Am the Light - 202
I Am the Resurrection - 207
I Am the Truth - 212
I Am the Vine - 208–09
I Am the Way - 211
Image of God - 248
Immanuel - 259
Immortal God - 260
Invisible God - 261–62
Jealous God - 115
Jesus - 263
Judge - 116

King - 118
King of Kings, Lord Lords - 265
King of the Jews - 266
Lamb of God - 267
Last Adam - 214
Lawgiver - 119
Leader and Commander - 121
Lifter of My Head - 122
Lion of Judah - 268
Living and True God - 269
Living God, Lord of Hosts - 124
Lord Almighty - 272
LORD God - 10, 46
LORD God Most High - 25
LORD God of Father David - 88
LORD God of Hosts – 27, 47, 124
LORD God, My God - 89
LORD God, the Almighty - 189
LORD Horn of My Salvation - 112
LORD is My Deliverer - 110
LORD is My Rock - 107
LORD is My Shepherd - 35
LORD is My Shield - 111
LORD is My Strength - 106
LORD is My Stronghold - 113
LORD Is Our Healer - 37
LORD Is There - 31
Lord Jesus Christ - 190
LORD Jesus Who Acts - 5
LORD Most High - 28
LORD My God - 128
Lord of All - 273

Lord of Glory - 274–75
Lord of Heaven and Earth - 277
LORD of Host, of Israel - 127
LORD of Hosts - 29, 38–39
LORD of Hosts, King/God - 125
LORD of Kings - 129
LORD of Lords - 130
Lord of the Harvest - 278
LORD Our Banner - 34
LORD Our God - 131
LORD Our Maker - 133
LORD Our Peace - 40
LORD Our Provider - 32
LORD Our Righteousness - 43
LORD Our Sanctifier - 33
LORD Who Acts - 3–4
LORD Who Heals - 176
LORD Who Is Present - 41
LORD Your God - 134
LORD, Everlasting God - 26
LORD, God of All Flesh - 74
LORD, God of Justice - 80
LORD, Holy God - 101
LORD, Rock of Israel - 81
LORD, the God of Heaven - 73
LORD/Lord - 44–45, 271
Loving-Kind God - 135
Magnifier of God - 245
Majestic Glory - 279
Majestic, Judge, Lawgiver - 139
Man of Sorrows - 280

Mediator - 281
Melchizedek - 283
Merciful God - 136
Messiah the Prince - 137
Mighty God - 17, 237
Mighty God of Israel - 15
Mighty One, God, LORD - 16
Morning Star - 284
Most High - 14, 140, 285
My Confidence - 141
My Counselor - 142
My Cup - 143
My Exceeding Joy - 145
My Glory - 146
My Help - 147
My Hope - 148
My Keeper - 179
My King - 149
My Light - 151
My Portion - 152
My Redeemer - 153
My Refuge - 154
My Salvation - 155
My Shade - 181
My Song - 157
My Tower of Strength - 177
My Witness - 178
Nazarene - 286
One Enthroned in Heaven - 158
One of Sinai - 159
One to Be Feared - 160

One Who Goes With You - 161
One Who Remembers - 163
Only Begotten Son - 287, 289
Our Passover - 290
Priest - 165
Prince of Life - 292
Prince of Peace - 239
Prophet - 293
Radiance of God's Glory - 242–43
Righteous God - 167
Righteous Mighty One - 117
Rock of Our Salvation - 100
Root, Descendant of David - 296
Ruler - 297–98
Ruler of Kings - 291
Savior - 169, 299
Shiloh - 170
Slow to Anger - 52
Son of David - 301
Son of Man - 302–03
Son of the Blessed - 305
Son of the Highest - 307
Son of the Living God - 304
Source of Eternal Salvation - 308
Sovereign Lord - 309
Spiritual Rock - 295
Sun - 171
Sun of Righteousness - 172
Sunrise from on High - 310
Sustainer of My Soul - 173
The Living God - 123

Voice of LORD, God of Glory - 76
Wonderful Counselor - 236
Word in the Beginning - 184
Word Was God - 187–88
Word with God - 185

Old Testament

Gen. 1:1 - 8
Gen. 1:26, 3:22 - 9
Gen. 2:4 - 10
Gen. 4:26 - 7
Gen. 6:2-3 - 4
Gen. 14:18-23 - 13
Gen. 14:22–23 - 25
Gen. 16:13 - 19
Gen. 17:1 - 20
Gen. 21:33 - 26
Gen. 22:14 - 32
Gen. 24:7 - 73
Gen. 31:13 - 75
Gen. 31:42 - 63
Gen. 31:53 - 63, 71
Gen. 33:20 - 15
Gen. 49:10 - 170
Gen. 50:17 - 87
Ex. 3:13-15 - 1–3
Ex. 3:14–15 - 311
Ex. 3:18 - 83
Ex. 3:6 - 65, 67–70
Ex. 15:26 - 37, 176
Ex. 17:15–16 - 34
Ex. 20:4 - 4
Ex. 20:4–6 - 115
Ex. 31:12–13 - 33
Ex. 34:6–7 – 50–53, 55–56
Ex. 34:9 - 45
Num. 16:22 - 85

1 Sam. 20:12 - 178
1 Kings 19:10 - 27
1 Chron. 17:24 - 127
1 Chron. 28:20 - 89
1 Chron. 29:20 - 86
2 Chron. 2:4 - 128
Ezra 5:11 - 21
Neh. 9:17 - 64, 94
Neh. 9:31 - 94
Ps. 2:12 - 93
Ps. 2:4 - 158
Ps. 2:7 - 93
Ps. 3:2–4 - 122
Ps. 3:3–4 - 146
Ps. 4:1 - 166
Ps. 7:17 - 28
Ps. 10:16–17 - 149
Ps. 16:10 - 104
Ps. 16:5 - 143, 152
Ps. 16:7 - 142
Ps. 17:7 - 169
Ps. 18:1–2 - 106–07, 109–13
Ps. 22:19 - 147
Ps. 23:1 - 35
Ps. 27:1 - 59, 151, 155
Ps. 29:3 - 76
Ps. 42:1–2 - 123
Ps. 42:8 - 82
Ps. 43:4–5 - 145
Ps. 54:4 - 173

Ps. 95:1–2 - 100
Ps. 95:3 - 99
Ps. 95:6–7a - 133
Ps. 110:4 - 165
Ps. 113:3–5 - 164
Ps. 116:5 - 95
Ps. 118:14 - 157
Ps. 118:22 – 57–58
Ps. 121:5–7 - 179, 181
Ps. 136:23 - 163
Job 4:17 - 23
Job 19:25–27a - 153
Job 34:16–17 - 117
Isa. 3:15 - 47
Isa. 10:21 - 17
Isa. 6:1–3 - 38
Isa. 6:4–7 - 39
Isa. 9:6 - 17, 236-39
Isa. 12:2 - 44
Isa. 29:23 - 105
Isa. 30:18 - 80
Isa. 30:29–30 - 81
Isa. 33:21–22 - 139
Isa. 33:22 - 119
Isa. 38:5 - 88
Isa. 40:28 - 61
Isa. 42:1 - 235
Isa. 45:21 - 167
Isa. 53:3 - 280
Isa. 55:3–4 - 121

Num. 24:16 - 14	Ps. 59:10, 17 - 135	Isa. 65:16a - 91
Num. 27:16 - 85	Ps. 61:3 - 177	Jer. 23:36 - 124
Deut. 1:30–31 - 134	Ps. 68:35 - 79	Jer. 23:5–6 - 43
Deut. 4:31 - 136	Ps. 68:7–8 - 159	Jer. 32:27 - 74
Deut. 6:4 - 131	Ps. 71:22 - 103	Jer. 51:56 - 175
Deut. 7:9–10 - 62	Ps. 71:4–5 - 148	Eze. 48:35 - 31, 41
Deut. 10:17 - 77, 97–98	Ps. 71:5–6 - 141	Dan. 2:47 - 129
Deut. 10:17–18 - 130	Ps. 75:7–8 - 116	Dan. 3:26 - 22
Deut. 20:3–4 - 161	Ps. 76:11–12 - 160	Dan. 7:9–10 - 49
Josh. 22:22 - 16	Ps. 83:1-2, 18 - 140	Dan. 9:25–26 - 137
Josh. 7:7 - 46	Ps. 84:1–4 - 125	Amos 5:27 - 11
Judg. 6:22–24 - 40	Ps. 84:9–11 - 171	Zech. 9:9 - 118
1 Sam. 1:3 - 29	Ps. 91:1–2 - 154	Mal. 4:2 – 172
1 Sam. 6:19-20 - 101	Ps. 94:1 - 92	

New Testament

Matt. 1:1 - 301	John 6:66–69 - 255–56	Eph. 1:22 - 254
Matt. 1:21 - 263	John 8:12 - 201-02	Col. 1:15 - 248–249, 261–262
Matt. 1:23 - 259	John 8:58 - 5, 200	1 Thess. 1:9 - 269
Matt. 2:2 - 266	John 10:11 - 206	1 Tim. 1:11 - 226
Matt. 2:23 - 286	John 10:14 - 206	1 Tim. 2:5 - 281
Matt. 2:6 - 297–98	John 10:9–10 - 205	1 Tim. 6:14–16 - 265
Matt. 3:17 - 223–25	John 11:25–26 - 207	Heb. 1:2–3 - 241–45
Matt. 9:37–38 - 278	John 14:6 – 211–13	Heb. 2:10 - 227
Matt. 16:13–16 - 304	John 15:1, 5 - 208, 209	Heb. 3:1 - 220, 251
Matt. 16:15–17 - 230	Acts 3:14–15 - 292	Heb. 4:14 - 251
Matt. 18:11 - 302–03	Acts 3:22 - 293	Heb. 5:8–9 - 308
Matt. 22:29–32 - 197	Acts 10:36 - 273	Heb. 5:9–11 - 283
Matt. 22:42–44 - 301	Acts 15:24–26 - 190	Heb. 6:20 - 250
Matt. 27:37 - 263, 266	Acts 17:23 - 269	1 Peter 2:25 - 253
Mark 14:60–64 - 305	Acts 17:23–24 - 277	1 Peter 5:10 - 194
Luke 1:32 - 285, 307	Acts 17:28 - 269	1 Peter 5:4 - 229

Luke 1:69 - 257	Rom. 1:22–23 - 260	2 Peter 1:17 - 279
Luke 1:78 - 310	Rom. 1:25 - 232	1 John 2:1 - 215
Luke 2:11 - 299	Rom. 10:9–10, 13 - 271	Rev. 1:5 - 291
Luke 2:25 - 231	Rom. 11:26 - 233	Rev. 1:8 - 217–18
John 1:1 - 182–85, 187–88	1 Cor. 2:7–8 - 274–75	Rev. 3:14 - 219, 221, 247
John 1:3 - 232	1 Cor. 5:7 - 290	Rev. 4:8 - 189
John 1:9 - 201	1 Cor. 10:1–4 - 295	Rev. 5:5 - 268
John 1:18 - 287, 289	1 Cor. 15:45 - 214	Rev. 6:10 - 309
John 1:29 - 267	2 Cor. 1:20 - 219	Rev. 21:6 - 218
John 6:35 - 203	2 Cor. 1:3 - 191, 193	Rev. 22:13 - 218
Gen. 1:1 - 8	2 Cor. 6:18 - 272	Rev. 22:16 - 284, 296
Gen. 1:26, 3:22 - 9	2 Cor. 13:11 - 195–96	Rev. 22:6 – 199

Day by Day in the Gospel of Matthew

by Chuck Gianotti

When Matthew was called to discipleship by Jesus with the simple command, "Follow Me!" he was a Rome appointed tax collector and despised by his fellow Jewish countrymen. Now he holds a place of honor as one of the four authorized biographers of the life and ministry of Jesus Christ.

Matthew's gospel account portrays Jesus of Nazareth as the fulfillment of the Old Testament prophecies, giving ample proof that He was, indeed, the Messiah King whom God had promised to send to reign over His people, Israel.

These daily devotionals (spanning one whole year) follow the gospel of Matthew verse by verse. Each reading is accompanied by a brief commentary and a succinct, devotional prayer to ground your heart and will in an increasing desire to love, honor, and serve the Lord Jesus as one of His disciples today.

Call or go online for more information:
563-585-2070 or EmmausWorldwide.org

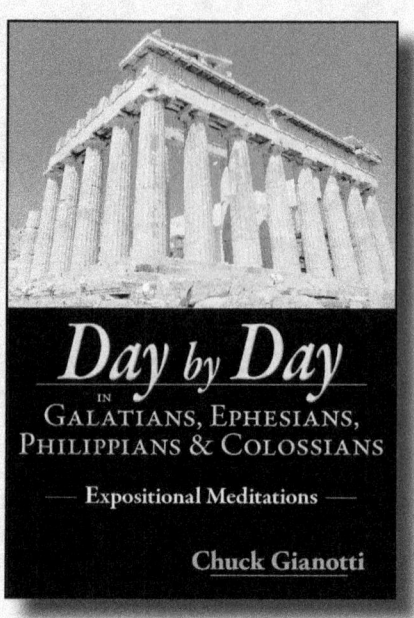

Day by Day in Galatians, Ephesians, Philippians & Colossians

by Chuck Gianotti

These verse-by-verse expositional meditations follow the four epistles of Paul to the Galatians, Ephesians, Philippians and Colossians. The Bible text is accompanied by short textual commentaries and devotional thoughts for each day, spanning an entire year.

The reader will notice that the devotionals are divided up to suit a typical five-day workweek. We have included suggested readings for the weekends from the four accounts of the Gospel of Christ: Matthew, Mark, Luke, and John.

May God use these brief daily thoughts to spur you on to greater discipleship of our Lord and King, Jesus Christ, and to enjoy ever-deepening contemplations about His person and work.

Call or go online for more information:
563-585-2070 or www.EmmausWorldwide.org

Day by Day in Hebrews
by Chuck Gianotti

By comparison with other books of the Bible, Hebrews can seem to be not so relevant for our everyday lives. Chapter 11 (the "Hall of Faith" chapter) and a few verses here and there amount to all that many Christians know about the book. In our world of "instant everything," digging for gold takes some effort. In the case of Hebrews, the abundance of spiritual gold to be found there is well worth the effort.

The magnificent Christ emerges from the text: He is better than angels, than Moses, than the High Priest, than the sacrificial system, than the tabernacle. And that mysterious individual Melchizedek turns out to be a very important biblical figure—the reason why is exciting!

May these expository meditations catapult you into greater enjoyment of our Lord Jesus. We can give no greater glory to God than to exalt His Son through our growing appreciation of His glory.

[Jesus] is the radiance of His [God's] glory . . . (Heb. 1:3a)

Call or go online for more information:
563-585-2070 or EmmausWorldwide.org

Day by Day in the Upper Room
by Chuck Gianotti

The atmosphere in the Upper Room turned dark and troubling. The twelve disciples (quickly reduced to eleven) had joined their Lord for what turned out to be His last meal before He died. Their dreams were dashed at the incomprehensible teachings as He spoke of His betrayal, death and departure. They could not understand that He was preparing them for life without His physical presence.

Yet for those who know the end of the story, the truths Jesus taught them are powerful and profound. The inspired author, John, in the Gospel account by his name (chapters 13–17) writes with simple words using elementary grammar and sentence structure. But God sovereignly appointed him to set us not only soaring, but also diving to profound depths. What he records almost exceeds human language to convey. No superficial reading will suffice to gain the heart of God as revealed in that dinner conversation. May your daily reading in this book help you go where you may not have gone before, as you listen in and contemplate the Upper Room experience.

Call or go online for more information:
563-585-2070 or www.EmmausWorldwide.org

Day by Day in Romans
by Chuck Gianotti

In this meditation on the Book of Romans you will see not only the forest, but also the trees. That is, as you spend time, day by day you will gain a good grasp on the flow of Paul's letter, the major themes and practical applications; and you will enjoy the details along the way. Each day will bring new reasons for praising God who is "just and the justifier of the one who has faith in Jesus" (Romans 3:26)

Call or go online for more information:
563-585-2070 or www.EmmausWorldwide.org

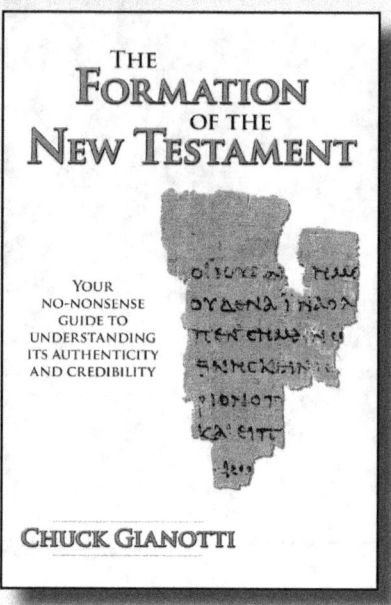

The Formation of the New Testament
by Chuck Gianotti

The Christian faith rises or falls on the historical credibility of the Bible, particularly the New Testament documents. In today's post-modern culture, Christians and those searching for answers face numerous questions including:

- Are the New Testament writings historically reliable?
- How do we know those books are authoritative?
- Who decided which documents to include?
- What about the apocryphal or deutero-canonical writings?
- Can we know for certain that the Bible is accurate and complete?

This book reduces the large volume of available (yet very technical) information on the subject by providing a concise analysis of the facts to help you gain confidence in the credibility of the New Testament canon.

Call or go online for more information:
563-585-2070 or EmmausWorldwide.org

www.ingramcontent.com/pod-product-compliance
Lightning Source LLC
Chambersburg PA
CBHW070127080526
44586CB00015B/1587